Audrey

Audrey

# Golden Treasury of Cooking

# Better Homes and Gardens®

# Golden Treasury of Cooking

© Meredith Corporation, 1973. All Rights Reserved.
Printed in the United States of America. First Edition. First Printing.
Library of Congress Catalog Card Number: 73-78908
SBN: 696-00640-5

# Contents

BETTER HOMES AND GARDENS BOOKS

Editorial Director: Don Dooley
Managing Editor: Malcolm E. Robinson    Art Director: John Berg
Asst. Managing Editor: Lawrence D. Clayton    Asst. Art Director: Randall Yontz
Food Editor: Nancy Morton
Senior Food Editor: Joyce Trollope
Associate Editors: Rosemary Corsiglia, Sharyl Heiken
Assistant Editors: Sandra Mapes, Elizabeth Strait
Designers: Harijs Priekulis, Tonya Rodriguez
Test Kitchen Director: Marion Viall    Asst. Test Kitchen Director: Kay Cargill
Test Kitchen Home Economists: Sharon Golbert, Marilyn Cornelius
Contributing Writers: Jean LemMon, Gerald Carson,
Shirley Sarvis, James Villas
Special Photography: George de Gennaro, Vince Maselli
Consultants: Myrna Johnston, Irwin Glusker

# Five Decades of Good Food

Out of the vast array of kitchen-tested, taste-tempting foods comes one representative from each of the five decades: a Roast Turkey with Oyster Stuffing from the '30s, Chocolate Chip Cake from the '40s, fabulous Cheesecake Supreme with Strawberry Glaze from the '50s, Beef Fondue from the '60s, and Honey-Oatmeal Bread from the '70s. Each recipe has been tested for today's ingredients and cooking equipment.

8

Here's a glimpse of the Tasting-Test Kitchen as it looked in the '30s. Using equipment like that in readers' kitchens, the editors tested thousands of recipes from all across the country. Those that proved their superiority were included in *My Better Homes and Gardens Cook Book.*

The Test Kitchen of the '70s is the home base of all current *Better Homes and Gardens* cook book recipes. It is the place where all recipe inspirations are put into working order, tasted, and judged carefully before publication.

# Your Golden Treasury of Cooking

A wealth of great recipes amassed over five decades awaits your eating pleasure in this *Golden Treasury of Cooking.* The recipes, like gemstones in any fine collection, have a story to tell. It is part of the *Better Homes and Gardens* heritage. Throughout the book, you'll find recipes surrounded by copy that not only reflects the nostalgia and flavor of each decade, but also sets the mood for your own excursions into the kitchen. Some of the incidents and dishes will jog your memory, while others will serve to introduce you to the delicacies of another decade. To put the recipe jewels in a setting you can use today, the dishes were retested in the *Better Homes and Gardens* Test Kitchens and adjusted to modern ingredients and up-to-date cooking equipment. In this way you can enjoy the foods of days gone by without the particular inconveniences of the times.

A frequent question is, "Where do those great *Better Homes and Gardens* recipes come from year after year?" The answer has two parts—inspiration and making inspiration work. The inspirations that start the tasty concoctions on their way to the printed page are as varied as the finished dishes themselves. A new recipe idea may have its beginnings in the food traditions of the past or the professional travels, curiosity, and expertise of food editors and Test Kitchen home economists. A contest entry or a letter from a reader with a cooking problem may trigger a new dish, too. To these add a feel for the taste and temper of the times and a dash of publishing philosophy that makes just as much sense now as it did in the 1920s. Then, because it is one thing to plan a magnificent dish on paper but quite another to make the proportions work, the Test Kitchen staff goes into action. Once the recipe is in working order, it is evaluated by a taste panel of home economists who judge the dish for its family appeal, deliciousness, and practicality.

The history of these recipes and the fifty million cook books they gave birth to really belongs to E. T. Meredith of Des Moines, Iowa. In the early 1920s his magazine, *Successful Farming,* was well established in rural America. Meredith caught sight of the then 12 million families who lived in cities, towns, and suburbs. For them he produced a magazine he called *Fruit, Garden and Home.* He saw its audience as people eager to do something now, within their means, to make their homes more comfortable and attractive. Besides the garden and decorating tips, he included recipes. He knew his market. Families wanted this practical approach to home life in 1922 and they still want it today.

Like everything in *Fruit, Garden and Home,* the food articles reflected the doing something now within one's means. Food writers of the day contributed articles to help readers increase their culinary skills while staying within a moderate budget. The magazine also requested and printed favorite recipes submitted by readers in an ongoing section called Cooks' Round Table. (See feature on page 25.)

By the fall of 1924, the magazine's name changed to *Better Homes and Gardens.* The scope of the food articles broadened and recipe contributions to the Cooks' Round Table continued to roll in. After publication, these recipes were filed, then collected and reprinted in pamphlet form as *The 202 Best and Most Interesting Recipes from Cooks' Round Table.*

**A**s the magazine's circulation climbed and the volume of recipes submitted went up, a long-range means of evaluating recipes was necessary. The solution was, and still is, a practical one—a test kitchen. Women with home economics degrees were employed to prepare and judge recipes, then to write them in clear, understandable language so that homemakers across the country could duplicate the dish with the same success. The Cooks' Round Table page in February, 1929, stated that recipes from readers were tested in the *Better Homes and Gardens* kitchens. The pictures on page 8 give you a then and now look at the decor and equipment in the *Better Homes and Gardens* Test Kitchens.

The stage was now set for a cook book. The October, 1930 issue of the magazine announced *My Better Homes and Gardens Cook Book*, changed in 1953 to the *New Cook Book*. Some 10,000 copies were ordered before the book was released. By December of the same year, the book also could be obtained through a magazine subscription offer.

*My Better Homes and Gardens Cook Book* was a new kind of cook book for a new kind of homemaker. The difference—it was designed for the home-business woman, the woman interested in bringing the same efficiency of a well-run business into the home. Automatic cooking devices and improved equipment for food storage and meal preparation were necessary tools as was an attitude that adopts the new when it proves efficient or is ready to discard the old when something is better.

The book championed level measurements and the listing of ingredients in order of use. In fact, homemakers who wished to submit their own recipes to the Tasting-Test Kitchen, were requested to follow these same techniques. A chart of equivalents inside the back cover came to the aid of the homemaker unfamiliar with standard measurements.

This first *Better Homes and Gardens* cook book was new to cook book publishing, too. It was ringbound to open flat for ease in following recipe directions. Although cover color and design have changed with the succeeding seven editions, the ringbound feature has been retained. In addition, since 1937, the magazine has been printing punched recipe pages. These pages can be pulled out and put into the cook book so that homemakers can keep their books up to date each month.

**T**o those who have grown up with one or more editions of the *Better Homes and Gardens Cook Book* in a handy place in the kitchen, the book's popularity is of no surprise. However, the number of copies sold sometimes is. To date, more than 17 million copies have rolled off the presses, making it the No. 1 best seller of all time excluding Bibles and dictionaries.

Keeping this cooking 'bible' up to date presents a constant challenge. At intervals, the red and white plaid cook book is completely revised to incorporate new interests, equipment, foods, and techniques. For example, in the 1953 edition a section on Outdoor Cooking was added. Barbecuing was taking the country by storm, and *Better Homes and Gardens* magazine was in the forefront with the kinds of helpful tips and recipes that make barbecuing fun for the whole family.

The space available in the *New Cook Book* was soon too limited to contain all of the information and enthusiasm the backyard grill generated. As a result, in 1957, the *Better Homes and Gardens Barbecue Book* was created. It was the first of many cook books devoted to specific topics. Today, this line includes books for salad lovers, calorie counters, fondue enthusiasts, working homemakers who want meals in minutes, as well as blender owners, devotees of the electric skillet, and many more. All of the recipes that are published in these volumes undergo the same inspiration and testing process that was outlined earlier.

**A**s you page through the decades in the *Golden Treasury of Cooking,* notice the times, equipment, or food preferences that made the recipes popular. Many of the dishes are coming around again for entirely different reasons. Others have never really lost their flavor appeal.

*In the '30s* you'll learn what families enjoyed at the dinner table via the Cooks' Round Table. There is also a collection of recipes associated with celebrities. The flavor of Walt Disney's Macaroni Mickey Mousse is as likable as the cartoon character for which it was named. In addition, those ice creams capitalizing on the mechanical refrigerator in the 1930s kitchen work mighty well in today's models.

*In the '40s* train travel was the way to go, and food in the dining cars rivaled that of great restaurants in the cities along the way. The trains are but a memory. The foods, such as Union Pacific Fruit Salad Dressing, need not be. Victory Gardens of the war years and subsequent home-canned foods are enjoying a revival as satisfying do-it-yourself projects. Saving fuel with oven meals is in style again, too.

*In the '50s* many new cooking techniques were learned at the backyard barbecue grill. They were good preparation for the leisure-time living of today. The backyard now is the beach, the mountains, or other playgrounds a weekend's worth of miles away. It was also during this decade that main dish salads really moved out of California and onto the luncheon plates of the nation. Today, he-men and dieters alike take a hearty salad's crisp goodness for granted.

*In the '60s* fondue pots came on the market, and women learned that cooking at the table is not only fun for the guests, but frees the hostess from kitchen duties. Gourmet cooking and convenience foods court the cook as more people travel and more women are employed outside the home.

*In the '70s* doing your own thing in the kitchen puts a creative emphasis on cooking. The satisfactions of making breads, granola, and other time-consuming foods are balanced by the speed of microwave ovens and by all of the other timesaving appliances now available. New products and new ideas come thick and fast.

**R**eading about good food is decidedly second best to tasting it. After you have savored all the pieces of information about the dishes, take the *Golden Treasury of Cooking* into your kitchen and translate some of its riches into eating enjoyment for your family and guests.

The red-plaid seal assures you that every recipe in the *Golden Treasury of Cooking* is endorsed by the *Better Homes and Gardens* Test Kitchen. Each of the recipes is tested for family appeal, practicality, and deliciousness.

JULY 1933 10 CENTS

# BETTER HOMES
# & GARDENS

Meredith Publishing Company · Des Moines, Iowa
More Than 1,400,000 Circulation

The ups and downs of the '30s are legendary. The Wall Street "crash" was followed by the Great Depression; but it also was a time of uncomplicated living—instead of a television, the family surrounded the radio for the Saturday night play or variety program, or spent the evening at the Bijou watching a double-feature of the new "talking" pictures. And family fare centered around macaroni and cheese, potatoes, fish, veal, and pork. In the kitchen, new innovations in equipment began making life easier and speedier. And with the introduction of the mechanical refrigerator, the door was opened to such delights as freezer tray ice creams, gelatin salads, and desserts.

# THE 30s

The Great Depression scarred the thirties. It was a time of breadlines curling through city streets and the barter system operating in farming communities. Cottage cheese paid for dentistry. Butter settled the plumber's bill. And the theme song of the decade seemed to be "Brother, Can You Spare a Dime." Or was it?

Though three million workers were unemployed in 1930, many more millions *didn't* lose their jobs, *didn't* lose their homes, and somehow muddled through. By 1935, the worst was over and the economy had started an upward climb. Alphabetized agencies of government — the WPA (Works Progress Administration), NRA (National Recovery Act), CCC (Civilian Conservation Corps), and all the rest — were creating jobs, and thereby, generating new hope and confidence.

Life in the thirties proved once again that the only thing we can be sure of is change. As prices went down, so did skirts. Bobbed hair became passé along with the flat-chested, leggy figure of John Held's red-hot baby. Twenty-five cents at the local Bijou bought escape into never-never land with Jean Harlow, Carole Lombard, or Clark Gable. In addition to the screen entertainment, movie-goers got coupons good for marcel waves — or, on what was called 'Dish Night,' a chance to win a free set of dishes.

The dollar-conscious woman planned everyday menus around macaroni and cheese, scalloped potatoes, cabbage, root vegetables, and the abundantly available fish, or veal and pork as substitutes for chicken. The homemaker still made her own pies and cakes, and dried fruits appeared in many variations such as prune whip, apple cobbler, or raisin pie.

Entertaining was done at home because of the tight economic situation, and the rituals of formal hospitality became more and more relaxed for club meetings or sorority socials. At an evening buffet, the man of the house often pitched in to help and got a kick out of his new skills. In certain limited circles, he may have offered an aperitif. But until the repeal of Prohibition in 1933, the perfectly legal grenadine was more likely to appear, if at all, in a fruit cup.

If love was sweeping the country, as was asserted in one of Ira Gershwin's lyrics for the 1931 Pulitzer Prize-winning musical *Of Thee I Sing*, so were such things as contract bridge, Mah-Jongg, miniature golf, and home-based diversions such as jigsaw puzzles and Monopoly.

As pocket books grew heavier and hearts lighter, travel became everyone's sport. Twenty million visitors flocked to Chicago in 1933 to take in the Century of Progress exposition. Here, they viewed with awe the newest wonders of science, including the irradiation of foods with vitamin D. Perhaps it was also awe those visitors felt who took the opportunity to get a good, close look at Sally Rand's fan dance.

Americans who weren't sailing off to foreign countries toured the United States in the family car, enjoying a touch of luxury in a new facility called a motel — lounge and dining facilities added to the earlier tourist cabin concept. Motels spread rapidly from California eastward. (The word originated, according to one account, because the owner of The Milestone Motor Hotel at San Luis Obispo couldn't get the full name of his motor court on his roadside sign.)

Technology was on the march, too. It brought better automobiles, big ticket items such as improved washing machines, and new consumer conveniences including Clarence Birdseye's frozen fruits and vegetables. Perhaps no technological advance of the decade had more impact on the American family than the mechanical refrigerator, which put the ice man out of business in short order. Homemakers started enjoying a new world of food preservation and preparation. Now, anything that could be made in a gelatin mold soared to the top spot on Americans' menus. Ice cream could be made effortlessly in freezer trays instead of by the old muscle-building, hand-cranking method that was necessary before.

The thirties were radio's great years, and Bing Crosby, Kate Smith, and Major Bowes were familiar friends. Regular visitors in every home were Rudy Vallee singing "Your Time is My Time," The Quiz Kids, Edgar Bergen and Charlie McCarthy, Fred Allen, and Amos 'n Andy. It became a national sport to fish for distant stations on the Philco or RCA 'consoles.' But kids of the time left that 'fishing' to adults. The young set had their own listening preferences, which included the adventures of Superman, Orphan Annie, and Jack Armstrong, that wholesome all-American boy who would send any of a variety of secret rings and decoding devices in exchange for a Wheaties boxtop. News from all over the world came into American homes via radio—with the fireside chats by FDR and reports of such important events as Edward VIII's abdication and the Japanese movements in China. Other not exactly entertaining radio features centered around the actions of Hitler and Mussolini. As the decade ran out, the economic threat to the United States gave way to another threat—war!

But for the moment, world problems didn't affect Americans as they flocked to the decade's largest exhibition, the New York World's Fair, dedicated to the "World of Tommorw. The idea had ironic overtones when viewed in the perspective of Pearl Harbor and its aftermath. The Fair may have been the last carefree fling. The scene was lively, with fountains and flags (except Germany's), fireworks, foreign restaurants for the adventurous, and waterfalls for all. General Electric offered its vision of the future, a television studio. And General Motors provided an unforgettable ride on its Futurama. However, it was all slightly unreal as Eleanor Holm and a flock of pretty girls swam to waltz time at the Aquacade while the blitzkrieg was destroying Poland.

Throughout the ups and downs of these roller-coaster years, *Better Homes and Gardens* held steadily to its editorial program of providing practical service material, news from the country's most prestigious cooking schools, and developments in kitchen management that could bring a better way of living to American families. The best recipes from all over the United States were collected from readers of the popular monthly feature, Cooks' Round Table. All of these were kitchen- and panel-tested by expert cooks and tasters before they were admitted to one of the nation's greatest treasuries of recipes: *My Better Homes and Gardens Cook Book.*

Whatever people do, first they must eat. *Better Homes and Gardens* was committed to the idea that its readers should eat well, be well nourished, and enjoy what they ate. The pages of the magazine displayed a judicious mingling of the old and the new. Visual excitement was added by the new technique of direct color photography. Some of the traditional ideas that the magazine thought worth saving included home preserving and canning, and that smacking-good cream, vinegar, and sugar salad dressing that dates all the way back to 1900. Pie was a big favorite, particularly concord grape, squash, raisin crisscross, and milk chocolate.

While it preserved the best of the past, *Better Homes and Gardens* continued to pioneer new ideas. One was the main dish salad, a menu idea the magazine pushed strongly with an assist from Irene Castle, the famous —and slim—dancer. Jellied and molded salads also appeared frequently. The tossed green salad with the simple oil-and-vinegar dressing was still only a gleam in his eye, yet the editor of the magazine—a man—sensed the wave of the future when he personally wrote 'The Eatin' o' the Green.'

Though *Better Homes and Gardens* could (and did) offer advice on how to select a servant and pictured a trim, starchy-aproned maid telephoning in a grocery order, the servantless household was the prevailing mode and the magazine gave every encouragement to the do-it-yourself trend. This new 'get-involved' philosophy also stressed male participation. And to inspire husbands to try their hand with the mixing bowl and the gas or electric range, the editors printed recipes from such admired achievers as Enrico Caruso (Mushrooms Sautes) world-famed explorer and news commentator Lowell Thomas (Lamb en Brochette à l'Armenia), and the Sole Marguery of Raymond Orteig, the French-born proprietor of New York's Lafayette Hotel and the man who had put up the prize money for the first solo flight across the Atlantic, which Charles Lindberg won. Walt Disney came up with an appetizing dish and a dandy pun—Macaroni Mickey Mousse. And men also found a creative outlet in the new, relaxed custom of the cookout, called 'outdoor supper.' A charcoal steak with a bacon lattice top in the San Francisco style clearly signalled the arrival of the patio and grill. "Mere men," said *BH&G* slyly, "but they can cook."

**F**olks in the thirties were very much caught up in regional cookery, and *Better Homes and Gardens* mirrored this keen interest. Menus and recipes celebrated Boston food customs (fresh salmon, new potatoes, and green peas, traditional on Bunker Hill Day and the Fourth of July). There were mouth-watering foods from the Pennsylvania Dutch country, and from across the continent came California-style meals utilizing such familiar western foods as prunes, raisins, dates, walnuts, head lettuce, and citrus fruits along with newcomers such as avocados and pomegranates. *Better Homes and Gardens* also culled recipes from the Great Northwest with its baked Idaho potatoes and Olympia oysters. From the midwestern heartland the magazine extolled the virtues of the fried chicken dinner, fluffy whipped potatoes and speckled gravy, roasting ears, luscious sliced tomatoes, cucumber, and onion.

But regional American cooking wasn't the only source of new recipes for *Better Homes and Gardens'* readers. Cosmopolitan foods found their way into many American kitchens. Favorites among Francophiles were bouillabaisse and chocolate soufflé from the legendary cuisine at the very French Lafayette Hotel restaurant near New York's Washington Square. In an intriguing article, "Eating-Around-The-World Tour," a spectacular arroz con pollo recipe from Spain rated cheers from cooks and diners. Also in the spotlight was the radical chic of Russian foods. Readers even learned not to flinch when garlic was mentioned seriously—or shish kabob or yelmi. American tastes were becoming more sophisticated.

Throughout the thirties, *Better Homes and Gardens* continued to pioneer. It stressed the importance of level measurements, explained allergies, warned of cholesterol and pointed out the versatility of the new ranges, electric mixers, and refrigerators that brightened the advertising pages. Vitamins were known, but the magazine made them better known. Spinach, with help from Popeye, got a boost. So did herb cookery and the new trimmed, packaged, and frozen meats. The editors thought highly of liver, too. Gone forever were the days when the butcher, wrapping up a meat order, would toss in a free slice of liver for the family cat.

The thirties brought with them economic depression then reconstruction —limited budgets even for necessities, then an improved financial climate that encouraged travel and provided some of the previously denied luxuries. In foods, too, the thirties swung from budget-minded staple foods to experimenting with regional and foreign dishes. So, the decade that came in at such a low ebb bowed out with promises of better things ahead.

← *Unfold this section for three-page foldout illustration in full color*

# Recipe Features of the Thirties

## Cooks' Round Table

Swap your favorite recipes with the homemakers of the thirties by reading the Cooks' Round Table. This feature, which appeared in the *Better Homes and Gardens* magazine each month, encouraged everyone to participate. It served as a forum for exchanging readers' recipes, which ranged from an elegant cheese rarebit to a homey Ozark pudding.

## Personalities

Make a journey back in time to meet some of the famous personalities of the thirties. One way is to try the foods they enjoyed most. This collection of recipes includes the favorite dishes of notables such as President Franklin Roosevelt, Mme. Schumann-Heink, Lowell Thomas, Henry A. Wallace, Walt Disney, and Oscar of the Waldorf.

## Ice Creams and Sherbets

Join the homemakers of the thirties in making ice creams and sherbets in your own refrigerator trays. These homemakers were eager to try recipes that used their newest appliance— the refrigerator. This assortment of ice creams and sherbets is a delightful mixture of those made in refrigerator trays as well as those made in ice cream freezers.

Homemakers of the thirties enjoyed cooking and were eager to try new recipes. Sometimes, though, they became confused. This homemaker turned to an early edition of *My Better Homes and Gardens Cook Book* for help.

# Cooks' Round Table

Cooks' Round Table, now called Prize-Tested Recipes, started in 1924 as a country-wide reader recipe exchange. From it grew the Tasting-Test Kitchen, a magazine's reputation for appealing recipes, and a series of best-selling cook books. Through the years, this feature has kept food editors in touch with the kinds of foods that families enjoy.

In the 1930s, as later, page space in the magazine and the cook book limited the number of submitted recipes that could actually appear in print. However, any recipe that passed the test kitchen's standards of taste, dependability, and family usefulness was awarded a signed Certificate of Endorsement. Because it established her as a good cook, this certificate, with six copies of her recipe for friends, meant as much as the prize money to many women. Today, Certificates and recipe copies are awarded only to winners in the Prize-Tested Recipe contest.

To those submitting recipes in the '30s, the editors cautioned about "the evils of housewives' recipes...'scant,' 'heaping,' 'rounding,' and 'pinch.'" They further counseled that "unless a recipe is accurate as to measurements and clear as to method, it is not dependable for other women to follow." Level measurements are no longer a novelty, but accurate measurements and clearly written methods are still among the standards any recipe bearing the *Better Homes and Gardens* seal must meet.

## Daffodil Cake

½ cup sifted cake flour
½ cup sifted powdered sugar
6 egg whites
½ teaspoon cream of tartar
½ teaspoon vanilla
⅛ teaspoon salt
½ cup granulated sugar

¾ cup sifted cake flour
¾ teaspoon baking powder
6 egg yolks
2 tablespoons lemon juice
1 tablespoon cold water
½ cup granulated sugar
Powdered sugar

*White part:* Sift ½ cup cake flour and ½ cup powdered sugar together three times. Beat egg whites till frothy; add cream of tartar, vanilla, and salt. Beat till soft peaks form. Gradually beat in ½ cup granulated sugar. Sift a fourth of the flour mixture at a time over top; fold in.

*Yellow part:* Sift ¾ cup cake flour and baking powder together three times. Beat yolks with juice and water till thick, 5 to 7 minutes; gradually beat in ½ cup granulated sugar. Sift a fourth of the flour mixture at a time over top; fold in.

Alternately spoon yellow and white mixtures into an ungreased 9- or 10-inch tube pan. Bake at 375° for 35 to 40 minutes. Invert and cool. Dust cake with powdered sugar.

*Appearing with spring's first jonquils was the Daffodil Cake (pictured opposite), also known as Easter Dinner Cake. A beauty to behold, this sunny yellow and white marbled sponge cake and angel food was thrifty, too. It handily used both the yolks and whites of 6 eggs, a very popular feature with women who always wondered what to do with the 12 egg yolks left from baking an angel food cake.*

## Ozark Pudding

1 cup sugar
2 slightly beaten eggs
1 teaspoon vanilla
⅓ cup all-purpose flour
3 teaspoons baking powder

⅛ teaspoon salt
2 cups chopped, peeled apple (3 medium)
½ cup chopped walnuts
Whipped cream

Combine sugar, beaten eggs, and vanilla. Stir in flour, baking powder, and salt. Add apple and walnuts to egg mixture; mix well. Turn into greased and floured 9x9x2-inch baking pan. Bake at 325° for 30 to 35 minutes. Serve warm with whipped cream. Serves 6 to 8.

*Outstanding, homey dishes of many nationalities appeared on the pages of Cooks' Round Table. Each recipe benefited from the touch of originality applied by the woman who submitted it. In Italian Polenta the something extra in flavor is the cheese stirred into the cornmeal mixture.*

## Italian Polenta

3¾ cups water
1 cup yellow cornmeal
½ teaspoon salt
½ cup shredded process American cheese
½ teaspoon paprika
½ pound ground beef
½ cup chopped onion
½ cup sliced mushrooms

3 slices bacon, chopped
½ clove garlic, minced
2 tablespoons all-purpose flour
1 28-ounce can tomatoes, cut up
½ teaspoon salt
⅛ teaspoon pepper
Grated Parmesan cheese

In large saucepan bring *2¾ cups* of the water to full rolling boil. Combing remaining 1 cup water, cornmeal, and ½ teaspoon salt. Slowly stir into boiling water. Cook till thick, stirring frequently. Cover and cook over low heat for 10 to 15 minutes. Stir in American cheese and paprika. Turn into greased 10x 6x2-inch baking dish. Cool; cover and chill. To prepare sauce, cook beef, onion, mushrooms, bacon, and garlic till beef is browned. Sprinkle with flour; mix well. Stir in tomatoes, ½ teaspoon salt, and pepper. Simmer, covered, for 20 minutes. Bake cornmeal mixture, covered, at 350° for 25 to 30 minutes. Cut in squares; top with sauce. Sprinkle with Parmesan. Serves 6.

*From the genial cook of a quaint tearoom in New Orleans came this recipe for Deep Sea Delight. Tuna is the, then unusual, deep sea ingredient in this forerunner of today's standby, the tuna-noodle casserole.*

## Deep Sea Delight

2 tablespoons butter or margarine
2 tablespoons all-purpose flour
1½ cups milk
1 cup shredded process American cheese
1 6½- or 7-ounce can tuna, drained and flaked

4 ounces fine noodles, cooked and drained
1 3-ounce can sliced mushrooms, drained
¼ cup chopped green pepper
¼ teaspoon salt
Dash pepper
1 cup cooked cut asparagus

In saucepan melt butter; blend in flour. Add milk all at once. Cook and stir till thickened and bubbly. Stir in ¾ *cup* cheese, tuna, noodles, mushrooms, green pepper, salt, and pepper. Turn *half* the mixture into a 1½-quart casserole. Top with asparagus. Top with remaining noodle mixture. Bake at 350° for 35 to 40 minutes. Sprinkle with remaining shredded American cheese. Bake 5 minutes longer. Makes 6 servings.

## Corned Beef Cakes

2 cups mashed cooked potatoes
1 tablespoon butter or margarine, melted
1 teaspoon Worcestershire sauce
½ teaspoon dry mustard
½ teaspoon salt
⅛ teaspoon pepper

1 12-ounce can corned beef, flaked
2 slightly beaten eggs
¼ cup finely chopped onion
½ clove garlic, minced
Milk
Shortening
6 poached eggs (optional)

Combine mashed potatoes, butter, Worcestershire, dry mustard, salt, and pepper. Add corned beef, beaten eggs, onion, and garlic. Mix thoroughly. (Add 1 to 2 tablespoons milk if mixture seems dry.) Shape mixture into 6 patties. Fry in hot shortening till browned, turning once. Top each patty with a poached egg, if desired. Serves 6.

## Scalloped Chicken with Mushroom Sauce

4 cups diced cooked chicken
2½ cups soft bread crumbs
(3 slices bread)
1 cup cooked rice
4 beaten eggs
¼ cup diced canned pimiento

¼ cup butter or margarine,
melted
1¼ teaspoons salt
2 cups chicken broth
1 cup milk
Mushroom Sauce

Mix chicken, bread crumbs, cooked rice, eggs, pimiento, butter, and salt. Combine chicken broth and milk. Stir into chicken mixture. Pour into 12x7x2-inch baking dish. Bake at 350° till set, 45 to 50 minutes. Serve immediately with Mushroom Sauce. Serves 8 to 10.

*Mushroom Sauce:* In saucepan melt ¼ cup butter or margarine. Add 3 cups sliced mushrooms; cook till tender, about 5 minutes. Blend in ¼ cup all-purpose flour. Add 2 cups chicken broth to mushrooms. Cook, stirring constantly, till thickened and bubbly. Add 2 tablespoons snipped parsley and 1 teaspoon lemon juice. Combine 2 beaten egg yolks and ¼ cup whipping cream; stir mixture into sauce. Cook and stir over low heat, 2 minutes more. Season with salt and pepper.

## Tomato-Cheese Rarebit

3 tablespoons butter or
margarine
3 tablespoons all-purpose
flour
1 cup milk
1 8-ounce can tomato sauce

¼ teaspoon dry mustard
¼ teaspoon prepared
horseradish
2 cups shredded process
American cheese
Toast *or* saltine crackers

In a saucepan melt the butter; blend in flour. Add milk all at once. Cook and stir over medium heat till thickened and bubbly. Stir in the tomato sauce, dry mustard, and horseradish. Mix thoroughly. Stir in shredded cheese. Cook over low heat till the cheese is melted and sauce is smooth, stirring occasionally. (If cheese is slow to blend, beat with rotary beater till smooth.) Serve at once on toast. Serves 6.

*Rink-tum-tiddy and Blushing Bunny were whimsical names for versatile Tomato-Cheese Rarebit. The flavor combination, too good to limit to a bed of crisp crackers or toast triangles, was also enjoyed over mashed potatoes or as the topper for a bacon and tomato supper sandwich.*

## Barbecued Limas

2 cups dry lima beans
6 ounces salt pork, cut in
½-inch cubes
½ cup chopped onion
1 clove garlic,
minced
1 10¾-ounce can condensed
tomato soup

2 tablespoons vinegar
1 tablespoon packed brown
sugar
2 teaspoons prepared
mustard
2 teaspoons Worcestershire
sauce
½ teaspoon chili powder

Rinse lima beans; combine with 5½ cups cold water in a saucepan. Bring to boiling; boil for 2 minutes. Remove from heat and cover. Soak 1 hour. (Or, combine beans and 5½ cups water; soak overnight.) Do not drain. In skillet fry the salt pork till browned. Remove from skillet, reserving drippings. Add pork to limas. Simmer, covered, till beans are tender, about 45 minutes. Drain, reserving 1½ cups liquid. In reserved drippings cook onion and garlic till onion is tender but not brown. Stir in reserved bean liquid, tomato soup, vinegar, brown sugar, mustard, Worcestershire, and chili powder. Bring to boiling; simmer 5 minutes. Add beans. Turn into 2-quart casserole. Bake, uncovered, at 350° for 45 minutes, stirring twice. Serves 8.

# Personalities

Radio brought musicians, commentators, and politicians right into the family living rooms of the '30s. Down at the local Bijou you could see these people in action via newsreel, travelogue, or feature film. This new closeness sparked a lively interest in the notables of the day, often extending to their lives offstage, including what they liked to eat.

Throughout the decade, *Better Homes and Gardens* chronicled the food likes of many famous people. In 1935, the magazine announced to millions of Americans that the late Enrico Caruso, a famous tenor, loved mushrooms. Another time, Mme. Schumann-Heink, one of the world's leading sopranos, was pictured creaming a cake in her sunny California garden and advocating housework as the means to a hardy constitution. And from Walter Damrosch, whose 'musical university of the air' did much for music appreciation, came his recipe for Mutton with Caper Sauce.

Not all the people featured were musicians. For example, the table for a country luncheon at the Roosevelt home in Hyde Park was set with blue willowware and graced with a silver pitcher of pink roses flanked by silver compotes containing peaches. In another issue, Lowell Thomas shared exotic recipes he acquired during his globe-trotting jaunts.

Restaurants produced culinary celebrities, too. One was Oscar of the Waldorf. Another was Raymond Orteig of New York's Lafayette Hotel in Washington Square. Meanwhile, Herr August Luchow was building an enviable reputation for fine German specialties.

The selection of recipes on the following pages is a sample of the good food recommended by well-known personalities of the 1930s.

## Caruso's Mushrooms Sautes

*Bootblack to bank president knew Enrico Caruso as Italy's greatest tenor. Once, when asked for an I.D. in a New York bank, he threw back his head and sang a high B that startled every bank clerk. "That's who I am." To keep this magnificent voice in trim, he took great care of his body. But even operatic tenors need to splurge once in a while. Caruso did this with his favorite Mushrooms Sautes. Maybe you don't have the voice, but you can still enjoy this succulent appetizer.*

1¼ cups sliced mushrooms
¼ cup cooking oil
⅛ teaspoon pepper
2 tablespoons butter or
   margarine

¼ cup chopped green onion
2 tablespoons snipped
   parsley
1 teaspoon anchovy paste
Small toast triangles

Combine sliced mushrooms, cooking oil, and pepper. Marinate several hours; stir often. Drain well. Melt butter in saucepan; add onion and cook till tender but not brown. Add mushrooms, parsley, and anchovy paste. Heat through. Spread on toast triangles. Makes 32 canapés.

## Henry A. Wallace's Cheese Soufflé

3 tablespoons butter or
   margarine
3 tablespoons all-purpose
   flour
½ teaspoon salt
⅛ teaspoon white pepper

1 cup milk
1 cup shredded process
   American cheese
   (4 ounces)
3 egg yolks
3 egg whites

In saucepan melt butter or margarine; blend in flour, salt, and white pepper. Add milk. Cook and stir over medium heat till mixture is thickened and bubbly. Remove from heat. Add cheese; stir till melted. Beat egg yolks till thick and lemon-colored. *Slowly* add the cheese mixture, stirring constantly; cool slightly. Beat egg whites till stiff peaks form; fold into the cheese mixture. Bake in an *ungreased* 5½-cup soufflé dish at 325° for 25 to 30 minutes. Serve immediately. Serves 4.

Looking for a really special dish? Try *President Roosevelt's Boiled Salmon with Egg Sauce* (see recipe, page 30). This presidential favorite features a dressed salmon accented by a creamy egg sauce. Sprinkle with paprika and garnish with parsley and lemon slices.

Treat your guests to the rich goodness of *Henry A. Wallace's Cheese Soufflé*, a favorite of the former vice president. This puffy creation of eggs, milk, and cheese tastes as good as it looks. It's sure to please even the most critical gourmet.

*Creative cooking was the rage of the '30s. Everyone had their own homespun favorites, even Mme. Ernestine Schumann-Heink, whose lilting soprano voice was heard on early radio. When a tour was over, she would go into the kitchen and make hearty Potato Soup.*

*Globe-trotting news commentator, Lowell Thomas, likes lamb en brochette. He first sampled it in the desert while watching the exploits of Lawrence of Arabia.*

*Boiled Salmon with Egg Sauce was one of Franklin D. Roosevelt's favorite dishes. When the Roosevelts moved into the White House, the First Lady asked Henrietta Nesbitt to go along, too. She believed her former Hyde Park neighbor was the only woman who could supervise the preparation of the President's favorite foods — including salmon.*

*Walter Damrosch, who was familiar to many children of the '30s for his music appreciation classes via radio, loved Mutton with Caper Sauce. Because mutton isn't readily available in the United States today, the test kitchen changed it to Lamb with Caper Sauce. Either way, it's a musical dish for you, too.*

## Mme. Schumann-Heink's Potato Soup

4 large potatoes, peeled
2 large onions
3 bay leaves
4 cups milk

2 beaten egg yolks
¼ cup whipping cream
White pepper
Toast points

Quarter potatoes and onions. Combine vegetables, bay leaves, 4 cups water, and 1 teaspoon salt; simmer till vegetables are tender, about 25 minutes. Do not drain. Remove bay leaves. Put mixture through food mill. Add milk; heat through. Beat yolks with cream; stir into soup and heat through. Season with salt and pepper. Serve with toast. Serves 12.

## Lowell Thomas' Lamb en Brochette à l'Armenia

1 cup finely chopped onion
⅓ cup lemon juice
2 tablespoons cooking oil

1 teaspoon salt
2 pounds boneless lamb, cut into 1-inch cubes

Combine onion, lemon juice, oil, and salt. Add lamb. Chill several hours or overnight. Drain lamb; thread onto skewers. Broil 4 inches from heat 10 to 12 minutes; turn frequently. Serves 6 to 8.

## President Roosevelt's Boiled Salmon with Egg Sauce *(see photo, page 29)*

1 4- to 5-pound fresh or frozen dressed salmon*
2 cups water
1 stalk celery, cut up

1 slice lemon
1 slice onion
1 bay leaf
Egg sauce

Thaw frozen salmon. Wrap salmon in cheesecloth. Place in large, shallow pan; add water, celery, lemon, onion, bay leaf, and 1 teaspoon salt. Simmer till fish flakes easily when tested with fork, 25 to 30 minutes. Reserve 1 cup fish stock. Remove skin, being careful to preserve shape of fish. Discard skin. Transfer fish to serving plate. Top with Egg Sauce. Makes 8 to 10 servings.

*Or, substitute 8 to 10 salmon steaks; simmer 5 to 10 minutes.
*Egg Sauce:* In saucepan melt ¼ cup butter or margarine; blend in 3 tablespoons all-purpose flour, ½ teaspoon salt, and ⅛ teaspoon white pepper. Add reserved fish stock and 1 cup light cream. Cook and stir till thickened and bubbly. Add 2 chopped hard cooked eggs to cream mixture and heat through.

## Walter Damrosch's Lamb with Caper Sauce

1 4- to 5-pound leg of lamb
1 clove garlic, sliced
½ cup chopped onion
3 tablespoons all-purpose flour

¼ teaspoon salt
1 cup water
½ cup light cream
3 tablespoons capers, drained

Trim excess fat from lamb. Cut slit into each side of leg; insert a piece of garlic clove in each slit. Place meat, fat side up, on rack in shallow roasting pan. Sprinkle with onion. Season with salt and pepper. Roast at 325° till meat thermometer registers 175° to 180°, about 3½ hours. Remove meat to platter. Pour ½ cup pan juices into saucepan; stir in flour and salt. Add water and cream; cook and stir till bubbly. Add capers. Serve with lamb. Serves 10 to 12.

## Raymond Orteig's Sole Marguery

2 pounds fresh or frozen
    sole fillets, cut in 6
    portions
12 fresh or frozen
    shelled shrimp
12 shucked oysters *or*
    mussels, drained

¼ cup sliced mushrooms
½ teaspoon salt
¼ teaspoon white pepper
½ cup dry white wine
4 slightly beaten egg yolks
½ cup whipping cream
¼ cup butter or margarine

Thaw frozen fish; place sole in baking dish. On each portion of sole, place two shrimp and two oysters. Top with mushrooms; sprinkle with salt and white pepper. Add wine. Cover and bake at 450° for 15 minutes. Pour off stock, reserving 1 cup. Keep fish hot. In top of double boiler boil stock rapidly till reduced to ¼ cup. Add egg yolks and cream. Cook and stir over hot, not boiling, water till thickened. (Upper pan should not touch water.) Beat in butter, a little at a time; continue cooking till thickened and smooth. Pass sauce. Serves 6.

*Good recipes don't have to be complicated. Sole Marguery is a case in point. A famous restaurateur sent his son all the way to France just to learn how to put the recipe together. But you can dine with wine and eat with the best with this simple version from Raymond Orteig, owner of New York's old Lafayette Hotel.*

## Macaroni Mickey Mousse

Cook 1 cup elbow macaroni in boiling, salted water till tender; drain. Melt ¼ cup butter or margarine in 1½ cups hot milk. Pour over 1 cup soft bread crumbs. Add 1½ cups shredded sharp process American cheese, 2 tablespoons finely chopped onion, 2 tablespoons minced canned pimiento, 1 tablespoon snipped parsley, ½ teaspoon salt, ⅛ teaspoon pepper, dash paprika, and cooked macaroni. Blend in 3 beaten eggs. Turn into a greased 9x5x3-inch loaf pan. Bake at 325° for 45 to 50 minutes. Let stand a few minutes before serving. Serves 6.

*Walt Disney, working late at a Kansas City art studio, shared his cheese sandwich with mice that scampered about. One clambered up on his drawing board, inspiring his cartoon character.*

## Luchow's Potato Pancakes

6 large potatoes, peeled
3 slightly beaten eggs
¼ cup grated onion
1 tablespoon all-purpose
    flour

1 tablespoon finely crushed
    saltine crackers
2 teaspoons sugar
1½ teaspoons salt
Dash pepper

Grate potatoes into cold water. Drain; squeeze in cheesecloth to remove excess water. Mix with remaining ingredients. Drop mixture from a ¼-cup measure onto lightly greased hot skillet. Spread to 4-inch diameter. Bake till browned, about 5 minutes on each side. Makes 18.

*It's hard to associate music with potato pancakes, but Herr August Luchow accomplished this when he borrowed $1,500 from William Steinway of the piano company to open the restaurant now known for good German food and Potato Pancakes.*

## Oscar of the Waldorf's Orange Charlotte

¾ cup sugar
1 envelope unflavored
    gelatin
½ teaspoon grated orange
    peel
1 cup orange juice

½ cup water
2 tablespoons lemon juice
2 egg whites
2 medium oranges, peeled
    and sectioned

Combine sugar and gelatin. Add orange peel and juice, water, and lemon juice. Stir over low heat till gelatin and sugar are dissolved. Chill till partially set. Add to egg whites. Beat till fluffy, 2 to 3 minutes. Line a 4-cup bombe mold with orange segments. Gently pour in egg mixture. Chill till set. Unmold. Garnish with crystalized orange flowers or maraschino cherries, if desired. Serves 6 to 8.

*The legendary Oscar was better known by the Waldorf Salad he created for the hotel's opening in 1893 than by his last name—Tschirky—yet the real Oscar touch lies in the simplicity of this Orange Charlotte.*

# Ice Creams and Sherbets

When the mechanical refrigerator replaced the icebox, the 'Great American Dessert' became more than a Fourth of July treat. Enjoyment of easy-to-make ice creams became part of the American way of life.

The ice man still patrolled the streets with his cry of, "icee," but it was the freezing tray tucked away in the ice-cube compartment of the refrigerator that stirred the imagination and creativity of more than 7,800 homemakers who submitted recipes to the frozen dessert recipe contest in August, 1932. Six shiny new refrigerators were moved into the Test Kitchen to test the entries.

In that first contest a creamy Vanilla Ice Cream was the winner. In succeeding years luscious variations, such as Date-Nut and Chocolate-Macaroon, capitalized upon the goodness of that basic recipe. Still other versions relied on gelatin or sweetened condensed milk for smoothness.

*English Toffee Ice Cream (see recipe, page 34), Cranberry Sherbet (see recipe, page 37), and Apricot Chiffon Ice Cream (all pictured opposite) are ideal for taking the heat off a hot summer afternoon. These flavors will be favorites for ice cream fans of all ages.*

## Vanilla Ice Cream

2 cups milk
¾ cup sugar
2 slightly beaten egg
    yolks

2 teaspoons vanilla
2 stiffly beaten egg
    whites
1 cup whipping cream

In a heavy saucepan combine milk, sugar, egg yolks, and ¼ teaspoon salt. Cook the mixture over medium-low heat, stirring constantly, till mixture coats a metal spoon. Stir in vanilla. Fold custard mixture into the stiffly beaten egg whites. Chill thoroughly. Whip the cream till thick and custardlike. Fold cream into the chilled custard mixture. Pour into two 3-cup refrigerator trays. Place in freezer; stir every 30 minutes the first 1½ hours. Freeze till firm. Makes 5½ cups.

**Chocolate-Macaroon Ice Cream:** Prepare Vanilla Ice Cream as above, *except* fold 1 cup coarsely crumbled chocolate wafers and 1 cup crumbled soft macaroons along with the whipped cream into the custard.

**Date-Nut Ice Cream:** Prepare Vanilla Ice Cream as above, *except* fold 1 cup chopped walnuts and ½ cup chopped dates along with the whipped cream into the custard.

**Orange Marmalade Ice Cream:** Prepare Vanilla Ice Cream as above, *except* fold ⅓ cup orange marmalade along with cream into custard.

**Fresh Fruit Ice Cream:** Prepare Vanilla Ice Cream as above, *except* fold 1 cup mashed fresh fruit along with whipped cream into the chilled custard mixture.

*The twin delights of the '30s were ice cream from the refrigerator and movies that talked. Sitting around the kitchen table with a dish of homemade ice cream was a happy setting for recounting the latest troubles of Mickey Rooney as Andy Hardy or the adventures of Judy Garland in the Land of Oz. Movies featuring a winsome Shirley Temple, the singing of Deanna Durbin, or the skating of Sonja Henie were popular with young and old. And in 1939, the all-time big picture, Gone With the Wind, was released—it's still drawing crowds to movie theaters today.*

## Apricot Chiffon Ice Cream

1 cup dried apricots
3 beaten egg yolks
3 egg whites

½ cup sugar
1 cup whipping cream

Cook apricots without adding sugar; drain. Puree in blender (makes about ¾ cup purée). In saucepan combine purée, egg yolks, and ¼ cup water. Cook and stir till thickened. Cool. Beat egg whites till soft peaks form. Gradually add sugar, beating till stiff peaks form. Fold into cooled apricot mixture. Whip cream till soft peaks form. Fold whipped cream into apricot mixture. Spoon into two 3-cup refrigerator trays and freeze till firm. Do not stir during freezing. Makes about 5½ cups.

## Favorite Ice Cream

*This refrigerator delight, a tropical tutti-frutti, gets its flavor from pineapple, banana, and chopped red cherries. No wonder it was labeled favorite when it first appeared in print.*

1 8¼-ounce can crushed
    pineapple, drained
½ cup mashed ripe banana
½ cup sugar
¼ cup chopped maraschino
    cherries

2 tablespoons lemon
    juice
1 teaspoon vanilla
⅛ teaspoon salt
2 cups whipping cream

Combine the drained crushed pineapple, mashed ripe banana, sugar, chopped maraschino cherries, lemon juice, vanilla, and salt. Whip the cream till thick and custardlike. Fold the whipped cream into the fruit mixture. Pour the ice cream mixture into two 3-cup refrigerator trays. Freeze till the mixture is firm, 5 to 6 hours or overnight. Do not stir. Let the ice cream stand in refrigerator 10 to 15 minutes before serving. Cut into squares. Makes about 6 cups ice cream.

## Peppermint Ice Cream

⅔ cup *sweetened condensed*
    milk
½ cup water
½ teaspoon peppermint
    extract

3 drops red food
    coloring
1 cup whipping
    cream

Combine the milk, water, extract, and food coloring. Whip cream till thick and custardlike; fold into peppermint mixture. Pour mixture into a 3-cup refrigerator tray. Freeze till partially frozen. Break mixture into chunks into a chilled mixer bowl. Beat till smooth. Return to cold refrigerator tray. Freeze till firm. Makes 3 cups.

## Apricot Mousse

1 17-ounce can unpeeled
    apricot halves,
    drained and mashed
    (1 cup pulp)
½ cup sifted powdered sugar

½ teaspoon vanilla
¼ teaspoon almond
    extract
Dash salt
1 cup whipping cream

In a large mixing bowl combine the mashed apricots, sifted powdered sugar, vanilla, almond extract, and dash salt. Whip the cream till thick and custardlike. Fold the whipped cream into the apricot mixture. Turn the ice cream mixture into a 3-cup refrigerator tray and freeze till the mixture is firm, about 4 hours. Makes about 3 cups.

## English Toffee Ice Cream *(see photo, page 32)*

*"If there's a better refrigerator-made ice cream than this one, I haven't found it," said the Connecticut contributor of English Toffee Ice Cream. "I'd vote twice for this one any day." The English toffee gives it a grand flavor. You'll vote twice for it today, too.*

4 1⅛-ounce chocolate
    coated English toffee
    bars
1 14-ounce can *sweetened
    condensed* milk

½ cup strong coffee
    cooled
2 cups whipping cream
1½ teaspoons vanilla

Crush toffee bars by placing them between two pieces of waxed paper and crushing with rolling pin; set aside. Combine milk, coffee, whipping cream, and vanilla. Chill thoroughly. Whip the mixture to custardlike consistency. Fold in crushed toffee bars. Spoon into three 3-cup refrigerator trays. Freeze firm. Makes 8 cups.

## Toasted Almond Ice Cream

½ cup sugar
4 ounces slivered almonds
    (about ¾ cup)
2 cups light cream

2 cups whipping cream
¾ cup sugar
1 teaspoon vanilla
¼ teaspoon salt

In a small, heavy skillet melt the ½ cup sugar till caramelized (golden brown), stirring constantly to prevent scorching. Add slivered almonds, stirring till thoroughly coated. Spread almond mixture on foil. Cool mixture to room temperature. Chop the toasted almonds into pieces. Combine the almonds, light cream, whipping cream, ¾ cup sugar, vanilla, and salt. Freeze almond mixture in ice cream freezer according to freezer manufacturer's directions. Makes 6 cups.

*From Washington's Crossing Inn, Buck's County, Pa., came our recipe for Toasted Almond Ice Cream in 1931. The Inn is where Washington made plans for crossing the Delaware that cold December night during the Revolutionary War.*

## Graham Cracker Ice Cream

2 cups light cream
1 cup finely crushed
    graham crackers

½ cup sugar
1 teaspoon vanilla

Combine the light cream, finely crushed graham crackers, sugar, and vanilla. Pour cream mixture into a 3-cup refrigerator tray. Freeze until the mixture is partially frozen. Break mixture into chunks into a chilled mixer bowl. Beat at medium speed with an electric mixer till mixture is smooth and fluffy. Quickly return ice cream to cold refrigerator tray and freeze till firm. Makes about 2½ cups ice cream.

*Little did Sylvester Graham, a food reformer of the 1850s, dream of the imaginative ways that the wafers bearing his name would be used in recipes so many decades later. One fond mama even added crumbled crackers to the ice cream for son Jimmie's birthday.*

## Chocolate Chip Ice Cream

½ cup sugar
2 tablespoons cornstarch
2 cups milk
2 beaten eggs
2 cups whipping cream

1 tablespoon vanilla
3 1-ounce squares semi-
    sweet chocolate, finely
    chopped or grated

In a medium saucepan combine the sugar and cornstarch. Stir in milk all at once. Cook and stir over medium heat till mixture is thickened and bubbly. Stir a moderate amount of the hot mixture into the beaten eggs; return to the remaining hot mixture in saucepan. Cook and stir over low heat 1 to 2 minutes longer. Cool mixture to room temperature. Stir whipping cream, vanilla, and chopped or grated chocolate into the mixture. Freeze mixture in an ice cream freezer according to freezer manufacturer's directions. Makes about 6 cups.

## Banana Freeze

1 14-ounce can *sweetened condensed* milk
⅓ cup lemon juice

1 cup mashed ripe banana
    (2 bananas)
1 cup whipping cream

In a large bowl combine sweetened condensed milk and lemon juice; stir just till milk begins to thicken. Stir in mashed banana. Whip the cream until thick and custardlike. Fold the whipped cream into the banana mixture. Freeze mixture in two 3-cup refrigerator trays for 1 hour. Break into chunks into a chilled mixer bowl. Beat with an electric mixer till smooth. Return to cold refrigerator trays. Freeze 1 hour; repeat beating procedure. Freeze firm. Makes 5 cups.

## Green Gage Ice Cream

½ cup sugar
1 teaspoon unflavored
  gelatin
1 cup light cream
½ teaspoon vanilla

1 17-ounce can green gage
  plums, drained
1 teaspoon lemon juice
½ cup whipping cream

In saucepan blend sugar and gelatin. Stir in light cream. Heat and stir till gelatin is dissolved. Cool; stir in vanilla. Turn into a 3-cup refrigerator tray. Freeze till mushy. Turn into a chilled mixer bowl and beat with an electric mixer, about 2 minutes. Sieve plums or puree in a blender. Stir purée and lemon juice into frozen mixture. Whip cream till custardlike; fold into plum mixture. Return to cold refrigerator tray. Freeze; stir once when partially frozen. Makes 3 cups.

## Honey-Orange Ice

1 envelope unflavored
  gelatin
1¾ cups sugar
2 tablespoons honey

1 tablespoon grated orange
  peel
2 cups orange juice
2 stiffly beaten egg whites

In a bowl soften gelatin in ¼ cup cold water. In saucepan combine 2 cups boiling water, sugar, honey, and orange peel. Heat to boiling. Pour over gelatin; stir till gelatin dissolves. Strain. Add orange juice. Pour into three 3-cup refrigerator trays; freeze firm. Break into chunks into a chilled mixer bowl; beat till light. Fold in egg whites. Return to cold refrigerator trays and freeze firm. Makes 8 cups.

*Gelatin and egg whites take care of the texture, while honey and oranges look after the flavor and color of this refreshing ice. You'll like it best escorted with crisp little cookies as an interlude on a hot afternoon.*

## Oahu Frappé

½ cup sugar
1 12-ounce can unsweetened
  pineapple juice

¾ cup orange juice
  Grated orange peel
  (optional)

Bring ¾ cup water and the sugar to boiling; simmer over medium heat 5 minutes. Cool slightly. Add fruit juices. Pour into 3-cup refrigerator tray. Freeze till firm. To serve, break in chunks and stir till mushy. Trim with grated orange peel, if desired. Makes 3 cups.

## Peach Ice Cream

2 cups finely chopped
  peaches
¼ cup sugar
  Red food coloring
  Yellow food coloring

1 14-ounce can *sweetened
  condensed* milk
1 cup whipping cream
⅓ cup slivered almonds,
  toasted

In bowl combine peaches, sugar, and ¼ cup water; mash peaches. Add 1 to 2 drops *each* of the red and yellow food colorings. Drain peach mixture, reserving the juice. Add enough water to the reserved juice to make ¾ cup. Combine drained peaches, reserved juice, and sweetened condensed milk; pour mixture into two 3- or 4-cup refrigerator trays. Freeze till firm. Break mixture into chunks into a chilled mixer bowl. Beat till fluffy with an electric mixer. Whip cream till custardlike. Fold whipped cream and almonds into ice cream. Return to cold refrigerator trays. Freeze till firm. Makes 5 cups.

## Cranberry Sherbet *(see photo, page 32)*

1 16-ounce package
    cranberries (4 cups)
2 cups sugar

1 teaspoon unflavored
    gelatin
2 cups ginger ale

In large saucepan cook cranberries, uncovered, in 2 cups water till skins pop. Press mixture through a sieve or food mill. Combine sugar and unflavored gelatin; stir into cranberry mixture till sugar and gelatin are completely dissolved. Cool to room temperature. Stir in ginger ale. Pour into two 3-cup refrigerator trays; freeze till partially frozen. Break sherbet mixture into chunks into chilled mixer bowl. Beat till smooth with an electric mixer. Pour mixture into cold refrigerator trays or into paper cups. Freeze till sherbet is firm. Serve either as a main dish accompaniment or dessert. Makes 5 cups.

## Ginger Ale-Pineapple Sherbet

2 cups water
1½ cups sugar
1 3-ounce package lemon-
    flavored gelatin

2 cups unsweetened pine-
    apple juice
2 cups ginger ale
¼ cup lemon juice

In medium saucepan combine water, sugar, and lemon-flavored gelatin. Heat and stir till gelatin and sugar are completely dissolved. Cool to room temperature. Add the unsweetened pineapple juice, ginger ale, and lemon juice. Freeze mixture in a 5-quart ice cream freezer according to manufacturer's directions. Makes about 4 quarts.

## Lemon-Nut Sherbet

2 eggs
½ cup sugar
2 cups light cream
½ cup light corn syrup

2 teaspoons grated lemon
    peel
¼ cup lemon juice
½ cup chopped walnuts

Beat eggs till thick and lemon-colored. Add the sugar gradually; beat till thick. Stir in light cream, corn syrup, grated lemon peel, and lemon juice. Pour mixture into two 3-cup refrigerator trays; freeze about 2½ hours. Break sherbet into chunks into chilled mixer bowl. Beat till smooth with an electric mixer. Stir in walnuts. Return quickly to cold refrigerator trays and freeze till firm. Makes 5 cups.

## Grape-Cream Sherbet

1 cup light cream
½ cup sugar
2 tablespoons light corn
    syrup

1 cup grape juice
2 stiffly beaten egg
    whites
1 cup whipping cream

Heat together the light cream, sugar, and light corn syrup, stirring just till the sugar is dissolved. Cool to room temperature. Add grape juice to cooled mixture. Fold in stiffly beaten egg whites. Whip the whipping cream just till thick and custardlike. Fold whipped cream into grape juice mixture. Pour mixture into two 3-cup refrigerator trays. Freeze mixture till partially frozen. Break sherbet into chunks into a chilled mixer bowl. Beat till smooth with rotary beater. Return sherbet to cold refrigerator trays. Freeze firm. Makes 4 cups.

*When Sunday dinner was a regular family gathering, sherbets weren't always relegated to the end of the meal. Mother knew that a small portion of Cranberry Sherbet or Ginger Ale-Pineapple Sherbet was exceedingly good with the Sunday roast. You can revive this pleasant custom on holiday occasions by serving one of these tasty sherbets along with the turkey, beef, or ham. Both sherbets are easy to make. The cranberry version is frozen in a refrigerator tray. Although the ginger ale sherbet does require an ice cream freezer, there are electric models available that take no hand power to turn the freezer crank.*

# Good Eating during the Thirties

## Tempting Appetizers and Refreshing Drinks

Treat your guests to a variety of canapés, appetizers, and beverages that will start any meal with a flair.

## Main Dish Medleys

For a perfect main dish choose from chicken, goose, turkey, veal, beef, lamb, pork, ham, or oyster recipes.

## Vegetables with Variety

Select vegetables to tempt even the fussiest eater—including potatoes, turnips, acorn squash, and cauliflower.

## Salad Roundup

Try an inviting salad to perk up your menu. Included here are molded and tossed salads, salad dressings, even pickles.

## Bakery Classics

It's hard to pass up warm-from-the-oven breads when you have these rolls, popovers, muffins, and breads to choose from.

## Old-Fashioned Confections

Pick your favorites from these cookies, candies, puddings, cakes, pies, and refrigerator desserts. They're easy to make and sure to be a hit with the whole family.

For those special occasions, try elegant *Hollyhock-House Roast Lamb* (see recipe, page 45), *Citrus-Avocado Salad* (see recipe, page 56), *Feather Rolls* (see recipe, page 58), and *Apricot-Wafer Dessert* (see recipe, page 67).

# Tempting Appetizers and Refreshing Drinks

## Olympia Oyster Cocktail

1 pint shucked oysters
Lettuce
¾ cup chili sauce
1 to 2 tablespoons prepared
  horseradish

1½ teaspoons lemon juice
½ teaspoon salt
¼ teaspoon pepper
  Dash Worcestershire sauce

Chill oysters. Drain and place in 6 cocktail glasses or sherbets lined with lettuce. Combine chili sauce, prepared horseradish, lemon juice, salt, pepper, and Worcestershire. Spoon over oysters. Serves 6.

## Waldorf Paste for Crackers

¾ cup crumbled blue cheese
  (3 ounces)
¼ cup butter or margarine,
  softened
1 tablespoon catsup

1 tablespoon Worcestershire
  sauce
1 teaspoon snipped chives
  Assorted crackers

Combine blue cheese, butter, catsup, Worcestershire sauce, and snipped chives. Beat with electric mixer till smooth. Chill. Just before serving, spread paste on assorted crackers. Makes 1¼ cups paste.

## Pineapple-Mint Cup

In a mixing bowl combine one 30-ounce can pineapple chunks, drained; 1 cup seeded, halved Tokay grapes; and ½ cup white after-dinner mints, broken. Cover and chill fruit mixture thoroughly. At serving time, spoon the pineapple mixture into chilled sherbets; pour a little chilled ginger ale over the fruit in each glass. Serves 8.

## Mushroom Canapés

12 1½-inch bread rounds
½ pint mushrooms, thinly
  sliced
3 tablespoons butter or
  margarine
1 tablespoon all-purpose
  flour

¼ teaspoon salt
⅔ cup light cream
¼ cup shredded process
  American cheese
  (1 ounce)
Watercress

Toast the bread rounds on both sides under broiler. In medium saucepan cook sliced mushrooms in butter or margarine till tender, 1 to 2 minutes. Remove cooked mushrooms from butter, and place them on toasted bread rounds. Stir flour and salt into butter in saucepan. Add light cream all at once. Cook and stir over medium heat till mixture is thickened and bubbly. Spoon the cream sauce over mushrooms and bread rounds. Sprinkle shredded cheese over each canapé. Place on baking sheet. Heat at 400° till cheese melts and sauce is bubbly, 4 to 5 minutes. Serve very hot on watercress nests. Makes 12.

## Honeyed Chocolate

1 4-ounce package sweet
  cooking chocolate
1 cup water
¼ cup honey

½ teaspoon salt
7 cups milk
1 teaspoon vanilla

Chop the sweet chocolate. In a 3-quart saucepan combine the chocolate, water, honey, and salt. Cook and stir the mixture over low heat till smooth. Gradually add milk. Cook and stir till heated through. Stir in vanilla. Serve hot in mugs. Makes sixteen 4-ounce servings.

*Ceramic mugs, though high-style today, can't match the status value of yesterday's chocolate set with its graceful china pot and tall cups holding court from the sideboard. Luckily, the Honeyed Chocolate tastes just as great from a pottery mug.*

## Grape Iceberg

2 cups grape juice
¾ cup sugar
1½ cups orange juice,
  chilled

½ cup lemon juice, chilled
1 28-ounce bottle ginger
  ale, chilled

Pour grape juice into a 4-cup refrigerator tray; freeze into ice cubes. In medium saucepan combine sugar and 1¾ cups water. Bring the mixture to boiling, stirring constantly till sugar dissolves. Remove from heat; chill. Add chilled orange juice and lemon juice. Slowly add ginger ale, stirring gently, using an up-and-down motion. Remove the grape juice cubes from refrigerator tray. Place in tall glasses. Pour fruit juice mixture over grape juice cubes. Serve immediately. Makes 8 cups.

## Pin-Gin Punch

2 cups water
1¼ cups sugar
2 cups unsweetened grape-
  fruit juice, chilled
2 cups orange juice,
  chilled

2 cups unsweetened pine-
  apple juice, chilled
2 12-ounce cans or bottles
  ginger ale, chilled
Crushed ice
Fresh mint sprigs

In medium saucepan combine the water and sugar. Bring the sugar mixture to boiling, stirring constantly, till the sugar is completely dissolved. Chill the sugar syrup several hours. Combine chilled sugar syrup, grapefruit juice, orange juice, and pineapple juice. Slowly pour the chilled ginger ale into the fruit juice mixture. Fill tall glasses about half full with crushed ice. Pour in enough fruit juice mixture to fill. Trim glasses with the fresh mint sprigs. Makes 12 cups.

*The name sounds intoxicating, but a glance at the ingredients shows that Pin-Gin Punch could go to a church reception without hesitation. The gin is short for ginger ale, which gives the fruit juice mixture a special sparkle.*

## Iced Fruited Tea

6 cups orange juice
1 cup lemon juice
6 cups boiling water
5 tea bags

1 cup sugar
Ice cubes
Lemon slices (optional)

Combine the orange juice and lemon juice. Strain fruit juice mixture. Pour the boiling water over the tea bags; let stand about 5 minutes. Remove the tea bags from the water. Add the sugar, stirring constantly, till the sugar is dissolved. Fill tall glasses with ice cubes. Pour tea mixture into the tall glasses till about half full. Add enough fruit juice mixture to fill the glasses. Stir to blend the ingredients. Garnish with lemon slices, if desired. Serve immediately. Makes 13 cups.

# Main Dish Medleys

### Arroz con Pollo

1 8-ounce package brown-and-serve sausage links
1 2½- to 3-pound ready-to-cook broiler-fryer chicken, cut up
¼ cup all-purpose flour
1¾ cups water
1 cup chopped onion

½ cup chopped celery
1 cup long grain rice
1 8-ounce can tomatoes, cut up
1 8½-ounce can peas, drained
½ cup sliced pimiento-stuffed green olives

Brown the sausages in a Dutch oven. Drain, reserving 3 tablespoons drippings; set sausages aside. Coat chicken with mixture of flour, 1¼ teaspoons salt, and ¼ teaspoon pepper; brown in reserved drippings. Add water, onion, and celery to chicken. Cover and simmer till chicken is nearly tender, about 30 minutes. Add rice, tomatoes, and sausages. Simmer till rice is tender, about 20 minutes more. Skim off excess fat. Add peas; heat through. Garnish with olives. Serves 4 to 6.

### India Chicken Curry

*Curry, long an Indian specialty, came to this country via World War II when G.I.s stationed in India learned to like Chicken Curry 'hot hot.' The dish gets its pungency from curry powder, a blend of spices based on combinations of turmeric, cumin, coriander, fenugreek, and red pepper. To get the most flavor from curry powder, heat it in butter before adding it to other ingredients.*

½ cup finely chopped onion
½ cup finely chopped celery
¼ cup butter or margarine
⅓ cup all-purpose flour
1 tablespoon curry powder
2 cups chicken broth

1 cup tomato juice
1 teaspoon Worcestershire sauce
3 cups cubed, cooked chicken *or* turkey
Hot cooked rice
Condiments

In saucepan cook onion and celery in butter till tender but not brown. Stir in flour and curry powder. Add chicken broth, tomato juice, and Worcestershire sauce. Cook and stir over medium heat till thickened and bubbly. Add salt and pepper to taste. Stir in chicken; heat through. Serve over hot cooked rice. Pass condiments (chutney, chopped hard-cooked egg white, sieved hard-cooked egg yolk, chopped peanuts, grated coconut, and/or crumbled, crisp-cooked bacon). Makes 6 servings.

### Creamed Chicken and Ham

¼ cup butter or margarine
5 tablespoons all-purpose flour
1½ cups chicken broth
1 cup light cream *or* evaporated milk
1½ cups cubed, cooked chicken
1 cup diced, fully cooked ham

2 hard-cooked egg yolks, mashed
2 hard-cooked egg whites, chopped
⅓ cup sliced pimiento-stuffed green olives
⅛ teaspoon paprika
⅛ teaspoon Worcestershire sauce
Toast, biscuits, waffles, *or* baked patty shells

Melt butter; blend in flour. Add broth and cream or evaporated milk. Cook and stir till thickened and bubbly. Stir in chicken, ham, egg yolks, egg whites, olives, paprika, and Worcestershire. Heat through. Serve on toast, biscuits, waffles, or in patty shells. Serves 6.

## Elegant Chicken à la King

1 cup sliced mushrooms
¼ cup chopped green pepper
6 tablespoons butter or
    margarine, softened
2 tablespoons all-purpose
    flour
2 cups light cream
3 cups cubed, cooked
    chicken

3 egg yolks
½ teaspoon paprika
2 tablespoons dry sherry
1 tablespoon lemon juice
1 teaspoon onion juice
2 tablespoons chopped
    canned pimiento
Toast points

In saucepan cook mushrooms and green pepper in *2 tablespoons* of the butter till tender but not brown; push vegetables to one side. Blend flour and ¾ teaspoon salt into butter in saucepan. Stir in cream; cook and stir till thickened and bubbly. Add chicken; heat, stirring occasionally.

Meanwhile, in small bowl blend remaining butter, egg yolks, and paprika; set aside. To chicken mixture add sherry, lemon juice, and onion juice; bring to boiling. Add yolk mixture, stirring till blended. Remove from heat. Stir in pimiento. Serve over toast points. Serves 6 to 8.

*At the turn of the century, Chef George Greenwald of the old Brighton Beach Hotel outside New York City tempted the proprietor with a new chicken dish covered with a smooth cream sauce and served on toast. The reaction? "More please." The next day, the chef put Chicken à la King on the menu, naming it not for European royalty but for the hotelier, Charles E. King II.*

## Roast Goose with Bread Stuffing *(see photo, page 46)*

⅓ cup chopped onion
½ cup butter or margarine
8 cups dry bread cubes
1 teaspoon poultry
    seasoning
1 teaspoon ground sage

½ teaspoon salt
½ teaspoon pepper
¼ to ½ cup water *or* chicken
    broth
1 10- to 12-pound ready-to-
    cook domestic goose

Cook onion in butter till tender. Combine with bread and seasonings. Toss with enough liquid to moisten. Stuff cavity of goose; thoroughly prick legs and wings with fork to

let fat escape. (Do not oil the bird.) Place, breast side up, on rack in shallow roasting pan. Roast, uncovered, at 325° for 3¾ to 4¼ hours. Spoon off fat. Serves 5 or 6.

## Chicken Tetrazzini

3 tablespoons butter
3 tablespoons all-purpose
    flour
2 cups milk
1 cup light cream
1½ cups sliced mushrooms
2 tablespoons butter
3 cups cubed, cooked
    chicken

Dash paprika
2 egg yolks
1 tablespoon milk
7 ounces spaghetti, cooked
    and drained
¼ cup butter or margarine
½ cup grated Parmesan
    cheese
Parsley

In saucepan melt 3 tablespoons butter; stir in flour, 1 teaspoon salt, and ⅛ teaspoon pepper. Add 2 cups milk and light cream. Cook and stir till thick and bubbly; set aside. Cook mushrooms in the 2 tablespoons butter for 1 to 2 minutes. Add chicken, paprika, *2 cups* of the white sauce, and ¼ teaspoon salt. Heat 10 minutes, stirring occasionally. Beat egg yolks with 1

tablespoon milk. Stir into chicken mixture. Keep hot. Combine hot spaghetti, ¼ cup butter, ¼ *cup* of the Parmesan cheese, and remaining white sauce. Pour into 6-cup ring mold. Turn spaghetti ring out onto ovenproof platter. Spoon chicken mixture into center. Sprinkle with remaining Parmesan cheese. Bake at 350° for 5 minutes. Garnish with parsley. Serves 5 or 6.

*Creating a special dish and naming it for an opera star was a chef's way of paying tribute to an artist in another field. Madame Luisa Tetrazzini, a famous Italian soprano, was thus honored with Chicken Tetrazzini. This excellent spaghetti dish with its creamy chicken sauce has become as well known in its own right as the diva from whom it gets its name.*

## Roast Turkey *(see photo, pages 6-7)*

*"Better than ever" is the way to describe a tender turkey fairly bursting with Oyster or Brazil Nut Stuffing. The stuffings live up to the fondest memories of the past, but today's broad-breasted turkey is practically a new creation by comparison. All are bred to have more white meat, and many of those on the market also have built-in basting to ensure juiciness.*

Rinse one 10- to 12-pound ready-to-cook turkey; pat dry. Salt cavity. Stuff with Oyster Stuffing *or* Brazil Nut Stuffing. Truss and place, breast side up, on rack in shallow roasting pan. Rub skin with cooking oil. Insert meat thermometer in center of inside thigh muscle, not touching bone. Cover loosely with foil. Roast at 325° for 3½ hours, basting occasionally. Cut band of skin or string between legs and tail; uncover. Continue roasting till drumstick moves easily in socket and meat thermometer registers 185°, about 45 minutes more. Remove from oven; let stand 15 minutes before carving. Serves 12 to 14.

*Oyster Stuffing:* Cook ½ cup chopped celery, ½ cup chopped onion, and 1 bay leaf in ¼ cup butter till vegetables are tender. Discard bay leaf. Add 6 cups dry bread crumbs (about 12 slices) and 1 tablespoon snipped parsley; mix thoroughly. Drain 3 cups oysters, reserving liquid. Add oysters, 2 beaten eggs, 1 teaspoon poultry seasoning, 1 teaspoon salt, and dash pepper to crumb mixture; mix thoroughly. Stir in enough of the reserved oyster liquid to moisten.

*Brazil Nut Stuffing:* Cook ½ cup chopped onion in ½ cup butter till tender. Combine with 8 cups toasted bread cubes (12 slices); 1½ cups chopped, toasted Brazil nuts (about 8 ounces); 1 tablespoon rubbed sage; and 1 teaspoon salt. Toss lightly with 1 cup chicken broth to moisten.

## Minestrone à la Genovese

1 cup dry navy beans
1 cup chopped carrots
2 cups finely shredded cabbage
4 ounces fine noodles (2 cups)
1 8½-ounce can peas, drained
1 8-ounce can cut green beans, drained
1 8-ounce can tomatoes

1 teaspoon dried basil, crushed
¼ cup light cream
3 tablespoons butter
3 tablespoons grated Parmesan cheese
3 tablespoons olive oil *or* cooking oil
2 tablespoons snipped parsley
1 clove garlic, minced

Wash navy beans. Combine beans and 10 cups cold water; soak overnight. (Or simmer 2 minutes; remove from heat. Cover and let stand 1 hour.) Don't drain. Add carrots; simmer, covered, 2½ to 3 hours. Add cabbage, noodles, peas, green beans, tomatoes, basil, and 2 teaspoons salt; simmer till noodles are cooked, 20 to 25 minutes more. Stir in cream, butter, Parmesan, oil, parsley, and garlic. Heat. Serves 10.

## City Chicken *(see photo, page 47)*

*City Chicken was a hit long before kabob cookery came to town. Made from pork and veal cubes alternated on wooden skewers, the mock drumsticks are much like their namesakes for fine, delicate flavor.*

1 pound pork, cut in 1½-inch cubes
1 pound veal, cut in 1½-inch cubes
⅔ cup finely crushed saltine crackers (18)
1 teaspoon paprika

¾ teaspoon poultry seasoning
1 slightly beaten egg
2 tablespoons milk
3 tablespoons shortening
1 chicken bouillon cube
½ cup boiling water

Thread pork and veal cubes alternately onto 6 skewers. Mix crumbs, paprika, poultry seasoning, and 1½ teaspoons salt. Combine egg and milk. Dip meat in egg mixture, then in crumbs. Brown in hot shortening. Dissolve bouillon cube in boiling water; add to meat. Bake, covered, at 350° for 45 minutes. Uncover; bake 30 minutes more. Serves 6.

## Tyrolienne Alps Ragout

3 tablespoons butter or
    margarine
1 cup sliced mushrooms
1 cup chopped onion
2 pounds beef tenderloin,
    sliced in thin strips

Brown Sauce
¼ cup dry sherry
¼ teaspoon salt
¼ teaspoon Worcestershire
    sauce
Hot cooked rice

In a 12-inch skillet melt the butter or margarine. Add sliced mushrooms and onion; cook and stir over medium heat till tender but not brown. Push vegetables to one side of the skillet. Quickly cook about a third of the meat strips at a time in the butter till browned. When all the strips are browned, add Brown Sauce, dry sherry, salt, Worcestershire sauce, and dash pepper. Cook till heated through, 5 to 10 minutes. Serve over hot cooked rice. Makes 6 to 8 servings.

*Brown Sauce:* In saucepan melt 2 tablespoons butter or margarine; blend in 2 tablespoons all-purpose flour. Cook and stir over medium heat till lightly browned, 2 to 3 minutes. Remove from heat; stir in one 10½-ounce can condensed beef broth and 1 cup water. Cook and stir till thickened and bubbly. Simmer 30 minutes; stir occasionally.

## Hollyhock-House Roast Lamb *(see photo, page 38)*

1 4- to 5-pound leg of
    lamb
1 clove garlic, halved
1 tablespoon snipped
    parsley
1 teaspoon salt
1 teaspoon celery salt
½ teaspoon pepper
¼ teaspoon paprika

¼ cup butter or margarine,
    softened
2 tablespoons all-purpose
    flour
¼ cup finely chopped carrot
1 tablespoon finely chopped
    onion
¼ bay leaf, crumbled
Plum Jelly Sauce

Rub leg of lamb all over with cut side of garlic. Combine parsley, salt, celery salt, pepper, and paprika; rub into lamb. Place lamb, fat side up, on rack in shallow roasting pan. Roast at 325° for 2 hours. Combine butter, flour, carrot, onion, and bay leaf; spread over lamb. Continue roasting till meat thermometer registers 175° to 180°, about 1 hour. Serve with warm or cool Plum Jelly Sauce. Serves 8 to 10.

*Plum Jelly Sauce:* Combine ¾ cup plum jelly, ¼ cup unsweetened pineapple juice, 1 tablespoon orange juice, 1 teaspoon all-purpose flour, ¼ teaspoon dry mustard, and dash ground mace. Cook and stir till thickened and bubbly. Simmer 2 to 3 minutes, stirring occasionally.

*Hollyhock-House Roast Lamb rated the accolade, "Food Just A Bit Different" because the celery salt, salt, pepper, paprika, and parsley rubbed in before roasting gave it flavor. The Plum Jelly Sauce served with it in place of mint jelly was also a touch unique to the Hollyhock House.*

## Stuffed Frankfurters

3 cups toasted bread cubes
    (4 slices bread)
1 cup chopped celery
½ cup evaporated milk
2 tablespoons chopped onion
⅛ teaspoon pepper

⅛ teaspoon rubbed sage
2 tablespoons butter or
    margarine, melted
10 frankfurters
10 slices bacon, partially
    cooked

Mix bread cubes, celery, evaporated milk, onion, and seasonings. Add butter; mix thoroughly. Split frankfurters lengthwise, *cutting to but not through* opposite side. Fill the cavities with stuffing. Wrap each frank with a slice of bacon. Secure with wooden picks. Place in a 13x9x 2-inch baking pan. Bake at 400° for 20 minutes. Serves 10.

An elegant way to please guests at a holiday meal is to serve *Roast Goose with Bread Stuffing* (see recipe, page 43). Garnish the goose with spicy *Cinnamon Apples* (see recipe, page 55) filled with cream cheese and walnuts.

*Orange-Glazed Ham* (see recipe, page 49) makes a perfect center of attraction for any meal. Round out the tangy goodness of the ham with *Jellied Cider Molds* (see recipe, page 56) placed on top of colorful apple wedges.

Try *City Chicken* (see recipe, page 44). This delicious combination of pork and veal on a skewer was used by city dwellers of the thirties as a substitute for chicken, which was very expensive. Warm spiced peaches are a perfect accompaniment.

Hard-cooked eggs, ham, prepared mustard, Worcestershire sauce, and onion all go into *Savory Deviled Eggs* (see recipe, page 49). This simple but elegant dish makes a perfect main dish for a special luncheon or a late-evening supper.

48

Long before the white man came to North America, sweet potatoes grew where Charleston, South Carolina now stands. Although a far cry from today's hybrids, these potatoes were good enough to tide the first English settlers over during those lean first years. Later, with the coming of Huguenot refugees, sweet potatoes got a real break. It never takes a Frenchman or a Southerner long to discover possibilities in foods. They promptly put them into their famous biscuits, like these with Pork Pie.

## Pork Pie

1½ pounds ground pork
½ cup chopped onion
½ cup chopped celery
3 tablespoons all-purpose flour
1 teaspoon dried savory, crushed
1 teaspoon paprika

1 teaspoon instant chicken bouillon granules
¾ teaspoon salt
1 tablespoon brown sugar
3 medium tart cooking apples, peeled, cored, and sliced
Sweet Potato Biscuits

Cook pork, onion, and celery till meat is browned and vegetables are tender. Blend in flour, savory, paprika, bouillon granules, salt, and ⅛ teaspoon pepper. Add 1½ cups water. Cook and stir till thickened and bubbly. Sprinkle sugar over apples; stir to coat. In a 2-quart casserole alternately layer apples and meat, ending with meat. Cover; bake at 425° for 20 minutes. Top with Sweet Potato Biscuits. Bake, uncovered, till biscuits are done, 20 to 25 minutes. Serves 6.

*Sweet Potato Biscuits:* Stir together 1 cup all-purpose flour, 3 teaspoons baking powder, and ½ teaspoon salt. Cut in ¼ cup shortening till the size of small peas. Add 1 cup mashed, cooked sweet potatoes. Add ¼ cup milk and blend. Roll on a lightly floured surface to ½ inch thickness. Cut with floured 2½-inch biscuit cutter.

## Favorite Meat Loaf

1 beaten egg
½ cup coarsely crumbled saltine crackers (8)
½ cup milk
1 3-ounce can chopped mushrooms, drained
2 tablespoons chopped green pepper

2 tablespoons catsup
1 to 2 tablespoons prepared horseradish
½ teaspoon salt
1 pound ground veal
½ pound ground fully cooked ham
3 slices bacon

Combine egg, cracker crumbs, milk, mushrooms, green pepper, catsup, horseradish, and salt. Add the veal and ham. Mix well. Shape into a 9x4½-inch loaf, and place in an 11x7x1½-inch baking pan. Arrange bacon slices on top. Bake at 350° for 1 hour. Makes 6 servings.

## Twin Meat Loaves

2 beaten eggs
4 slices bread, cubed
¾ cup milk
¼ cup finely chopped onion
2 tablespoons finely chopped celery
1 tablespoon Worcestershire sauce
1½ teaspoons salt
¼ teaspoon dry mustard

¼ teaspoon ground sage
¼ teaspoon poultry seasoning
¼ teaspoon pepper
1 pound ground beef
½ pound ground pork
½ pound ground veal
½ cup fine dry bread crumbs
1 cup chili sauce
½ cup boiling water

Combine beaten eggs, bread cubes, milk, onion, celery, Worcestershire sauce, and seasonings. Add beef, pork, and veal. Mix thoroughly. Form into two loaves. Roll in dry bread crumbs, and place in 13x9x2-inch baking pan. Spread ½ *cup* chili sauce over *each* loaf. Pour boiling water around but not over loaves. Bake at 350° for 1 hour. Baste with liquid in pan every 15 minutes. Makes 8 to 10 servings.

## Orange-Glazed Ham *(see photo, page 46)*

Insert meat thermometer in a 10- to 14-pound fully cooked ham. Bake in a roasting pan at 325° for 2½ to 3 hours. Brush with orange marmalade. Bake till thermometer registers 140°, 30 minutes more.

## Savory Deviled Eggs *(see photo, page 47)*

8 hard-cooked eggs, halved
½ cup finely chopped fully
    cooked ham
¼ cup butter, softened
1 tablespoon chopped onion
1 teaspoon snipped parsley
½ teaspoon Worcestershire
    sauce

¼ teaspoon prepared mustard
3 tablespoons butter
¼ cup all-purpose flour
⅛ teaspoon paprika
1 cup chicken broth
1 cup milk
1 cup shredded process
    American cheese

Mash egg yolks; add ham, ¼ cup butter, onion, parsley, Worcestershire, and mustard. Fill egg whites with yolk mixture. Arrange eggs in blazer pan of a chafing dish. Melt 3 tablespoons butter; blend in flour, paprika, ¼ teaspoon salt, and dash pepper. Add chicken broth and milk. Cook and stir till thickened and bubbly. Pour over eggs. Heat atop range for 20 to 25 minutes. Sprinkle with cheese. Heat 5 minutes more. Keep warm over hot water (bain-marie). Serves 4 or 5.

*Sunday evening was a good time for young people to entertain in the '30s. Out came the chafing dish, unabashedly dubbed 'the beau catcher' by young ladies who filled it with creamed seafood mixtures or ham-filled Savory Deviled Eggs to serve to a special boyfriend.*

## Salmon Croquettes

1 16-ounce can salmon
2 cups mashed cooked
    potatoes
1 beaten egg
½ teaspoon salt

⅛ teaspoon pepper
1 beaten egg
1 cup fine dry bread crumbs
    Fat for frying
    Creamed Pea Sauce

Drain the salmon; remove bones and skin. Mash fish well with a fork. Add mashed potatoes, 1 beaten egg, salt, and pepper. Chill. Form into 12 cones. Combine remaining beaten egg and 2 tablespoons water. Roll salmon cones in bread crumbs, then in egg mixture. Roll in crumbs again. Fry a few at a time in deep, hot fat (350°) till brown and hot, 2½ to 3 minutes. Drain on paper toweling. Serve warm with Creamed Pea Sauce. Makes 4 to 6 servings.

*Creamed Pea Sauce:* Cook one 10-ounce package frozen peas according to package directions; drain well. Melt 2 tablespoons butter. Blend in 1 tablespoon all-purpose flour, ¼ teaspoon salt, and dash white pepper. Add 1 cup milk; cook and stir till thickened and bubbly. Cook 1 minute more. Stir in peas.

*During the '30s, plentiful canned salmon was a mealtime standby coast to coast. Good cooks of the day creamed it, sauced it, souffleed it, or incorporated it into crusty croquettes.*

## Salmon Soufflé

½ cup butter or margarine
6 egg yolks
½ teaspoon onion juice
1 7¾-ounce can salmon,
    drained and flaked

2 tablespoons light cream
    *or* milk
    Dash pepper
3 stiffly beaten egg whites

Cream butter; add egg yolks one at a time, beating well after each. Add onion juice. Cook and stir over low heat till thickened. Remove from heat. Stir in salmon, cream, and pepper. Fold in egg whites. Pour into an *ungreased* 5-cup soufflé dish. Bake at 325° till knife inserted off-center comes out clean, about 35 minutes. Serves 6.

50

*A Gay '90s favorite at Delmonico's and the Waldorf, Lobster Newburg was named for an American tycoon, Wenburg. The chef simply reversed part of the name of his favored customer to christen the rich seafood sauce he served from chafing dish into puff pastry shells.*

## Lobster Newburg

¼ cup butter or margarine
1 cup light cream
3 slightly beaten egg yolks
1 5-ounce can lobster, drained, broken up, and cartilage removed

2 tablespoons dry sherry
¼ teaspoon salt
¼ teaspoon paprika
Dash ground nutmeg
Toast points

Melt butter or margarine in a saucepan. Combine cream and egg yolks. Add to butter. Cook over low heat, stirring constantly, till mixture begins to thicken. Add lobster; heat through. Stir in sherry, salt, paprika, and nutmeg. Serve over toast points. Makes 4 servings.

## Surprise Tuna Pie

1 cup packaged biscuit mix
½ cup shredded process American cheese (2 ounces)
2 tablespoons butter or margarine
2 tablespoons all-purpose flour
¼ teaspoon salt
Dash pepper
1¾ cups milk
1 teaspoon instant chicken bouillon granules

1 9¼-ounce can tuna, drained and flaked
1 cup diced, cooked potatoes
½ cup chopped, cooked carrot
½ cup cooked peas or 1 8½-ounce can peas, drained
⅓ cup chopped green pepper
2 tablespoons chopped canned pimiento
2 tablespoons chopped onion

Prepare the biscuit mix according to package directions for biscuits, using 1 cup mix. Roll dough on a lightly floured surface to a 7½x5-inch rectangle. Sprinkle with American cheese. Roll as for jelly roll, beginning at long end. Cut into ten ¾-inch slices. Set biscuits aside. In saucepan melt butter or margarine. Blend in the flour, salt, and pepper. Add milk and chicken bouillon granules all at once. Cook and stir over medium heat till thickened and bubbly. Add tuna, potatoes, carrots, peas, green pepper, pimiento, and onion. Heat to boiling; pour into a 2-quart casserole. Place biscuits atop hot mixture. Bake at 425° till biscuits are golden, 20 to 25 minutes. Serves 4.

## Shrimp-Tuna Bake

3 beaten eggs
½ cup finely crushed saltine crackers (14)
3 tablespoons butter or margarine, melted
2 tablespoons chopped celery

1 tablespoon finely chopped onion
⅛ teaspoon paprika
1 6½- or 7-ounce can tuna, drained and flaked
1¾ cups milk
Shrimp Sauce

Mix eggs, crackers, butter, celery, onion, paprika, ½ teaspoon salt, and ¼ teaspoon pepper. Add tuna. Stir in milk. Turn into 1½-quart casserole. Bake at 325° for 55 to 60 minutes; stir occasionally. Serve with Shrimp Sauce. Serves 4 to 6.
*Shrimp Sauce:* Melt 2 tablespoons butter or margarine in medium saucepan; stir in 2 tablespoons all-purpose flour. Add 1¼ cups water, 1 teaspoon lemon juice, and 1 chicken bouillon cube all at once. Cook and stir over medium heat till thick and bubbly. Stir in one 4½-ounce can shrimp, drained, and 1 tablespoon chopped sweet pickle *or* capers. Heat through.

## Oyster Stew

2 tablespoons all-purpose
   flour
2 teaspoons salt
⅛ teaspoon pepper
   Dash ground mace
   (optional)
2 tablespoons cold water

1 quart shucked oysters,
   undrained
2 cups light cream
1 cup milk
¼ cup butter or margarine
   Paprika
   Oyster crackers

In a 3-quart saucepan blend together flour, salt, pepper, and mace, if desired. Stir in cold water. Add undrained oysters. Simmer over very low heat, stirring gently, till edges of oysters curl, 3 to 4 minutes. Stir in the cream and milk; heat mixture through. Ladle into soup bowls; float butter or margarine atop and sprinkle with paprika. Serve immediately with oyster crackers. Serves 6 to 8.

## Deviled Oysters

¼ cup butter or margarine
¼ cup all-purpose flour
⅔ cup milk
1 slightly beaten egg yolk
½ pint shucked oysters,*
   drained and chopped
1 tablespoon snipped parsley

1 teaspoon lemon juice
¼ teaspoon dry mustard
   Dash cayenne
¾ cup soft bread crumbs
2 teaspoons butter or
   margarine, melted

In saucepan melt the ¼ cup butter; blend in flour. Add milk all at once. Cook and stir till thickened and bubbly. Stir some of the hot mixture into the egg yolk; return to mixture in saucepan. Cook and stir 1 minute more. Add oysters, parsley, lemon juice, dry mustard, cayenne, and ¼ teaspoon salt. Pour into four 6-ounce custard cups. Combine the crumbs and 2 teaspoons melted butter; sprinkle over oyster mixture. Bake at 400° for 25 minutes. Serves 4.

*Or use one 10-ounce can of oysters and increase milk to 1 cup.

## Oyster Shortcake

1½ cups sliced mushrooms
    (about 4 ounces)
½ cup diced celery
2 tablespoons chopped onion
¼ cup butter or margarine
⅓ cup all-purpose flour
½ teaspoon salt
¼ teaspoon paprika

1 cup milk
1 pint small shucked
   oysters, undrained
1 tablespoon snipped
   parsley
1 teaspoon lemon juice
   Baking Powder Biscuits

Cook the mushrooms, celery, and onion in butter till tender. Blend in flour, salt, and paprika. Stir in milk. Cook and stir till thick. Add the undrained oysters, parsley, and lemon juice. Cook over medium heat till edges of the oysters begin to curl, about 5 minutes. Serve hot between and over split Baking Powder Biscuits. Makes 4 servings.

*Baking Powder Biscuits:* Stir 2 cups all-purpose flour, 3 teaspoons baking powder, and ½ teaspoon salt together in a bowl. Cut in ⅓ cup shortening till like coarse crumbs. Make a well; add ¾ cup milk all at once. Stir quickly with fork just till dough follows fork around bowl. Turn onto lightly floured surface. Knead gently 12 strokes. Roll dough ½ inch thick. Cut dough with floured biscuit cutter. Bake on ungreased baking sheet at 450° for 10 to 12 minutes. Makes 10.

*If you are lucky and the day is shining on you, you'll crack open an oyster and a pearl will pop out, leaving you gasping at the wonder glistening in a bed of iridescent matter. If that happens, you've tasted of a tropical oyster. These are wholly unlike oysters found in American waters, which are bred in the Atlantic for the cooking pot and your eating enjoyment. If you do come across a small, hard pearl-like stone, sadly throw it away, and count the rings of the shell to determine the age of the oyster. The stone is worthless and is called a calcareous concretion. The real pearl is the oyster. Add more oysters to it, and prepare one of the specialties on this page — Oyster Stew, Deviled Oysters, or Oyster Shortcake.*

# Vegetables with Variety

## Sweet Potatoes in Orange Cases

3 large oranges, halved
2 cups mashed, cooked sweet
    potatoes (1¼ pounds)
¼ cup butter or margarine

Salt
Pepper
3 marshmallows, halved

Squeeze juice from the orange halves, reserving juice. Scrape out inside of orange halves, removing as much of the white membrane as possible. Combine mashed sweet potatoes, butter, and enough of the reserved orange juice (about 4 teaspoons) to make a fluffy consistency.

(Use remaining juice as a beverage.) Season to taste with salt and pepper. Fill orange cups with sweet potato mixture. Top each cup with a marshmallow half. Place on baking sheet. Before serving, heat at 400° till marshmallows are melted, 8 to 10 minutes. Serves 6.

## Acorn Squash Wedges with Creamed Onions

3 acorn squash, quartered
Salt
Pepper
1 tablespoon butter or
    margarine
1 tablespoon all-purpose
    flour

Dash salt
¾ cup milk
1 15½-ounce can boiled
    onions, drained
2 tablespoons chopped
    canned pimiento

Remove seeds from acorn squash, and arrange squash wedges in a single layer in a large shallow baking pan or a 13x9x2-inch baking dish. Sprinkle with salt and pepper. Cover with foil; bake at 350° till squash is tender, 35 to 40 minutes. Meanwhile, melt butter in a medium saucepan. Stir in flour and dash salt. Add milk all at once. Cook and stir mixture over medium heat till thickened and bubbly. Stir onions and pimiento into creamed mixture. Heat through. Serve sauce and vegetables with baked squash. Serves 8.

## Turnips au Gratin

2 pounds turnips, peeled
    and diced (about
    6 cups)
¼ cup butter or margarine
3 tablespoons all-purpose
    flour
¾ teaspoon salt
    Dash pepper

2 cups milk
½ cup shredded process
    American cheese
    (2 ounces)
1½ cups soft bread crumbs
    (about 2 slices)
2 tablespoons butter or
    margarine, melted

Cook diced turnips in boiling, salted water till almost tender, about 5 minutes. Drain well. In medium saucepan melt the ¼ cup butter or margarine. Stir in the flour, salt, and pepper. Add milk all at once. Cook quickly, stirring constantly, over medium heat till thickened and bubbly. Remove from heat and add the shredded cheese, stirring till completely melted. Stir in the cooked turnips. Turn into a 10x6x 2-inch baking dish. Combine the bread crumbs and 2 tablespoons melted butter or margarine. Sprinkle atop turnip mixture. Bake at 375° till crumbs are golden brown, about 30 minutes. Serves 6 to 8.

## Goldilocks Potatoes

**4 or 5 medium potatoes, peeled and quartered**
**¼ cup hot milk**

**½ cup whipping cream**
**½ cup shredded process cheese spread (2 ounces)**

Cook potatoes in boiling, salted water till tender, 20 to 25 minutes. Drain well. Shake over low heat till thoroughly dry. Mash; measure 2½ cups. Beat in enough of the hot milk to make potatoes fluffy. Season with salt and pepper to taste. Spoon into six 6-ounce custard cups. Whip cream; fold in cheese. Spoon mixture atop potatoes. Bake at 350° till lightly browned, about 15 minutes. Makes 6 servings.

*Goldilocks Potatoes are a tasty example from the era of twice-cooked vegetables. One step usually involved top-of-the-range cookery. Then, a sauce, cheese, or an interesting topper was added just before the dish was put in the oven to brown, blend flavors, or just heat.*

## Yelmi

**1 16-ounce can whole green beans**
**2 small tomatoes, washed and cut up**
**½ cup thinly sliced onion**

**¼ cup chopped fully cooked ham**
**1 tablespoon olive oil**
**⅛ teaspoon salt**
**⅛ teaspoon paprika**

Drain beans, reserving ¼ cup liquid. Combine beans, reserved liquid, tomatoes, onion, ham, olive oil, salt, and paprika in a 1-quart saucepan. Cover and bring to boiling. Reduce heat; simmer over low heat till flavors are blended, about 45 minutes. Makes 4 or 5 servings.

*A fine Polish touch with vegetables is evident in both Yelmi and Cauliflower Polonaise. The recipe for Yelmi was shared with Americanization classmates by an immigrant from Poland. One of the classmates sent it to the magazine. And Polonaise is the French menu term that denotes foods prepared in the Polish style — with a liberal sprinkling of buttered crumbs and chopped hard-cooked egg.*

## Cauliflower Polonaise

**1 medium head cauliflower**
**1 tablespoon butter**
**¼ cup fine dry bread crumbs**

**1 hard-cooked egg, finely chopped**
**1 tablespoon snipped parsley**

Remove leaves from cauliflower; trim base. Cook whole, covered, in boiling, salted water for 15 to 20 minutes. (Or cut into flowerets and cook 10 to 15 minutes.) Drain well. Heat butter till lightly browned; add crumbs, egg, and parsley. Spoon over cauliflower. Serves 5 or 6.

One way to spark up your favorite fruit salad is with *Tango Dressing* (see recipe, page 56). This blend of chili sauce, whipping cream, and mayonnaise enhances color and flavor of almost any fruit.

*Tomato Rose Salads* brought Philadelphia cream cheese to cooking school audiences. To prepare the salads, deftly shape the cheese into petals around whole tomatoes and garnish with sieved egg yolk. Serve on lettuce and accompany with sliced, boiled ham.

# Salad Roundup

### Cinnamon Apples *(see photo, page 46)*

2 cups water
½ cup sugar
½ cup red cinnamon candies
6 large apples, peeled and
cored

1 3-ounce package cream
cheese, softened
2 tablespoons chopped
walnuts

In large saucepan or medium skillet mix water and sugar. Bring to boiling; boil gently 5 minutes. Add candies; stir till melted. Add apples; cover and simmer till tender, 10 to 12 minutes, turning occasionally.

Remove from heat. Let apples stand in syrup till a deep red color, turning once or twice. Remove apples and drain well. Combine cream cheese and walnuts; stuff center of apples. Chill. Makes 6 servings.

### Tomato Rose Salads

1 8-ounce package cream
cheese, softened
2 tablespoons milk
½ teaspoon onion juice
6 small tomatoes

Mayonnaise or salad
dressing
1 hard-cooked egg yolk,
sieved

Blend softened cream cheese with milk and onion juice. Insert a fork in the stem end of tomato. Dip a teaspoon into cheese mixture and level off the teaspoon. Holding tomato by the fork, place cheese side of teaspoon against side of tomato near the top and draw away the

spoon. (Cheese will have formed one petal of a rose.) Continue around tomato till petal circle is complete. Repeat for remaining 5 tomatoes. Garnish with a dollop of mayonnaise or salad dressing in the center of each tomato. Top with sieved yolk. Makes 6 servings.

*When lacy, hand-crocheted place mats were in vogue, a salad that looks like a rose with soft white petals of cream cheese, was also the rage. Used by manufacturers of cream cheese to promote the product, this eye-catching specialty caught the fancy of ladies all over the country, many of whom planned luncheon menus around it.*

### Pickled Carrot Sticks

4 cups carrot sticks (about
1¼ pounds)
¾ cup vinegar
¾ cup sugar

1 tablespoon mustard seed
1½ teaspoons celery seed
1 teaspoon salt

Cook carrot sticks in boiling water 5 minutes. Drain well. In saucepan combine vinegar, sugar, mustard seed, celery seed, salt, and ½ cup water. Bring to boiling. Add carrot

sticks; cover and simmer, stirring frequently, till carrots are crisp-tender, about 10 minutes. Chill in vinegar mixture, turning occasionally. Makes 3½ cups pickles.

*It didn't take the woman with a new refrigerator long to discover that she could make and store small batches of quick pickles and relishes. You can do it, too. The fact that these tasty accompaniments are not canned or processed and must be used within a short time presents no problem. The products are so good they are sure to disappear in a hurry.*

### Cranberry Relish

2 medium oranges
1 pound cranberries

2 cups sugar
¼ cup chopped walnuts

Peel and section oranges; reserve peel of one orange. Remove as much white membrane from peel as possible. Grind orange sections, orange

peel, and cranberries, using a coarse blade. Stir in sugar and nuts. Chill. Serve as meat accompaniment. Makes about 3½ cups.

## Jellied Cider Molds *(see photo, page 46)*

1 3-ounce package lemon-
flavored gelatin

2 cups apple cider *or*
apple juice

In medium saucepan combine gelatin and cider. Bring to boiling, stirring to dissolve gelatin. Pour into eight ¼-cup individual molds. Chill till firm. Unmold. Serve cider molds with baked ham. Makes 8 molds.

## Tango Dressing *(see photo, page 54)*

¾ cup mayonnaise or salad
dressing
¼ cup chili sauce
½ cup whipping cream

Dash salt
1 tablespoon finely chopped
green pepper (optional)

Combine mayonnaise and chili sauce. Whip cream till soft peaks form; fold into mayonnaise mixture. Add salt. Serve with fruit salads. To serve with tossed salads add green pepper. Makes 1¾ cups.

## Borsch French Dressing

*You can read history in recipe titles like Borsch French Dressing. This was French dressing with beets. But Borsch was Russian, and things Russian were radical chic in the '30s. This included restaurants. Russian restaurants were opened in American cities after the revolution — by refugees hungry for foods of home. They provided employment for exiled nobility. You never knew when a princess would serve the cracked wheat pilaf while a balalaika orchestra played.*

1 cup olive oil *or* salad
oil
½ cup cider vinegar
1 teaspoon salt
1 teaspoon sugar
¼ teaspoon Worcestershire
sauce

Dash paprika
½ cup chopped, cooked beets
2 hard-cooked eggs, chopped
2 tablespoons chopped
onion
1 tablespoon snipped
parsley

In a screw-top jar combine the oil, vinegar, salt, sugar, Worcestershire, and paprika. Shake well. Add the beets, eggs, onion, and parsley; mix thoroughly. Serve over tossed greens. Makes 2⅓ cups dressing.

## Spinach-Tuna Salad Special

2 cups coarsely chopped
fresh spinach
½ cup French salad dressing
1 6½- or 7-ounce can tuna,
drained and flaked

¼ cup chopped onion
1 medium head lettuce, torn
in bite-size pieces
Pimiento-stuffed green
olives

Combine spinach and French dressing. Chill ½ hour. Add tuna and onion. Toss with lettuce. Garnish with olives. Makes 3 or 4 servings.

## Citrus-Avocado Salad *(see photo, page 38)*

Peel and section 4 medium oranges and 2 grapefruits over a bowl, reserving juice. Dice orange sections. Cut 4 small ripe avocados in half lengthwise. Remove seeds and peel. Slash rounded end of each about three-fourths the length of fruit. Brush avocados with reserved fruit juices. Heap oranges into avocado halves. Garnish with grapefruit sections and ¼ cup pomegranate seeds. Serve on lettuce with Celery Seed Dressing. Serves 8.

*Celery Seed Dressing:* Combine ½ cup sugar, ⅓ cup lemon juice, 1 teaspoon celery seed, 1 teaspoon dry mustard, 1 teaspoon paprika, and ½ teaspoon salt. Slowly add ¾ cup salad oil, beating with electric or rotary beater till thick.

## Tomato-Cheese Salad

1 envelope unflavored
    gelatin
¼ teaspoon salt
1 10½-ounce can condensed
    tomato soup
1 cup cream-style cottage
    cheese

½ cup mayonnaise or salad
    dressing
1 cup chopped celery
½ cup shredded cucumber
¼ cup sliced radishes
¼ cup sliced green onion
    with tops

In medium saucepan soften gelatin in ¼ cup cold water. Stir over low heat till gelatin is dissolved. Add salt. Blend in tomato soup. Beat in cottage cheese and mayonnaise or salad dressing. Chill till partially set. Fold in celery, cucumber, radishes, and onion. Pour into 4-cup mold. Chill till firm, 5 to 6 hours or overnight. Makes 8 to 10 servings.

*Cooking with tomato soup was big news in 1937. Women liked to make use of the flavor blend of ingredients developed by chefs at the cannery. There was a tomato soup cake, several appealing tomato soup-based salad dressings, and this pretty and flavorful Tomato-Cheese Salad.*

## Frozen Vegetable Salad

1 cup cream-style cottage
    cheese
¼ cup mayonnaise or salad
    dressing
¾ teaspoon salt
1 cup diced, peeled tomato

½ cup chopped, cooked green
    beans
¼ cup finely chopped green
    pepper
1 teaspoon grated onion
1 cup whipping cream

Sieve cottage cheese; stir in mayonnaise or salad dressing and salt. Stir in tomato, beans, green pepper, and onion. Whip cream till soft peaks form; fold into vegetable mixture. Pour into a 5-cup refrigerator tray or a 10x6x2-inch baking dish. Freeze mixture for 30 minutes; stir. Freeze 30 to 60 minutes more. (Do not freeze solidly.) Serves 6 to 8.

## Bermuda Salad Bowl

1 small head cauliflower,
    broken into flowerets
½ large Bermuda onion
    sliced
½ cup sliced pimiento-
    stuffed green olives

⅔ cup French salad dressing
1 small head lettuce, torn
    in bite-size pieces
½ cup crumbled blue cheese
    (2 ounces)

Slice cauliflowerets into a large salad bowl. Separate onion slices into rings; add to cauliflower. Add olives. Pour dressing over; toss. Chill 30 minutes. Just before serving, add the lettuce and cheese; toss lightly. Pass extra French dressing, if desired. Serves 8 to 10.

## Creamy Lettuce Salad

3 slices bacon
2 tablespoons vinegar
2 teaspoons sugar
½ teaspoon salt
1 cup dairy sour cream

1 tablespoon all-purpose
    flour
1 medium head lettuce, torn
    in bite-size pieces
    (6 cups)

In a skillet cook the bacon till crisp. Drain well, reserving drippings. Crumble bacon; set aside. Stir vinegar, sugar, and salt into bacon drippings. Combine sour cream and flour; stir into vinegar mixture. Cook over *low* heat just till heated through. Stir in crumbled bacon. Spoon over torn lettuce; toss thoroughly. Serve at once. Serves 4 or 5.

# Bakery Classics

### Feather Rolls *(see photo, page 38)*

*(see photo, page 38)*

*Mashed potatoes make Feather Rolls light as feather-beds, hence the name for these puffy pan rolls that were a '30s Sunday dinner tradition from Maryland to California.*

5 cups all-purpose flour
1 package active dry yeast
½ cup mashed, cooked
    potatoes

⅓ cup cooking oil
¼ cup sugar
1 teaspoon salt

In mixer bowl combine *2 cups* of the flour and the yeast. Combine potatoes, oil, sugar, salt, and 1½ cups warm water (110°). Add to dry ingredients; beat at low speed with electric mixer for ½ minute, scraping sides of bowl constantly. Beat 3 minutes at high speed. By hand, stir in remaining flour. Cover; refrigerate for at least 2 hours or up to 3 days. Punch down; turn out on lightly floured surface. Cover; let rest 10 minutes. With lightly floured hands, shape into 24 buns. Place in greased 13x9x2-inch baking pan. Cover; let rise till almost double (40 minutes). Bake at 400° for 16 to 20 minutes. Makes 24.

### Sour Milk Doughnuts

*In the pre-refrigerator '30s when sour milk was plentiful, so were homemade doughnuts. Today, buttermilk substitutes for sour milk, unless you want to stir vinegar into sweet milk. Either way, doughnuts are a fine way to welcome winter's first snowfall.*

Beat 2 eggs till thick and lemon-colored. Add 1 cup sugar and beat till smooth. Stir in ¼ cup cooking oil and 1 teaspoon vanilla. Stir together 4 cups all-purpose flour, 4 teaspoons baking powder, ¾ teaspoon salt, and ¼ teaspoon baking soda. Add to the egg mixture alternately with 1 cup sour milk *or* buttermilk, beating thoroughly. Turn out on a lightly floured surface; pat or roll dough ½ inch thick. Cut with floured doughnut cutter. Fry in deep, hot fat (375°) till doughnuts are golden brown, about 3 minutes, turning once. Drain on paper toweling. Serve plain or coat with sugar. Makes 2 dozen.

### Graham Popovers

*"The time to eat a popover is when it has just popped over" was advice for brides in the '30s. It's still true today. These quick and easy batter breads, similar to but smaller than the Yorkshire puddings served by the English with roast beef, can be enjoyed at any meal of the day.*

Stir together thoroughly ⅔ cup all-purpose flour, ⅓ cup whole wheat flour, and ½ teaspoon salt. Add 1 cup milk, 2 eggs, and 1 teaspoon cooking oil; beat with electric mixer or rotary beater for 30 seconds. Fill six well-greased 5-ounce custard cups half full. Bake at 475° for 15 minutes. Reduce heat to 350° and bake till browned and firm, 40 to 45 minutes more. Serve immediately with butter. Makes 6 popovers.

### Onion Shortcake

1½ cups chopped onion
¼ teaspoon salt
¼ cup butter or margarine
1 cup all-purpose flour
1½ teaspoons baking powder

¼ teaspoon salt
¼ cup shortening
½ cup milk
1 beaten egg
½ cup dairy sour cream

Sprinkle onion with ¼ teaspoon salt. Melt butter or margarine in skillet. Add chopped onions; cover and simmer, stirring occasionally, till onions are tender. Set aside. Stir together flour, baking powder, and ¼ teaspoon salt. Cut in shortening till like coarse crumbs. Make a well in center. Add milk all at once. Stir with fork just till dough follows fork around bowl. Spread in greased 8x1½-inch round baking pan. Cover with cooked onions. Mix egg and sour cream; pour atop onions. Bake at 425° for 25 to 30 minutes. Serve hot. Serves 6 to 8.

## Health Muffins

Soften 1 cup whole bran cereal and ½ cup chopped pitted dates in ⅔ cup boiling water. Stir in ⅓ cup dark corn syrup, 3 tablespoons cooking oil, and 1 beaten egg. Stir together 1 cup all-purpose flour, 2 tablespoons sugar, 4 teaspoons baking powder, and ¼ teaspoon salt. Stir in ½ cup chopped walnuts. Stir into date mixture. Fill greased muffin pans ⅔ full. Bake at 400° for 30 minutes. Makes 12.

*Back in the days when muffins were baked in black cast iron instead of today's Teflon-lined aluminum muffin pans, health muffins were known as 'gems.'*

## Orange Nut Bread

   2 cups all-purpose
      flour
   ¾ cup sugar
   ½ teaspoon salt
   ½ teaspoon baking soda
   ½ cup coarsely chopped
      walnuts
   1 beaten egg

   1 tablespoon grated orange
      peel
   ¾ cup orange juice
   ¼ teaspoon grated lemon
      peel
   2 tablespoons lemon juice
   2 tablespoons melted short-
      ening *or* cooking oil

Stir together flour, sugar, salt, and baking soda; stir in chopped walnuts. Combine beaten egg, orange peel, orange juice, lemon peel, lemon juice, and melted shortening or oil. Add to dry ingredients, stirring just till moistened. Turn batter into a greased 8½x4½x2½-inch loaf pan. Bake at 350° till done, 50 to 60 minutes. Remove from pan; cool. Wrap with foil and store overnight before slicing. Makes 1 loaf.

The fresh flavors of orange and lemon give *Orange Nut Bread* a tangy goodness that makes it the perfect complement for many breakfast foods. Try it plain or spread with lots of butter.

# Old-Fashioned Desserts

## Chocolate Crinkles

1½ cups granulated sugar
½ cup cooking oil
3 1-ounce squares
    unsweetened chocolate,
    melted and cooled
2 teaspoons vanilla

3 eggs
¼ cup milk
2 cups all-purpose flour
2 teaspoons baking powder
Sifted powdered sugar

Combine granulated sugar, oil, melted chocolate, and vanilla. Beat in eggs one at a time, beating well after each. Stir in milk. Stir flour and baking powder together thoroughly. Stir into chocolate mixture.

Chill. Using 1 tablespoon dough for each, shape into balls; roll in powdered sugar. Bake on a greased cookie sheet at 375° for 10 to 12 minutes. While still warm, roll again in powdered sugar. Makes 4 dozen.

At your next party offer guests a variety of sweets (pictured opposite) such as *Cherry Divinity* (see recipe, page 62), *Chocolate Crinkles, Gumdrop Bars,* and raisin-filled *Brambles*—confections that are sure to please everyone.

## Brambles

1 slightly beaten egg
⅔ cup sugar
½ cup raisins
¼ cup finely crushed
    saltine crackers (about 7)
¼ cup butter or margarine,
    melted and cooled

¼ cup lemon juice
1½ cups all-purpose flour
½ teaspoon salt
½ cup shortening
4 to 5 tablespoons cold
    water

Combine egg, sugar, raisins, cracker crumbs, butter, and lemon juice; set aside. Stir flour and salt together thoroughly. Cut in shortening till pieces are the size of small peas. Sprinkle the cold water over flour mixture, one tablespoon at a time, tossing mixture after each addition. Form pastry into a ball; flatten on a

lightly floured surface. Roll ⅛ inch thick; cut into 3-inch rounds, using a floured biscuit cutter. Place rounds in 1¾-inch muffin pans. Place about 1 tablespoon raisin mixture in each. Bake at 400° for 15 to 18 minutes. Let cool a few minutes before removing from pans. Makes 2 dozen cookies.

*In 1930, Brambles were raisin-filled cookies made from 3-inch rounds of pastry folded over like a turnover. A child could eat them on the playground and not get messed up. Today, Brambles are tea-table style, baked in tiny muffin pans or tassies.*

## Gumdrop Bars

2 cups all-purpose flour
1 cup finely chopped gum-
    drops of assorted flavors,
    except licorice flavor
    (6 ounces)
½ cup chopped pecans
4 eggs

1 tablespoon water
2 cups packed light brown
    sugar
1 teaspoon ground cinnamon
¼ teaspoon salt
Orange Icing

Thoroughly mix flour, gumdrops, and pecans; set aside. Beat eggs with water till foamy. Gradually add brown sugar, beating till light. Beat in cinnamon and salt. Stir in gumdrop mixture. Spread mixture evenly in greased 15½x10½x1-inch baking pan. Bake at 375° till done, 15 to 20 minutes. While still warm,

spread with Orange Icing and cut into 2-inch squares. Remove from pan. Garnish with sliced gumdrops, if desired. Makes about 3 dozen.
*Orange Icing:* Melt 3 tablespoons butter. Stir in 1 teaspoon grated orange peel and 2 tablespoons orange juice. Add enough sifted powdered sugar to make a thin icing.

Knowing how to make good Christmas candies was both a matter of pride and a necessity during the lean years. However, once you'd mastered Cherry Divinity, you could also take advantage of this know-how come St. Valentine's Day to fill a frilly heart-shaped box with this fluffy, cloudlike sweet.

## Cherry Divinity *(see photo, page 60)*

2½ cups sugar
½ cup light corn syrup
½ cup water
¼ teaspoon salt

2 egg whites
1 teaspoon vanilla
½ cup chopped maraschino
   cherries, well drained

In 2-quart saucepan combine sugar, corn syrup, water, and salt. Cook to hard-ball stage (260°), stirring only till sugar dissolves. Meanwhile, beat egg whites till stiff peaks form. Gradually pour syrup over egg whites, beating at high speed on electric mixer. Add vanilla; beat till candy holds its shape, 4 to 5 minutes. Quickly stir in cherries, and drop from a teaspoon onto waxed paper. Makes 40 pieces.

## Butterscotch Cookies

2½ cups packed brown sugar
1½ cups butter or margarine
1 teaspoon vanilla
3 beaten eggs
5 cups all-purpose flour

¾ teaspoon baking soda
¾ teaspoon cream of tartar
1 cup flaked coconut
½ cup chopped walnuts
   Date Filling

Cream sugar, butter, and vanilla till fluffy. Beat in eggs. Stir together flour, soda, and cream of tartar. Add to creamed mixture, blending thoroughly. Divide the dough in quarters. To one quarter of the dough, stir in flaked coconut. To the second quarter, add chopped walnuts. Leave remaining two quarters plain. Form dough into 4 separate rolls (6x2 inches). Wrap in waxed paper; chill thoroughly. Remove 1 roll from refrigerator at a time. Slice the coconut and walnut rolls into thin slices (⅛ to ¼ inch thick). Bake on ungreased cookie sheet at 375° till golden brown, 10 to 12 minutes. Remove immediately to cooling rack. Use rolls of plain dough to make date-filled cookies. Slice the dough into very thin slices (⅛ inch thick). Place small amount of Date Filling on *half* of the dough slices. Cover with remaining dough slices. Seal. Bake on lightly greased cookie sheet at 375° till golden brown, about 10 minutes. Remove immediately to cooling rack. Store each kind of cookie in a separate container. Makes 8½ to 9 dozen.

*Date Filling:* Mix 1 cup chopped pitted dates, ½ cup granulated sugar, and ¼ cup water. Bring to boiling. Cover; simmer 5 minutes, stirring often. Add 1 tablespoon lemon juice. (Should be thick enough to hold shape on cookies.) Stir in ½ cup chopped walnuts. Cool.

As anyone who has ever harvested black walnuts can tell you, cracking and picking out the nuts is hard, tedious work that takes patience. But the special flavor the nuts impart to this old-fashioned Black Walnut Candy is worth every bit of effort.

## Black Walnut Candy

Butter or margarine
2 cups sugar
½ cup milk
½ cup light cream
1 tablespoon light corn
   syrup

½ teaspoon salt
1 tablespoon butter or
   margarine
1 teaspoon vanilla
1 cup chopped black walnuts

Butter sides of a heavy 2-quart saucepan. In it combine the sugar, milk, cream, corn syrup, and salt. Cook over medium heat, stirring constantly, till sugar dissolves and mixture comes to boiling. Then cook to soft-ball stage (238°). Immediately remove from heat and cool to lukewarm (110°) without stirring. Add 1 tablespoon butter and vanilla. Beat vigorously until mixture becomes very thick and starts to lose its gloss. Quickly stir in the nuts, and spread in a buttered 8x8x2-inch pan. Score in squares while warm; cut when cool and firm. Makes 36.

## Plum Omelet

4 egg yolks
1 tablespoon granulated
    sugar
¼ teaspoon water
⅛ teaspoon salt

4 stiffly beaten egg whites
2 tablespoons butter or
    margarine
¼ cup plum preserves
    Sifted powdered sugar

In mixer bowl beat the egg yolks till thick and lemon-colored. Add sugar, water, and salt to egg yolks. Beat till smooth. Fold in stiffly beaten egg whites. Melt butter or margarine in an omelet pan. Pour in egg mixture and spread evenly with spatula, leaving the sides slightly higher. Cook slowly till puffed and set, 8 to 10 minutes. The bottom of the omelet should be golden. Bake at 325° till knife inserted in the center comes out clean, 6 to 10 minutes. Loosen sides and make a shallow cut across center. Carefully spread half the omelet with plum preserves. Tilt pan. Fold upper half over lower half. Using spatula, slip omelet onto platter. Sprinkle with powdered sugar. Serve at once. Pass additional powdered sugar. Serves 3 or 4.

*"Plum Omelet, reaching back to 1823, is 'tried, true, and treasured,'" said the Estherville, Iowa, woman who sent it. In those days, Iowa was wild prairie sod, unbroken by plow and alive with pasque (Easter) flowers, or windflowers as the first brave blooms to come out in the spring were known. In this part of the Louisiana Territory and as far west as the Rockies, plums for the omelet's filling grew wild.*

## Cheese Torte

1¼ cups crushed zwieback
    (about 11 slices)
3 tablespoons butter or
    margarine, melted
1 tablespoon sugar
3 3-ounce packages cream
    cheese, softened
⅓ cup sugar

2 tablespoons all-purpose
    flour
⅛ teaspoon salt
2 egg yolks
½ cup milk
1 teaspoon vanilla
2 stiffly beaten egg whites
    Sliced fresh fruit

Combine crushed zwieback, butter, and 1 tablespoon sugar. Press into the bottom of a 9-inch springform pan. Cream together softened cream cheese and ⅓ cup sugar. Mix in flour and salt. Beat in egg yolks; blend in milk and vanilla. Fold in stiffly beaten egg whites. Spoon mixture into crumb-lined pan. Bake at 325° till knife inserted off-center comes out clean, 30 to 35 minutes. Cool about 20 minutes before removing the sides of the pan. Chill. Serve with fresh fruit. Serves 6 to 8.

## Peanut Waffles with Butterscotch Sauce

2 cups sifted cake flour
2 tablespoons granulated
    sugar
3 teaspoons baking
    powder
1 teaspoon salt
1¼ cups milk
2 slightly beaten egg yolks

⅓ cup cooking oil
½ cup chopped peanuts
2 stiffly beaten egg
    whites
    • • •
Butter or margarine
Butterscotch Sauce

In a mixing bowl sift together the cake flour, sugar, baking powder, and salt. Combine the milk, beaten egg yolks, and cooking oil; blend thoroughly. Stir into dry ingredients. Stir chopped peanuts into batter. Fold in egg whites. Bake in preheated waffle baker (use ⅓ cup batter for each waffle). Serve hot with butter or margarine and Butterscotch Sauce. Makes 12 waffles.

*Butterscotch Sauce:* In a medium saucepan combine 1¼ cups packed brown sugar, ⅔ cup light corn syrup, ¼ cup milk, and ¼ cup butter or margarine. Bring to boiling; reduce heat. Simmer, stirring occasionally, for 20 minutes. Serve hot.

*Pineapple Meringue Cake* offers an interesting blend of textures. It combines the fluffiness of gold cake with the crunchiness of meringue. The pineapple filling spread between the layers helped make this a winner among 7,000 entries in the magazine's first recipe contest.

## Pineapple Meringue Cake

*The first recipe in the 1930 edition of the* Cook Book *was Pineapple Meringue Cake. A generation of youngsters, knew it as 'Lindy's Cake,' named for the young pilot who first soloed across the Atlantic in 1927.*

¼ cup butter or margarine, softened
½ cup granulated sugar
2 egg yolks
½ teaspoon vanilla
1 cup all-purpose flour
1½ teaspoons baking powder
¼ teaspoon salt
½ cup milk
2 egg whites
1 teaspoon vanilla
½ cup granulated sugar
⅓ cup chopped pecans
1 cup whipping cream
2 tablespoons sifted powdered sugar
1 teaspoon vanilla
1 8¼-ounce can crushed pineapple, drained

In a mixer bowl cream together butter and ½ cup sugar; add egg yolks and ½ teaspoon vanilla. Beat with electric mixer till light and fluffy. Stir together thoroughly flour, baking powder, and salt. Add to creamed mixture alternately with milk. Pour into two greased, paper-lined 8x1½-inch round baking pans. Beat egg whites and 1 teaspoon vanilla till soft peaks form; gradually add ½ cup sugar. Beat till stiff peaks form. Carefully spread egg white mixture over unbaked layers. Sprinkle pecans over egg whites. Bake at 350° till wooden pick inserted in center comes out clean, 25 to 30 minutes. Cool in pans 10 minutes. Carefully remove from pans. Turn cake layers meringue side up; cool thoroughly. Meanwhile, for filling combine whipping cream, powdered sugar, and 1 teaspoon vanilla. Beat till soft peaks form. Fold in pineapple. Place one layer, cake side down, on cake plate. Top with filling. Place second layer on top, with meringue side up. Chill. Serves 8.

The rich goodness of *Concord Grape Pie* will be hard for anyone to resist. This combination of Concord grapes, sugar, lemon juice, and butter makes a delightfully different filling. The grape pastry leaves add just a bit of elegance to the piecrust.

## Concord Grape Pie

Slip skins from 4 cups Concord grapes (1½ pounds); set skins aside. In large saucepan bring pulp to boil. Reduce heat; simmer 5 minutes. Press through sieve to remove seeds. Add skins to pulp. Combine 1 cup sugar, ⅓ cup all-purpose flour, and ¼ teaspoon salt. Stir in 2 tablespoons butter or margarine, melted; 1 tablespoon lemon juice; and grape mixture. Pour into unbaked 9-inch pastry shell. Stir together ½ cup all-purpose flour and ½ cup sugar. Cut in ¼ cup butter till crumbly. Sprinkle over pie. Bake at 400° till done, about 40 minutes. Top with Pastry Grape Leaves.

*Pastry Grape Leaves:* Cut leaf design from pastry with a knife. Make leaf veins with top of knife. Bake on baking sheet at 450° for 8 to 10 minutes. Arrange on hot pie.

## Yum-Yum Date Loaf

2¼ cups finely crushed
　　graham crackers
16 marshmallows, cut in
　　eighths

1⅓ cups chopped pitted dates
1 cup chopped walnuts
1 cup whipping cream

Reserve ¼ *cup* crushed graham crackers. Combine remaining crumbs with marshmallows, dates, and walnuts. Moisten with unwhipped cream and blend well. Form into a 6x3-inch roll. Roll in reserved crackers. Cover with clear plastic wrap and chill 6 hours. Cut into 8 slices; serve with whipped cream, if desired. Serves 8.

*On the tombstone of Ephraim Wales Bull is inscribed, "He sowed — others reaped." You might wonder what this has to do with Concord Grape Pie. Mr. Bull developed the Concord grape from more than 22,000 seedlings of wild grapes growing in the rugged New England soil. At one time, he was able to sell cuttings of this firm, fragrant, delectable grape for $1,000 each. Yet, Mr. Bull died a poor man. You can still enjoy the fruits of his labor when you cut into this aromatic pie.*

## Squash Pie

2 cups mashed cooked squash
½ cup sugar
1 tablespoon butter or
    margarine, melted
½ teaspoon ground cinnamon
¼ teaspoon ground ginger

⅛ teaspoon ground nutmeg
1¾ cups milk
2 slightly beaten eggs
1 unbaked 9-inch pastry
    shell with edges
    crimped high

Combine squash, sugar, butter, cinnamon, ginger, nutmeg, and ½ teaspoon salt. Add milk and eggs. Pour mixture into unbaked pastry shell.

Bake at 400° till knife inserted halfway between center and edge comes out clean, about 50 minutes. (Filling may seem soft.) Cool.

## Raisin Crisscross Pie

1 cup packed brown sugar
3 tablespoons cornstarch
2 cups raisins
1⅓ cups water
1 teaspoon grated orange
    peel
½ cup orange juice

1 teaspoon grated lemon
    peel
2 tablespoons lemon juice
½ cup broken walnuts
    Pastry for a 9-inch
    lattice-top pie

In medium saucepan combine brown sugar and cornstarch. Stir in the raisins, water, orange peel, orange juice, lemon peel, and lemon juice. Cook and stir over medium

heat till thickened and bubbly. Remove from heat; stir in the walnuts. Turn into pastry-lined 9-inch pie plate. Adjust lattice top; seal. Bake at 350° about 30 minutes. Cool.

## Milk Chocolate Pie

¾ cup sugar
5 tablespoons cornstarch
2½ cups milk
3 1-ounce squares semisweet
    chocolate, melted
2 tablespoons butter or
    margarine

Dash salt
3 slightly beaten egg yolks
2 teaspoons vanilla
1 *baked* 9-inch pastry
    shell
3 egg whites
6 tablespoons sugar

In saucepan combine ¾ cup sugar and the cornstarch. Stir in milk. Cook and stir over medium heat till thickened and bubbly. Add chocolate, butter, and salt. Stir some of the hot mixture into egg yolks; return to remaining hot mixture. Cook and stir 1 to 2 minutes more.

Add vanilla. Put waxed paper over pudding, touching surface. Cool. Spread in baked pastry shell. Beat egg whites till soft peaks form; gradually add 6 tablespoons sugar, beating till stiff peaks form. Spread atop pie, sealing to edge. Bake at 350° for 12 to 15 minutes. Cool.

## Lemon Pudding Cake

Combine ¾ cup sugar, ¼ cup all-purpose flour, and dash salt; stir in 3 tablespoons melted butter or margarine, 1 teaspoon grated lemon peel, and ¼ cup lemon juice. Combine 1½ cups milk and 3 well-beaten egg yolks; add to lemon mixture.

Fold 3 stiffly beaten egg whites into lemon mixture. Pour into an 8x8x-2-inch baking pan. Place in a larger pan on oven rack. Pour hot water into larger pan till 1 inch deep. Bake at 350° for 40 minutes. Serve warm or chilled. Serves 9.

*Hannibal set a record for crossing the Alps, which still stands as one of the greatest feats in military history. He also ate raisins. Many of his raids on the sunbaked valleys of Asia Minor and the low-lying plains of Tibet around 200 B.C. were to secure supplies of the luscious dried grapes that weighed little yet sustained well.*

*About 1860, a man named Thompson went to Hannibal's source of supply, Smyrna (now called Turkey), for grape cuttings. These were heat-propagated into what are known as Thompson seedless grapes, a variety used in producing raisins.*

## Chocolate-Nut Dessert

1 cup sugar
¼ cup unsweetened cocoa
   powder
3 tablespoons cornstarch
¼ teaspoon salt
2 cups light cream
3 slightly beaten eggs

2 tablespoons butter
½ teaspoon vanilla
1 cup finely crushed graham
   crackers
½ cup chopped walnuts
3 tablespoons butter or
   margarine, melted

In medium saucepan stir together sugar, cocoa powder, cornstarch, and salt. Add cream. Cook and stir over medium heat till thickened and bubbly. Add some of the hot mixture to the slightly beaten eggs. Return to remaining hot mixture; cook and stir 2 minutes more. Remove from heat; add the 2 tablespoons butter and vanilla. Combine crushed crackers, walnuts, and 3 tablespoons melted butter. Pour *half* of the chocolate mixture into an 8x8x2-inch baking pan. Top with *half* the crumb mixture. Repeat layers. Chill till firm. Serves 8 or 9.

## Orange Icebox Cake

½ cup sugar
1 envelope unflavored
   gelatin
¼ teaspoon salt
2 egg yolks
¾ cup milk
1 teaspoon grated orange
   peel

¼ cup orange juice
   Few drops yellow food
   coloring
2 egg whites
¼ cup sugar
½ cup whipping cream
12 ladyfingers, split

In saucepan mix ½ cup sugar, gelatin, and salt. Beat yolks with milk; add to gelatin mixture. Cook and stir over low heat till gelatin dissolves and mixture is slightly thickened. Add peel, juice, and food coloring. Chill till partially set. Beat whites till soft peaks form; gradually add ¼ cup sugar, beating till stiff peaks form. Whip cream. Beat gelatin mixture till frothy; fold in egg whites and whipped cream. Line 9x5x3-inch loaf pan with waxed paper; then line with ladyfingers. Fill with gelatin mixture; chill till set, at least 4 hours. Garnish with additional whipped cream, if desired. Serves 8 to 10.

*The word icebox lingered in the vocabulary long after gas and electric refrigerators were well established in the kitchen. The name icebox dessert still is applied to the elegant layered creations consisting of crumbs, whipped cream, and fruit made the night before and refrigerated till time to serve the bridge club or women's society meeting.*

## Apricot-Wafer Dessert *(see photo, page 38)*

½ cup butter or margarine
2 slightly beaten eggs
1½ cups dried apricots
½ cup granulated sugar
1½ cups crushed vanilla
   wafers

3 tablespoons butter or
   margarine, melted
1½ cups sifted powdered
   sugar
1 cup whipping cream

Have ½ cup butter and eggs at room temperature. Place apricots in medium saucepan. Add water to 1 inch above apricots. Bring to boiling. Simmer till very tender, about 20 minutes. Drain. Sieve to make a purée. Stir in granulated sugar. Set aside. Combine wafers and melted butter. Reserve ½ cup crumb mixture; press remaining mixture in bottom of 10x6x2-inch baking dish. Cream the ½ cup butter and powdered sugar till fluffy. Beat in eggs. Spoon atop wafer crust. Spread apricot purée over butter mixture.

Whip cream. Spread over apricot layer. Sprinkle with reserved crumbs. Chill 12 hours or overnight. Remove from refrigerator about 15 minutes before serving. Serves 8.

*California's fabulous dried fruit industry, which peaked in the '30s, began when plum trees for prunes were planted by the padres around their missions. They also brought apricot, peach, almond, olive, and grape cuttings from their native Spain, whose soil and climate resemble California's. The miners of '49 took cuttings from these and started orchards that eventually bore crops for desserts like Baked Prune Whip.*

## Baked Prune Whip

**1½ cups whole prunes**
**4 egg whites**
**¼ teaspoon cream of tartar**
**4 tablespoons sugar**

**1½ teaspoons grated lemon peel**
**2 teaspoons lemon juice**
**Velvet Custard Sauce**

In saucepan combine prunes and 1½ cups water; bring to boiling. Cover and simmer 10 minutes. Cool in liquid; drain. With kitchen shears snip prunes from pits in small pieces; set aside. In large mixer bowl beat egg whites with cream of tartar and ¼ teaspoon salt to soft peaks. Gradually add *3 tablespoons* of the sugar, beating to stiff peaks. In small mixer bowl combine prunes, the remaining sugar, lemon peel, and juice; beat till blended. Gently fold mixture into egg whites. Turn into greased 1½-quart soufflé dish (or a 5-cup dish with collar). Bake at 350° till knife inserted off-center comes out clean, 25 to 35 minutes. Serve with Velvet Custard Sauce. Serves 6 to 8.

*Velvet Custard Sauce:* In a heavy saucepan beat together 4 egg yolks, 2 cups light cream, ¼ cup sugar, and ⅛ teaspoon salt. Cook over low heat, stirring constantly, till egg mixture coats a metal spoon.

## Easter Dessert

**¼ cup sugar**
**3 tablespoons quick-cooking tapioca**
**2 cups milk**
**½ teaspoon vanilla**
**2 stiffly beaten egg whites**

**¼ cup sugar**
**3 tablespoons quick-cooking tapioca**
**2 cups milk**
**2 beaten egg yolks**

In saucepan combine first ¼ cup sugar, 3 tablespoons tapioca, and ⅛ teaspoon salt. Stir in 2 cups milk. Let stand 5 minutes. Bring to boiling, stirring constantly. Cook and stir 6 minutes. Remove from heat; add vanilla. Fold into egg whites; set aside. In another saucepan combine remaining ¼ cup sugar and tapioca. Add ⅛ teaspoon salt. Stir in 2 cups milk and yolks. Cook and stir 6 minutes. Cool. Spoon white and yellow mixtures alternately into parfait glasses. Serves 8.

## Steamed Chocolate Pudding with Butterscotch Hard Sauce

**⅔ cup granulated sugar**
**3 tablespoons shortening**
**1 egg**
**2 1-ounce squares unsweetened chocolate, melted and cooled**

**2¼ cups all-purpose flour**
**4 teaspoons baking powder**
**¼ teaspoon salt**
**1 cup milk**
**Butterscotch Hard Sauce**

Cream sugar and shortening. Add egg; beat thoroughly. Beat in melted chocolate. Stir together thoroughly flour, baking powder, and salt. Add to creamed mixture alternately with milk, beating well. Pour into a well-greased 6-cup mold. (Do not use ring mold or tube pan.) Cover. Place on rack in a kettle; add boiling water to a depth of 1 inch. Cover kettle and steam till wooden pick inserted in the center comes out clean, 1¾ to 2 hours. Unmold pudding. Serve warm with Butterscotch Hard Sauce. Serves 8.

*Butterscotch Hard Sauce:* Using an electric mixer, cream ½ cup softened butter. Gradually add ⅔ cup packed light brown sugar; beat until fluffy. Beat in 1 egg yolk and 1 teaspoon vanilla. Add 3 tablespoons milk gradually, beating well. Beat 1 egg white till stiff peaks form. Fold into mixture. Chill well.

## Mother's Orange-Raisin Cake

1 cup raisins
½ cup chopped walnuts
   Peel of 1 medium orange,
     with white membrane
     removed
1 cup sugar
½ cup butter or margarine
2 eggs

1 teaspoon vanilla
2 cups sifted cake flour
1 teaspoon baking soda
½ teaspoon salt
1 cup buttermilk
1 cup sugar
⅓ cup orange juice

Combine the raisins, nuts, and orange peel. Put mixture through food grinder; set aside. Cream together 1 cup sugar and the butter. Add eggs and vanilla, beating till fluffy. Stir in orange-raisin mixture. Sift together the cake flour, baking soda, and salt. Add dry ingredients to creamed mixture alternately with buttermilk, beating well after each addition. Turn batter into a greased 9x9x2-inch baking pan. Bake at 350° till done, about 45 minutes. In small saucepan heat together 1 cup sugar and orange juice till sugar is dissolved. Prick top of cake all over with fork. Spoon sugar mixture over warm cake.

*Pouring an orange juice-sugar mixture over Mother's Orange-Raisin Cake while it is warm gives it a sugary glaze. This cake is also known as Williamsburg Cake.*

## Caramel Angel Food Cake

1½ cups egg whites (about
     10 to 12)
1¼ teaspoons cream of
     tartar
1 teaspoon vanilla

2 cups sugar
1½ cups sifted cake flour
   Burnt-Sugar Syrup
   Burnt-Sugar Frosting

Beat egg whites, cream of tartar, and vanilla till stiff peaks form. Sift together sugar and cake flour twice. Sift *a fourth at a time* over egg whites; fold in. Carefully fold in ¼ *cup* Burnt-Sugar Syrup. Spoon into an *ungreased* 10-inch tube pan. Bake at 375° till done, about 40 minutes. Invert cake in pan; cool completely. Remove from pan. Frost with Burnt-Sugar Frosting.

*Burnt-Sugar Syrup:* In a heavy skillet melt ¾ cup sugar, stirring constantly. When a deep golden brown syrup, remove from heat. Slowly add 1 cup boiling water. Cook and stir till all dissolves and syrup is reduced to ½ cup. Cool.

*Burnt-Sugar Frosting:* Place 1¼ cups sugar, 2 unbeaten egg whites, ¼ cup Burnt-Sugar Syrup, ¼ cup cold water, ¼ teaspoon cream of tartar, and dash salt in the top of a double boiler (don't place over boiling water). Beat ½ minute at low speed of electric mixer to blend. Now place mixture over, but not touching, boiling water. Cook, beating constantly, till frosting forms stiff peaks, *about* 7 minutes.

*Caramel Angel Food Cake was a Sigma Nu sweetheart — the cake that housemothers made for college boys when first we printed it, with the admonition that making angel food cake takes a gentle touch.*

## Applesauce Cake

½ cup butter or margarine
2 cups sugar
2 eggs
2½ cups all-purpose flour
1½ teaspoons baking soda
1 teaspoon salt

1 teaspoon ground cinnamon
½ teaspoon ground nutmeg
¼ teaspoon ground allspice
1½ cups canned applesauce
½ cup raisins
½ cup chopped pecans

Cream butter; gradually add sugar, creaming till light and fluffy. Add eggs one at a time, beating well after each. Stir together dry ingredients. Add to creamed mixture alternately with applesauce. Stir in raisins and nuts. Turn batter into greased and lightly floured 13x9x2-inch baking pan. Bake at 350° till done, about 45 minutes. Cool.

# Better Homes & Gardens

MORE THAN 2,400,000 CIRCULATION

JULY 1942 15¢

★ Home is the Strength of the Nation

PLANNING FOR TODAY AND TOMORROW—Page 18

SUMMER COOK BOOK – Frosty drinks · Steps to canning · Meals-in-a-basket · and more

"It was the best of times, it was the worst of times," wrote Charles Dickens more than 100 years ago. And for Americans this wraps up the '40s. The flush of prosperity and the bleakness of war were wrapped up in one decade. The early '40s were comfortable years. The depression over, we were beginning to enjoy the foods and recipes we hadn't seen in almost a decade. New kitchen appliances hit the market, and advertising cried out "buy"— and we did. Then came the war and with it food shortage and denial. Food rationing was relieved only by Victory Gardens. Not until late in the decade did the pendulum swing full-circle, with food and spending power both available again.

# THE 40s

The forties came in without fanfare or fireworks. As a matter of fact, 1940, like several of the years ahead of it, came in with nothing more momentous than the strains of "Auld Lang Syne" droned by Guy Lombardo and his Royal Canadians direct from the Roosevelt Hotel and into America's living rooms via radio. But no one was complaining. The country had pulled itself up out of the Depression of the 1930s, and the rosy view ahead looked pretty nice. There was a war going on in Europe, but that didn't really affect things here—certainly not the things everyone took for granted such as cars, houses, and food.

It was comfortable in the early forties just sitting around the oilcloth-covered kitchen table. Talk revolved around popular subjects such as the new movie, *Gone with the Wind*; the sensational singing rage, Frank Sinatra; teen-age bobby-soxers and their wild dance, the jitterbug; or the family vacation and traveling on one of the famous trains of the day. And talk definitely included foods and cooking.

Shrimp and avocado were enjoying newfound popularity everywhere, zucchini was an exciting, brand-new vegetable, vacuum-packed nuts of all kinds were the newest wrinkle for nibblers, and custards were making their first appearance as 'respectable' desserts—not just as baby food and hospital fare. Chocolate chips made their debut, too, and the whole country seemed to be munching Toll House Cookies.

There was time to fuss with fancy dishes and garnishes, time to serve attractive meals—and women were geared for it. At this time, a woman's place was unquestionably in the home, and even a college education for girls was viewed with great apprehension. A *Better Homes and Gardens* article of the time raised the question, "What kind of homemaker, wife, and mother will a college turn out?" There certainly was not much thought of women as surgeons, engineers, or business executives. Besides, new appliances were being developed and old ones improved considerably, adding considerable excitement to the career of homemaking. Ranges were being equipped with smokeless broilers, food blenders had come out of the soda fountains and into the kitchen, barbecue equipment was a red-hot item throughout the country, and to make even cleaning up palatable, there was a newfangled gadget called a 'dishwasher.'

And, of course, the kitchen table talk went to money. Every generation complains about the high cost of living, and things were no different in the early forties. "Imagine, butter costs 40 cents a pound, milk 13 cents a quart, and meat cuts anywhere from 25 to 45 cents a pound."

But the time was just ahead when money wasn't as limiting a factor as availability and food ration stamps counted as much, if not more, than dollars in planning the family's menus. The presence of the Food for Britain program already was starting to reveal possible shortages in certain foods areas, and with the bombing of Pearl Harbor in December, 1941, Americans headed into half a decade of belt-tightening unlike anything most of the population had ever experienced.

January, 1942, brought food and gas rationing. Every family had to learn to cope with the complex system of ration coupons, and foods on market shelves now carried two designations—the price and the amount of ration points needed to purchase the item. Thus, the great age of culinary improvisation was launched. Substituting one food for another became a necessity, and a nation that was used to eating what it pleased learned to eat what was available. Margarine replaced butter, while jellies, marmalades, and various 'spreads' were called into play to make butterless bread tasty. America's sweet tooth suffered only slightly, as the scarce sugar was replaced by honey, corn syrup, or molasses in desserts. Fruits became a standard dessert to save sugar. And the imaginative cook learned to make do with variety meats and to extend what meat she had.

Despite shortages, foods were making strides in improved quality and nutrition. The country was now vitamin conscious; the result was the introduction of fortified margarine and enriched flour and bread. Non-fat dried milk and spray-dried eggs, developed primarily for servicemen in distant spots around the globe, made their appearances, too, and were destined to speed up the development of the wide variety of mixes enjoyed today. By 1944, there were six mixes on the market—muffin, gingerbread, biscuit, pudding, pastry, and pancake/waffle.

Cooking, eating, and entertaining styles were changing dramatically under the impact of war. When Mom took up blowtorch or soldering gun and went to work in the war plant, cooking had to be simplified. Time and timing became important, and the pressure cooker made its own contribution to the war effort by speeding up the kitchen operation. Informality was the order of the day. Place mats replaced tablecloths to cut down laundry, pottery was just fine—there was no need to use the good china—stainless steel flatware became standard for the table—no time to polish silver—and Dad and the kids learned to cook and pack lunch buckets while Mom worked. Once Mom realized the size of her paycheck at the war plant, there was no getting her back to the range. So the trend was toward quick, easy, spur-of-the-moment meals and recipes.

Women who didn't work outside the home were making their own kind of contribution. Fuel was limited, so the patriotic woman cooked oven meals to conserve the limited heating fuels. She saved waste fat and turned it back in to her grocer so it could be collected for use in making explosives. She flattened tin cans, saved empty toothpaste tubes, even turned in her silk or nylon stockings to aid in making gun powder bags for naval guns. And she may very well have been the power behind the hoe in the nation's great Victory Gardening success.

The Victory Garden did more than grow vegetables. It cultivated a sense of national patriotism that went deeper than the carrots and beets. This was something everyone from grandparents to housewives to kids could get involved in and feel they were doing something to win the war. 'Food Fights for Freedom' was everyone's battle cry. At this time, Victory Gardens sprouted up in every inch of available space as well as in some spots that might, in less critical times, have been considered unavailable. Tomatoes, beans, carrots, peas, beets, and radishes flourished in such unlikely spots as Chicago's Arlington Racetrack, the Cook County Jail, the Portland, Oregon Zoo, and along railroad rights-of-way.

By 1943, home-front farmers were producing at least one-third of all the fresh vegetables being consumed in the country. This, in turn, triggered a tremendous increase in home canning. *Better Homes and Gardens* catered to the Victory Gardeners. It provided articles and booklets on vegetable planting and growing, and service articles on home canning and dehydrating foods. The pages of the magazine were filled with recipes for pickling, preserving, and canning, and advice on how to get the most mileage out of homegrown fruits and vegetables.

The war years honed the fighting edge of the *Better Homes and Gardens* staff. They produced articles to help mothers raise their children without fathers and provided home-medical information during the scarcity of civilian doctors. A regular monthly feature was a column titled 'Tips on Wartime Living,' telling readers how to repair and prolong the life of hard-to-get items that included just about everything. *Better Homes and Gardens* also served as a U. S. Treasury Agency in the sale of War Bonds and

Stamps by mail. And throughout the years of the war, the magazine offered encouragement to readers by featuring articles on 'coming attractions' — new developments, new techniques, and new life-styles.

The war went on. But somehow Americans were fed better than ever before. They ate more food and spent more money on food than at any other time in history. Nonetheless, when the war ended in 1945, America was more than ready to dump food rationing, swing shifts in shipyards, and the Victory Gardening many considered a pain in the back.

The country that had lived with tight food supplies and tight nerves was starting to relax. It did so with work-saving appliances such as the new automatic washer and the electric clothes dryer, introduced in 1946. It relaxed with entertainment, too. *Oklahoma* and *South Pacific* played to full houses on Broadway, while *Forever Amber*, *The Robe*, and *The Egg and I* topped the best-seller lists. America also grew fond of the new 'drive-in' movies where attractively attired 'carhops' served refreshments through windows of Kaiser and Studebaker cars. By 1947, American women were out of the war plant safety snoods and going all-girl again with the first home permanents and the shocking new look from Dior that dropped hemlines to 12 inches above the floor.

Television started to make inroads in several major cities, offering significant viewing 'firsts' such as coverage of the 1947 World Series and the 1948 presidential election. It also offered less significant viewing in the form of wrestling matches and kinescope recordings that were sometimes too fuzzy to know for sure what was on the screen. But only a relatively small percentage of U.S. homes had TV sets, or even access to its signal, by the decade's close.

Dinner hours were graced with an abundance and a variety of foods again. Chocolate, coconut, pineapple, and bananas were back. Chiffon cake, the first really new cake in a hundred years, was launched, and so were fancy, fluffy desserts such as chiffon pies, airy gelatins, and whipped cream confections. Instants found a ready market, and, for the first time, homemakers could enjoy the convenience of instant pudding, coffee, and tea. Mixes were making things easier, too. By 1949, there were dozens to choose from, including butter cake, corn bread, brownies, hot roll, and angel food cake. Frozen foods were becoming more and more popular as home freezers became more and more common.

The salad department offered only limited variety: tomato aspic or lime gelatin, potato, coleslaw, and chef's. Even the choice of dressings was slim. French and mayonnaise didn't create much excitement.

Barbecuing started to grow. Steak was back, and, for the first time, a shopper could buy chicken by the parts. Supermarkets, which had started to replace the independent grocer, were cutting up chickens and bagging the 'most desirable' cuts together. Up to this time, chicken breasts for company dinner meant buying four to six chickens, serving the breasts to guests, then serving the backs, necks, and wings to the family for a week.

Turkey was available 'by the part,' too, and the development of the Beltsville broad-breasted turkey gradually turned the gobbler into the traditional Thanksgiving bird. Until then, a brace of roasting chickens, ducks, or a pork roast had been holiday feast fare.

By the time the forties were doing their swan song, foods were not only plentiful again, they were better than ever before. New methods and equipment made cooking easier and the results tastier. All in all, the forties had made its mark on Americans' eating habits. Just as 'war turned boys into men,' the war years had matured and seasoned our food styles. And a little seasoning never hurt anything.

← *Unfold this section for three-page foldout illustration in full color*

FOR PRESIDENT
THOMAS E. DEWEY

# Recipe Features of the Forties

## Foods from Famous Trains

Travel the rails of the forties by trying some of the Foods from Famous Trains. Your trip will carry you all over the country and will include a nostalgic look at some of the most famous railroad lines, which reached their peak in the forties. Choose from the food of the Union Pacific, Milwaukee Road, Great Northern, New York Central, or Burlington.

## Home Canning

Capture the fresh goodness of the summer harvest by canning your own fruits and vegetables. The process of home canning became almost routine in the forties to help preserve the fruits and vegetables grown in victory gardens. This collection of recipes includes some of the best pickles, relishes, jams, and preserves of that era.

## Oven Meals

Save time by fixing a whole meal in the oven at once. This method of cooking was popular during the war years of the forties because it was a way to save precious fuel. In addition, it was ideal for working homemakers who had to prepare meals in a hurry. There were many different types of oven meals. Three of the best feature chicken, meat loaf, or ham.

In the forties *Better Homes and Gardens* used this kitchen to illustrate the ideal kitchen. It was planned for maximum working and storage area. It included a baking center, ample counter space, and a dishwasher.

# Foods from Famous Trains

Chefs on the Challenger served *Union Pacific Fruit Salad Dressing* (pictured opposite) to accompany a fruit and cottage cheese luncheon plate. Travelers completed the meal with a cup of tomato soup, a pot of coffee, and chocolate pudding with custard sauce for dessert.

From the Northern Pacific in the West to the Baltimore and Ohio in the East, American trains promoted regional food specialties in the '40s. The Northern Pacific annually gobbled up 265 tons of 2-pound tubers, and turned a marketing man's headache into a boon by perfecting a cooking technique that baked the mealy Goliaths in two hours—they pierced both ends with an ice pick. Another super-size dish, Rome Beauties, was baked by the Great Northern, which trekked through Washington State apple country. Apples were glazed with syrup made by cooking cores and peels.

Also in the West, the Union Pacific, famous for the golden spike wedding it to the Central Pacific in 1869, which made coast-to-coast railroad travel possible, served a fruit plate with a special fruit salad dressing. The Santa Fe Super Chiefs swept the tracks with revolving headlights. Their Harvey Girls, who were to railroads then what stewardesses are to airlines today, served old-fashioned boneless chicken pies with marvelously crisp Fred Harvey crusts. The Burlington Zephyrs served trout as the rail cars sliced past cold mountain streams.

But Western trains had no corner on good food. Rolling through Wisconsin dairyland, the Milwaukee Road roasted chicken with plenty of butter, and the Panama Limited, silverstreaking Illinois' flat farmland at 90 miles an hour on the way to New Orleans, featured succulent Gulf shrimp. Along the Eastern seaboard, the Baltimore and Ohio enticed young appetites with "The Flagman's Signal Dinner," and the New York Central served Custard with Apricot Sauce.

It was food at its best served in gracious surroundings—the rival of many of the day's finest restaurants. Etiquette was a spoon in your cup to keep the coffee from spilling over going 'round the curves. And the ingredients were plucked seemingly along the way. Though the red carpet is no longer rolled out for the New York Central's 20th Century Limited, fine food and Zephyr Vista Domes are back on Amtrak.

## Union Pacific Fruit Salad Dressing

| | |
|---|---|
| 1 clove garlic | 3 tablespoons lemon juice |
| 1½ teaspoons sugar | 2 tablespoons vinegar |
| ½ teaspoon salt | 1 egg |
| ½ teaspoon paprika | 1 cup salad oil* |
| ¼ teaspoon dry mustard | ¼ cup chili sauce |

Cut garlic clove in half, and rub a small mixer bowl with cut side. Mix sugar, salt, paprika, and dry mustard in bowl to absorb garlic flavor. Add lemon juice, vinegar, and egg. Beat with mixer. Very slowly add oil, beating constantly with mixer. Beat until oil is blended in, then beat in the chili sauce. Serve with fruit. Makes 1½ cups.

*For vegetable salads, use ½ cup salad oil and ⅓ cup olive oil.

*Broiled Steak* (pictured opposite), flattered with mushrooms, bacon, tomatoes, and sweet pickle fans, was the Great Northern's welcome aboard. Accompaniments were new potatoes blanketed with cream sauce, Brussels sprouts, lettuce-orange salad, relishes, and biscuits.

## Broiled Steak

Have a porterhouse, T-bone, or club beef steak cut 1½ inches thick. Slash fat edge (not into meat) at 1-inch intervals to prevent steak from curling. Place steak on cold rack in broiler pan. Broil so surface of meat is 3 to 4 inches from heat for 7 to 8 minutes on *each side* for rare, or 9 to 10 minutes on *each side* for medium. To test steak for doneness, slit center of steak and note inside color: red—rare; pink—medium. Season the steak with salt and pepper as desired.

A *Challenger* LUNCHEON ON THE UNION PACIFIC

THE GREAT NORTHERN'S *Empire Builder* SERVES A STEAK

84

## Southern Pacific Salad Bowl

*The Southern Pacific's scenic route along the sparkling blue ocean and through California's 'salad bowl' inspired it to toss crisp iceberg lettuce, tomatoes, cucumber, radishes, and green pepper with French salad dressing. This quickly became America's everyday, home-style salad.*

1 medium head lettuce
4 medium tomatoes
1 cucumber
½ bunch radishes, thinly
  sliced (¾ cup)

½ green pepper, cut in
  strips (½ cup)
1 teaspoon sugar
Dash salt
⅓ cup French salad dressing

Break lettuce into salad bowl in bite-size pieces. Peel and quarter tomatoes. Peel cucumber; score with tines of a fork and slice thinly. Arrange quartered tomatoes, sliced cucumber, sliced radishes, and green pepper strips over lettuce pieces. Sprinkle with sugar and salt. Pour French salad dressing over salad, and toss lightly till vegetables are coated. Serve immediately. Makes 8 to 10 servings.

## Supreme of Chicken Washington — Milwaukee Road-Style

½ cup chopped green pepper
2 tablespoons butter
1 17-ounce can whole kernel
  corn, drained
2 tablespoons chopped
  canned pimiento
1 4-pound ready-to-cook
  roasting chicken
1 cup sliced onion

1 cup sliced carrots
2 tablespoons butter,
  melted
Canned artichoke hearts,
  drained
Butter
Hot cooked asparagus tips
Canned pimiento strips
Watercress

Cook green pepper in 2 tablespoons butter till tender. Stir in corn, the 2 tablespoons pimiento, ¼ teaspoon salt, and dash pepper. Heat 5 minutes. Stuff cavity of chicken with corn mixture; skewer closed and lace shut. Place onion and carrots in roasting pan. Place chicken on top of vegetables. Brush 2 tablespoons melted butter over chicken. Roast at 375° till chicken tests done, 1½ to 2 hours, basting frequently with pan drippings. If desired, prepare gravy, using pan drippings. Dice cooked vegetables from roasting pan and stir into the gravy. Serve chicken on platter garnished with artichoke hearts warmed in butter. Atop artichoke hearts place a small bouquet of asparagus tips and pimiento strips. Trim with watercress. Serves 4.

## Colorado Mountain Trout — Burlington Zephyr-Style

¼ cup all-purpose flour
1 teaspoon salt
½ teaspoon pepper
2 pan-dressed mountain
  trout, ½ pound each
¼ cup milk

3 tablespoons butter or
  margarine
2 tablespoons lemon juice
1 teaspoon snipped parsley
Lemon wedges
Parsley *or* watercress

Combine the all-purpose flour, salt, and pepper. Dip pan-dressed trout in milk, then roll in flour mixture until evenly coated. In heavy skillet heat *2 tablespoons* of the butter or margarine. Fry trout in hot butter over medium heat till browned on one side, about 4 minutes. Turn and brown other side, cooking till fish flakes easily when tested with a fork, 4 to 5 minutes longer. Remove trout from skillet to hot platter and keep warm. Add the remaining 1 tablespoon butter or margarine to skillet. Stir in the lemon juice and 1 teaspoon snipped parsley; heat through. Drizzle the lemon-butter mixture over the pan-fried trout. Serve lemon wedges with the cooked fish. Garnish the platter with sprigs of parsley or watercress. Makes 2 servings.

## Gulf Coast Shrimp, Creole-Style—Illinois Central

2 quarts water
1 stalk celery, cut up
1 small onion, cut up
¼ cup vinegar
1 tablespoon salt
¼ teaspoon pepper

3 whole cloves
2 bay leaves
3 pounds shrimp in shells
    Creole Sauce
    Hot cooked rice
    Parsley

In large saucepan or Dutch oven combine water, celery, onion, vinegar, salt, pepper, whole cloves, and bay leaves; bring mixture to boiling. Add shrimp. Heat to boiling; reduce heat and simmer till shrimp turn pink, 1 to 3 minutes. Drain. Peel and devein shrimp. Add to Creole Sauce; heat through, about 5 minutes. Serve in individual casseroles with a mound of rice. Garnish with parsley. Makes 8 servings.

*Creole Sauce:* In large saucepan cook 3 slices bacon till crisp; drain, reserving 2 tablespoons drippings. Cook 1 cup chopped onion, 1 cup chopped green pepper, ½ cup chopped celery, and 1 clove garlic, minced, in bacon drippings till vegetables are tender but not brown. Blend in 1 tablespoon all-purpose flour. Stir in one 28-ounce can tomatoes, 3 whole cloves, 1 bay leaf, 1½ teaspoons salt, 1 teaspoon sugar, and ⅛ teaspoon pepper. Bring to boiling; reduce heat and simmer 30 minutes. Crumble cooked bacon; stir into sauce.

## Custard with Apricot Sauce—New York Central-Style

1 17-ounce can unpeeled
    apricot halves
4 slightly beaten eggs
⅓ cup sugar
¼ teaspoon salt
¼ teaspoon grated or ground
    nutmeg

2 cups milk
¼ teaspoon grated lemon peel
¼ teaspoon grated orange
    peel
2 tablespoons finely chopped
    almonds, toasted
    (optional)

Drain apricots, reserving ½ cup syrup. Combine eggs, sugar, salt, and nutmeg. Stir in milk, lemon peel, and orange peel. Generously butter six 6-ounce custard cups. If desired, divide almonds among the custard cups. Place one apricot half, cut side up, on top of nuts in each cup. Fill cups with egg mixture. Set in shallow pan on oven rack; pour hot water into pan, 1 inch deep. Bake at 325° until knife inserted in custards off-center comes out clean, 40 to 45 minutes. Cool before removing from cups.

In blender container combine remaining apricot halves and the reserved ½ cup syrup; blend till smooth. Heat in saucepan. Serve warm with custards. Serves 6.

## Baked Wenatchee Apples—Great Northern-Style

6 large Rome Beauty
    apples

1⅓ cups sugar
2 cups water

Remove cores from apples and peel one round from the top of each apple; reserve cores and peel. Place apples in a 10x6x2-inch baking dish, and fill each apple with about *1 tablespoon* of the sugar. Sprinkle *½ cup* of the sugar around the apples. Bake at 350° till apples are done, 45 to 60 minutes. After juices form in pan, baste apples once or twice. Cool apples before serving.

Meanwhile, prepare syrup by cooking cores and peels in 2 cups water with remaining sugar. Simmer syrup, uncovered, until mixture thickens, about 10 minutes. Strain to remove skins. Serve syrup over apples. Serves 6.

*Washington State is synonymous with the crisp Delicious apples, but it also grows Rome Beauties, the best baking apples. The Great Northern made them memorable by sprinkling liberally with sugar and basting with juices during baking.*

# Home Canning

That ill wind, World War II, blew some good—the pickle, preserve, jam, jelly, and canning recipes that resulted from putting up Victory Garden produce. The pressure canner got a workout in homes, and canning centers were set up in church basements or community centers. Never in the decades of Cooks' Round Table contests have there been better recipes than these 'war babies,' which form the nucleus of this collection. Tangerine Marmalade, one of the spreads-of-the-month that appeared as butter extenders, has continued to make toast a treat. Crisp Pickle Slices have stood the test of time. They still appear in the current *Cook Book* edition.

Today, homemakers can fruits and vegetables for various reasons. There are those women who want to capture the freshness of their home-grown produce for year-round enjoyment. Others prepare special recipes to stock on their cupboard shelves, specialties that aren't available at the supermarket. And still others put up jams, jellies, pickles, and preserves in attractive containers to give as hostess or holiday gifts.

Assorted homemade jams, jellies, and preserves, and *Mixed Pickles* (pictured opposite) recapture a corner from Grandmother's cupboard, just as the delightful fragrance of vinegar and spices boiling in a kettle brings back memories of her kitchen.

## Pickled Beets

6 pounds small whole beets*
(3½ pounds without tops)
4 cups cider vinegar
1 cup sugar

6 inches stick cinnamon, broken
2 teaspoons whole allspice
12 whole cloves

Wash beets, leaving root and 1 inch of tops. Cover with boiling water; simmer about 25 minutes. Drain, reserving 2 cups cooking liquid. Slip off skins and trim; keep hot. In large kettle combine vinegar, reserved cooking liquid, and sugar. Tie spices in cheesecloth. Add spice bag to pickling liquid. Bring to a boil; simmer 15 minutes. Discard spice bag. Pack hot beets loosely into hot pint jars, leaving ½-inch headspace. Cover beets with boiling pickling liquid, leaving ½-inch headspace. Wipe jar rims; adjust lids. Process in boiling water-bath canner 30 minutes (start timing when water covering jars returns to boiling). Makes 3 pints.

*For large beets, wash, remove tops, and cook 25 minutes. Slip off skins; cube and process as directed.

## Mixed Pickles

10 cucumbers, cut in strips
(4½ quarts)
6 green peppers, cut in
strips (2½ quarts)
6 sweet red peppers, cut in
strips (2½ quarts)
6 cups water
¾ cup pickling salt

6 large carrots, peeled and
cut in strips (1 quart)
6 cups sugar
4 cups cider vinegar
3 tablespoons celery seed
3 tablespoons mustard seed
1 tablespoon salt
2 teaspoons turmeric

Cover cucumbers and peppers with mixture of water and pickling salt. Let stand in cool place overnight. Drain; rinse. Cook carrots in boiling salted water 5 minutes. Drain; add carrots to drained cucumber mixture. Combine sugar, vinegar, celery seed, mustard seed, salt, and turmeric. Pour over *drained* vegetables. Bring to boil. Fill hot pint jars to ½ inch from top. Wipe jar rims; adjust lids. Process in boiling water-bath canner for 5 minutes (start timing when water covering jars returns to boiling). Makes 10 pints.

## Crisp Pickle Slices

4 quarts sliced, unpeeled, medium cucumbers
6 medium white onions, sliced (6 cups)
2 green peppers, sliced (1⅔ cups)
3 cloves garlic
⅓ cup pickling salt
Cracked ice
5 cups sugar
3 cups cider vinegar
2 tablespoons mustard seed
1½ teaspoons celery seed
1½ teaspoons turmeric

Combine cucumbers, onions, peppers, and garlic. Add pickling salt. Cover with ice; mix well. Let stand 3 hours; drain well. Remove garlic. Combine sugar, vinegar, mustard seed, celery seed, and turmeric; pour over cucumber mixture. Bring to a boil. Fill hot pint jars loosely with boiling hot cucumber mixture to ½ inch from top. Wipe jar rims; adjust lids. Process in boiling water-bath canner for 5 minutes. (Count time after water covering jars returns to boiling.) Makes 8 pints.

## Best Tomato Catsup

1 cup white vinegar
1½ inches stick cinnamon, broken
1½ teaspoons whole cloves
1 teaspoon celery seed
8 pounds tomatoes
1 medium onion, chopped
¼ teaspoon cayenne
1 cup sugar
4 teaspoons salt

In small saucepan combine vinegar, cinnamon, cloves, and celery seed. Cover; bring to a boil. Remove from heat; let stand. Wash, core, and quarter tomatoes into large kettle or Dutch oven. Add onion and cayenne. Bring to a boil; cook 15 minutes, stirring occasionally. Put tomatoes through food mill or coarse sieve. Add sugar to tomatoes. Bring to a boil; reduce heat and *simmer* briskly till mixture is reduced to half (measure depth with wooden ruler at beginning and end), 1½ to 2 hours.

Strain vinegar mixture into tomato mixture; discard spices. Add salt. Simmer till of desired consistency, about 30 minutes, stirring often. Fill hot pint jars with hot tomato mixture to within ½ inch of top; wipe jar rims and adjust lids. Process in boiling water-bath canner 5 minutes (count time after water covering jars returns to boiling). Makes 2 pints.

## Honey Corn Relish

9 cups fresh corn kernels
3 cups chopped cabbage
3 cups chopped celery
3 cups chopped onion (6 medium)
3 cups chopped, unpeeled, seeded cucumbers
2 cups chopped green pepper (2 large)
1 cup chopped sweet red pepper (1 large)
½ cup sugar
3 tablespoons salt
1 tablespoon dry mustard
1 tablespoon turmeric
1 tablespoon celery seed
3 cups cider vinegar
1 cup honey

Combine vegetables in very large kettle or Dutch oven. Combine sugar, salt, mustard, turmeric, and celery seed. Mix vinegar, honey, and 1 cup water; stir into sugar mixture, then into vegetables. Boil gently, uncovered, 15 minutes. Loosely fill hot pint jars to ½ inch from top. Wipe jar rims; adjust lids. Process in boiling water-bath canner 15 minutes (count time when water covering jars returns to boiling). Drain before serving. Makes 8 or 9 pints.

## Red Sauce

9 pounds tomatoes
1½ cups cider vinegar
1¼ cups sugar

½ cup ground onion (2 small)
½ cup ground green pepper
1 tablespoon salt

Wash, core, and cut up tomatoes. Cook in large kettle till soft. Turn into colander and drain off juice. (Use juice elsewhere.) Press tomatoes through food mill. Add remaining ingredients. Bring to boil. Reduce heat; simmer till thick, about 1 hour. Stir occasionally. Fill hot pint jars with hot mixture to within ½ inch of top; wipe jar rims and adjust lids. Process in boiling water-bath canner 5 minutes (count time after water covering jars returns to boil). Makes 2 pints.

## Hot Dog Relish

5 cups ground cucumber
(5 medium)
3 cups ground onion
3 cups chopped celery
2 sweet red *or* green
peppers, ground (1 cup)
2 hot red peppers, ground

¼ cup pickling salt
3 cups sugar
3 cups white vinegar
1 cup water
1 tablespoon celery seed
2 teaspoons mustard seed

Combine ground cucumber, onion, celery, sweet peppers, and hot peppers; add pickling salt. Mix thoroughly. Let stand 3 hours or overnight. Rinse well. Drain. Heat sugar, white vinegar, water, celery seed, and mustard seed to boiling. Add vegetables; bring to boiling. Reduce heat and simmer 10 minutes. Pack relish loosely while boiling hot into hot pint jars, filling to ½ inch of top. Wipe jar rims. Adjust lids. Process in boiling water-bath canner 5 minutes (count time after water covering jars returns to boiling). Makes 6 pints.

## Pickled Dilled Beans

2 pounds green beans
Boiling water
3 cups water
1 cup white vinegar

2 cloves garlic, crushed
2 tablespoons pickling salt
2 teaspoons dried dillweed
¼ teaspoon cayenne

Wash beans. Trim ends. Cut beans to fit jars. Cover beans with boiling water; cook 3 minutes. Drain. Pack lengthwise into hot jars, leaving ½-inch headspace. Combine remaining ingredients; bring to boil. Cover beans with boiling liquid; leave ½-inch headspace. Wipe jar rims; adjust lids. Process in boiling water-bath canner 10 minutes (count time after water covering jars returns to boiling). Makes 4 pints.

## Pineapple Spears

In 4- to 6-quart kettle or Dutch oven combine 4 cups water and 3 cups sugar; cook and stir till sugar dissolves. Keep hot but not bubbling. Wash two 4-pound pineapples well; cut off crowns and peel. Remove eyes. Quarter and core the fruit. Cut fruit in spears ½ inch shorter than pint jars. Add pineapple spears to sugar syrup; bring to boil. Boil about 7 minutes. Pack hot fruit into hot pint jars. Cover with boiling syrup, leaving ½-inch headspace. Wipe rim of jars. Adjust lids. Process in boiling water-bath canner 30 minutes (count time after water covering jars returns to boiling). Makes 3 pints.

*"Play up those gold-plated garden vegetables" was wartime advice when steaks and chops were in short supply. It's pertinent today, too. Make hamburgers better with Red Sauce from your tomato crop, or Hot Dog Relish from cucumbers, onions, and peppers.*

## Carrot Circles Relish

2 pounds carrots, peeled
2 cups sugar
2 cups cider vinegar

1½ teaspoons salt
1½ teaspoons dried basil,
  crushed

Bias-cut carrots in ½-inch pieces. Cook in boiling salted water till crisp-tender, 5 minutes. Drain; pack into hot pint jars, filling to ½ inch of top. Bring remaining ingredients and 2 cups water to boil; simmer 3 minutes. Pour over carrots, filling to ½ inch of top. Wipe jar rims; adjust lids. Process in boiling water-bath canner 15 minutes (count time after water returns to boil). Makes 3 pints.

## Pear-Peach Jam

1 pound pears, peeled
1 pound peaches, peeled
2 tablespoons lemon juice

1 1¾-ounce package
  powdered fruit pectin
5½ cups sugar

Core pears; pit peaches. Grind fruits (should be 4 cups). In 10-quart kettle combine fruits, lemon juice, and pectin; bring to boiling. Stir in sugar. Again bring to full rolling boil; boil hard 1 minute, stirring constantly. Remove from heat. Skim off foam and stir jam 5 minutes. Fill hot sterilized half-pint jars. Seal. Makes 7 half-pints.

## Pineapple-Mint Jam

2 medium pineapples
2½ cups sugar

8 drops green food coloring
1 drop oil of peppermint

Cut crowns from pineapples. Peel; remove eyes. Quarter and core. Cut in chunks to make 4 cups. Put half at a time into blender container; blend till coarsely chopped. Transfer to 3-quart saucepan. Add sugar and 1 cup water. Boil gently, stirring often, till thick, about 45 minutes. Stir in remaining ingredients. Ladle into hot sterilized half-pint jars; seal with vacuum lids or paraffin. Makes 3 half-pints.

## Corn and Tomato Relish

2 medium onions
2 medium green peppers
3 stalks celery, cut up
1 cup cider vinegar
½ cup sugar
2 or 3 small dried hot red
  peppers (optional)

2 tablespoons salt
1 tablespoon turmeric
2 teaspoons mustard seed
1 16-ounce can tomatoes
2 16-ounce cans whole
  kernel corn, drained
2 tablespoons cornstarch

Cut up onions and green peppers; put in blender container. Cover with *cold* water; blend till vegetables are coarsely chopped. Drain thoroughly and put in 10-quart kettle. Chop celery in blender as above. Drain. Put vinegar, sugar, hot red peppers, salt, turmeric, and mustard seed in blender container; blend till combined. Add tomatoes; turn blender on and off quickly. Add to kettle. Add corn; bring to boil. Reduce heat; simmer, uncovered, 30 to 35 minutes. Mix ¼ cup cold water into cornstarch; add to vegetable mixture. Cook and stir till thick, 3 to 4 minutes. Fill hot jars to within ½ inch of top. Wipe jar rims; adjust lids. Process in boiling water-bath canner 15 minutes (count time when water returns to boil). Makes 4½ pints.

## Grape Conserve

4 pounds Concord grapes,
washed
3 large oranges

2 large lemons
8 cups sugar
1 cup broken walnuts

Separate grape skins from pulp; reserve skins. Cook pulp till soft, about 5 minutes; sieve to remove seeds. Squeeze 1½ cups orange juice and ½ cup lemon juice; reserve peels from 2 oranges and 1 lemon. Scrape off excess white; slice peels very thin. Cover peels with water and cook till tender; drain. Combine grape skins and pulp, juices, peels, and sugar. Boil till thick enough to sheet from metal spoon, 35 to 40 minutes. Add nuts. Fill hot sterilized jars to within ½ inch of top. Seal with paraffin or vacuum lids. Makes 10 half-pints.

## Tangerine Marmalade

8 to 10 tangerines
7 cups sugar

1 6-ounce bottle liquid
fruit pectin

Peel tangerines, reserving peel; remove membrane from pulp. Dice pulp, removing seeds (should be 3½ cups pulp). Scrape excess white from peel. Cut peel in very fine shreds to make ¾ cup. In large saucepan combine diced pulp, peel, and sugar. Mix well. Heat to a full rolling boil over high heat, stirring constantly. Boil hard 1 minute, stirring constantly. Remove from heat and stir in pectin. Stir and skim for 5 minutes to prevent the fruit from floating. Pour into hot sterilized jars filling to within ½ inch of top. Seal at once with vacuum lids or paraffin. Makes ten 6-ounce jars.

*Tangerine Marmalade started life as a butter stretcher during the war years when the magazine ran a spread-of-the-month feature. Now it's a breakfast brightener.*

## Old-Fashioned Tomato Preserves

2 pounds ripe tomatoes (6)
1 teaspoon grated lemon
peel
¼ cup lemon juice

6½ cups sugar
1 6-ounce bottle liquid
fruit pectin

Wash, peel, and core tomatoes; cut in eighths or crush. Measure 3 cups tomatoes into 6-quart kettle or Dutch oven; simmer over low heat 10 minutes. Add lemon peel and lemon juice. Add sugar; bring to full rolling boil over high heat, stirring constantly. Boil hard 1 minute. Remove from heat; stir in liquid fruit pectin. Skim off foam with metal spoon. Ladle into hot sterilized jars to within ½ inch of top; seal at once with vacuum lids or paraffin. Makes about 8 half-pints.

*Once families discovered how extraordinarily good Old-Fashioned Tomato Preserves were on toast or to pep up a small portion of meat, no shelf of home-canned tomato products was complete without them. You can make the same tasty discovery by putting up a batch from your own garden surplus or from tomatoes offered at a nearby vegetable stand.*

## Pear Conserve

6 medium Bartlett pears
1 13¼-ounce can pineapple
tidbits, drained
2 teaspoons grated orange
peel

⅓ cup orange juice
4 cups sugar
1 4-ounce jar maraschino
cherries, drained and
chopped (⅓ cup)

Wash, quarter, and core, but do not peel pears. Grind or finely chop pears and pineapple. Add orange peel and juice. Add sugar. Bring to boiling. Boil till syrup sheets from metal spoon, 25 to 30 minutes. Add cherries. Ladle into hot sterilized jars to within ½ inch of top; seal at once with vacuum lids or paraffin. Makes 7 half-pints.

# Oven Meals

Oven meals, in which the main dish, vegetable, and dessert all bake at the same time, became popular during the World War II fuel shortages. Chicken Fricassee, the Sunday dinner treat pictured at left, meat loaf, and ham steak were oven favorites back when the thickness of the ham slice was determined by the number of meat ration points on hand. Desserts were cobblers, cornstarch-thickened fruit mixtures topped with biscuits, or crumb-topped crisps, all of which are as well-liked today as they were then because they free women from pot-watching.

Dovetail recipe preparations for oven meals so that all foods will finish baking at the same time. Begin with the *Chicken Fricassee* and, if the oven is large enough, *Oven Rice.* Next, prepare the *Scalloped Spinach.* The last dish to go into the oven is the *Peaches 'n Cream Crisp* (pictured opposite).

## MENU
*Chicken Fricassee*
*Oven Rice (optional)*
*Scalloped Spinach*
*Carrot Sticks   Olives*
*Peaches 'n Cream Crisp*
*Beverage*

## Chicken Fricassee

1 3- to 4-pound ready-to-
  cook fryer chicken, cut
  in serving-size pieces
½ cup all-purpose flour
¼ cup shortening
½ cup chopped celery

¼ cup chopped onion
1 10½-ounce can condensed
  cream of mushroom soup
2 tablespoons chopped
  canned pimiento
Oven Rice (optional)

Coat chicken with a mixture of the flour, 1 teaspoon salt, and ⅛ teaspoon pepper. Brown chicken in hot shortening in skillet; remove to 3-quart casserole. Cook celery and onion in skillet till tender but not brown. Drain off excess fat. Stir in soup, pimiento, and ¾ cup water. Pour over chicken in casserole.

Cover and bake at 350° until tender, about 1 hour. Serve with Oven Rice or hot cooked rice. Serves 6.

*Oven Rice:* Place 1 cup long grain rice in 1-quart casserole. Add 2½ cups water and 1 teaspoon salt. Cover; bake at 350° for 30 minutes. Fluff with fork. Cover; bake till tender, 20 to 30 minutes more.

## Scalloped Spinach

2 10-ounce packages frozen
  chopped spinach
¾ cup milk
¾ cup shredded process
  American cheese

3 beaten eggs
3 tablespoons chopped onion
1 cup coarse soft bread
  crumbs
1 tablespoon butter, melted

Cook spinach following package directions; drain well. Mix with milk, ½ *cup* of the cheese, eggs, onion, ½ teaspoon salt, and dash pepper. Turn into greased 8x8x2-inch baking pan. Bake at 350° for 25 min-

utes. Combine crumbs, remaining cheese, and butter; sprinkle atop spinach. Bake till knife inserted off-center comes out clean, 10 to 15 minutes more. Let stand 5 minutes before serving. Serves 6.

## Peaches 'n Cream Crisp

1 29-ounce can peach slices,
  drained
¾ cup quick-cooking rolled
  oats

½ cup packed brown sugar
½ cup all-purpose flour
6 tablespoons butter
  Vanilla ice cream

Arrange drained peaches in an 8x1½-inch round baking dish. Combine oats, brown sugar, flour, and

butter. Sprinkle over peaches. Bake at 350° for 30 minutes. Serve warm with ice cream. Serves 6.

## MENU

*Meat Loaf Ring*
*Corn*
*Baked Potatoes*
*Cabbage-Pepper Slaw*
*Date-Nut Pudding*
*Beverage*

*Slaw comes from the Dutch who planted cabbages where Wall Street now stands, and who shredded them with salt. From Manhattan the cabbages, the Dutch, and coleslaw traveled to the Midwest, bastion of this crisp cabbage salad. Traditionally made with a boiled mustard dressing, it's now tossed with mayonnaise thinned with cream, or with oil and vinegar. It may include red or green peppers; sliced radishes, celery, or carrots; diced red apple; or pineapple. If made with red cabbage, it's Calico Slaw.*

## Meat Loaf Ring

2 beaten eggs
2 cups soft bread crumbs
1 8-ounce can tomatoes, cut up
½ cup finely chopped onion
½ cup finely chopped celery
1 tablespoon prepared horseradish
1½ teaspoons salt
½ teaspoon dry mustard
⅛ teaspoon pepper

1½ pounds ground beef
½ pound ground pork
• • •
½ cup catsup
1 tablespoon light corn syrup
1 teaspoon Worcestershire sauce
• • •
2 12-ounce cans whole kernel corn

In mixing bowl combine beaten eggs, bread crumbs, tomatoes, onion, celery, horseradish, salt, dry mustard, and pepper. Add ground beef and ground pork; mix well. Press meat mixture into a 6½-cup ring mold. Bake at 350° for 1 hour. Carefully drain off fat. Turn meat ring out onto a baking sheet. Combine catsup, corn syrup, and Worcestershire sauce; spread over meat. Return meat ring to oven and bake 15 minutes longer.

Heat corn in saucepan. Drain off liquid; season to taste. Transfer meat from baking sheet to serving plate. Fill center of meat ring with corn. Makes 6 to 8 servings.

## Cabbage-Pepper Slaw

1 small head cabbage, shredded (3 cups)
¾ cup sliced green olives
1 medium green pepper, cut in thin strips (½ cup)
¼ cup sliced canned pimiento

¼ cup salad oil
2 tablespoons vinegar
¼ teaspoon salt
¼ teaspoon celery salt
Dash pepper
Dash cayenne

In a bowl toss together cabbage, olives, green pepper, and pimiento. Combine oil, vinegar, salt, celery salt, pepper, and cayenne in a screw-top jar. Cover and shake thoroughly. Pour dressing over cabbage mixture. Toss until vegetables are coated. Serves 6 to 8.

## Date-Nut Pudding

1 cup chopped pitted dates
½ cup boiling water
1 tablespoon butter or margarine
1 beaten egg
½ cup sugar
½ cup dark corn syrup
1 teaspoon vanilla

1½ cups all-purpose flour
1½ teaspoons baking powder
½ teaspoon salt
1 cup chopped walnuts
• • •
¾ cup dark corn syrup
¼ cup light cream
½ teaspoon vanilla

Combine dates, boiling water, and butter; set date mixture aside. Combine egg, sugar, ½ cup dark corn syrup, and 1 teaspoon vanilla; beat thoroughly. Stir in date mixture. Stir together thoroughly the flour, baking powder, and salt. Add to date mixture; mix well. Stir in the walnuts. Pour into a greased 11x- 7½x1½-inch baking pan. Bake at 350° till mixture is done, 30 to 40 minutes. Prepare sauce by combining the ¾ cup dark corn syrup and light cream in a saucepan. Bring just to boiling. Reduce heat and simmer 3 minutes. Stir in ½ teaspoon vanilla. Serve warm sauce with pudding. Serves 6 to 8.

## Double-Deck Ham Bake

¾ cup long grain rice
2 tablespoons butter
1 10½-ounce can condensed
    beef broth
½ cup water
2 tablespoons chopped onion

½ teaspoon poultry
    seasoning
2 fully cooked ham slices,
    cut ¾ inch thick (about
    2½ pounds)
1 teaspoon prepared mustard

In a skillet slowly brown uncooked rice in the butter. Remove from heat. Stir in condensed beef broth, water, chopped onion, and poultry seasoning. Bring to boiling. Reduce heat; cover and simmer 15 minutes.

Spread one ham slice with mustard. Cover with the rice mixture and top with the second ham slice. Place ham in a 13x9x2-inch baking pan. Cover pan with foil. Bake at 350° about 50 minutes. Serves 8.

**MENU**

*Double-Deck Ham Bake*
*Green Beans*
*(oven-heated)*
*Angel Salad*
*Hot Rolls   Butter*
*Apricot Cobbler*
*Beverage*

## Apricot Cobbler

1½ cups all-purpose flour
3 teaspoons baking powder
1 tablespoon sugar
½ teaspoon salt
⅓ cup shortening
½ cup milk
1 beaten egg
2 30-ounce cans unpeeled
    apricot halves (4 cups)
2 tablespoons sugar

2 tablespoons all-purpose
    flour
½ teaspoon ground cinnamon
2 tablespoons lemon juice
1 tablespoon butter
½ teaspoon vanilla
1 tablespoon sugar
    Vanilla ice cream *or* light
    cream

For topper stir together thoroughly 1½ cups flour, baking powder, 1 tablespoon sugar, and salt. Cut in shortening till mixture resembles coarse crumbs. Combine the milk and beaten egg. Add all at once to dry ingredients, stirring just to moisten. Set aside. Drain apricots, reserving 1 cup of the syrup. In a saucepan combine the 2 tablespoons sugar, 2 tablespoons flour, and cin-

namen. Stir in the reserved apricot syrup, lemon juice, and butter. Cook and stir till thick and bubbly. Stir in the apricots and vanilla. Pour hot filling into an 8x8x2-inch baking dish. Immediately spoon on topper in 8 or 9 mounds. Sprinkle the 1 tablespoon sugar over topper. Bake at 350° for 40 minutes. Serve warm with vanilla ice cream or light cream. Makes 8 or 9 servings.

## Angel Salad

1 13¼-ounce can pineapple
    tidbits
2 egg yolks
2 tablespoons sugar
1 tablespoon vinegar
    Dash salt
3 cups tiny marshmallows

2 cups grapes, seeded and
    halved
2 tablespoons sliced mara-
    schino cherries
½ cup whipping cream
    • • •
    Lettuce

Drain pineapple tidbits, reserving 3 tablespoons of the syrup. In heavy saucepan beat egg yolks. Stir in the reserved pineapple syrup, sugar, vinegar, and salt. Cook and stir over low heat until mixture is thickened. Set aside to cool. Combine the marshmallows, grapes, drained

pineapple tidbits, and maraschino cherries; pour egg mixture over and mix well. Refrigerate several hours or overnight. Whip the cream. Fold whipped cream into fruit mixture. Serve salad on lettuce and garnish with additional seeded grapes, if desired. Makes 8 servings.

*Angel Salad is also called Heavenly Hash or 24-Hour Salad, the time it takes for the marsh-mallows to get squashy. Any version usually has five things: marsh-mallows, whipping cream, and pineapple are the basics, plus other fruits which vary. The homemade dressing of egg yolks, pineapple syrup, and sugar marks this an 'old reliable.'*

# Good Eating during the Forties

## Party-Perfect Appetizers and Beverages

Spark your appetite with a cheese ball, canapés, lemonade, cider, and eggnog—all from the forties.

## Main Dishes for Hearty Appetites

When company comes, feature a hearty shrimp, sole, chicken, beef, oxtail, sparerib, ham, or veal main dish.

## Vegetables—Plain and Fancy

Serve several of these tempting vegetables soon. They include onions, zucchini, corn, and tomatoes.

## Salad Specials

Add a salad to your menu. There's quite a selection. Choose anything from egg or potato salads to frozen and molded salads. You'll find dressing recipes, too.

## Fresh Breads from the Oven

If you enjoy making and eating breads, try these rolls, breads, and biscuits. You won't be disappointed.

## Praise-Winning Desserts

The pie, sherbet, cheesecake, cookie, fruitcake, gingerbread, pudding, soufflé, torte, and cake recipes in this collection will win the praise of all who try them.

For your next family meal, try this trio: *Ham Loaf* (see recipe, page 105), *Orange Bowknots* (see recipe, page 114), and *Grandma's Chocolate Cake* (see recipe, page 124). Trim the ham loaf with pineapple and green pepper.

# Party-Perfect Appetizers and Beverages

## Mystery Cheese Ball

In mixer bowl combine three 5-ounce jars process cheese spread with blue cheese, 1 cup shredded process cheese spread (4 ounces), 1 teaspoon chopped onion, and 1 teaspoon Worcestershire sauce. Beat with electric mixer till smooth. Chill several hours or overnight. Shape into a ball. Roll in ½ cup chopped walnuts and 2 tablespoons snipped parsley. Serve with crackers. Makes 2 cups spread.

## Cheese Rounds

1½ cups shredded process
American cheese
(6 ounces)
1 beaten egg
Dash Worcestershire sauce

¼ cup butter, softened
2 teaspoons prepared mustard
24 bread rounds (1¾ inches
in diameter)
24 dill pickle slices

Combine cheese, egg, and Worcestershire. Blend butter and mustard. Toast bread on one side. Spread other side with mustard mixture; top with pickle slice and 1 teaspoon cheese mixture. Broil 3 inches from heat till lightly browned, about 3 minutes. Makes 24 rounds.

## Deviled Eggs

Halve 6 hard-cooked eggs lengthwise. Remove yolks and mash; combine with ¼ cup mayonnaise, 1 tablespoon chopped sweet pickle, 1 teaspoon prepared horseradish, 1 teaspoon prepared mustard, and ¼ teaspoon salt. Refill egg whites. Sprinkle with paprika. Makes 12.

## Hot Mulled Cider

In saucepan combine 8 cups apple cider, ½ cup honey, the peel of one lemon, 3 inches stick cinnamon, and 1 teaspoon whole cloves. Bring to boiling; reduce heat and simmer 20 minutes. Strain; discard peel and spices. Serve hot cider mixture in mugs. Top each serving with a thin orange slice and a maraschino cherry slice. Makes 8 servings.

## Aunt Susan's Lemonade

2½ cups water
2 cups sugar
3 oranges
6 lemons

¼ cup lightly packed fresh
mint leaves (optional)
Water
Ice cubes

Heat 2½ cups water and sugar till sugar dissolves. Cool. Grate 2 tablespoons of peel from oranges. Squeeze juice from oranges and lemons (should be 1½ cups each). Add juices and peel to cooled syrup; pour over mint, if used. Cover and steep 1 hour. Strain into jars; refrigerate. To serve, mix equal parts fruit syrup and water. Serve over ice. Garnish with fruit slices and mint leaves, if desired. Makes 6 cups concentrate.

## Crab-Bacon Rolls

1 cup cooked crab meat or
    1 7½-ounce can crab
    meat, drained
½ cup fine dry bread crumbs
¼ cup tomato juice
1 well-beaten egg
1 tablespoon lemon juice

1 tablespoon snipped
    parsley
¼ teaspoon salt
¼ teaspoon Worcestershire
    sauce
9 slices bacon, cut in half

Flake crab and remove cartilage. Combine crab, crumbs, tomato juice, egg, lemon juice, parsley, salt, Worcestershire, and dash pepper; mix well. Roll into 18 fingers about 2 inches long. Wrap each with ½ slice bacon. Fasten with wooden picks. (Rolls may be made ahead of time and refrigerated till ready to broil.) Broil 5 inches from heat about 10 minutes, turning often to brown evenly. Serve hot. Makes 18 rolls.

*Any kind of crab will work in this recipe for Crab-Bacon Rolls — Pacific Coast Dungeness, Alaskan King, or the Atlantic and Gulf Coast blue crabs, which are all available fresh, frozen, or canned. King crab wasn't available outside Alaska when the recipe originated, but it was being flown all over the United States frozen by the '60s.*

## Holiday Eggnog

12 egg yolks
½ cup sugar
4 cups cold milk
½ to ¾ cup light rum*

½ cup bourbon*
¼ teaspoon salt
12 egg whites
2 cups whipping cream

In mixer bowl beat egg yolks with electric mixer. Gradually add sugar and continue beating till thick and lemon colored. Add milk, rum, bourbon, and salt. In very large bowl beat egg whites till stiff but not dry. Whip cream. Fold egg yolk mixture and whipped cream into beaten egg whites. Serve immediately in chilled punch bowl. Sprinkle ground nutmeg over each serving, if desired. Makes 25 (5-ounce) servings.

*If desired, substitute 1 cup cold milk for the bourbon and light rum.

There's wicked glee in outwitting the weatherman. The higher he bubbles his mercury, the more cool drinks clink on shady porches. Before bottled drinks and frozen concentrates, *Aunt Susan's Lemonade* was made by squeezing oranges and lemons, and by blending the juice with a sugar syrup.

# Main Dishes for Hearty Appetites

## Golden Omelet Layers

*Firsthand observations from the world-famous Cordon Bleu cooking school in Paris: The omelet is the triumph of the egg. When the chef has a large front and leans backward, he's a general chef in the omelet department. He has acquired this pose by keeping away from the fire so that he does not burn the omelet, or himself. To see him beat out a rhythm with a whisk egg beater is equal to watching a conductor at the Metropolitan Opera House.*

8 eggs, separated
3 tablespoons all-purpose
   flour

Cheese Sauce
½ cup shredded process
   cheese spread (2 ounces)

Beat egg whites and ¾ teaspoon salt till stiff but not dry. Beat egg yolks until thick and lemon colored. Add flour and ⅛ teaspoon pepper; blend thoroughly. Fold egg yolk mixture into egg whites. Pour mixture into two well-greased *hot* 8x1½-inch round baking pans. Spread lightly in pan, having mixture higher around edge. Bake at 350° until knife inserted off-center comes out clean, about 15 minutes. Mean-while, prepare Cheese Sauce. Invert one omelet layer on warm serving platter. Sprinkle with ½ cup shredded cheese spread. Top with second omelet layer, right side up. Garnish top with currant jelly, if desired. Cut in wedges. Serve with Cheese Sauce. Serves 6.

*Cheese Sauce:* In saucepan combine 2 cups diced process cheese spread, ½ cup milk, and dash pepper. Stir over low heat till cheese melts.

## Rice Croquettes

¾ cup long grain rice
   Thick White Sauce
2 beaten egg yolks
¼ cup grated process
   American cheese
⅛ teaspoon cayenne

2 slightly beaten egg
   whites
1 cup fine dry bread crumbs
   Fat for frying
1 10¾-ounce can condensed
   tomato soup

Cook rice according to package directions. Prepare Thick White Sauce. Combine cooked rice, white sauce, egg yolks, cheese, cayenne, and ½ teaspoon salt. Chill mixture thoroughly. Using about ¼ cup for each, form into 6 to 8 cone-shaped croquettes. Dip in beaten egg whites, then roll in bread crumbs. Fry in deep hot fat (365°) until golden brown, about 2½ to 3 minutes. Drain on paper toweling. Heat the tomato soup. Pass soup with croquettes. Makes 6 to 8 servings.

*Thick White Sauce:* Melt 2 tablespoons butter in saucepan. Stir in 2 tablespoons all-purpose flour, ⅛ teaspoon salt, and dash pepper. Add ½ cup milk. Cook and stir till mixture thickens and bubbles.

## French-Fried Shrimp

*From a Japanese restaurant in Chicago in the '40s came this superb French-Fried Shrimp recipe. The owner agreed to share it if the door of the photography studio was locked while she prepared it for the picture so no one could steal her secret—ice water in the batter.*

2 pounds fresh or frozen
   shrimp in shells
1 cup all-purpose flour
½ teaspoon sugar

1 cup ice water
1 slightly beaten egg
2 tablespoons cooking oil
   Fat for frying

Thaw frozen shrimp. Combine flour, sugar, and ½ teaspoon salt. Add water, egg, and oil. Beat till smooth. Remove shells from shrimp, leaving last section and tail intact. Butterfly shrimp by cutting almost through center back without cutting tail end; remove black vein. Dry shrimp well. Dip into batter. Fry in deep hot fat (375°) till golden. Drain. Serve with cocktail sauce, if desired. Serves 4 to 6.

## Baked Sole à la Thermidor

1½ pounds fresh or frozen
  sole fillets
¾ teaspoon salt
  Dash pepper
½ cup milk
2 tablespoons butter

2 tablespoons all-purpose
  flour
¾ cup milk
¼ cup shredded process
  American cheese
2 tablespoons dry sherry

Thaw frozen fish. Place fillets in greased 10x6x2-inch baking dish. Season with salt and pepper. Add ½ cup milk. Bake, uncovered, at 350° till fish flakes easily when tested with a fork, about 15 minutes. Drain off milk. In saucepan melt butter; blend in flour. Add ¾ cup milk. Cook and stir till thickened and bubbly. Add cheese and wine. Pour over fish. Place under broiler till golden brown. Serves 4 to 6.

*Thermidor is not a chef, but a season—July 19 to August 17 in the French revolutionary calendar—when lobsters are most abundant in the English Channel. It's also a style of cooking, for sole as well as lobster.*

## Fish Chowder *(see photo, page 103)*

1 pound fresh or frozen fish
  fillets
2 cups cubed potatoes
2 teaspoons salt
⅛ teaspoon pepper

3 slices bacon
½ cup chopped onion
2 cups milk
3 tablespoons all-purpose
  flour

Thaw frozen fish. Cut into 2-inch pieces. Cook potatoes in 2 cups water for 5 minutes. Add fish, salt, and pepper. Simmer, covered, 10 to 12 minutes. In skillet cook bacon till crisp. Drain bacon and crumble; reserve drippings in skillet. Cook onion in drippings till tender. Add bacon and onion to fish-potato mixture. Combine milk and flour; add to chowder. Cook and stir till thick and bubbly. Serves 6.

## Yakima Special Baked Beans

2 cups dry navy beans
  (16 ounces)
2 tart apples, peeled,
  cored, and chopped
2 small onions, quartered

4 ounces salt pork, diced
½ cup dark molasses
2 tablespoons sugar
2 teaspoons salt
1 teaspoon dry mustard

Rinse beans; add to 8 cups cold water. Bring to boiling; simmer 2 minutes. Remove from heat. Cover and let stand 1 hour. (Or, add beans to water; soak overnight.) Simmer beans until tender, 30 to 45 minutes. Drain, reserving cooking water. Put *half* of the beans in 2½-quart casserole. Add apples, onions, and *half* of the salt pork. Add remaining beans. Combine dark molasses, sugar, salt, dry mustard, and 2½ cups of the cooking water; pour over beans. Top with the remaining salt pork. Cover and bake at 300° for 5 to 6 hours. Add more bean liquid or boiling water, if necessary. During last ½ hour, uncover to brown. Serve with brown bread, if desired. Serves 6 to 8.

*Out in the great Pacific Northwest homemakers believe that almost any recipe can be improved with the addition of apples. You'll like what chopped apple does to Yankee pork and beans as they become a Yakima special.*

## Bean-Stuffed Onions *(see photo, page 102)*

Hollow out 6 medium onions; chop enough of centers to make 2 tablespoons (use remaining centers elsewhere). Salt cavities of the onions. Combine 2 cups baked beans, ⅓ cup catsup, ¼ cup molasses, and the chopped onion. Spoon the bean mixture into hollowed-out onions. Place onions in an 8x8x2-inch baking pan. Add 2 tablespoons water. Cover pan tightly with foil. Bake at 400° for 1 hour. Makes 6 servings.

102

Spark up leftover baked beans by creating *Bean-Stuffed Onions* (see recipe, page 101). Garnish the serving platter with attractive carrot curls, radish roses, and sprigs of parsley. For the final touch, serve slices of *Boston Brown Bread* (see recipe, page 115).

A good oxtail stew has established more than one chef's reputation, so this wartime dish with dumplings (to extend the meat) was no hardship to eat. Fortunate families today enjoy *Oxtail Stew with Parsley Dumplings* (see recipe, page 104).

Good eating is guaranteed when you add a hearty New England-style chowder to your supper menu. You will tantalize your family as well as your guests with steaming bowls of *Fish Chowder* (see recipe, page 101).

Perk up interest and appetites by serving savory *Veal Birds* (see recipe, page 105). A tasty bread stuffing is rolled up in tender veal and wrapped with bacon slices. Pass the piping hot gravy. Serve with cooked carrots that are garnished with snipped parsley.

A prizewinning family casserole, *Hamburger Pie* is the most popular recipe *Better Homes and Gardens* magazine has ever published. Enjoy this thrifty, easy, and great-tasting casserole often.

For an intriguing yet delightfully tempting main dish, try *Pineapple Spareribs* served with hot cooked rice. An especially tasty sweet-sour sauce glazes the ribs.

## Tamale Casserole

1 pound bulk pork
   sausage
1 28-ounce can tomatoes,
   cut up
1 17-ounce can whole kernel
   corn, undrained
1 cup chopped onion
2 cloves garlic, minced

1 tablespoon chili powder
3 beaten eggs
1 cup milk
¾ cup yellow cornmeal
1 3¼-ounce can pitted ripe
   olives, drained and
   chopped (about ¾ cup)
2 teaspoons salt

In 12-inch skillet brown the pork sausage; drain off excess fat. Add cut up tomatoes, corn with liquid, chopped onion, minced garlic, and chili powder. Bring mixture to boiling; reduce heat and simmer, covered, for 15 minutes. In a mixing bowl combine the beaten eggs, milk, cornmeal, chopped olives, and salt. Stir cornmeal mixture into the sausage mixture. Heat through. Turn the mixture into a 3-quart casserole. Cover and bake at 350° for 45 minutes. Serves 8 to 10.

*Californians make Tamale Pie. They line a casserole with cornmeal mush like a pie shell, fill it with a ground beef mixture including ripe olives and onions, then bake it. When the recipe moved eastward across the country, the cornmeal mush and ground beef were mixed together and called Tamale Casserole. Either way, a generation of young cooks have favored it to entertain in-laws and to show off wedding-gift casseroles.*

## Hamburger Pie

1 pound ground beef
½ cup chopped onion
½ teaspoon salt
   Dash pepper
1 16-ounce can cut
   green beans,
   drained (2 cups)

1 10¾-ounce can condensed
   tomato soup
5 medium potatoes, cooked*
½ cup warm milk
1 beaten egg
½ cup shredded process
   American cheese

In large skillet cook the meat and onion till meat is lightly browned and onion is tender. Add salt and pepper. Stir in drained beans and soup; pour into greased 1½-quart casserole. Mash potatoes while hot; add milk and egg. Season to taste with salt and pepper. Spoon in mounds over casserole. Sprinkle potatoes with cheese. Bake at 350° for 25 to 30 minutes. Serves 4 to 6.

*Or, prepare 4 servings packaged instant mashed potatoes according to packaged directions, except *reserve the milk*. Add egg and season to taste with salt and pepper. Add enough reserved milk so potatoes are stiff enough to hold shape.

## Pineapple Spareribs

4 pounds pork spareribs,
   cut in 2-rib portions
¼ cup cornstarch
¼ cup dark molasses
¼ cup soy sauce
   Fat for frying
1 20-ounce can pineapple
   chunks

3 tablespoons brown sugar
2 tablespoons cornstarch
¼ teaspoon salt
3 tablespoons vinegar
2 tablespoons soy sauce
2 small green peppers, cut
   in 1-inch squares
   Hot cooked rice

In Dutch oven simmer ribs in 8 cups water and 2 teaspoons salt for 45 minutes. Drain ribs and cool. Combine ¼ cup cornstarch, molasses, and ¼ cup soy sauce. Brush on ribs. Fry in deep hot fat (375°) till golden, 1 to 2 minutes. Keep ribs warm. Drain pineapple, reserving ⅔ cup syrup. In saucepan combine reserved syrup, brown sugar, 2 tablespoons cornstarch, and ¼ teaspoon salt; stir in vinegar, 2 tablespoons soy sauce, and 1 cup water. Cook and stir till thick and bubbly. Add pineapple and green pepper. Heat through. Spoon sauce over ribs to glaze. Serve with rice. Pass sauce. Serves 4 or 5.

*Trader Vic's Pineapple Spareribs in 1949 were followed with other Victor J. Bergeron Polynesian foods through the years. The good glazes that style his meats — Oriental, Hawaiian, Chinese, or South Seas — were ideal for barbecuing then and still are today.*

## Chow Mein

¾ pound veal, diced
½ pound pork, diced
½ pound beef, diced
2 tablespoons shortening
½ cup soy sauce
3 cups bias-cut celery
    slices (½ inch wide)
2½ cups Home-Grown Bean
    Sprouts (see recipe
    below) *or* 2½ cups
    canned bean sprouts

½ cup chopped onion
3 tablespoons cornstarch
1 cup cold water
2 5-ounce cans water
    chestnuts, drained
    and sliced
Salt
Pepper
Hot cooked rice *or* chow
    mein noodles, warmed
Soy sauce

In large skillet brown the veal, pork, and beef in hot shortening. Add 1¼ cups water and the ½ cup soy sauce. Simmer the meat mixture about 30 minutes. Add the celery, bean sprouts, and chopped onion. Simmer the mixture 30 minutes longer. Combine cornstarch and 1 cup cold water; stir into the meat mixture. Cook and stir till thickened and bubbly. Add sliced water chestnuts and cook slowly until heated through. Season with salt and pepper. Serve with rice or chow mein noodles. Pass additional soy sauce. Serves 8.

## Home-Grown Bean Sprouts

*Sprouting mung beans or soybeans turns them into fresh vegetables rich in vitamin C and moderately rich in vitamin B, calcium, and iron, without destroying their original high protein content. Use in Chow Mein.*

Buy mung beans that have not been chemically treated. (These can be found in a health food store or a gourmet shop that stocks oriental foods.) Carefully sort through the beans, selecting ⅓ cup of clean, whole beans. Wash them thoroughly. Place the beans in a bowl and cover them with lukewarm water, allowing enough water for the beans to swell. (They will almost double in size.) Let stand overnight. Drain; rinse well.

Wash four 1-quart jars; place ¼ cup of the soaked beans in each jar. Cover top of the jar with two layers of cheesecloth or nylon netting; fasten with two rubber bands or a screw-type canning lid band. Store in a warm, dark place (68° to 75°). Place the jars on their sides so the beans form a layer. Once a day rinse the sprouts by pouring lukewarm water into the jars, swirling to moisten all the beans, then pouring off the water. Sprouts take about three or four days. Optimum sprout length is 1½ to 2½ inches.

The whole sprouts — seeds, roots (if they develop), stems, and outer hulls — may be eaten. But hulls may be removed, if preferred. To do so, stir sprouts vigorously in a bowl of cold water. Skim away husks that rise to top or collect at sides. Repeat rinsing several times.

## Shish Kabob

*Shish Kabobs, chaslick, shaslik, and lamb en brochette are some of the versions of lamb on a stick the magazine has printed over the years. World traveler-commentator Lowell Thomas contributed the Lamb en Brochette á l'Armenia on page 30.*

1½ pounds boneless lamb
    shoulder
½ cup chopped onion
⅓ cup dry sherry
2 tablespoons cooking oil

1 teaspoon salt
½ teaspoon dried rosemary,
    crushed
⅛ teaspoon pepper
Hot cooked rice

Cut lamb into 1½-inch cubes. In large bowl combine onion, sherry, oil, salt, rosemary, and pepper. Add meat and stir to coat. Refrigerate for several hours or overnight, stirring occasionally. Drain well. Thread meat on long metal skewers. Grill meat 5 inches from *hot* coals, turning to brown meat on all sides and basting occasionally with remaining marinade, till done, about 15 minutes. Slide the cooked meat off the skewers onto hot plates. Serve with rice. Serves 4 to 6.

# Vegetables—Plain and Fancy

## Stuffed Zucchini

6 medium zucchini
  (3 pounds)
Salt
2 cups soft bread crumbs
1 beaten egg
3 tablespoons finely
  chopped onion

2 tablespoons butter or
  margarine, melted
1 tablespoon snipped
  parsley
⅛ teaspoon pepper
½ cup shredded process
  American cheese

Wash zucchini and cut off ends. Do not peel. Cook whole zucchini in boiling salted water for 7 minutes (begin timing when water returns to boiling). Cut in half lengthwise. Scoop out *half* of the pulp from each with paring knife to form boats. Sprinkle inside of shells with salt.

Chop pulp; combine with bread crumbs, egg, onion, butter, parsley, pepper, and 1 teaspoon salt. Fill zucchini shells with mixture. Place in shallow baking dish. Bake, uncovered, at 350° till tender, 25 to 30 minutes. Sprinkle with cheese; bake 1 minute more. Serves 6.

*Plant a zucchini seed; grows like a weed; zucchini is a very 'in' vegetable right now because it's low calorie. Stuffed zucchini first appeared in Cooks' Round Table in 1937, but it was not generally served outside Washington and California until the late '40s. This Italian green squash is best eating when cucumber-size and less seedy.*

## Corn-Tomato Casserole

3 slices bacon,
  diced (⅓ cup)
⅓ cup finely chopped onion
3 tablespoons chopped green
  pepper
1 16-ounce can tomatoes,
  cut up (2 cups)
2 tablespoons packed brown
  sugar

1 teaspoon salt
⅛ teaspoon pepper
1 17-ounce can whole kernel
  corn, drained
½ cup shredded process
  cheese spread (2 ounces)
1 cup croutons
1 tablespoon butter or
  margarine, melted

Fry bacon in skillet until crisp; remove bacon to 1½-quart casserole. Cook onion and green pepper in bacon drippings until tender but not brown. Add tomatoes, brown sugar, salt, and pepper. Stir in corn

and cheese. Turn into casserole and mix with bacon. Toss croutons with butter; sprinkle around edge of casserole. Bake at 350° till hot, about 30 minutes. Serve in sauce dishes. Serves 6.

*No wonder corn or maize holds its head higher than any other vegetable. The Mayas of central Mexico worshiped it, sculpting its tassels into the heads of their famous warriors. Columbus carried the first samples of corn to the Old World when he returned from exploring America. The Spaniards thought it an excellent food and planted some right away. From then on, corn was grown wherever soil and climate were suitable, in northern Italy for example.*

*Tomatoes also were first eaten by the Indians, the Incas of Peru, so the Corn-Tomato Casserole is really a native American dish.*

## Perfect French-Fried Onions

3 Bermuda or mild white
  onions, sliced ¼ inch
  thick
⅔ cup milk

1 egg
1 cup all-purpose flour
Fat for frying

Separate onion slices into rings. In bowl combine milk and egg; beat thoroughly. Pour mixture into shallow pan. Drop some onion rings into the pan. With fingers, swish rings around till each is well coated with liquid. Lift onions out of liquid; shake over pan to drain. Then drop rings in pan of flour, a few rings at a time, coating each ring well.

Shake the rings to remove the excess flour. Fill French-frying basket ¼ full so onions will brown evenly. Set the basket in deep hot fat (375°). Stir onion rings once with a fork to separate. When onion rings are golden brown, remove from fat and drain on paper toweling. To keep onions crispy, salt rings just before serving. Serves 8.

# Salad Specials

## Old-Fashioned Egg Salad

*This egg salad with natural cheese was a protein-stretching salad for hot summer days. The eggs were cooked and the dressing made in the cool of the evening and refrigerated till the next day. This tossed salad was distinctive because of its vinegar and oil dressing rather than mayonnaise or boiled dressing.*

6 cups torn lettuce
   (1 medium head)
6 hard-cooked eggs, sliced
1 small onion, thinly
   sliced
¼ cup shredded sharp
   natural Cheddar cheese
¼ cup salad oil

2 tablespoons vinegar
1 tablespoon snipped
   parsley
1 teaspoon Worcestershire
   sauce
½ teaspoon salt
⅛ teaspoon pepper
Dash paprika

In large salad bowl combine the lettuce, egg slices, sliced onion, and shredded cheese. Cover and chill thoroughly. Combine salad oil, vinegar, parsley, Worcestershire sauce, salt, pepper, and paprika. Pour dressing over chilled salad. Toss salad lightly. Serves 6.

## Chef's Potato Salad

*A good chef's salad should be about one-third protein. With diced luncheon meat, cheese, and hard-cooked eggs, this Chef's Potato Salad is.*

3 medium potatoes
1 clove garlic, halved
1 12-ounce can luncheon
   meat, diced or cut
   into sticks (2¼ cups)
1 cup diced process
   American cheese
1 cup diced celery
⅓ cup chopped onion

1 cup mayonnaise or salad
   dressing
2 tablespoons vinegar
1 teaspoon snipped parsley
1 teaspoon chopped green
   onion
¼ teaspoon salt
2 hard-cooked eggs,
   cut in wedges

Cook potatoes in boiling salted water till tender; peel and dice. Rub salad bowl with garlic. In bowl combine potatoes, luncheon meat, cheese, celery, and the ⅓ cup onion. Blend together the mayonnaise, vinegar, parsley, 1 teaspoon onion, salt, and dash pepper. Toss salad with mayonnaise mixture. Chill. Trim with egg wedges. Serves 6.

## Perfection Salad

½ cup sugar
2 envelopes unflavored
   gelatin
1 teaspoon salt
1½ cups water
1½ cups cold water
⅓ cup white vinegar
2 tablespoons lemon juice
2 cups finely shredded
   cabbage
1 cup chopped celery

⅓ cup sliced pimiento-
   stuffed green olives
¼ cup chopped green pepper
¼ cup chopped canned
   pimiento
Lettuce
Carrot curls
Ripe olives
Parsley
Mayonnaise or salad
   dressing

In a medium saucepan combine sugar, gelatin, and salt. Add 1½ cups water and stir over medium heat till gelatin is dissolved. Stir in 1½ cups cold water, vinegar, and lemon juice; chill till partially set. Fold cabbage, celery, sliced green olives, green pepper, and pimiento into gelatin. Pour gelatin mixture into 8½x4½x2½-inch loaf pan. Chill till firm. Unmold the salad onto lettuce; trim with carrot curls, ripe olives, and parsley. Pass mayonnaise. Serves 8 to 10.

Luca della Robbia did beautiful fruit-wreathed terracotta plaques in fifteenth-century Italy; hence, the name *Della Robbia Wreath Salad* (see recipe, page 113). The salad features frosted grapes, pineapple, crab apples, apricots, and peach and pear halves piped together with cream cheese.

*Perfection Salad* won a gelatin cooking contest in 1903, judged by Fannie Farmer of Boston Cooking School fame. Ever since, lemon-vinegar tart gelatin with shredded cabbage, celery, and carrots has been on America's tables.

*Through the years, American aspic has ranged from a mild jelly mold to a highly spiced one. In the '20s it was a 'tomato' jelly—whole strained canned tomatoes simmered with onion and celery, added to gelatin, and poured over shredded cabbage. During the war years, aspic was combined with jellied cottage cheese in a ring mold. It became highly spiced during the early '70s when taste buds attuned to hot barbecue sauces demanded that whole cloves and bay leaf be added to seasoned tomato sauce. With or without spice, aspic is often served with cold, baked ham and potato salad, or with shrimp.*

## Cottage Cheese-Tomato Aspic Mold

¾ cup cream-style cottage
  cheese
1 3-ounce package cream
  cheese, softened
1 teaspoon finely chopped
  onion
4 teaspoons unflavored
  gelatin
2½ cups tomato juice

2 tablespoons chopped onion
2 tablespoons chopped celery
  leaves
1 tablespoon packed brown
  sugar
2 whole cloves
1 small bay leaf
2 tablespoons lemon juice

Beat cheeses together till fluffy. Stir in the 1 teaspoon chopped onion and ¼ teaspoon salt. Soften *1 teaspoon* gelatin in ½ cup cold water. Stir over low heat till gelatin dissolves. Stir into cheese mixture. Pour into a 4-cup ring mold. Chill until *almost* firm. Meanwhile, in saucepan combine *1½ cups* of the tomato juice, 2 tablespoons onion, celery leaves, brown sugar, cloves, bay leaf, and ½ teaspoon salt. Bring to boil; reduce heat and simmer 5 minutes. Strain. Soften remaining 3 teaspoons gelatin in the remaining tomato juice; dissolve in hot mixture. Stir in lemon juice. Chill till partially set. Pour over cheese layer. Chill till firm. Unmold. Serves 8.

## Frozen Fruit Salad

Blend 1 cup mayonnaise or salad dressing and two 3-ounce packages softened cream cheese till smooth. Whip 1 cup whipping cream and fold into mayonnaise mixture. Fold in 2½ cups diced marshmallows (about 24); one 20-ounce can crushed pineapple, drained; ½ cup chopped red maraschino cherries; and ½ cup chopped green maraschino cherries. Pour into two 3-cup refrigerator trays. Freeze till firm. Serves 12.

## Cranberry Squares

½ cup sugar
1 3-ounce package cherry-
  flavored gelatin
1 cup boiling water
1 8¼-ounce can crushed
  pineapple
1 tablespoon lemon juice

1 cup cranberries
½ small orange, seeded
½ cup chopped celery
¼ cup chopped walnuts
  Lettuce leaves
  Mayonnaise or salad
  dressing

Dissolve sugar and gelatin in boiling water. Add undrained pineapple and lemon juice; chill till mixture is partially set. Put cranberries and orange through food grinder, using a fine blade. Fold cranberry mixture, celery, and walnuts into gelatin. Pour mixture into a 10x6x2-inch dish or individual molds. Chill 5 to 6 hours or overnight. Serve on lettuce-lined plates. Pass mayonnaise. Makes 6 to 8 servings.

## Black Cherry Salad

Dissolve one 3-ounce package orange-flavored gelatin in ½ cup boiling water. Drain one 16-ounce can pitted dark sweet cherries, reserving syrup. Combine syrup, 2 tablespoons lemon juice, and enough water to make 1¼ cups liquid. Stir into gelatin. Chill until partially set. Fold in cherries, ½ cup chopped pecans, and ¼ cup sliced pimiento-stuffed green olives. Pour into 6 individual molds or into a 3½-cup mold. Chill till firm. Unmold. Pass mayonnaise. Serves 6.

## Fruit Salad Dressing

½ cup sugar
1 tablespoon all-purpose
    flour
½ cup vinegar

1 tablespoon grated onion
2 teaspoons paprika
2 teaspoons celery seed
¾ cup salad oil

In saucepan mix sugar and flour together; add vinegar. Cook and stir over low heat till thickened and bubbly. Add onion, paprika, celery seed, and 1 teaspoon salt; mix thoroughly. Slowly pour in oil, beating constantly with rotary beater or electric mixer. Makes 1⅓ cups.

## Della Robbia Wreath Salad *(see photo, page 111)*

1 29-ounce can peach
    halves (8 halves)
1 29-ounce can pear
    halves (8 halves)
1 28-ounce jar spiced crab
    apples (11 or 12)
1 20-ounce can pineapple
    slices (8 slices)
1 17-ounce can peeled
    whole apricots

1 8-ounce package cream
    cheese, softened
8 red maraschino
    cherries
Curly endive
Pineapple Dressing
    (see below)
Frosted Grapes
    (see below)

Drain canned fruits; chill. Dry chilled peaches and pears well on paper toweling. Fill peach and pear hollows with *half* of the softened cream cheese. Put a maraschino cherry in center of *half* the cheese-filled fruit. Press peach halves together; repeat with pears. Pipe remaining cream cheese through pastry tube to seal the halves. Arrange bed of endive on large platter. Arrange all fruit around bowl of Pineapple Dressing. Garnish with Frosted Grapes. Serves 10 to 12.

## Pineapple Dressing

In small saucepan combine ⅓ cup sugar, 4 teaspoons cornstarch, and ¼ teaspoon salt. Gradually blend in 1 cup unsweetened pineapple juice, ¼ cup orange juice, and 2 tablespoons lemon juice. Cook and stir over medium heat till thickened and bubbly. Blend moderate amount of the hot mixture into 2 beaten eggs. Return the mixture to saucepan and cook over low heat 1 to 2 minutes more. Remove mixture from the heat. Gradually stir hot mixture into two 3-ounce packages cream cheese, softened. Chill thoroughly. Makes about 2¼ cups.

## Frosted Grapes

Dip 1½ pounds red and green grapes into 2 slightly beaten egg whites. Drain. Dip grapes in ½ cup sugar. Place on rack to dry for 2 hours.

## Cloverleaf Dressing

In blender container combine 1½ cups salad oil; one 10¾-ounce can condensed tomato soup; ½ cup vinegar; 2 tablespoons sugar; 1 tablespoon Worcestershire sauce; 1 teaspoon dry mustard; 1 teaspoon salt; 1 teaspoon paprika; ½ small onion, cut up; ¼ green pepper, cut up; and ¼ clove garlic. Blend ingredients until smooth, about 1 minute. Chill. Serve dressing on crisp salad greens. Makes 3½ cups.

*In the '30s and '40s, tearooms were favorite eating places, often run by women who needed to support themselves when a husband died or became ill. The owners parlayed skill as cooks and hostesses into successful businesses. A Des Moines woman made her tearoom famous by serving Fruit Salad Dressing with fresh fruit and sticky buns.*

*Don't look for green in Cloverleaf Dressing. The lucky name comes from the shape of the blender container in which it was buzzed up.*

# Fresh Breads from the Oven

### Orange Bowknots *(see photo, page 96)*

*(see photo, page 96)*

*Make the most of your bread-making know-how with Orange Bowknots. The bowknots were selected as one of the seven all-time best recipes when used to celebrate the magazine's 25th anniversary.*

4¾ to 5 cups all-purpose
  flour
2 packages active dry yeast
1¼ cups milk
½ cup shortening
⅓ cup sugar

1 tablespoon grated orange
  peel
¼ cup orange juice
1 teaspoon salt
2 eggs
  Orange Topping

In large mixer bowl combine *2 cups* of the flour and the yeast. Heat milk, shortening, sugar, orange peel, orange juice, and salt just till warm (115° to 120°), stirring constantly to melt shortening. Add to dry mixture in mixer bowl; add eggs. Beat mixture at low speed with electric mixer for ½ minute, scraping sides of bowl constantly. Beat 3 minutes at high speed. By hand, stir in enough of the remaining flour to make a moderately soft dough. Knead on lightly floured surface till smooth (5 to 8 minutes). Place in greased bowl, turning once. Cover; let rise in warm place till double (45 to 60 minutes). Punch down. Cover; let rest 10 minutes. Roll into an 18x10-inch rectangle, ½ inch thick. Cut into strips 10 inches long and ¾ inch wide. Roll strips back and forth lightly; loosely tie in knots. Put on greased baking sheet. Cover and let rise till double (30 minutes). Bake at 400° for 10 to 12 minutes. Spread with Orange Topping. Makes 24.

*Orange Topping:* Blend together 1 cup sifted powdered sugar, 1 teaspoon grated orange peel, and 2 tablespoons orange juice.

### Squash Biscuits

*These biscuits hail from the Toll House Inn, Whitman, Massachusetts, which has a heritage of more than 264 years of hospitality.*

3½ cups all-purpose flour
1 package active dry yeast
1 cup milk
¼ cup sugar

¼ cup shortening
1 teaspoon salt
1½ cups strained, cooked
  winter squash

In large mixer bowl combine *2 cups* of the flour and the yeast. In saucepan heat milk, sugar, shortening, and salt till warm (115° to 120°), stirring constantly to melt shortening. Add to dry mixture in mixer bowl. Beat at low speed with electric mixer for ½ minute, scraping sides of bowl constantly. Beat 3 minutes at high speed. Beat in the squash. By hand, stir in enough of the remaining flour to make a soft dough. Place in lightly greased bowl, turning once to grease surface. Cover; let rise in warm place till double (about 1 hour). Punch dough down. Turn out on lightly floured surface. Cover; let rest 10 minutes. Roll dough to ½-inch thickness. Cut with 2½-inch biscuit cutter. Place on greased baking sheet. Let rise in a warm place till double (about 45 minutes). Bake at 375° for 20 minutes. Makes 18.

### Spoon Bread Soufflé

In saucepan combine 4 cups milk, 1 cup yellow cornmeal, ¼ cup chopped onion, ¼ cup chopped celery, 1 tablespoon sugar, 1¼ teaspoons salt, and dash pepper. Cook 10 minutes; stir constantly. Remove from heat. Add moderate amount of hot mixture to 3 well-beaten egg yolks; return to the hot mixture. Fold in 3 stiffly beaten egg whites. Turn into greased 2-quart casserole. Dot with 1 tablespoon butter or margarine. Bake at 325° for 1 hour. Serve with butter. Serves 6 to 8.

## Boston Brown Bread *(see photo, page 102)*

1 cup whole wheat flour
½ cup all-purpose flour
½ cup yellow cornmeal
1 teaspoon baking powder
½ teaspoon baking soda
½ teaspoon salt
½ cup molasses
¼ cup sugar

1 beaten egg
1 tablespoon butter or
   margarine, melted
1½ cups buttermilk or sour
   milk
¼ cup chopped walnuts
¼ cup raisins
3½ cups boiling water

Combine flours, cornmeal, baking powder, soda, and salt. Combine molasses, sugar, egg, and butter. Add flour mixture alternately with buttermilk to molasses mixture. Beat well. Stir in nuts and raisins. Mix well. Fill 3 well-greased 16-ounce food cans half full. Cover cans with foil; tie string around each tightly. Place on rack in 4-quart pressure cooker. Add boiling water. Close cover securely; cook without pressure for 20 minutes. Put pressure regulator in place; cook 40 minutes with pressure regulator rocking gently (15 pounds pressure). Reduce pressure under cold running water. Makes 3 loaves.

*The introduction of the pressure cooker dramatically reduced cooking time for foods like Boston Brown Bread, which steams in 1 hour instead of the 3 hours it would take in a kettle. "No more difficult to operate than the baby's bath," said the pleased owner of one of the first pressure cookers.*

## Upside-Down Orange Biscuits

¾ cup sugar
3 tablespoons butter or
   margarine
1 tablespoon grated orange
   peel
2 tablespoons orange juice
2 cups all-purpose flour

3 teaspoons baking powder
½ teaspoon salt
⅓ cup shortening
¾ cup milk
¼ cup sugar
½ teaspoon ground cinnamon

In small saucepan combine the ¾ cup sugar, butter or margarine, orange peel, and orange juice. Bring to full boil over medium heat; cook and stir 1 minute more. Reserve 2 tablespoons orange mixture; pour remainder into foil-lined 8x8x2-inch baking pan. Stir together flour, baking powder, and salt. Cut in shortening till mixture resembles coarse crumbs. Add milk all at once, stirring just till dough follows fork around bowl. Turn dough out onto lightly floured surface. Knead dough gently 15 to 20 strokes. Roll the dough into a 12x9-inch rectangle, about ¼ inch thick. Spread the dough with the reserved orange mixture. Mix the ¼ cup sugar and cinnamon; sprinkle over dough. Roll up from long side as for jelly roll. Slice into 9 pieces; place, cut side down, atop orange mixture in pan. Bake at 425° till golden, about 20 minutes. Invert onto plate; remove foil. Makes 9.

## Cowboy Coffee Cake

1½ cups all-purpose flour
1 cup packed brown sugar
⅓ cup shortening
¼ teaspoon salt
1 teaspoon baking powder

¼ teaspoon baking soda
¼ teaspoon ground cinnamon
¼ teaspoon ground nutmeg
½ cup buttermilk
1 beaten egg

Mix flour, brown sugar, shortening, and salt till crumbly; reserve ½ cup of the crumb mixture to sprinkle over batter. To remaining crumb mixture add baking powder, baking soda, cinnamon, and nutmeg; mix well. Add buttermilk and egg; mix well. Pour into a greased and floured 8x8x2-inch baking pan; sprinkle with reserved crumb mixture. Bake at 375° about 25 minutes. Serve warm. Makes 1 coffee cake.

# Praise-Winning Desserts

## Lemon Custard in Meringue Cups

3 egg whites
½ teaspoon vinegar
¼ teaspoon vanilla
⅛ teaspoon salt
2 cups sugar
⅓ cup cornstarch
⅛ teaspoon salt

1½ cups hot water
3 beaten egg yolks
1 tablespoon grated lemon
    peel
6 tablespoons lemon juice
2 tablespoons butter
    Sweetened whipped cream

Combine egg whites, vinegar, vanilla, and salt; beat till soft peaks form. Gradually add *1 cup* of the sugar; beat till very stiff peaks form. Cover baking sheet with plain ungreased brown paper. Spoon egg white mixture in 8 mounds on paper. Shape into cups with a spoon. Bake at 300° for 45 minutes. Remove from paper immediately. Cool. In saucepan combine remaining 1 cup sugar, cornstarch, and salt. Slowly add hot water, stirring constantly. Cook and stir till thick and bubbly, about 2 minutes. Add small amount of hot mixture to egg yolks; stir into remaining hot mixture. Cook and stir 2 minutes longer. Remove from heat; blend in lemon peel and juice. Stir in butter; chill. Just before serving, fill meringue shells. Top with whipped cream. Serves 8.

## High Citrus Pie

½ cup sugar
1 teaspoon unflavored
    gelatin
    Dash salt
4 egg yolks
½ teaspoon grated lemon
    peel (set aside)
⅓ cup lemon juice

½ teaspoon grated orange
    peel (set aside)
3 tablespoons orange juice
2 tablespoons water
4 egg whites
¼ cup sugar
1 *baked* 8-inch pastry
    shell, cooled

In saucepan combine the ½ cup sugar, gelatin, and salt. Beat egg yolks, lemon juice, orange juice, and water together. Stir into gelatin mixture. Cook and stir just till mixture boils. Remove from heat; stir in lemon and orange peels. Chill, stirring occasionally, till partially set. Beat egg whites till soft peaks form. Gradually add ¼ cup sugar, beating till stiff peaks form. Fold in gelatin mixture. Pour into pastry. Chill till firm. Trim with shredded orange peel, if desired.

## Super Lemon Sherbet

1 cup water
¾ cup sugar
    Dash salt
½ cup light cream

½ cup lemon juice
2 egg whites
¼ cup sugar
    Lemon candies (optional)

In saucepan combine water, ¾ cup sugar, and salt; bring to boiling. Reduce heat; simmer 5 minutes. Cool. Stir in cream and juice. Freeze in refrigerator tray. Beat egg whites till soft peaks form. Gradually add ¼ cup sugar, beating till stiff peaks form. Break frozen mixture into chunks. Turn into chilled bowl. Beat smooth with electric mixer or rotary beater. Fold in egg whites. Return quickly to cold refrigerator tray; freeze till firm. Serve with candies, if desired. Serves 6.

The freshness of lemon marks these desserts: *Lemon Custard in Meringue Cups, High Citrus Pie,* and *Super Lemon Sherbet* (pictured opposite). Once known as sorbet, the sherbet was one of seven best recipes in the 25th anniversary issue of the magazine in 1947. The other recipes are equally praiseworthy.

The exotic fragrance of *Royal Plum Pudding* brings to mind Grandmother's Christmas larder. It is here that she stored her delectable plum pudding, with its mixture of spices, fruits, syrups, and nuts, for several weeks before Christmas.

## Royal Plum Pudding

2 cups all-purpose flour
2 teaspoons baking powder
½ teaspoon ground cinnamon
½ teaspoon ground nutmeg
¼ teaspoon baking soda
¼ teaspoon ground allspice
3 beaten eggs
4 ounces suet, ground
¾ cup milk

½ cup light molasses
1 cup chopped, peeled apple
½ cup raisins
½ cup dried currants
½ cup chopped pitted dates
½ cup diced mixed candied
    fruits and peels
¼ cup chopped almonds
    Foamy Sauce

Stir together flour, baking powder, cinnamon, nutmeg, soda, allspice, and ½ teaspoon salt. Combine eggs, suet, milk, and molasses; add to dry ingredients. Beat well. Add next 6 ingredients. Grease 6-cup mold (do not use ring mold or tube pan). Fill ⅔ full. Cover with foil; tie with string. Place on rack in deep kettle; add boiling water 1 inch deep. Cover and steam 3¼ hours, adding more water if needed. Cool 10 min-utes; remove from pan. Cool. Wrap in brandy-soaked cheesecloth, if desired; wrap in foil. Store 3 weeks in cool, dry place. Reheat by steaming 1½ hours in mold. Serve with Foamy Sauce. Serves 8.

*Foamy Sauce:* Beat 1 cup sifted powdered sugar into 2 stiffly beaten egg whites. Beat 2 egg yolks and ¼ teaspoon vanilla till thick; fold into egg whites. Whip ½ cup whipping cream; fold into egg mixture.

No magic in creating fine pastry for *Apple Dumplings*. All it takes is a light hand. Piecrust is as delicate as chiffon; it needs to be treated accordingly. The coarser and mealier the fat/flour mixture, the better the crust will be.

## Apple Dumplings

2¼ cups all-purpose flour
½ teaspoon salt
⅔ cup shortening, chilled
6 to 8 tablespoons cold
    water
6 small apples, peeled and
    cored
⅔ cup granulated sugar

¼ cup light cream
¾ cup hot maple or maple-
    blended syrup
Currant jelly (optional)
Hard sauce, hot maple
    syrup, light cream, *or*
    vanilla ice cream

Mix flour and salt. Cut in shortening till mixture resembles coarse crumbs. Sprinkle water over, a little at a time; mix lightly till all is moistened. Form into ball; roll out on lightly floured surface to 18x12-inch rectangle. Cut into six 6-inch squares. Place an apple in center of each square. Mix granulated sugar and ¼ cup cream; spoon into centers of apples. Moisten edges of pastry. Fold corners to center; pinch together. Place 1 inch apart in ungreased 11x7½x1-inch baking pan. Bake at 450° for 15 minutes. Reduce oven temperature to 350°. Baste dumplings with ¾ cup hot maple syrup. Bake till apples are done, about 30 minutes, basting with hot syrup every 15 minutes. Garnish with jelly, if desired. Serve with Hard Sauce, syrup, cream, or ice cream. Serves 6 to 8.

*Hard Sauce:* Cream 6 tablespoons butter with 1 cup sifted powdered sugar till fluffy. Chill in mounds.

## Grandma's Chocolate Cake *(see photo, page 96)*

| | |
|---|---|
| 1 cup granulated sugar | ½ cup hot water |
| ½ cup packed brown sugar | 1¾ cups all-purpose flour |
| ½ cup shortening | 1 teaspoon baking soda |
| 2 eggs | ¼ teaspoon salt |
| 1 teaspoon vanilla | ⅔ cup buttermilk |
| 3 1-ounce squares | Mocha Frosting |
| unsweetened chocolate | Chopped walnuts |

Cream sugars and shortening till light and fluffy. Add eggs, one at a time, beating well after each. Add vanilla. Melt chocolate in the hot water over low heat; blend thoroughly and cool slightly. Add to creamed mixture. Stir flour, soda, and salt together. Beat into creamed mixture alternately with milk, beating well after each addition. Pour into 3 greased and floured 8x1½-inch round baking pans. Bake at 350° for 20 to 25 minutes.

Cool 10 minutes; remove from pans. Cool; fill and frost with Mocha Frosting. Sprinkle nuts atop cake.

*Mocha Frosting:* Sift together one 16-ounce package powdered sugar, ½ cup unsweetened cocoa powder, and ½ teaspoon instant coffee powder. Beat *2 cups* of the mixture into 6 tablespoons butter and 1 teaspoon vanilla. Add remaining sugar mixture alternately with milk to make of spreading consistency (about 2 tablespoons milk); beat well.

## Silver White Layer Cake

*Hydrogenated vegetable shortening and the electric mixer made one-bowl cakes like Silver White Layer Cake possible. The dry ingredients (including sugar), shortening, and milk are all beaten together. The old way was to cream butter and sugar by hand, then add eggs, and then the sifted dry ingredients alternately with milk, beating 150 strokes between each addition, and 300 after the last addition.*

| | |
|---|---|
| 2 cups all-purpose flour | 2 teaspoons vanilla |
| 1½ cups sugar | ½ cup shortening |
| 4 teaspoons baking powder | 4 egg whites |
| 1 teaspoon salt | Cooked White Frosting |
| 1 cup milk | (see recipe, page 127) |

Have all ingredients at room temperature. In large mixer bowl stir together the flour, sugar, baking powder, and salt. Combine milk and vanilla. Add ⅔ *cup* of the milk mixture and the shortening all at once to dry ingredients. Beat at low speed of electric mixer for 2 minutes. Add unbeaten egg whites and the remaining milk mixture. Beat 2 minutes longer; scrape sides of bowl frequently. (Batter will be thin.) Pour batter into 2 greased and floured 8x1½-inch round baking pans. Bake at 350° for 30 to 35 minutes. Cool 10 minutes; remove from pans. Cool on racks. Fill and frost with Cooked White Frosting.

## Chocolate Chip Cake *(see photo, pages 6-7)*

| | |
|---|---|
| 1¾ cups sugar | 3 teaspoons baking powder |
| ⅔ cup shortening | 1¼ cups milk |
| 1 teaspoon grated lemon | 1½ cups semisweet chocolate |
| peel | pieces |
| 5 egg whites | Fluffy Frosting (see |
| 3 cups sifted cake flour | recipe, page 125) |

Cream the sugar, shortening, and lemon peel till light. Add unbeaten egg whites one at a time; beat well after each. Sift cake flour, baking powder, and ½ teaspoon salt; add to creamed mixture alternately with milk, beating till smooth after each addition. Pour *half* batter into 2 greased and floured 9x1½-inch round baking pans. Sprinkle *half* the chocolate over batter. Add remaining batter; sprinkle with remaining chocolate. Bake at 350° for 30 to 35 minutes. Cool 10 minutes; remove from pans. Cool. Fill and frost with Fluffy Frosting.

## Lady Baltimore Cake

2 cups sugar
¾ cup shortening
½ teaspoon vanilla
½ teaspoon lemon extract
3 cups sifted cake flour

3 teaspoons baking powder
1 cup milk
6 egg whites
　Fluffy Frosting
　Lady Baltimore Filling

Cream 1½ cups sugar, shortening, vanilla, and lemon extract. Sift flour, baking powder, and ¾ teaspoon salt. Add to creamed mixture alternately with milk, beating after each addition. Beat egg whites to soft peaks. Gradually add remaining sugar; beat to stiff peaks. Fold into batter. Spread in 3 greased and floured 9x1½-inch round pans. Bake at 375° for 18 to 20 minutes. Cool for about 10 minutes; remove from pans. Cool. Prepare Fluffy Frosting and Lady Baltimore Filling. Fill and frost the cake layers.

*Fluffy Frosting:* Combine 1½ cups sugar, 2 unbeaten egg whites, 5 tablespoons cold water, ¼ teaspoon cream of tartar, and dash salt in top of double boiler (do not place over boiling water). Beat egg mixture ½ minute at low speed of electric mixer. Place over, but not touching, boiling water. Cook, beating constantly, till stiff peaks form, about 7 minutes. Remove from boiling water. Add ½ teaspoon vanilla. Beat frosting till of spreading consistency, about 2 minutes more.

*Lady Baltimore Filling:* To one-fourth of the Fluffy Frosting, add 1 cup chopped figs, ½ cup raisins, ½ cup chopped candied cherries, and ½ cup chopped pecans. Stir well.

*Lady Baltimore is a white cake put together with figs, nuts, candied cherries, and fluffy white frosting. Some say the Lady Baltimore Cake came from Owen Wister's novel,* The Virginian. *It's definitely a south of the Mason-Dixon Line recipe.*

## Gold Cupcakes

Cream 1 cup sugar, ½ cup shortening, and 1 teaspoon vanilla till light. Add 3 beaten egg yolks; beat well. Stir together 2 cups all-purpose flour, 2 teaspoons baking powder, and ½ teaspoon salt. Add to creamed mixture alternately with ¾ cup milk, beating well after each addition. Fill paper bake cups in muffin pans half full. Bake at 350° for 30 minutes. Frost with Fluffy Frosting (see above). Makes 18.

## Lincoln Log

4 egg yolks
⅓ cup granulated sugar
½ teaspoon vanilla
4 egg whites
½ cup granulated sugar

⅔ cup sifted cake flour
1 teaspoon baking powder
　Sifted powdered sugar
　Chocolate Frosting
¼ cup sliced almonds

Beat egg yolks till thick; gradually beat in ⅓ cup sugar and vanilla. Beat egg whites till soft peaks form. Gradually add ½ cup sugar; beat till stiff peaks form. Fold yolks into whites. Sift together flour, baking powder, and ¼ teaspoon salt; fold into egg mixture. Spread batter in greased and floured 15½x10½x1-inch jelly roll pan. Bake at 375° for 10 to 12 minutes. Immediately turn out on towel sprinkled with sifted powdered sugar. Starting at narrow end, roll cake and towel together; cool on rack. Trim edges. Unroll; remove cloth and spread with *1 cup* of the Chocolate Frosting. Reroll. Frost with remaining frosting. To make bark, draw tines of fork through frosting in uneven lines. Sprinkle with almonds. Refrigerate. Before serving, let stand at room temperature 15 minutes. Slice. Serves 8.

*Chocolate Frosting:* Melt four 1-ounce squares unsweetened chocolate. Add 1 cup sifted powdered sugar and 2 tablespoons hot water; blend. Add 2 eggs; beat well after each. Add 2 tablespoons *each* shortening and softened butter; beat well. Chill till partially set.

## Hot Milk Sponge Cake

2 eggs
1 cup sugar
1 cup all-purpose flour
1 teaspoon baking powder
¼ teaspoon salt
½ cup milk
1 tablespoon butter
Broiled Frosting

Beat eggs till thick and lemon-colored. Slowly add sugar and beat at medium speed of mixer 4 to 5 minutes. Stir flour, baking powder, and salt together. Add to egg mixture; stir just till blended. Heat milk and butter till butter melts; stir into batter. Mix well. Pour into greased 9x9x2-inch baking pan. Bake at 350° for 20 to 25 minutes.

Frost with Broiled Frosting. Cut into squares; serve warm or cold.

*Broiled Frosting:* Combine 1 cup flaked coconut; ½ cup packed brown sugar; 6 tablespoons butter or margarine, melted; ¼ cup light cream; and ½ teaspoon vanilla. Spread over baked cake; place under broiler 4 or 5 inches from heat. Broil till brown and bubbly, about 3 minutes.

## Pineapple Chiffon Cake

*Chiffon cakes were introduced in May, 1948, the biggest cake news in 100 years because it was so different from butter cake. It used cooking oil instead of shortening and it was beaten, not creamed. Flavors were myriad, but none surpassed those made with fruit juice, like this Pineapple Chiffon Cake.*

2¼ cups sifted cake flour
1½ cups sugar
3 teaspoons baking powder
½ cup cooking oil
5 egg yolks
¾ cup unsweetened pineapple juice
1 cup egg whites (8)
½ teaspoon cream of tartar
Pineapple Topping

Sift together flour, sugar, baking powder, and 1 teaspoon salt. Make well in center and add in order: cooking oil, egg yolks, and unsweetened pineapple juice. Beat till smooth. In large mixer bowl beat egg whites with cream of tartar till *very stiff peaks* form. Pour batter in thin stream over entire surface of egg whites; fold in gently. Bake in *ungreased* 10-inch tube pan at 350° for 60 minutes. Invert; cool thoroughly. Split into 2 layers. Fill and frost with Pineapple Topping.

*Pineapple Topping:* Whip 2 cups whipping cream. Fold one 20-ounce can crushed pineapple, well drained, into whipped cream.

## Martha Washington Cake

1¼ cups granulated sugar
⅔ cup shortening
3 egg yolks
1 teaspoon vanilla
2 cups all-purpose flour
2½ teaspoons baking powder
¼ teaspoon salt
1 cup milk
3 egg whites
• • •
Cream Filling
Powdered sugar

Cream *1 cup* of the granulated sugar and shortening. Add egg yolks and vanilla; beat well. Stir together dry ingredients. Add to creamed mixture alternately with milk, beating well after each addition. Beat egg whites till soft peaks form. Slowly add the remaining granulated sugar and beat till stiff peaks form. Fold into batter. Bake in 2 greased and floured 9x1½-inch round baking pans at 350° about 25 minutes. Cool 10 minutes; remove from pans. Cool completely. Fill

with Cream Filling. Hold a paper doily firmly in place on top of cake. Lightly sift powdered sugar over top. Rub in gently. Lift doily.

*Cream Filling:* In saucepan combine ⅓ cup sugar, ¼ cup all-purpose flour, and ¼ teaspoon salt. Stir in 1½ cups milk. Cook and stir till thick. Remove from heat. Stir a moderate amount of hot mixture into 1 beaten egg; return to hot mixture. Cook and stir 2 minutes more. Remove from heat; add 1 teaspoon vanilla. Cool.

## Orange Delight Cake

1½ cups sugar
¾ cup shortening
1 teaspoon grated orange
    peel
3 eggs, separated

2 cups all-purpose flour
3 teaspoons baking powder
¼ cup orange juice
    Orange Filling
    Orange Frosting

Cream sugar, shortening, and peel till light. Add egg yolks; beat well after each. Stir together flour, baking powder, and ½ teaspoon salt. Add to creamed mixture alternately with juice and ¾ cup water, beating after each addition. Beat egg whites till stiff but not dry; fold into batter. Bake in 2 greased and floured 9x1½-inch round pans at 350° for 30 to 35 minutes. Cool 10 minutes; remove from pans. Cool. Fill with Orange Filling; frost with Orange Frosting.

*Orange Filling:* Grate 1½ teaspoons orange peel (set aside). Combine 1 cup sugar, ¼ cup cornstarch, and ½ teaspoon salt; add 1 cup orange juice. Tint orange with food coloring. Cook and stir till thick; add 2 tablespoons butter, 1½ tablespoons lemon juice, and grated orange peel. Cool.

*Orange Frosting:* In saucepan cook 1 cup sugar and ¼ cup orange juice to thread stage (234°). Pour syrup over 2 stiffly beaten whites; beat till thick enough to spread.

*Many a queen of the kitchen reigns today, as 100 years ago, by right of divine cakes—the eye-tempting, melt-in-the-mouth variety like Orange Delight Cake. Today, few cakes are made from scratch, but a fine cake—tender, fragile, light, velvety, and with a delicate golden crust—still takes a light hand, a good recipe, the right equipment, and the best of ingredients.*

## George Washington Cake

1½ cups sugar
¾ cup shortening
1½ teaspoons vanilla
2¾ cups sifted cake flour
1 teaspoon baking powder

½ teaspoon baking soda
¼ teaspoon salt
1¼ cups buttermilk
4 stiffly beaten egg whites
    Cooked White Frosting

Cream sugar, shortening, and vanilla. Sift together dry ingredients. Add to batter alternately with buttermilk, beating well after each addition. Fold in egg whites. Bake in 2 greased and floured 9x1½-inch round pans at 350° for 25 minutes. Cool 10 minutes; remove from pans. Cool. Fill and frost with Cooked White Frosting.

*Cooked White Frosting:* Cook 2 cups sugar, ½ cup water, and ⅛ teaspoon cream of tartar over low heat; stir till sugar dissolves. Cover pan 2 to 3 minutes; *do not stir.* Uncover; cook to soft-ball stage (240°). Beat 2 egg whites to soft peaks. Slowly add hot syrup, beating constantly. Add 1 teaspoon vanilla; continue beating till spreadable, 7 minutes.

*The George Washington Cake is based on Virginia's fine old white cake. The amounts have been changed to match modern ingredients, but the proportions are still the same—twice as much sugar as shortening. The buttermilk and soda are as the old recipe called for.*

## Pineapple Upside-Down Cake

1 8¼-ounce can pineapple
    slices
¼ cup butter or margarine
½ cup packed brown sugar
    Milk
½ cup granulated sugar

⅓ cup shortening
1 teaspoon vanilla
1 egg
1 cup all-purpose flour
1½ teaspoons baking powder
¼ teaspoon salt

Drain pineapple, reserving syrup. Cut slices in half. Melt butter in 8x8x2-inch baking pan; stir in brown sugar and *2 tablespoons* of the reserved syrup. Arrange pineapple in pan. Add milk to remaining syrup to make ½ cup liquid. Cream together the granulated sugar, shortening, and vanilla. Add egg; beat well. Stir together dry ingredients; add to creamed mixture alternately with liquid, beating after each addition. Spread over pineapple. Bake at 350° for 35 to 40 minutes. Cool 5 minutes; invert on plate. Serve warm.

November 1955 · **25c** In Canada 35c

# Better Homes
## and Gardens
®

▶ How to plan a family room
▶ Indoor plants—8 pages to clip

Serving more than 4,000,000 families

The fun and excitement of the '50s is still with us. These exuberant years of Sputnik, rock 'n roll, and television were also landmark years for food. Gone was the rationing of the war years. Americans now had the time and money to enjoy eating. And enjoy they did. Millions devoured submarine sandwiches, pizzas, and hamburgers. The blossoming supermarkets displayed many new wonders such as out-of-season fruits and vegetables, boxed cake mixes, dry soup mixes, bottled sauces, and frozen orange juice. Americans also began using new conveniences such as dishwashers, hand mixers, blenders, and electric skillets in a big way. All these innovations added to the wonderful flavors that came out of the '50s. And most of them are still around today.

# THE 50s

The frenetic fifties was a decade of fun, excitement, and gusto. Except for the Korean conflict at the very beginning of the decade, there were few earthshaking problems—or so people believed. Unlike the preceding turbulent years of world war, disease, food rationing, and the start of general reconstruction, the fifties were mostly carefree, peaceful, and prosperous years—a time when people were neither rationed nor recessioned and when they could relax, rebuild their lives, and enjoy leisure activities. The period was headlined by rock 'n roll, a home building boom, fast sports cars, and chrome-bedecked sedans with fins. Sputnik, the miraculous Salk vaccine, and oval-shaped TV screens were all part of the fifties. So were hamburgers, pancakes, pizzas, and sandwiches called submarines. Ike was our president for eight of these years. And sports boomed. Youngsters generally held to the same beliefs as their parents, and parents at least tolerated the latest tunes of Elvis blaring from new portable hi-fi's. Perhaps everyone was trying to blot out memories of the past, but it's more probable that they were simply savoring the return to good times and taking advantage of every frolicking moment.

Except for the major advances in medical research and air travel, no general aspect of the period fascinated the public more than the revolutionary innovations in food styles, eating habits, and cooking methods. Although by the late forties foods were again plentiful and kitchen equipment was becoming sophisticated, it was not until the early fifties that people enjoyed real prosperity and culinary adventure. The rapid growth of supermarkets and food chains, as well as the improvements in air freight and rail shipping, allowed homemakers not only to purchase a greater number of products, but also to experiment with a wide variety of out-of-season goods previously unavailable on a nationwide basis. As early as 1950, strawberries, Mexican cantaloupe, cherry tomatoes, Hawaiian papaya, mangoes, and other exotica were just a few of the items available.

The convenience foods of the fifties made putting together complete meals enjoyable. By 1951 boxed mixes to make jiffy-quick batters and doughs, bottled sauces, dry milk products, canned meats, and packaged dry soups were overflowing the grocery shelves. Equally important were frozen foods, which made their debut in the forties but were now considered absolutely essential in preparing meals. Frozen orange juice had become a breakfast staple. Following close behind was an expanding variety of frozen vegetables, fruits, meats, even jams, and by 1953, supermarkets featured entire frozen dinners—an item that effected radical changes in the nation's eating habits. With more food preparation done outside the home, the average housewife was in a position to cut down kitchen responsibilities and to spend more time with the family.

Particularly impressive in this area of leisure and convenience was the incredible number of new kitchen appliances introduced. These helped to reduce the daily workload, and, at the same time, to inspire a cook's ingenuity. With the increased availability of the dishwasher, even cleanup was made easier. If Dad wanted to spend time in the kitchen, now he could devote more of it to the art of cooking. Giant freezers enabled the housewife to shop once a week and stock up enough food for an almost endless variety of dishes. And what chef didn't crave the luxury of a hand mixer, a blender, an electric skillet and roaster, or a rotisserie? It's no wonder that by 1958 the kitchen skills of Americans amazed Russians at the Moscow Trade Fair, while shortly before, Russia had amazed the world by orbiting Sputnik, the first spacecraft.

Above all, the trend toward informality typified the eating styles of Americans during the early fifties. Accelerated interest in barbecuing (or 'blue sky meals' as they were called), for example, on outdoor grills presented a new meal pattern that involved every member of the family and that established a tradition as popular today as it was 20 years ago. Dad would grill the steaks or hamburgers, Mom made the scalloped potatoes, and the youngsters sometimes tossed green salads or churned fresh ice cream for dessert. On football weekends, the tailgate of the family station wagon turned server for picnic fare, and all over the nation families, friends, and neighbors got together for potluck suppers of fried chicken, tossed salad, bread, potato salad, and juicy apple pie.

Nothing epitomized the nation's eating habits or disturbed nutritionists more than the casual stop at one of the pancake houses, pizza places, or food drive-ins that had sprouted up all over the country by the mid-fifties. Previously, the pancake had been no more than a breakfast dish served with maple syrup. But no longer! Silver-dollar size buckwheats, buttermilk flapjacks with whipped butter, and fruit-filled Swedish pancakes transformed the pancake into an all-American, anytime food. Equally impressive was the amazing choice of syrups, which ranged from boysenberry to crème de menthe. The same was true at pizza parlors, where a small amount of money could buy a full meal of giant pizzas prepared simply with tomato sauce and mozzarella cheese or spiced up with pepperoni, sausage, onions, green peppers, anchovies, or what-have-you. Hamburger haunts produced tasty sandwiches fast, charged low prices, and quickly capitalized on the idea that French fries and malts are good go-withs.

Health consciousness was raised to an all-time high level by President Eisenhower's heart attack. Scarcely a magazine or newspaper failed to make special efforts to educate the public on progress being made in the treatment of heart disease and on the treatment of infections with wonder drugs such as Aureomycin and Terramycin. Health became a major topic of social conversation as people became more concerned over how what they ate might affect how they felt.

During World War II, people had heard about something called cholesterol, and *Better Homes and Gardens* was in the vanguard with a series of diets for calorie-watchers and others wondering about their intake of fats. The magazine also dealt with other diet-related health questions. "Was it true that citrus fruits would strengthen blood vessels and fight off colds and flu?" "Could allergies be controlled by eliminating certain foods?" "What was the effect of nutritional intake on mental health?" "How much salt should be consumed per day and what advantages were there in foods with low sodium content?"

A large segment of the population did heed the advice offered by experts and, to some degree, began gradually to modify food and cooking styles. Efforts were made to find meat with less fat; salads containing fruit or high-protein ingredients became a rage; seafood (especially the newly fashionable South African rock lobster tails and Alaska king crab) gained considerable popularity; and artichokes, broccoli, and Brussels sprouts served with seasoned herb butters joined the ABCs of vegetables.

Medical news and discoveries did indeed make people conscious of how much—of which foods—prepared in what ways—they consumed. But it would be misleading to suggest that consumers in the mid- to late-fifties were as obsessed with weight watching and dieting as they are today. It was all right to think about calories and cholesterol some of the time, but certainly not all the time. Besides, who cared about going to a cocktail party where there were no canapés or snacks to nibble on? Who wanted to sit through Sid Caesar's "Show of Shows," "Playhouse 90," or "Alfred

Hitchcock Presents" without at least a big bowl of ice cream and a piece of rich fudge cake? Who was willing to forfeit the adventure of testing recipes with exciting new ingredients? Commercial sour cream, for example, took America by storm in the mid-fifties, and it was used not only as the preferred topping (mixed with chives) for baked potatoes, but also in dunks with onion soup mix and in foreign recipes for dishes like stroganoff and chicken paprika. Caesar Salad had gained popularity in California during the forties, but by 1956 chefs throughout the nation were tossing their greens with coddled egg, croutons, and rich dressings. Salads in general were on the upswing as people became more weight conscious. And with the trend toward lighter eating came the main dish salad — long promoted by *Better Homes and Gardens,* now an established menu idea throughout the nation. Main dish salads, first served by West Coast hostesses, evolved from the small first-course salads into whole meals atop crisp lettuce. Headliners in this area were — and still are — Stuffed Tomato-Crab Meat Salad, Fruited Tuna Salad, and Chef's Salad Bowl.

As the decade moved along, people everywhere were demanding more interesting recipes, more flavorful ingredients and exciting seasonings, and more showmanship in the preparation of food. Hamburgers and hot dogs were still great for a quick lunch or snack, but when it came to the evening meal at home, a little more culinary imagination was expected. Meats were flamed in chafing dishes, on skewers, or cooked on hibachis. Vegetables were stuffed with everything from chicken salad to crumbled blue cheese, and by the end of the decade, bold cooks were mixing vegetables in previously unheard-of combinations: lima beans and mushrooms, fried corn and onions, and peas and water chestnuts.

Of course, the topping on all the gastronomic fun was desserts, and even those people who were painfully conscious of tooth decay and calories found it difficult to resist the delectable creations featured in the sweet-toothed recipes of the period. Without doubt, the most sensational success of the decade was cheesecake, that sinfully rich specialty that won its initial glory at New York's old Lindy's Restaurant. Its popularity soon spread throughout the country. Chocolate, so scarce during the war years, was the major ingredient for literally hundreds of desserts, from chocolate cake to brownies to Mrs. Claus' famous fudge.

Ice cream remained as popular as ever, but at the end of the decade most of it was being scooped from cartons bought in supermarkets and used for parfaits and fruit-flavored gelatin desserts. A promotion by a flour mill and a gelatin manufacturer resulted in the parfait pie, which combined the best of both — pie and a refrigerator dessert.

In more than one respect, the food and eating styles of the fifties were possibly the most intriguing of any decade thus far in the century, and the reasons are fairly simple. People who had been forced by necessity to compromise during most of the forties were now in the position to live and eat well. Confronted with a different life-style, they kicked up their heels, closed one eye to the various health problems, which in the following decade would be taken very seriously, and treated themselves fully to multiple amenities. Foreign travel by fast jets allowed greater and more frequent opportunity to taste new flavors and witness different methods of preparing food. And this foreign exposure so influenced Americans that by 1959 traditional eating habits and cooking techniques were considerably modified and in some ways completely changed. The peace and joy of the fifties finally drifted away, but the imprint made on America by the decade's culinary styles and innovations was as indelible as memory itself.

← *Unfold this section for three-page foldout illustration in full color*

# Recipe Features of the Fifties

## Main Dish Salads

Choose a crisp main dish salad for lunch. In the fifties the main dish salad became a hit when businessmen found it to be a happy alternative to hearty fare. These salads range from molded ones with tuna to the tossed lettuce ones with ham.

## Backyard Barbecues

Come out to the backyard for a barbecue. This invitation was heard often during the fifties. For it was then that Americans really began to enjoy cooking outdoors. They eagerly tried preparing all types of foods on the barbecue including kabobs, ribs, roasts, vegetables, and desserts.

## Pancake Parade

Start your morning off right with pancakes. During the fifties pancakes became national favorites with the opening of pancake houses across the country. Soon they became not only a breakfast food, but fun to eat any time of day.

## Pastries and Pies

Looking for just the right dessert? Try a piece of pie.
The fifties was famous for double fruit flavor pies like pineapple-rhubarb. The parfait pie was a hit also.
A combination of gelatin, fruit, and ice cream, the parfait pie proved to be a light, refreshing finale for a summer meal.

The honey-maple cabinets are the outstanding feature of this fifties kitchen. They give the illusion of fine furniture. Other striking elements are the double-bowl sink and the copper hood and ventilator over the range.

# Main Dish Salads

The changing life-style of the '50s brought with it several food innovations. One was the main dish salad. These salads began as a simple arrangement of fruits, vegetables, and meat on a platter. Later, people turned to natural containers such as tomatoes or avocado halves. They were perfect for holding chicken or crab salad. Hostesses also introduced salads in wooden salad bowls. Salads grew bigger and bigger until they were a meal in themselves. Soon, Americans began creating still other types of main dish salads such as gelatin molds using meat or seafood. Here are just a few main dish favorites of the '50s.

*Highlight a summer luncheon with crisp and fresh-tasting Stuffed Tomato-Crab Meat Salad (pictured opposite). Simply fill firm, ripe tomatoes with a mixture of crab meat, celery, cucumber, and hard-cooked eggs. Round out the meal with crisp potato chips, corn relish, and fresh fruit.*

## Stuffed Tomato-Crab Meat Salad

| | |
|---|---|
| 4 medium tomatoes | ½ cup chopped celery |
| 1 7½-ounce can crab meat, drained, flaked, and cartilage removed | ¼ cup diced cucumber<br>Dash pepper<br>1 tablespoon lemon juice |
| 2 hard-cooked eggs, coarsely chopped | ⅓ cup mayonnaise or salad dressing |

With stem end down, cut each tomato into 6 wedges, *cutting to, but not through* base of tomato. Spread wedges apart slightly. Sprinkle insides with salt; chill. Combine crab meat, eggs, celery, cucumber, and pepper. Sprinkle mixture with lemon juice. Chill. Before serving, blend mayonnaise into crab mixture. Fill each tomato with ¼ of the crab mixture. If desired, garnish each salad with additional mayonnaise or salad dressing and sprigs of parsley. Makes 4 servings.

*The first fresh crab of the season is heralded with banners on cable cars to Fisherman's Wharf in San Francisco. 'Natives' buy crabs right from steaming kettles on the sidewalk and take them home to eat with fingers, sucking the last and sweetest morsel from the cracked claws.*

*Enjoyment of crab, however, is not limited to areas where it can be purchased fresh. Excellent frozen and canned crab meat is available in supermarkets everywhere as are the other ingredients for Stuffed Tomato-Crab Meat Salad.*

## Fruited Tuna Salad

| | |
|---|---|
| 1 8¾-ounce can pineapple tidbits, drained | ½ cup sliced celery |
| 1 6½- or 7-ounce can tuna, drained and flaked | ⅓ cup mayonnaise or salad dressing |
| ½ cup seedless green grapes, halved | ¼ cup chopped pecans<br>Lettuce |

Combine pineapple tidbits, tuna, green grapes, celery, mayonnaise, and pecans. Mix lightly; chill. Serve on lettuce. Serves 4.

## Salami-Cheese Salad

| | |
|---|---|
| 1 medium head lettuce, torn in pieces (6 cups) | 1 2-ounce can anchovy fillets, drained and chopped |
| 1 cup sliced salami cut in quarters | 3 tablespoons chopped canned pimiento |
| 4 ounces natural Swiss cheese, cut in strips | ⅓ cup salad oil<br>3 tablespoons wine vinegar |
| ½ cup sliced pitted ripe olives | ½ clove garlic, crushed |

Combine lettuce, salami, cheese, olives, anchovies, and pimiento. In screw-top jar combine oil, vinegar, and garlic for dressing. Cover; shake vigorously. Pour dressing over salad; and toss lightly. Makes 8 servings.

## Chicken Salad—Williamsburg-Style

In top of double boiler beat 2 egg yolks till thick and lemon-colored. Beat in 2 tablespoons lemon juice. Cook and stir over *hot, not boiling,* water till thickened. Remove from heat. Beat in 2 teaspoons prepared mustard, ¾ teaspoon salt, ½ teaspoon sugar, and ⅛ teaspoon cayenne. Cool. Gradually beat in ¼ cup salad oil. Chill. Toss dressing with 2 cups diced cooked chicken, 1 cup chopped celery, and 2 hard-cooked eggs, chopped. Serve in lettuce cups. Serves 4.

## Chef's Salad Bowl

1 clove garlic, halved
1 medium head lettuce, torn
   in bite-size pieces
1 cup chopped cucumber
2 tomatoes, cut in wedges
3 small carrots, cut in
   strips (1 cup)
1 cup fully cooked ham cut
   in strips (5 ounces)
1 cup cooked chicken cut
   in strips

3 hard-cooked eggs,
   quartered
Freshly ground pepper
½ cup salad oil
3 tablespoons vinegar
1 tablespoon prepared
   horseradish
½ teaspoon Worcestershire
   sauce
2 drops bottled hot pepper
   sauce

Rub large salad bowl with cut clove of garlic. Combine lettuce, cucumber, and tomatoes in bowl. Arrange carrots, ham, chicken, and hard-cooked eggs on top. Sprinkle with freshly ground pepper and salt. Combine remaining ingredients, ½ teaspoon salt, and ⅛ teaspoon pepper. Mix well. Pour over salad and toss lightly. Makes 8 servings.

## Henny-Penny Salad

2 cups cubed cooked chicken
1½ cups sliced celery
1 cup mayonnaise
½ cup chopped toasted
   almonds

2 tablespoons lemon juice
2 teaspoons grated onion
½ cup shredded sharp
   process American cheese
1 cup crushed potato chips

Combine chicken, celery, mayonnaise, nuts, lemon juice, onion, and ½ teaspoon salt. Spoon into six 6-ounce custard cups. Sprinkle with cheese, then chips. Bake at 400° till hot, about 15 minutes. Serves 6.

## Shrimp Mousse

2 envelopes unflavored
   gelatin
1 cup mayonnaise
½ cup chopped cucumber
¼ cup lemon juice
3 tablespoons chopped
   pimiento-stuffed green
   olives

2 teaspoons sugar
2 teaspoons prepared
   horseradish
½ teaspoon onion juice
¼ teaspoon paprika
½ cup whipping cream
2 4½-ounce cans shrimp,
   drained and cut in half

Soften gelatin in 1½ cups cold water. Heat till gelatin dissolves. Beat in mayonnaise; chill till partially set. Combine cucumber, lemon juice, olives, sugar, horseradish, onion juice, paprika, and ¼ teaspoon salt. Fold into gelatin mixture. Whip cream; fold into gelatin. Fold in shrimp. Pour into 5½-cup mold. Chill till firm. Serves 8.

## Tuna Salad Mold

1 envelope unflavored
   gelatin
1 tablespoon lemon juice
1 teaspoon drained capers
1 teaspoon snipped parsley
¼ teaspoon paprika

2 6½- or 7-ounce cans tuna,
   drained and flaked
1 cup chopped celery
¼ cup mayonnaise
1 teaspoon prepared mustard
½ cup whipping cream

Soften gelatin in ¼ cup cold water. Add ¾ cup water; heat till gelatin dissolves. Add lemon juice, capers, parsley, paprika, and ½ teaspoon salt. Chill till partially set. Fold in tuna and celery. Combine mayonnaise and mustard; fold in. Whip cream; fold into gelatin mixture. Spoon into 6 individual ¾-cup molds. Chill till firm. Serves 6.

## Corned Beef Salad Mold

2 envelopes unflavored
   gelatin
2 cups tomato juice
2 teaspoons lemon juice
1 12-ounce can corned beef,
   flaked

¾ cup mayonnaise or salad
   dressing
3 hard-cooked eggs, chopped
1 cup chopped celery
½ cup chopped cucumber
1 tablespoon chopped onion

In saucepan soften gelatin in tomato juice. Heat till gelatin dissolves. Stir in lemon juice and ½ teaspoon salt. Chill till partially set. Combine remaining ingredients; fold into gelatin mixture. Pour into 8½x4½x2½-inch loaf pan. Chill till firm. If desired, garnish salad with tomato wedges and hard-cooked egg slices. Makes 8 servings.

## Marinated Vegetable Salad

1 9-ounce package frozen
   cut green beans, cooked
1 cup cooked carrot strips
½ cup French salad dressing
6 cups torn curly endive
1 cup fully cooked ham cut
   in strips (5 ounces)
3 hard-cooked eggs, sliced

½ cup mayonnaise or salad
   dressing
2 tablespoons chopped sweet
   pickle
1½ teaspoons prepared
   mustard
1 teaspoon prepared
   horseradish

Drain beans. Marinate beans and carrots in dressing for 2 hours. Place endive in salad bowl. Arrange marinated vegetables, ham, and eggs on top. Combine remaining ingredients; spoon over. Toss. Serves 6.

## Black-Eyed Susans

8 hard-cooked eggs, chopped
½ cup chopped pitted ripe
   olives
⅓ cup chopped celery
¼ cup mayonnaise
3 tablespoons prepared
   mustard

2 tablespoons chopped green
   onion
½ teaspoon salt
8 unsplit frankfurter buns
   Butter or margarine,
   melted
   Leaf lettuce

Combine eggs, olives, celery, mayonnaise, mustard, onion, and salt. Chill. Hollow out buns to within ½ inch of edge. Brush buns with melted butter; line with lettuce. Fill with egg mixture. Serves 8.

*Main dish salads became make-aheads with the happy marriage of meat or seafood and unflavored gelatin. Season to taste with salad dressing, horseradish, lemon juice, vinegar, or other complementary ingredients. What an easy job it is to turn the mixture into a fancy-shaped mold, put it in the refrigerator to set overnight, then just before the party, unmold the masterpiece onto a bed of crisp greens.*

# Backyard Barbecues

Barbecuing has long been a speciality of *Better Homes and Gardens*. Early magazine articles told the fundamentals of outdoor cookery. By the '50s, however, the barbecue grill had become a permanent backyard fixture all over country. The key to success of barbecuing is that it provided a simple but fun activity for the whole family. Dad would cook the meat; Mom would prepare the salad and dessert; and the kids would bring it all to the table. These recipes show the wide variety barbecuing offers.

## Barbecued Steak

At intervals slash fat edge of one beef porterhouse, T-bone, *or* sirloin steak, cut 1½-inches thick. Grill steak over *hot* coals till desired doneness, turning once with tongs.

Allow about 14 to 16 minutes total cooking time for rare; 18 to 20 minutes for medium; and 25 to 30 minutes for well-done. Season grilled steak with salt and pepper.

## Onioned Potatoes

**½ cup butter or margarine, softened**

**1 envelope onion soup mix**
**6 medium baking potatoes**

Blend butter and onion soup mix. Cut each unpeeled potato into 3 or 4 lengthwise slices. Spread butter mixture on each slice. Reassemble

potatoes. Wrap each in a square of foil, overlapping ends to seal. Grill over *medium* coals, turning once, till tender, 45 to 60 minutes. Serves 6.

Choose a tender, juicy beef steak, one of the most delicious and simple meats to barbecue, for your next outdoor meal. Broil *Barbecued Steak* over hot coals to capture that tempting smoky, charcoal-grilled flavor.

## Deviled Beef Patties

2½ pounds ground beef
¾ cup chili sauce
4 teaspoons prepared
    mustard
4 teaspoons prepared
    horseradish

4 teaspoons Worcestershire
    sauce
1 tablespoon chopped onion
2 teaspoons salt
    Dash pepper
12 hamburger buns, split

In mixing bowl combine ground beef, chili sauce, prepared mustard, prepared horseradish, Worcestershire sauce, chopped onion, salt, and pepper. Mix well. Form into 12 patties. Broil over *hot* coals for 5 minutes. Turn patties and broil till desired doneness, about 3 minutes longer. Serve grilled patties on hamburger buns. Serves 12.

## Gardenburgers

2 slightly beaten eggs
¾ cup soft bread crumbs
¼ cup finely chopped onion
¼ cup catsup
1 teaspoon salt
1½ pounds ground beef
1 6-ounce can chopped
    mushrooms, drained

6 slices process American
    cheese (6 ounces)
6 slices onion
6 slices tomato
    • • •
6 hamburger buns, split
    and toasted

Mix eggs, crumbs, onion, catsup, salt, and pepper. Add beef; mix well. Form into 12 patties. Top *half* the patties with mushrooms, leaving a border of meat. Top with remaining patties; seal edges. Grill over *medium* coals 5 to 6 minutes on each side. Top with cheese; heat just till melted. Top each with onion and tomato. Serve on buns. Makes 6.

*Resist the temptation to put food on the grill before the charcoal is coated with a gray ash. Hold your hand over the coals at the height the meat will cook and count the seconds — one thousand and one, one thousand and two. That's two seconds — hot enough for steaks, hamburgers, or kabobs.*

Barbecuing is a great way to entertain large groups of friends. Spicy *Deviled Beef Patties,* ground beef mixed with chili sauce, mustard, and horseradish, broil on the grill while frankfurters, buns, pie, and coffee heat at the edge of the grill.

## Marinated Rump Roast

2½ cups vinegar
2 medium onions, sliced
1 medium lemon, sliced
2 or 3 bay leaves

12 whole cloves
6 whole black peppercorns
1 tablespoon salt
1 3-pound beef rump roast

Combine vinegar, onions, lemon, bay leaves, cloves, peppercorns, salt, and 2½ cups water. Add meat; refrigerate 2 or 3 days, turning meat occasionally. Drain meat.

Center roast on spit and secure with holding forks. Roast over *slow* coals on motorized spit till done (medium, 160°, about 1½ hours). Baste with marinade. Serves 8.

## Saucy Lamb Riblets

3 to 4 pounds lamb riblets,
cut in serving-size
pieces
½ cup chopped onion
1 tablespoon cooking oil
¾ cup catsup
¼ cup water

3 tablespoons
Worcestershire sauce
2 tablespoons packed brown
sugar
2 tablespoons vinegar
Dash bottled hot pepper
sauce

Trim excess fat from riblets. Cook riblets, covered, in boiling salted water for 1 to 1¼ hours. Drain. Meanwhile, cook onion in oil till tender. Add catsup, ¼ cup water, Worcestershire, brown sugar, vinegar, hot pepper sauce, and ¾ tea-

spoon salt. Heat through. Brown riblets over *medium-hot* coals 10 to 15 minutes on each side. Brush with sauce; continue cooking till riblets are hot and glazed, 10 to 15 minutes. Brush with sauce before serving. Pass extra sauce. Serves 4.

## Grilled Island Chicken

2 2-pound ready-to-cook
broiler-fryer chickens,
split in half
lengthwise
½ cup cooking oil
1½ teaspoons salt
¼ teaspoon pepper

1 8¼-ounce can crushed
pineapple
¾ cup packed brown sugar
3 tablespoons lemon juice
1 tablespoon prepared
mustard

Brush chickens well with cooking oil; season with salt and pepper. Grill over *slow* coals, with bone side nearest the coals. When bone side is well browned, 20 to 30 minutes, turn skin side down and cook about 20 minutes longer. Meanwhile, drain pineapple, reserving 2

tablespoons syrup. Combine crushed pineapple, reserved syrup, brown sugar, lemon juice, and mustard. Brush both sides of chickens with pineapple glaze. Broil till chicken is tender, about 10 minutes, turning and brushing each side twice with glaze. Pass extra glaze. Serves 4.

## 1-2-3 Barbecue Sauce

1 14-ounce bottle hot-style
catsup
3 tablespoons vinegar

2 teaspoons celery seed
1 clove garlic, halved

Combine catsup, vinegar, celery seed, and garlic. Chill. Remove gar-

lic. Use to baste grilled hamburgers. Makes about 1½ cups sauce.

## Barbecued Ribs

| | |
|---|---|
| 4 pounds pork loin back ribs | ½ teaspoon salt |
| ¼ cup molasses | ⅛ teaspoon bottled hot pepper sauce |
| ¼ cup prepared mustard | • • • |
| ¼ cup vinegar | ½ lemon, thinly sliced |
| ¼ cup Worcestershire sauce | ½ large onion, thinly sliced |

Trim excess fat from ribs. Sprinkle meat with salt and pepper to taste. Place ribs in Dutch oven. Add ½ cup water; cover and simmer till ribs are tender, about 2 hours. (Add more water during cooking if needed.) Drain. Blend molasses and prepared mustard. Stir in vinegar, Worcestershire sauce, salt, and hot pepper sauce. Heat to boiling. Coat ribs with sauce. Grill over *slow* coals 10 minutes, brushing with sauce and turning frequently. Brush meat side with sauce. Attach lemon and onion slices to meat side of ribs with wooden picks. Continue to grill without turning till done, 5 to 10 minutes more. Serves 4.

*The barbecue, as an event, began in nineteenth-century America as a political gathering. The barbecue included roasted meats, political speeches, and a lively band. Little else was served besides meats, homemade bread, and plenty of beer, wine, or coffee. At all of these gatherings, longtime favorites such as Barbecued Ribs were often the center of attraction.*

## Ham Slice with Cranberry Sauce

| | |
|---|---|
| 1 8-ounce can jellied cranberry sauce | 2 teaspoons packed brown sugar |
| 2 tablespoons bottled steak sauce | 1 teaspoon prepared mustard |
| 1 tablespoon cooking oil | 1 1½-pound fully cooked ham slice, cut 1-inch thick |

Combine jellied cranberry sauce, steak sauce, cooking oil, brown sugar, and prepared mustard. Beat with electric or rotary beater till smooth. Slash fat edge of fully cooked ham slice. Grill over *slow* coals 20 to 25 minutes, turning once. Brush with sauce. Broil 10 minutes longer, turning and basting once again. Heat remaining sauce on the edge of grill; serve with ham. Makes 4 or 5 servings.

## Marinated Grill-Broiled Chicken

| | |
|---|---|
| ½ cup soy sauce | Dash pepper |
| ¼ cup lemon juice | 2 2½- to 3-pound ready-to-cook broiler-fryer chickens, split lengthwise |
| ¼ cup cooking oil | |
| ¼ cup wine vinegar | |
| 1 teaspoon dried oregano, crushed | |

Combine soy sauce, lemon juice, oil, wine vinegar, oregano, and pepper. Place chicken in shallow baking dish; pour marinade over. Marinate in refrigerator overnight, turning occasionally. Drain, reserving marinade. Place chicken, bone side down, on grill over *slow* coals. Brush with marinade. Grill 30 minutes. Turn skin side down and grill till done, 20 to 30 minutes, brushing frequently with marinade. Serves 4.

## Roasted Corn in Foil

Remove husks from six ears of corn. Remove silk with a stiff brush. Place each ear on a piece of heavy foil. Spread corn liberally with softened butter or margarine. Sprinkle with salt and pepper. Wrap corn securely in foil. Roast ears of corn directly on *hot* coals, turning frequently, till corn is tender, 12 to 15 minutes. Serves 6.

## Hawaiian Kabobs

½ cup soy sauce
¼ cup cooking oil
1 tablespoon dark corn
  syrup
2 cloves garlic, minced
1 teaspoon dry mustard
1 teaspoon ground ginger

2½ pounds boneless lamb *or*
  beef, cut in 1½-inch
  cubes
3 green peppers, cut in
  1-inch squares
5 small firm tomatoes,
  quartered

In large bowl combine soy sauce, oil, corn syrup, garlic, dry mustard, and ginger. Add meat; refrigerate several hours or overnight. Drain meat, reserving marinade. Alternate meat, green pepper, and tomato on skewers. Grill over *medium-hot* coals till desired doneness, about 15 minutes for rare. Baste occasionally with sauce. Serves 8.

*The backyard grill has given the Middle-Eastern shish kabob a whole new look and taste. Anything that can be cut into cubes, put on a long skewer, and cooked over charcoal is. It's a meal on a stick, as fruits and vegetables join meats in the lineup. Before grilling, marinate or baste the foods with a peppy sauce to moisten the surface and to spread the flavor around. At serving time, push the cooked foods off the stick onto a paper plate or pop them into a waiting frankfurter bun.*

## Angus Beef Kabobs

½ cup cooking oil
⅓ cup soy sauce
¼ cup lemon juice
2 tablespoons prepared
  mustard
2 tablespoons
  Worcestershire sauce

1 clove garlic, minced
1 teaspoon coarsely cracked
  pepper
1½ pounds lean beef round or
  chuck, cut in 1-inch
  cubes
12 to 16 mushroom caps

Mix oil, soy sauce, lemon juice, mustard, Worcestershire, garlic, pepper, and 1½ teaspoons salt. Add beef. Chill overnight; turn occasionally. Pour boiling water over mushrooms. Let stand a few minutes; drain. Put meat and mushrooms on skewers. Grill over *hot* coals till done, 15 minutes for medium rare; turn often. Serves 4 or 5.

## Company Cookout

1 13¼-ounce can pineapple
  chunks
1 17-ounce can sweet
  potatoes
1 pound fully cooked ham,
  cut in 1½-inch cubes

1 16-ounce can spiced crab
  apples, drained
• • •
¼ cup packed brown sugar
2 tablespoons butter or
  margarine

Drain pineapple, reserving ¼ cup syrup. Thread skewers with sweet potatoes, ham, crab apples, and pineapple. Grill over *medium* coals 10 minutes, turning frequently. Combine reserved syrup, brown sugar, and butter. Heat and stir till blended. Grill kabobs 5 to 10 minutes longer, brushing with sauce. Pass remaining sauce. Serves 4.

## Vagabond Kabobs

1 pound ring-style bologna,
  cut in 1½-inch pieces
5 small onions, cut in
  ¾-inch slices

5 medium dill pickles, cut
  in 1½-inch slices
2 tablespoons butter or
  margarine, melted

Thread long skewers alternately with bologna pieces, onion slices, and dill pickle slices. Brush with some of the melted butter. Grill kabobs over *medium* coals 8 to 10 minutes. Brush with the remaining melted butter; turn and cook 8 to 10 minutes longer. Serves 5.

## Rye-Herb Loaf

6 tablespoons butter or
   margarine, softened
3 tablespoons snipped
   parsley
1 clove garlic, minced
½ teaspoon salt
¼ teaspoon ground sage

¼ teaspoon dried rosemary,
   crushed
¼ teaspoon dried thyme,
   crushed
¼ teaspoon dry mustard
1 loaf sliced light rye
   bread

Mix butter, parsley, seasonings, and ¼ teaspoon pepper. Spread on one side of each bread slice. Reassemble loaf; wrap in foil. Heat at side of grill till hot, 15 to 20 minutes, turning often. Makes 1 loaf.

*The far side of the grill, away from direct heat, is just the spot to warm Rye-Herb Loaf for an outdoor meal. The herb butter melts as the rye bread slices warm in aluminum foil—the barbecuer's best friend.*

## Skillet Hominy in Sour Cream

2 tablespoons butter
2 16-ounce cans hominy,
   drained

1 cup dairy sour cream
1 cup shredded sharp
   process American cheese

In heavy skillet melt butter over *slow* coals. Add hominy; heat through. Add sour cream and cheese. Season with salt and pepper. Cook and stir till cheese melts *(do not boil)*. Serves 6 to 8.

*When outdoor cooking takes to the road, a skillet is a necessary utensil. Besides fixing the morning bacon and eggs or panfrying freshly caught fish, it comes in handy for hearty dishes such as Skillet Hominy in Sour Cream.*

## Peppy Barbecue Sauce

1 cup catsup
¼ cup tarragon vinegar
¼ cup olive *or* cooking oil
2 tablespoons instant
   minced onion
2 tablespoons
   Worcestershire sauce
1 tablespoon packed brown
   sugar
2 teaspoons mustard seed

2 teaspoons paprika
1 clove garlic, minced
1 bay leaf
1 teaspoon dried oregano,
   crushed
1 teaspoon chili powder
½ teaspoon freshly ground
   pepper
¼ teaspoon ground cloves
2 or 3 drops liquid smoke

Combine all ingredients, ¾ cup water, and ½ teaspoon salt. Mix well. Simmer gently till desired consistency, 15 to 20 minutes. Remove bay leaf. Use for basting grilled ribs or hamburgers. Makes 2 cups.

## Roasted Cinnamon Apples

Cut heavy foil into four 12-inch squares. Core 4 tart baking apples, enlarging center opening slightly. Place each on a piece of foil. Fill apples, using 1 tablespoon red cinnamon candies and 1 tablespoon raisins in each. Add 1 teaspoon water to each; dot with butter. Bring foil up loosely over apples; twist ends together. Cook directly on *medium-slow* coals, turning often, till done, 20 to 25 minutes. Serves 4.

## Cake Kabobs

Cut pound cake *or* angel cake into 1½-inch cubes. Spear cake cubes with fork. Dip cake in *either* ½ cup melted currant jelly; *or* ½ cup *sweetened condensed* milk; *or* a mixture of ½ cup honey and 1 tablespoon lemon juice. Roll cubes in 2 cups flaked coconut to coat. Thread on skewers; toast over *very hot* coals, turning often, till golden.

# Pancake Parade

Pancakes were a passion of the '50s. Pancake houses sprang up all over the country and transformed this simple breakfast food into a special treat any time of day. These restaurants featured elaborate main dish pancakes with meat and glamorous dessert pancakes as well as breakfast pancakes and waffles. The specialties were such hits that homemakers began making them at home. Here are just a few to sample.

*Your family will eagerly await breakfast when you serve Favorite Pancakes (pictured opposite). Top these fluffy, golden brown griddle cakes with pats of butter and plenty of syrup. Small sausages and steaming hot coffee round out the morning meal.*

## Mushroom-Sauced Luncheon Pancakes

1 cup all-purpose flour
2 teaspoons sugar
¾ teaspoon baking powder
½ teaspoon baking soda
2 beaten egg yolks
1¼ cups buttermilk
2 tablespoons butter or
  margarine, melted

2 stiffly beaten egg
  whites
• • •
Chicken Filling
Mushroom Sauce
¼ cup shredded process
  American cheese
  (1 ounce)

Stir together thoroughly flour, sugar, baking powder, soda, and ¼ teaspoon salt. Combine egg yolks, buttermilk, and melted butter or margarine; add to dry ingredients. Beat till smooth. Fold in stiffly beaten egg whites. Using 2 rounded tablespoons batter for each pancake, bake on hot, lightly greased griddle. Place about 1 tablespoon Chicken Filling on each pancake; roll up. Place pancakes, seam side down, in 12 x 7½ x 2-inch baking dish. Top with Mushroom Sauce. Sprinkle with cheese. Bake, covered, at 350° till hot, 20 to 25 minutes. Serves 6.

*Chicken Filling:* In saucepan melt 3 tablespoons butter or margarine. Stir in 3 tablespoons all-purpose flour and ½ teaspoon salt. Add 1⅓ cups chicken broth all at once. Cook broth mixture, stirring constantly, till thickened and bubbly. Reserve *half* of this mixture for Mushroom Sauce. Add 1½ cups chopped cooked chicken and ⅓ cup finely chopped celery to the remaining mixture.

*Mushroom Sauce:* Combine the reserved chicken broth mixture; one 3-ounce can sliced mushrooms, drained; and ¼ cup light cream. Heat mushroom sauce mixture to boiling.

## Favorite Pancakes

Stir together thoroughly 1¼ cups all-purpose flour, 3 teaspoons baking powder, 1 tablespoon sugar, and ½ teaspoon salt. Combine 1 beaten egg, 1 cup milk, and 2 tablespoons cooking oil; add to dry ingredients, stirring *just till moistened.* (For thinner pancakes, add 2 tablespoons more milk.) Bake on hot, lightly greased griddle using ¼ cup batter for each 4-inch pancake or 2 tablespoons batter for each dollar-size pancake. Makes eight 4-inch or 16 dollar-size pancakes.

## Cornmeal Pancakes

Stir together thoroughly 1½ cups all-purpose flour, ½ cup yellow cornmeal, 2 tablespoons sugar, 1 teaspoon baking soda, and 1 teaspoon salt. Add 2 cups buttermilk, 2 slightly beaten eggs, and 2 tablespoons butter or margarine, melted. Stir just till flour is moistened. Using ¼ cup batter for each pancake, bake on a hot, lightly greased griddle or electric skillet heated to 375°. Makes sixteen 4-inch pancakes.

*Back when circuses traveled to small towns, setting up the big top on the outskirts, the cook wagon baked pancakes six at a time for the roustabouts. To make the fire in the old iron cook stove hot enough, the cooks stoked it with corncobs and cord wood. The recipe was Favorite Pancakes, made light with extra baking powder.*

*Plain Jane pancakes Cinderella'd from silver-dollar size buckwheats with a side order of bacon and eggs into the glamour girl of the '50s. Variety, versatility, and setting accounted for it. In the Victorian elegance of San Francisco's Fairmont Hotel or Pancake Palace, and at Chicago's Palmer House all types of pancakes ranging from Sweden's egg-rich thin delicacies to Germany's crisp potato pancakes with applesauce were served. Native favorites at the Pancake Palace were best-seller buttermilk pancakes. Suitable for all occasions — breakfast, lunch, or dessert—pancakes had trappings of cherry sauce, flavored whipped cream, whipped orange butter, or syrups such as boysenberry or crème de menthe. One chef accounted for their popularity with the statement, "Pancakes stay happy even if they have to wait." He meant the batter, of course.*

## Palmer House Griddle Cakes

4 cups all-purpose flour
5 tablespoons sugar
3 tablespoons baking powder
3 beaten egg yolks
5 cups milk

3 stiffly beaten egg whites
¾ cup butter, melted
½ cup sugar
⅓ cup lemon juice
Cherry Sauce

Stir together thoroughly flour, 5 tablespoons sugar, baking powder, and 1 teaspoon salt. Combine egg yolks and milk; add to dry ingredients. Mix well. Fold in egg whites; stir in ¼ *cup* of the melted butter. Using ½ cup batter for each pancake, bake one at a time on hot, lightly greased griddle over low heat till golden brown. Turn and brown second side. Keep pancakes warm by placing in 250° oven on baking sheet; separate with double thickness paper toweling. To serve, brush *each* with ½ tablespoon melted butter. Sprinkle *each* with

*1 teaspoon* of sugar and 1 teaspoon lemon juice. Roll up and sprinkle *each* with ½ teaspoon of the remaining sugar. Place pancakes on a heat-proof platter; broil 4 to 5 inches from heat till sugar dissolves, 3 to 5 minutes. Serve with hot Cherry Sauce. Makes 16 pancakes.
*Cherry Sauce:* Drain one 20-ounce can frozen pitted tart red cherries, thawed, reserving 1 cup juice. Combine ¼ cup sugar and 4 teaspoons cornstarch; gradually stir in juice. Cook and stir over medium heat till thickened and bubbly. Stir in cherries; heat through.

## Pancake Oscar

1 cup all-purpose flour
3 teaspoons baking powder
1 teaspoon granulated sugar
1 slightly beaten egg
1¼ cups milk
6 tablespoons butter or margarine, melted

2 tablespoons packed brown sugar
Marshmallow Mix
•   •   •
1 10-ounce package frozen sliced strawberries, thawed

Stir together flour, baking powder, granulated sugar, and ¼ teaspoon salt. Combine egg, milk, and *2 tablespoons* of the melted butter; mix well. Add to dry ingredients; beat smooth. Using ⅓ cup batter for each pancake, bake on hot, lightly greased griddle. Brush each with some of the remaining melted butter; sprinkle each with some of the brown sugar. Stack pancakes. Top with Marshmallow Mix. Broil 3 to

4 inches from heat till golden. Cut stack into wedges and serve with strawberries. Makes 6 servings.
*Marshmallow Mix:* Combine ½ cup sugar and 2 tablespoons water; heat till sugar dissolves. Beat 2 egg whites till soft peaks form. Slowly pour sugar mixture over egg whites, beating constantly. Beat mixture till stiff peaks form. Cool slightly. Beat in 1 tablespoon butter or margarine, softened.

## Dessert Pancakes

1 cup all-purpose flour
Dash ground nutmeg
1 slightly beaten egg

1½ cups milk
Cherry jam *or* preserves
Sifted powdered sugar

Stir together thoroughly flour, nutmeg, and dash salt. Combine egg and milk; add to dry ingredients. Beat smooth. Using 2 tablespoons batter for each pancake, bake in

hot, greased crepe pan or 6-inch skillet, turning once. Spread *each* with 1 to 2 tablespoons jam; roll up. Sprinkle with powdered sugar. Makes sixteen 6-inch pancakes.

## Hot Mince Pancakes

1¼ cups all-purpose flour
2 teaspoons baking powder
1 slightly beaten egg
½ cup light cream

¼ cup milk
3 tablespoons cooking oil
1 cup prepared mincemeat
Orange Hard Sauce

Stir together thoroughly flour, baking powder, and ¼ teaspoon salt. Combine egg, cream, milk, and oil; stir into flour mixture, blending well. Stir in mincemeat. Using 1 rounded tablespoon batter for each pancake, bake on hot, lightly greased griddle about 1½ minutes on each side. Serve pancakes with Orange Hard Sauce. Serves 8.

*Orange Hard Sauce:* Cream ¼ cup butter; gradually add 1 cup sifted powdered sugar. Cream together till light and fluffy. Add ¼ teaspoon grated orange peel and 1 tablespoon orange juice; blend well.

## Blueberry Pancakes

2 cups all-purpose flour
2 tablespoons sugar
1 teaspoon baking soda
1 teaspoon salt
2 slightly beaten eggs
2 cups buttermilk

2 tablespoons butter or
  margarine, melted
• • •
1 15-ounce can blueberries,
  well drained
Whipped Orange Butter

Stir together thoroughly flour, sugar, baking soda, and salt. Add eggs, buttermilk, and melted butter; stir just till flour is moistened. Fold in blueberries. Using ¼ cup batter for each pancake, bake on hot, lightly greased griddle or electric skillet heated to 375°. Serve pancakes with Whipped Orange Butter. Makes 18 pancakes.

*Whipped Orange Butter:* Beat ½ cup butter, softened, till fluffy. Stir in 1 tablespoon powdered sugar and ¼ teaspoon grated orange peel.

## Apple Pancakes

2 cups all-purpose flour
2 tablespoons sugar
2 teaspoons baking powder
1 teaspoon salt
2 beaten eggs
1½ cups milk

2 tablespoons butter or
  margarine, melted
1 large apple, peeled and
  finely chopped (1 cup)
Hot applesauce *or*
  maple-flavored syrup

Stir together flour, sugar, baking powder, and salt. Mix eggs, milk, and butter; stir into dry ingredients. Stir in apple. Bake on hot, lightly greased griddle. Serve with applesauce or syrup. Makes 14.

## Jiffy Orange Pancakes

1 beaten egg
1 cup light cream
¾ cup frozen orange juice
  concentrate, thawed

1 cup pancake mix
1 cup sugar
½ cup butter or
  margarine

Combine beaten egg, cream, and ¼ *cup* of the orange juice concentrate. Add pancake mix; stir to remove most of the lumps. Bake batter on hot, greased griddle. Combine sugar, butter or margarine, and the remaining orange juice concentrate. Bring mixture to boiling, stirring occasionally. Serve warm sauce over pancakes. Makes 18.

*Much of the folklore about pancakes centers on Shrove Tuesday when women in Olney, England, hold a race. During this race, the women run to the Church of St. Peter and St. Paul, flipping their pancakes at least three times. The first woman to complete the course wins. In 1950 the town of Liberal, Kansas, challenged the town of Olney. Each year the two towns hold races at exactly the same time, with the pancake flipper with the best time chosen the cross-Atlantic winner. In other places in America, churches often hold pancake breakfasts on Shrove Tuesday at which pancakes are served with syrup and sausages.*

# Pastries and Pies

Pies were one of the favorite desserts of the '50s. This isn't surprising because there was a wide variety to choose from. In addition to the traditional apple or lemon pies, homemakers began serving double-flavor pies such as peach-orange or grape and red raspberry. Fluffy desserts were popular, too. The chiffon pie was a special favorite for ladies' luncheons everywhere. The biggest pie sensation of the decade, though, was the parfait pie. This entirely new kind of dessert was not only tasty, but easy and fun for the homemaker to make.

*"Four-and-twenty blackbirds baked in a pie" is an old fairy tale verse that may be more truth than fiction. The English word for a dish wrapped in a pastry crust, pie, is an abbreviated version of the word magpie. Scholars believe that pies were named after the birds because they were the first filling for pastry crusts.*

## Plain Pastry

*For one single-crust pie or 6 tart shells:*

| | |
|---|---|
| 1½ cups all-purpose flour | ½ cup shortening |
| ½ teaspoon salt | 4 to 5 tablespoons cold water |

*For one double-crust or lattice-top pie, or 8 tart shells:*

| | |
|---|---|
| 2 cups all-purpose flour | ⅔ cup shortening |
| 1 teaspoon salt | 5 to 7 tablespoons cold water |

Stir flour and salt together; cut in shortening with pastry blender till pieces are the size of small peas. (For extra-tender pastry, cut in *half* the shortening till like cornmeal. Cut in remaining shortening till like small peas.) Sprinkle 1 tablespoon water over part of mixture. Gently toss with fork; push to side of bowl. Repeat till all is moistened. Form into a ball. (For double-crust and lattice-top pies, divide dough for lower and upper crust and form into balls.) Flatten on lightly floured surface by pressing with edge of hand 3 times across in both directions. Roll from center to edge till ⅛ inch thick.

*To bake single-crust pie shells:* Fit pastry into pie plate; trim ½ to 1 inch beyond edge. Fold under and flute edge by pressing dough with forefinger against wedge made of finger and thumb of other hand. Prick bottom and sides well with fork. (If filling and crust are baked together, *do not prick*.) Bake at 450° till golden, 10 to 12 minutes.

*For double-crust pie:* Trim lower crust even with rim of pie plate. Cut slits in top crust. Lift pastry by rolling it over rolling pin; then unroll loosely over well-filled pie. Trim ½ inch beyond edge. Tuck top crust under edge of lower crust. Flute edge of pastry as desired.

If edge of crust browns too quickly, fold strip of foil around rim of crust, covering fluted edge.

*For lattice-top pie:* Trim lower crust ½ inch beyond edge of pie plate. Roll remaining dough ⅛ inch thick. Cut strips of pastry ½ to ¾ inch wide with pastry wheel or knife. Lay strips on filled pie at 1-inch intervals. Fold back alternate strips to center. Lay one strip crosswise. Return folded strips to original position. Repeat to complete lattice. Trim lattice even with outer rim of pie plate; fold lower crust over strips. Seal; flute edge.

## Graham Cracker Crust

Combine 1¼ cups finely crushed graham crackers, ¼ cup sugar, and 6 tablespoons butter, melted. Mix together thoroughly. Press firmly into 8- or 9-inch pie plate. Bake at 375° till edges are browned, 6 to 8 minutes; cool. For unbaked crust, chill 45 minutes; fill.

Refreshing is the word for cloud-light *Pineapple Parfait Pie* (see recipe, page 159). Hot coffee is the perfect complement for this tempting luncheon dessert.

Enjoy double-fruit flavor in *Peach-Orange Pie* (see recipe, page 156) with its delicately browned fluted lattice top. The flavor combination of peaches and oranges is doubly appealing.

## Peach-Orange Pie *(see photo, page 155)*

1 29-ounce can peach
    slices, drained
2 large oranges, peeled and
    sectioned (about ⅔ cup
    sections)
½ cup sugar

2 tablespoons all-purpose
    flour
Pastry for 9-inch
    lattice-top pie
2 tablespoons butter or
    margarine

In a bowl mix together drained peaches, orange sections, sugar, and flour. Line a 9-inch pie plate with pastry. Fill pastry shell with the peach mixture. Dot with butter or margarine. Adjust lattice top. Seal; flute the edge high. Bake the pie at 400° for 40 to 45 minutes.

## Pineapple-Rhubarb Pie

3 cups rhubarb, cut in
    ½-inch pieces
1 8¼-ounce can crushed
    pineapple, *undrained*
1¼ cups sugar
⅓ cup all-purpose flour

Dash salt
Pastry for 9-inch
    lattice-top pie
2 tablespoons butter
    or margarine

In a small bowl mix together the rhubarb pieces and undrained pineapple. Combine the sugar, flour, and salt; toss the mixture with the rhubarb and pineapple. Line a 9-inch pie plate with pastry. Turn the fruit mixture into the pastry shell. Dot the fruit with butter or margarine. Adjust lattice top; seal. Bake at 400° about 40 minutes.

## Grape and Red Raspberry Pie

*Two-fruit combinations were one of the pie-styles of the '50s. One special favorite was grape and red raspberry. This combination is not only delicious, it is a practical way to use precious red raspberries. These berries, which have always been popular in America, date back to the Swiss Glastonbury lake dwellings in Europe. The Greek writer Pliny prized them so much he recorded that they came only from Mt. Ida, Greece.*

2 cups seedless green
    grapes, halved *or* 2
    8¼-ounce cans light
    seedless grapes
2 10-ounce packages frozen
    red raspberries, thawed
    and drained

⅔ cup sugar
3 tablespoons all-purpose
    flour
Pastry for 2-crust
    9-inch pie
2 tablespoons butter
    or margarine

Drain canned grapes. Combine grapes, red raspberries, sugar, and flour. Line a 9-inch pie plate with pastry. Fill pastry shell with raspberry mixture. Dot with butter or margarine. Adjust top crust, cutting slits for escape of steam; seal. Bake at 400° for 40 to 45 minutes.

## Pineapple-Apricot Pie

2 cups dried apricots
Water
Pastry for 9-inch
    lattice-top pie
¾ cup sugar

1 tablespoon all-purpose
    flour
1 8¼-ounce can crushed
    pineapple, drained
1 tablespoon butter

Cover apricots with water; bring to boiling. Simmer gently, uncovered, till tender, 15 to 20 minutes. Drain. Line a 9-inch pie plate with pastry. Combine sugar and flour; sprinkle *1 tablespoon* mixture in pastry shell. Combine remaining mixture with drained apricots and pineapple. Toss mixture till fruit is coated. Turn into pastry shell; dot with butter. Adjust lattice top; seal. Bake at 425° for 40 to 45 minutes.

## Sour Cream-Apple Pie

1 slightly beaten egg
1 cup dairy sour cream
¾ cup granulated sugar
2 tablespoons all-purpose
   flour
1 teaspoon vanilla
¼ teaspoon salt

2 cups coarsely chopped,
   peeled tart apple
1 unbaked 8-inch pastry
   shell
3 tablespoons butter
⅓ cup packed brown sugar
⅓ cup all-purpose flour

Mix egg, sour cream, sugar, 2 tablespoons flour, vanilla, and salt. Add apple. Pour into pastry. Bake at 400° for 25 minutes. Melt butter; add brown sugar and flour. Sprinkle over pie. Bake 20 minutes.

*This Sour Cream-Apple Pie with streusel topping is typical of the Pennsylvania Dutch who make it with Summer Duchess apples just before they turn red. It was especially appealing to the tastes of the '50s because it combined an old favorite, apple pie, with a national rage, dairy sour cream.*

## Cranberry-Apple-Raisin Pie

Pastry for 2-crust
   9-inch pie
1⅓ cups sugar
1⅓ cups raisins
1⅓ cups finely chopped,
   peeled apple
1 8-ounce can jellied cranberry sauce, broken up

⅓ cup chopped walnuts
1 teaspoon grated lemon
   peel
3 tablespoons lemon juice
½ teaspoon salt
¼ teaspoon ground cinnamon
⅛ teaspoon ground cloves
⅛ teaspoon ground ginger

Line 9-inch pie plate with pastry. Combine remaining ingredients. Fill pastry shell with mixture. Adjust top crust, cutting slits for escape of steam; seal. Bake at 400° for 40 to 45 minutes. Serve warm.

## Chocolate Angel Pie

4 cups marshmallows
   (about 38)
1 cup milk
2 1-ounce squares unsweetened chocolate, cut up
1 teaspoon vanilla

⅛ teaspoon salt
1 cup whipping cream
½ cup chopped walnuts
1 *baked* 9-inch pastry
   shell, cooled
¼ cup shredded coconut

Heat marshmallows and milk over low heat till marshmallows are barely melted. Stir in chocolate, vanilla, and salt till chocolate melts. Cool. Whip cream. Fold into chocolate mixture with nuts. Chill till mixture mounds. Turn into pastry. Top with coconut. Chill.

## Lemon Eggnog Pie

2⅔ cups flaked coconut
3 tablespoons butter or
   margarine, melted
1 3-ounce package lemon-
   flavored gelatin
1 cup boiling water

1 pint vanilla ice cream
¾ teaspoon rum flavoring
¼ teaspoon ground nutmeg
2 well-beaten egg yolks
2 stiffly beaten egg whites

Combine coconut and melted butter; press into a buttered 9-inch pie plate, building up sides. Bake at 300° for 20 to 25 minutes. Cool.
   Dissolve gelatin in boiling water. Cut ice cream into sixths; add one-sixth at a time to gelatin and stir till melted. Chill till partially set. Add rum flavoring and nutmeg; stir in egg yolks. Fold in egg whites. Turn into cooled coconut shell. Chill the pie till firm.

## Caramel-Pecan Pie

1 envelope unflavored
  gelatin
¼ cup cold water
28 vanilla caramels
1¼ cups milk

1 teaspoon vanilla
1 cup whipping cream
½ cup chopped pecans
1 8-inch graham cracker
  crust

Soften unflavored gelatin in cold water. In heavy saucepan melt caramels in the milk over low heat, 20 to 30 minutes, stirring frequently. Add softened gelatin; stir till gelatin is dissolved. Stir in vanilla and dash salt. Chill till partially set. Whip cream. Fold whipped cream and pecans into gelatin mixture. Chill again till mixture mounds. Turn into graham cracker crust. Chill till firm.

## Maple-Nut Chiffon Pie

*Chiffon pie was invented by 16-year-old Monroe Strause. The son of a Los Angeles miller, Monroe went into business with an uncle who made cream pies. Not long afterwards, he began experimenting with pie fillings. Starting with French cream filling, he added beaten egg whites. Soon, his filling was so light that it nearly floated off the table. His mother commented that it looked like a pile of chiffon, and so chiffon pies were born.*

1 envelope unflavored
  gelatin
¼ cup cold water
¾ cup milk
½ cup maple-flavored syrup
⅛ teaspoon salt
2 beaten egg yolks

1 teaspoon vanilla
2 egg whites
¾ cup whipping cream
⅓ cup chopped walnuts
1 *baked* 9-inch pastry
  shell, cooled

Soften gelatin in cold water. Stir in milk, maple syrup, and salt. Heat till gelatin is dissolved. Stir a moderate amount of hot mixture into egg yolks; return to remaining hot mixture. Cook and stir till slightly thickened, 1 to 2 minutes more. Stir in vanilla. Chill till partially set. Beat egg whites till stiff peaks form; fold into gelatin mixture. Whip cream just to soft peaks; fold into maple mixture along with nuts. Chill again, if necessary, till mixture mounds. Turn into cooled pastry shell. Chill pie till firm, several hours or overnight.

## Pumpkin Ice Cream Pie

1 cup mashed, cooked pumpkin or canned pumpkin
½ cup packed brown sugar
½ teaspoon salt
½ teaspoon ground cinnamon
½ teaspoon ground ginger
¼ teaspoon ground nutmeg

1 quart vanilla
  ice cream
1 9-inch graham cracker
  crust
Whipped cream
Pecan halves

Combine pumpkin, brown sugar, salt, and spices. Stir vanilla ice cream to soften; then fold ice cream into pumpkin mixture. Turn into graham cracker crust. Freeze till firm. Remove from freezer about 15 minutes before serving. Garnish with whipped cream and pecans.

## Cranberry Chiffon Pie

Soften 1 envelope unflavored gelatin in ½ cup cold water. Stir over low heat till gelatin is dissolved. Mix with one 16-ounce can whole cranberry sauce, 1 teaspoon grated lemon peel, 1 tablespoon lemon juice, and dash salt. Chill till partially set. Beat 2 egg whites till soft peaks form; gradually add ¼ cup sugar. Continue beating till stiff peaks form. Fold into cranberry mixture. Pile into 1 *baked* 9-inch pastry shell, cooled. Chill till firm. Garnish with whipped cream.

## Peach Parfait Pie

3½ cups sliced peaches,
sweetened, *or* 1
29-ounce can peach
slices
1 3-ounce package lemon-
flavored gelatin

1 pint vanilla ice cream
• • •
1 *baked* 9-inch pastry
shell, cooled
½ cup whipping cream

If using fresh peaches, let stand about 15 minutes after mixing with sugar. Drain peaches (fresh or canned), reserving syrup.

Add water to syrup to make 1¼ cups; heat to boiling. Add gelatin; stir till gelatin is dissolved. Add ice cream by spoonfuls to hot liquid. Stir till melted. Chill till mixture mounds slightly when dropped from a spoon. Fold in peaches. Turn the peach filling into cooled pastry shell. Chill till firm. Whip cream. Top pie with whipped cream.

## Pineapple Parfait Pie *(see photo, page 155)*

1 8¼-ounce can crushed
pineapple
1 3-ounce package lemon-
flavored gelatin

1 pint vanilla ice cream
1 *baked* 8-inch pastry
shell, cooled
Whipped cream

Drain pineapple; reserve syrup. Add water to syrup to make 1¼ cups. Combine gelatin and syrup; bring to boiling. Stir till gelatin is dissolved. Remove from heat. Add ice cream by spoonfuls to hot liquid; stir till melted. Chill till partially set; fold in pineapple. Pile filling into pastry shell; chill till firm. Garnish with whipped cream.

## Party Parfait Pie with Coconut Shell

1 3½-ounce can flaked coconut (1⅓ cups)
2 tablespoons butter or
margarine, melted
1 10-ounce package frozen
red raspberries, thawed

Water
1 3-ounce package
raspberry-flavored
gelatin
1 pint vanilla ice cream

Combine coconut and butter. Press into an 8-inch pie plate. Bake at 325° for 15 minutes. Cool. Drain raspberries, reserving syrup. Add water to syrup to make 1¼ cups. In saucepan combine the gelatin and syrup mixture. Heat and stir till gelatin is dissolved. Remove from heat. Add ice cream by spoonfuls; stir till melted. Chill till mixture mounds. Fold in raspberries. Pour into coconut shell. Chill till firm.

## Orange-Coconut Parfait Pie

1 3-ounce package orange-
flavored gelatin
1¼ cups orange juice
1 pint vanilla ice cream
½ cup flaked coconut

1 *baked* 8-inch pastry
shell, cooled
¼ cup flaked coconut,
toasted

Combine gelatin and orange juice. Heat till gelatin dissolves. Add ice cream by spoonfuls; stir till ice cream is melted. Chill till partially set. Fold in the ½ cup flaked coconut. Turn mixture into cooled pastry shell. Garnish with ¼ cup toasted coconut. Chill pie till firm.

*Parfait pies, a trend-setter dessert of the '50s, originated in the United States as a promotion by a flour miller and a manufacturer of fruit-flavored gelatins. Single-crust concoctions with a fruit, gelatin, and ice cream filling, these pies were especially popular because they were so easy to make. Also, the large number of combinations of fruit and ice cream allowed for almost unlimited creativity. All of the pies on this page are just like their name— 'parfait' or perfect.*

# Good Eating during the Fifties

### Savory Snacks and Dips

Dips and snack mixes were the appetizers of the fifties. They were great then and they're great now.

### Time-Tested Main Dishes

Deciding on a main dish is sometimes a problem, but not with this group of delicious recipes to choose from.

### Vegetables with a Flair

Round out your meal with vegetable dishes made with Brussels sprouts, broccoli, cauliflower, or eggplant.

### Zesty Side-Dish Salads

Here are some salad ideas and recipes that will complement the flavor of almost any main dish you're planning.

### Bread and Sandwich Favorites

Delight your guests with any of these breads, rolls, or buns. The sandwiches are perfect for informal lunches.

### A Decade of Desserts and Sweets

Those of you with a sweet tooth will appreciate this assortment of cakes, puddings, refrigerator desserts, and candies. They'll give your family plenty of good eating.

Snacks and appetizers are more fun when you share them with friends. To start your next party, serve *Creamy Onion Dip* (see recipe, page 162), *Swedish Pickled Shrimp* (see recipe, page 162), and *Bridge Scramble* (see recipe, page 163).

# Savory Snacks and Dips

## Creamy Onion Dip *(see photo, page 160)*

1½ cups dairy sour cream
2 tablespoons dry onion
  soup mix
½ cup crumbled blue cheese

Sliced pimiento-stuffed
  green olives (optional)
Vegetable dippers

In mixing bowl combine dairy sour cream and dry onion soup mix. Mix until ingredients are thoroughly blended. Stir in crumbled blue cheese. Chill until ready to serve. Garnish with sliced olives, if desired. Serve dip with vegetable dippers. Makes 2 cups dip.

## Swedish Pickled Shrimp *(see photo, page 160)*

2 to 2½ pounds fresh or
  frozen shrimp in shells
Boiling water
½ cup celery leaves
¼ cup mixed pickling spices
2 cups sliced onion
7 or 8 bay leaves

1½ cups cooking oil
¾ cup white vinegar
3 tablespoons capers with
  juice
2½ teaspoons celery seed
3 drops bottled hot pepper
  sauce

In saucepan cover shrimp with boiling water; add celery leaves, pickling spices, and 1 tablespoon salt. Cover and simmer 5 minutes; drain. Peel and devein shrimp under cold water. Layer shrimp, onion, and bay leaves in shallow dish. Combine remaining ingredients and 1½ teaspoons salt; pour over shrimp. Cover and chill at least 24 hours, spooning marinade over shrimp occasionally. Serve in bowl over ice.

## Coral Shrimp Dip

1 cup cream-style cottage
  cheese
3 tablespoons chili sauce
2 teaspoons lemon juice
½ teaspoon Worcestershire
  sauce

½ teaspoon onion juice
1 4½-ounce can shrimp,
  drained and chopped
Milk
Potato chips, pretzels,
  *or* crackers

In blender container combine cream-style cottage cheese, chili sauce, lemon juice, Worcestershire, and onion juice. Blend mixture till smooth. Stir in shrimp; chill. (If needed, add milk for dipping consistency.) Serve with chips, pretzels, or crackers. Makes 1⅔ cups.

## Cheese-Nut Appetizers

2 3-ounce packages cream
  cheese, softened
½ cup crumbled blue cheese
  (2 ounces)
2 tablespoons mayonnaise
  or salad dressing

2 tablespoons finely
  chopped celery
1 tablespoon chopped onion
Dash cayenne
1 cup finely chopped
  walnuts

Beat together cheeses and mayonnaise. Stir in celery, onion, and cayenne; chill. Form into tiny balls; roll in nuts. Chill. Makes about 36.

## Chive Chip Dip

Mix 1 cup dairy sour cream, ⅓ cup mayonnaise, ¼ cup snipped chives, 1 tablespoon tarragon vinegar, ½ teaspoon salt, and dash white pepper. Chill. Serve with vegetable dippers or potato chips. Makes 1⅔ cups.

## Bridge Scramble *(see photo, page 160)*

6 cups puffed oat cereal
3 cups pretzel sticks
3 cups mixed salted nuts

½ cup butter, melted
1 envelope Parmesan salad
   dressing mix

In 13x9x2-inch baking pan heat cereal at 300° till warm, about 5 minutes. Remove from oven. Add pretzel sticks and mixed nuts. Pour the melted butter over mixture; sprinkle with salad dressing mix, stirring well. Heat mixture 15 to 20 minutes more. Makes about 12 cups.

*Scramble is one of the most famous appetizers of the '50s. Originally created for eating while playing scrabble, it was named scramble because of some difficulties with copyright laws.*

## East India Mix

2 tablespoons butter
3 cups bite-size shredded
   rice squares
1 cup salted peanuts

½ cup salted cashews
1 teaspoon curry powder
¼ teaspoon salt
¼ teaspoon ground cinnamon

In heavy skillet melt butter. Add remaining ingredients and dash pepper. Stir mixture constantly until cereal and nuts are heated through, about 5 minutes. Serve snack warm or cool. Makes 4½ cups.

## Crackle-Top Snack

1 8½-ounce package corn
   muffin mix
     • • •
1 cup chopped salted
   peanuts

½ cup grated Parmesan
   cheese
1 teaspoon garlic salt
3 tablespoons butter or
   margarine, melted

Prepare corn muffin mix according to package directions. Spread batter evenly in a well-greased and floured 15½x10½x1-inch baking pan. Sprinkle batter with salted peanuts, grated Parmesan cheese, and garlic salt. Drizzle melted butter over top. Bake at 375° till crisp and lightly browned, 18 to 20 minutes. Immediately cut into squares. Cool slightly; remove from pan. Serve warm. Makes 35 squares.

*TV viewing was the favorite home entertainment of the '50s. Along with it came the snack. In these mixtures all kinds of crisp cereals, nuts, herbs, and spices were tossed with melted butter and served around the TV set. Crackle-Top Snack was one of these delightful combinations that helped make snack time the fourth meal for many Americans.*

## Tricorn Snacks

2 packages refrigerated
   biscuits (10 biscuits
   each)
4 ounces braunschweiger
2 tablespoons chili
   sauce

2 tablespoons sweet pickle
   relish
1 tablespoon finely chopped
   green onion
1 teaspoon Dijon-style
   mustard

Roll each biscuit into a 3½- to 4-inch circle. Mix remaining ingredients. Place a generous teaspoon of braunschweiger mixture in the center of each circle. Moisten edges; bring sides up and pinch together, forming a triangular base. Place on greased baking sheet. Bake at 400° till done, 8 to 10 minutes. Serve warm or cool. Makes 20.

# Time-Tested Main Dishes

## Cheese and Mushroom Pizza

1 cup chopped onion
2 cloves garlic, minced
2 tablespoons cooking oil
1 15-ounce can tomato sauce
1½ teaspoons dried oregano, crushed
1 teaspoon dried thyme, crushed

1 13¾-ounce package hot roll mix
1 6-ounce package sliced mozzarella cheese
1 6-ounce can sliced mushrooms, drained
¼ cup grated Parmesan cheese

Cook onion and garlic in oil till onion is tender but not brown. Add tomato sauce, oregano, thyme, ½ teaspoon salt, and ⅛ teaspoon pepper. Bring to boiling; reduce heat and simmer till thick, about 15 minutes. Meanwhile, prepare hot roll mix, using *1 cup warm water and omitting egg.* Cover and let rest 10 minutes. *(Don't let rise.)* Divide dough in half. On lightly floured surface roll each half to a 12-inch circle. Place on greased pizza pan or baking sheet. Clip dough at 1-inch intervals around edge, and press so edge stands up slightly. Spread *half* of the sauce mixture on each circle. Top with mozzarella cheese slices and sliced mushrooms. Sprinkle with grated Parmesan cheese. Bake at 425° for 15 to 20 minutes. Serves 4 to 6.

Serve long-time favorite spicy *Lasagne* (pictured opposite) for your next company dinner. This delicious, layered main dish goes well with a crisp tossed green salad. *Cheese and Mushroom Pizza* (pictured opposite) will be well-received for any informal occasion. It's easy to fix, using hot roll mix for the crust.

## Speedy Pizza Pie

Prepare one 13¾-ounce package hot roll mix, using *1 cup warm water and omitting egg.* Cover; let rest 10 minutes. *(Don't let rise.)* Divide dough in half; roll each half to a 12-inch circle. Press dough into two greased pizza pans. Brush *each* with 1½ teaspoons cooking oil. Combine one 10¾-ounce can condensed tomato soup; ½ teaspoon dried oregano, crushed; ½ teaspoon dried thyme, crushed; and dash pepper. Spread *half* the sauce over each pizza. Using 3 cups shredded sharp process American cheese *or* mozzarella cheese, sprinkle *each* pizza with *half.* Using 8 ounces salami, chopped, sprinkle *each* pizza with *half.* Bake at 425° for 15 to 18 minutes. Serves 6.

*Pizza, a hearty hit of the '50s in America, was served in Naples as early as the sixteenth century. During this time, King Ferdinand, its biggest fan, commissioned a famous pizza chef to supply his court with pizza. It remained primarily an Italian favorite until soldiers returning from World War II brought it home to America. Soon, pizza was a sure-fire way to please guests at almost any party.*

## Lasagne

1 pound Italian sausage
1 16-ounce can tomatoes, cut up
2 6-ounce cans tomato paste
1 tablespoon dried basil, crushed
1 clove garlic, minced
10 ounces lasagne noodles
2 beaten eggs

3 cups ricotta *or* cream-style cottage cheese
½ cup grated Romano *or* Parmesan cheese
2 tablespoons dried parsley flakes
½ teaspoon pepper
16 ounces mozzarella cheese, very thinly sliced

Brown sausage slowly; drain off fat. Add tomatoes, tomato paste, basil, garlic, and 1½ teaspoons salt. Simmer, uncovered, 30 minutes; stir occasionally. Cook noodles in boiling, salted water till tender; drain. Combine remaining ingredients *except* mozzarella. Add 1 teaspoon salt. In 13x9x2-inch baking pan layer *half each* of the noodles, ricotta mixture, mozzarella, and meat mixture. Repeat layers. Bake at 375° for 30 minutes. Let stand 10 minutes. Serves 8 to 10.

*Ever since the first Beef
Stroganoff was created by
a French chef for a
Russian count in the late-
nineteenth century, many
variations of this popular
dish have been tried. One
is Greenbrier Beef
Stroganoff. Russian food
lovers claim, however, that
what Americans and
Europeans call Beef
Stroganoff is really an
imposter. The original
dish was made with a
mustard paste and sour
cream and was served on
thin potato strips.*

## Greenbrier Beef Stroganoff

1 pound beef tenderloin
3 tablespoons cooking oil
1½ cups sliced mushrooms
(4 ounces)

½ cup dry sherry
¼ cup beef broth
1 cup dairy sour cream
Hot cooked fine noodles

Cut beef tenderloin in ¼-inch-thick strips. In skillet heat cooking oil. Brown the meat quickly in oil, 2 to 4 minutes. Remove meat from skillet. Add sliced mushrooms and cook 2 to 3 minutes; remove mushrooms. Add sherry and beef broth to skillet; bring to boiling. Cook, uncovered, till liquid is reduced to ⅓ cup. Stir in dairy sour cream and ½ teaspoon salt; stir in meat and mushrooms. Cook slowly till heated through *(do not boil)*. Serve over hot cooked noodles. Makes 4 servings.

## Pepper Steak

1 pound boneless beef
sirloin tip, cut in
¼-inch slices
¼ cup chopped onion
1 clove garlic, minced
2 tablespoons cooking oil
1 cup hot water

1 teaspoon instant beef
bouillon granules
1 medium green pepper
1 16-ounce can tomatoes
2 tablespoons cornstarch
2 tablespoons soy sauce
Hot cooked noodles

Cook meat, onion, and garlic in hot oil till meat is browned. Sprinkle with ½ teaspoon salt and dash pepper. Add hot water and bouillon. Cover; simmer till meat is almost tender, 30 to 35 minutes. Slice green pepper into rings. Add green pepper and tomatoes to meat; cook 10 minutes. Blend cornstarch, soy, and ¼ cup cold water; stir into meat mixture. Cook and stir till thick. Serve over noodles. Serves 4.

*Although sauerkraut is
usually considered
German, it was originally
used in China where it
was fed to the workers on
the Great Wall to help
cure their dietary
deficiencies. Later, the
Tartars introduced
sauerkraut to eastern
Europe. From there it
traveled to Austria and
then to Germany where it
was named "saurkraut"
or "sour cabbage." Taste
the deliciousness of this
ancient food in Beef-
Sauerkraut Skillet.*

## Beef-Sauerkraut Skillet

Cook 1 cup chopped onion and ¾ cup chopped green pepper in 2 tablespoons butter or margarine till tender but not brown. Add 1½ pounds beef round steak, cut in 1-inch cubes; one 16-ounce can tomatoes, cut up; 1 tablespoon paprika; 2 teaspoons salt; 1 teaspoon caraway seed; 1 bay leaf; ½ teaspoon capers, drained; and ¼ teaspoon pepper. Cover; simmer about 1 hour. Add one 27-ounce can sauerkraut, drained. Simmer mixture, covered, 30 minutes. Remove from heat. Remove bay leaf. Stir in 1 cup dairy sour cream. Serves 6.

## Flank Steak with Sausage Stuffing

1½ to 2 pounds beef flank
steak
2 slightly beaten eggs
1 cup soft bread
crumbs
½ cup chopped onion

1 tablespoon snipped
parsley
1 teaspoon ground sage
½ pound bulk pork sausage
2 tablespoons cooking oil
1 8-ounce can tomato sauce

Pound steak thoroughly; score. Sprinkle with salt and pepper. Combine eggs, crumbs, onion, parsley, sage, ¼ teaspoon salt, and dash pepper. Mix in sausage; spoon onto steak. Roll up; secure with string. Brown in oil. Place, seam side down, in 11x7½x1½-inch baking pan. Spread with tomato sauce. Cover; bake at 350° about 1½ hours. Remove string. Skim fat from drippings; pass drippings. Serves 6.

## Dinner in a Pepper

8 large green peppers
1 pound ground beef
½ cup chopped onion
3 medium tomatoes, chopped
• • •
1 8-ounce can whole kernel
corn, drained

1 8-ounce can cream-style
corn
¾ teaspoon dried basil,
crushed
• • •
¾ cup soft bread crumbs
1 tablespoon butter, melted

Remove top and seeds from green peppers; chop enough of the tops to make ¼ cup. Cook whole green peppers in boiling water for 5 minutes; drain. Sprinkle the insides of peppers lightly with salt. In skillet cook ground beef, onion, and the ¼ cup chopped green pepper till meat is brown and vegetables are tender.

Add tomatoes; simmer till tomatoes are cooked, about 4 minutes. Drain. Add whole kernel and cream-style corn, basil, 1 teaspoon salt, and dash pepper. Stuff peppers with meat mixture. Toss crumbs with butter; sprinkle atop peppers. Bake in shallow baking dish at 350° for 35 to 40 minutes. Serves 8.

## Corned Beef Dinner *(see photo, page 171)*

1 3- to 4-pound corned beef
brisket
½ cup chopped onion
2 cloves garlic, minced
2 bay leaves
6 medium potatoes, peeled

6 medium carrots, peeled
6 cabbage wedges
Prepared mustard
¼ cup packed brown sugar
Dash ground cloves

In Dutch oven barely cover corned beef with hot water. Add chopped onion, minced garlic, and bay leaves. Cover; simmer till meat is tender, 3 to 4 hours. Remove meat from liquid. Add whole potatoes and carrots. Cover and bring to

boiling. Cook 10 minutes. Add cabbage; cook 20 minutes longer. Meanwhile, spread fat side of meat lightly with mustard. Combine brown sugar and cloves; sprinkle over meat. Bake in baking pan at 350° for 15 to 20 minutes. Serves 6.

*Corned Beef Dinner is a variation of the traditional New England boiled dinner. New England rumor has it that when men see a boiled dinner heaped on a large platter, it gives them confidence, and they feel that they are able to handle all the problems of life. While this recipe may not build your family's confidence, it's sure to cure any lagging appetites.*

## Meatballs Stroganoff

¾ cup finely crushed
saltine crackers
(20 crackers)
2 eggs
⅓ cup milk
Dash dried thyme, crushed
Dash dried oregano,
crushed
½ teaspoon salt
Dash pepper
• • •
1 pound ground beef

1 pound ground pork
1 tablespoon cooking oil
½ cup water
1 beef bouillon cube
1 cup dairy sour cream
½ cup water
1 6-ounce can sliced
mushrooms, drained
1 tablespoon all-purpose
flour
¼ teaspoon salt

Combine crackers, eggs, milk, thyme, oregano, ½ teaspoon salt, and pepper. Add ground meats; mix well. Form meat mixture into 1-inch balls. In skillet brown the meatballs in hot oil; drain off fat. Add ½ cup water and bouillon; stir

to dissolve bouillon. Cover and simmer 30 minutes. Remove meatballs from skillet; skim fat from drippings. Combine remaining ingredients. Stir into meat drippings. Return meatballs to skillet. Heat through. Serves 8 to 10.

## Fried Chicken *(see photo, page 170)*

⅓ cup all-purpose flour
2 teaspoons paprika
1 2½- to 3-pound ready-to-
cook broiler-fryer
chicken, cut up

3 to 4 tablespoons
shortening
1½ cups milk
3 tablespoons all-purpose
flour

Combine ⅓ cup flour, paprika, 1 teaspoon salt, and ¼ teaspoon pepper in paper bag. Add 2 to 3 pieces of chicken at a time; shake to coat. Place on rack to let coating dry. In skillet heat shortening till a drop of water sizzles. Brown chicken in hot shortening—meaty pieces first then remaining pieces (don't crowd). Brown one side; turn with tongs. Add additional shortening as needed. When chicken is lightly browned, 15 to 20 minutes, reduce heat; cover tightly. (If cover isn't tight, add 1 tablespoon water.) Cook chicken till tender, 30 to 40 minutes; uncover the last 10 minutes. Remove chicken. In screw top jar shake ¾ *cup* of the milk with 3 tablespoons flour, 1 teaspoon salt, and dash pepper till blended. Skim fat from pan drippings. Stir in flour mixture, scraping particles from pan. Add remaining milk; cook and stir till thick. Cook 3 minutes more; serve with chicken. Serves 4.

## Golden Paprika Chicken

*Paprika is ground from sweet, mild Capsicum peppers which are native to South America. Brought to Europe by Spanish explorers, paprika is made in two general types. One is the rose-colored spicy kind known as Hungarian paprika; the other is a milder and brighter red Spanish type, which is found in most American supermarkets. Either is great in all kinds of recipes including Golden Paprika Chicken.*

¼ cup all-purpose flour
2 teaspoons paprika
1½ teaspoons salt
1 2½- to 3-pound ready-to-
cook broiler-fryer
chicken, cut up

2 tablespoons cooking
oil
½ cup chopped onion
1 cup dairy sour cream
1 teaspoon grated lemon
peel

Combine flour, paprika, salt, and ⅛ teaspoon pepper in a paper or plastic bag. Add 2 or 3 chicken pieces at a time; shake to coat. Brown chicken in hot oil. Stir in onion and 1 cup water. Cover; simmer till chicken is tender, about 40 minutes. Remove chicken to warm platter. Stir sour cream and grated lemon peel into mixture in skillet. Heat through over low heat, stirring constantly. *Do not boil.* Season to taste with additional salt and pepper. Serve over chicken. Serves 4.

## Turkey Pie

10 to 12 tiny whole onions
½ cup chopped celery
2 tablespoons butter or
margarine
⅓ cup all-purpose flour
2 cups chicken broth
3 cups cubed cooked turkey

½ cup cooked peas
1 3-ounce can sliced
mushrooms, drained
1½ cups all-purpose flour
½ cup shortening
4 to 5 tablespoons cold
water

Cook onions and celery in butter till tender. Blend in the ⅓ cup flour. Add broth all at once. Cook and stir till thickened. Stir in turkey, peas, mushrooms, ½ teaspoon salt, and dash pepper. Heat through. Pour into 1½-quart casserole. For pastry, stir together 1½ cups flour and ½ teaspoon salt. Cut in shortening till pieces resemble small peas. Sprinkle water over, 1 tablespoon at a time, tossing gently with a fork till all flour is moistened. Roll pastry 2 inches larger than casserole. Adjust pastry atop turkey mixture; fold dough under to fit *inside* the rim. Press pastry against casserole dish with fork. Cut slits in pastry. Bake at 425° for 30 to 35 minutes. Serves 6 to 8.

## Ham Cornettes

1 cup all-purpose flour
2 teaspoons baking powder
½ teaspoon salt
⅛ teaspoon pepper
2 slightly beaten eggs
⅓ cup milk
1 tablespoon cooking oil
1 12-ounce can whole kernel
    corn, drained (1½ cups)

1 cup diced fully cooked
    ham
2 tablespoons chopped
    canned pimiento
2 tablespoons chopped green
    pepper
1 teaspoon grated onion
    Fat for frying
    Maple-flavored syrup

Stir together flour, baking powder, salt, and pepper. Mix eggs, milk, and oil; stir into dry mixture. Stir in remaining ingredients *except* fat and syrup. Carefully drop mixture from tablespoon into deep hot fat (375°). Fry 3 to 3½ minutes. Serve hot with syrup. Makes about 30.

*The next time you feed your family, try Ham Cornettes. This combination of ham, corn, and flour is a type of fritter. These come in all shapes and sizes. Some are made with puffy pastry, others with a yeast dough, and still others with a pancake-like mixture. Ham Cornettes fall in the pancake-batter group. They're ideal for informal dining.*

## Apple Pork Steaks *(see photo, page 171)*

6 pork steaks, cut ¾-inch
    thick (about 2 pounds)
2 tablespoons shortening

Raisin Stuffing
3 tart red apples, cored
1 tablespoon sugar

Slowly brown 3 steaks on both sides in hot shortening. Season well with salt and pepper. Place in shallow baking pan. Repeat with remaining steaks. Top each with a mound of Raisin Stuffing. Halve apples lengthwise; place atop stuffing. Sprinkle apple with sugar. Cover; bake at 350° about 1 hour. Serves 6.

*Raisin Stuffing:* Toss together 3 cups croutons, 1½ cups chopped unpeeled apple, ½ cup chopped celery, ½ cup chopped onion, ½ cup raisins, 1 teaspoon salt, 1 teaspoon poultry seasoning, and ¼ teaspoon pepper. Dissolve 1 beef bouillon cube in ½ cup boiling water; toss beef bouillon with the stuffing mixture.

## Curried Pork Chops

6 pork loin chops, cut
    ¾-inch thick (2 pounds)
1 tablespoon all-purpose
    flour

⅓ cup catsup
⅓ cup water
1½ teaspoons curry powder
1 teaspoon salt

Trim excess fat from chops. In skillet brown chops; reserve drippings. Place chops in 12x7½x2-inch baking dish. Sprinkle lightly with salt.

Combine reserved drippings and flour. Blend in the remaining ingredients; spoon atop chops. Cover and bake at 350° about 1 hour. Serves 6.

## Swiss Cheese and Onion Pie

6 slices bacon
1 cup chopped onion
¾ cup dairy sour cream
2 slightly beaten eggs
¼ teaspoon salt

12 ounces natural Swiss
    cheese, cut in ¼-inch
    cubes (2½ cups)
1 unbaked 9-inch pastry
    shell

Cook bacon till crisp. Drain; reserve drippings. Crumble bacon. Cook onion in drippings till tender but not brown; drain. Blend in sour cream, eggs, salt, and dash pepper.

Add cheese and bacon. Pour mixture into pastry shell. Bake at 375° till knife inserted off-center comes out clean, about 25 minutes. Serve pie at once. Makes 6 to 8 servings.

*Fried Chicken* (see recipe, page 168), one of the most popular family dishes, is perfect any time of the year. Carry along crisp, tender chicken, hot or cold, for a picnic, or fry up plenty for a family dinner. Use the chicken drippings to make a tasty cream gravy.

*Hot Crab Bake* (see recipe, page 172) in individual baking shells makes a distinctive and attractive seafood dish. The filling of crab meat, hard-cooked eggs, and pimiento is sprinkled with golden buttered crumbs and slivered almonds.

Serve *Apple Pork Steaks* (see recipe, page 169) for an impressive, yet easy-to-prepare oven main dish. Each steak is topped with a layer of raisin stuffing and a tart red apple half. Parsley makes a pretty garnish.

Hearty *Corned Beef Dinner* (see recipe, page 167) is almost a complete meal by itself. Corned beef simmers with onion and garlic, then bakes under a spiced mustard-brown sugar glaze. Potatoes, carrots, and cabbage round out this appetizing and hearty main dish.

## Chicken Divan

2 10- or 10½-ounce packages
    frozen cut asparagus
1 10½-ounce can condensed
    cream of chicken soup
1 teaspoon Worcestershire
    sauce
Dash ground nutmeg

½ cup grated Parmesan
    cheese
2 cups sliced cooked
    chicken
½ cup whipping cream
½ cup mayonnaise or salad
    dressing

Cook asparagus according to package directions; drain. Arrange in 12x7½x2-inch baking dish. Blend soup, Worcestershire, and nutmeg; pour *half* over asparagus. Sprinkle with *one-third* of the cheese. Top with chicken and remaining soup mixture. Sprinkle with another *one-third* of the cheese. Bake, uncovered, at 350° till heated through, about 20 minutes. Whip cream just till soft peaks form; fold in mayonnaise. Spread mixture over chicken. Sprinkle with remaining cheese. Broil 3 to 4 inches from heat till golden, 1 to 2 minutes. Serves 6.

## Deviled Shrimp

1 tablespoon chopped onion
1 tablespoon butter
1 tablespoon all-purpose
    flour
¾ cup milk
1 4½-ounce can shrimp,
    drained and halved

1 teaspoon prepared mustard
1 teaspoon Worcestershire
    sauce
3 English muffins, split
    and toasted
½ cup shredded process
    American cheese

Cook onion in butter till tender. Blend in flour. Add milk. Cook and stir till thickened and bubbly. Add shrimp, mustard, Worcestershire, and dash pepper; heat through. Spread mixture on muffins. Top with cheese. Broil till cheese melts, about 1½ minutes. Serves 6.

## Hot Crab Bake *(see photo, page 170)*

In skillet melt ¼ cup butter; blend in ¼ cup all-purpose flour. Add 2 cups milk all at once. Cook and stir quickly till thickened and bubbly. Add one 7½-ounce can crab meat, drained, flaked, and cartilage removed; ½ cup chopped canned pimiento; 2 hard-cooked eggs, chopped; 1 teaspoon salt; and ⅛ teaspoon pepper. Spoon mixture into 6 individual baking shells. Combine ½ cup fine dry bread crumbs and 2 tablespoons butter, melted. Sprinkle crumbs over crab mixture. Top with ¼ cup slivered almonds. Bake at 350° for 20 to 25 minutes. Serves 6.

## Red-Ribbon Cheese Casserole

1 7-ounce package macaroni
1 10¾-ounce can condensed
    tomato soup
1 10½-ounce can condensed
    cream of chicken soup
½ cup milk

8 slices process American
    cheese (8 ounces)
7 tomato slices
1 cup soft bread crumbs
2 tablespoons butter or
    margarine, melted

Cook macaroni according to package directions; drain. Mix soups and milk; add macaroni. Turn into 12x 7½x2-inch baking dish. Alternate cheese and tomato slices down center. Toss crumbs with butter; sprinkle atop casserole. Bake at 350° for 30 minutes. Serves 6 to 8.

## Potage Elegante

2½ to 3 pounds cracked
    beef soup bones
3 medium potatoes, peeled
    and cut in large pieces
    (about 3 cups)
3 medium carrots, coarsely
    chopped (about 1½ cups)
2 medium turnips, peeled
    and coarsely chopped
2 medium onions, quartered

½ cup snipped parsley
2 tablespoons butter
    or margarine
3 quarts water
4 teaspoons salt
    • • •
1 cup light cream
2 beaten egg yolks
    Grated Parmesan cheese
    Snipped parsley

Place soup bones in a shallow baking pan. Bake at 450° till browned, about 15 minutes. In large kettle cook potatoes, carrots, turnips, onions, and ½ cup parsley in butter till lightly browned. Add soup bones, water, and salt. Cover; simmer 1 hour. Remove any meat from bones; discard bones. Strain soup, reserving stock and vegetables. In blender puree vegetables. Combine stock, meat, and puréed vegetables. Boil gently until soup measures 2½ quarts. (Stock may be refrigerated 1 to 2 days.) Before serving, heat soup. Combine cream and egg yolks. Stir some of the hot soup into cream mixture. Return to soup. Cook till slightly thickened. Sprinkle with cheese and parsley. Serves 12.

*Potage Elegante is a French peasant soup that is flavorful enough to star at any dinner party. The secret that makes this hearty soup extra flavorful is browning the soup bones. A purée is made from the cooked vegetables and added along with egg yolks and cream. The final result is a rich, smooth delightful soup that would be the pride of any gourmet.*

## Cornmeal-Coated Franks

1 cup all-purpose flour
⅔ cup yellow cornmeal
2 tablespoons sugar
1½ teaspoons baking powder
2 tablespoons shortening
1 slightly beaten egg

¾ cup milk
1 pound frankfurters
    (8 to 10)
    Cooking oil
    Catsup
    Prepared mustard

Stir together thoroughly flour, cornmeal, sugar, baking powder, and 1 teaspoon salt. Cut in shortening till mixture resembles fine crumbs. Combine egg and milk. Add to dry mixture; blend well. Insert wooden skewer into the end of each frankfurter. Pour oil into skillet to depth of 1 inch; heat to 375°. Spread franks with batter. Fry in hot oil till brown, 3 to 4 minutes. Serve with catsup and mustard. Serves 4 or 5.

*To most Americans, Cornmeal-Coated Franks create long-forgotten images of kids having fun. They bring back memories of happy summer days spent at fairs and amusement parks. Traditionally, they hold a special place in American hearts along with other childhood favorites such as cotton candy, popcorn, ice cream cones with chocolate and nuts on them, and fruit-flavored slushes.*

## Roast Duck with Apple-Raisin Stuffing

1 4½- to 5-pound ready-to-
    cook frozen duckling,
    thawed
4 cups toasted bread cubes
    (9 slices bread)
2 cups chopped, peeled
    apple (4 apples)
½ cup raisins

⅓ cup sugar
¼ cup chicken broth
2 tablespoons butter or
    margarine, melted
1 teaspoon grated lemon
    peel
1 tablespoon lemon juice
½ teaspoon ground cinnamon

Remove wing tip and first joint from duckling. Sprinkle cavity with salt. Combine toasted bread cubes, apple, and raisins. Add sugar, chicken broth, melted butter, grated lemon peel, lemon juice, cinnamon, and ½ teaspoon salt; mix lightly. Stuff the duckling lightly with bread mixture. Prick skin all over. (Do not rub with oil.) Truss; place duckling, breast up, on rack in shallow baking pan. (Do not add water.) Roast, uncovered, at 375° for 1½ to 2 hours. If not brown, increase temperature to 425° and roast duckling 15 minutes more. Serves 3 or 4.

# Vegetables with a Flair

## Spiced Beets

*Spiced beets often play an important part in traditional Pennsylvania Dutch dinners. These dinners are planned around the idea of 'seven sweets and seven sours.' Also included among the dishes are such home-style favorites as spiced peaches, sweet potato relish, sauerkraut, homemade pickles, apple butter, fox-grape jelly, honey cake, and a variety of cakes, cookies, and pies.*

1 16-ounce can sliced beets
½ cup vinegar
¼ cup packed brown sugar

½ teaspoon ground cinnamon
¼ teaspoon salt
⅛ teaspoon ground cloves

Drain beets, reserving liquid. In saucepan combine reserved liquid, vinegar, brown sugar, cinnamon, salt, and cloves. Heat to boiling. Pour over beets; chill several hours or overnight. Makes 4 to 6 servings.

## Celery with Brussels Sprouts

1 10-ounce package frozen
Brussels sprouts
1½ cups sliced celery
4 tablespoons butter

3 tablespoons all-purpose
flour
1½ cups milk
¾ cup soft bread crumbs

Cook Brussels sprouts; drain. Cut sprouts in half. Meanwhile, cook celery in *3 tablespoons* of the butter till nearly tender but not brown. Blend in flour, ½ teaspoon salt, and dash pepper. Add milk; cook and stir till thickened and bubbly. Add sprouts. Turn into 1-quart casserole. Melt remaining butter; toss with crumbs. Sprinkle atop vegetables. Bake at 375° till bubbly, about 15 minutes. Makes 4 to 6 servings.

Begin with frozen vegetables to create elegant *Green Beans Supreme* and *Yogurt-Curry Sauce over Broccoli.* Sour cream and American cheese make the crumb-topped green bean casserole a delicious company dish. For a tempting flavor combination complement broccoli with tangy curry sauce.

## Green Beans Supreme

2 9-ounce packages frozen
   French-style green
   beans
1 small onion, sliced
1 tablespoon snipped
   parsley
2 tablespoons butter
2 tablespoons all-purpose
   flour

½ teaspoon grated lemon
   peel
½ cup milk
1 cup dairy sour cream
½ cup shredded process
   American cheese
   (2 ounces)
¼ cup fine dry bread crumbs
1 tablespoon butter, melted

Cook beans according to package directions; drain. Cook onion and parsley in 2 tablespoons butter till onion is tender. Blend in flour, lemon peel, ½ teaspoon salt, and dash pepper. Add milk; cook and stir till thickened and bubbly. Stir in sour cream and beans; heat till bubbly. Spoon into 1-quart casserole. Top with cheese. Mix crumbs and 1 tablespoon butter; sprinkle atop beans. Broil 4 to 5 inches from heat till cheese melts and crumbs brown, 1 to 2 minutes. Serves 8.

## Cauliflower with Cheese-Mushroom Sauce

Remove leaves and all of woody base from 1 medium head cauliflower. Separate into flowerets. Cook, covered, in a very small amount of boiling salted water till tender, 10 to 15 minutes. Drain well. Cook 1½ cups sliced mushrooms (4 ounces) in 2 tablespoons butter or margarine till tender. Blend in 2 tablespoons all-purpose flour. Add 1 cup milk. Cook and stir till thickened and bubbly. Stir in 1 cup shredded sharp process American cheese, ¼ teaspoon salt, and dash pepper. Heat till cheese melts. Serve over cauliflower. Serves 6.

## Yogurt-Curry Sauce over Broccoli

1 8-ounce carton plain
   yogurt (1 cup)
1 tablespoon prepared
   mustard
1 teaspoon seasoned salt

½ to 1 teaspoon curry
   powder
• • •
2 10-ounce packages frozen
   broccoli spears, cooked

Thoroughly combine yogurt, mustard, seasoned salt, and curry powder. Chill well. Serve over warm or cold cooked broccoli. Serves 6 to 8.

## Eggplant Casserole

1 medium eggplant, peeled
⅓ cup cooking oil
1½ cups chopped onion
2 tablespoons cooking oil
2 cups chopped green pepper
½ cup sliced pitted ripe
   olives

1½ cups shredded sharp
   process American
   cheese (6 ounces)
1 8-ounce can tomato sauce
1 cup soft bread crumbs
2 tablespoons butter or
   margarine, melted

Cut eggplant into ½-inch cubes. Cook in ⅓ cup oil till tender. Remove; drain. Cook onion in 2 tablespoons oil till tender. Add green pepper, olives, and ½ teaspoon *each* salt and pepper. Put *half* the eggplant in 1½-quart casserole. Add *half* the olive mixture and *half* the cheese. Repeat layers. Pour tomato sauce over. Mix crumbs with butter; sprinkle atop. Bake at 375° for 30 to 35 minutes. Serves 6 to 8.

*Americans love cheese — especially when it's used in a recipe such as Cauliflower with Cheese-Mushroom Sauce. Cheesemaking has always been a prosperous American industry, starting way back with small farm operations. Farmhouse cheesemakers, trying to preserve the abundance of milk resulting from spring's green pastures, started the cheesemaking industry in the United States. When these Yankee dairymen migrated beyond the eastern mountains, they took their knowledge of English Cheddaring with them. It soon was in such common usage that it became known as American cheese. By 1851, the first modern cheese factory was built on the Erie Canal in Herkimer County, New York. American cheese factories were off and running. And our taste for cheese has kept cheese factories going ever since.*

# Zesty Side-Dish Salads

## Strawberry Soufflé Salads

1 10-ounce package frozen
    sliced strawberries,
    thawed
1 3-ounce package
    strawberry-flavored
    gelatin

1 cup boiling water
2 tablespoons lemon juice
¼ cup mayonnaise
¼ cup chopped walnuts
    Lettuce
    Canned pineapple slices

Drain berries, reserving syrup. Add water to syrup to make ¾ cup. Dissolve gelatin and ¼ teaspoon salt in boiling water. Add reserved syrup and lemon juice. Beat in mayonnaise. Chill till partially set. Whip with electric mixer till fluffy. Fold in berries and nuts. Pour into individual molds. Chill till set. Unmold on lettuce-lined platter atop pineapple. Serve with additional mayonnaise, if desired. Serves 4 to 6.

Include individually molded *Strawberry Soufflé Salads* (pictured opposite) when planning the menu for your next luncheon. Lemon juice accents the strawberry flavor of frozen berries and strawberry-flavored gelatin.

## Company Salad Bowl with Garlic Dressing

2 heads Boston lettuce,
    torn in bite-size
    pieces (4 to 5 cups)
4 cups torn leaf lettuce
3 medium tomatoes, cut in
    wedges
2 7-ounce cans artichoke
    hearts, drained and
    cut up
2 avocados, peeled and
    sliced

2 hard-cooked eggs, sliced
    • • •
¾ cup salad oil
¼ cup vinegar
1 clove garlic, minced
¼ teaspoon white pepper
¼ teaspoon celery salt
¼ teaspoon dry mustard
    Several dashes bottled
      hot pepper sauce

In salad bowl combine torn greens. Arrange tomatoes, artichoke pieces, avocado slices, and egg slices on top of greens. Chill. In screw-top jar combine salad oil, vinegar, garlic, white pepper, celery salt, dry mustard, bottled hot pepper sauce, and 1 teaspoon salt. Cover and shake dressing vigorously. Toss salad with dressing. Makes 10 to 12 servings.

*Garlic is one of the most fascinating of all herbs. It was rumored to have grown up in the place where Satan's left foot touched as he fled from the Garden of Eden. Through the ages, garlic has been used in many ways. The ancient Egyptians offered it to their gods. The Chinese thought it increased intelligence, and Roman soldiers ate it for greater courage. Today, this flavorful herb is used for more ordinary purposes such as adding zip to Company Salad Bowl with Garlic Dressing.*

## Spinach-Cottage Cheese Salad

1 3-ounce package lemon-
    flavored gelatin
1 cup boiling water
½ cup cold water
1 tablespoon vinegar
¼ teaspoon salt
    Dash pepper
½ cup mayonnaise or salad
    dressing
1 cup chopped fresh spinach

¾ cup small curd cream-
    style cottage cheese
⅓ cup chopped celery
2 tablespoons chopped
    canned pimiento
1 tablespoon finely chopped
    onion
    Spinach leaves
    (optional)

Dissolve lemon-flavored gelatin in boiling water. Stir in cold water, vinegar, salt, and pepper. Beat in mayonnaise or salad dressing. Chill till partially set. Whip gelatin mixture with electric mixer till fluffy. Fold in chopped spinach, cottage cheese, celery, pimiento, and onion. Pour salad mixture into 4-cup mold. Chill till firm. Unmold. Serve salad on fresh spinach leaves, if desired. Makes 4 to 6 servings.

## Original Caesar Salad

Garlic Olive Oil
Caesar Croutons
3 medium heads romaine, chilled and broken into 2- or 3-inch widths
2 to 3 tablespoons wine vinegar
1 lemon, halved

1 or 2 1-minute coddled eggs
Dash Worcestershire sauce
Whole black pepper
6 tablespoons grated Parmesan cheese
Rolled anchovy fillets (optional)

One or more days before serving, prepare Garlic Olive Oil. Several hours before serving, prepare Caesar Croutons. At serving time, place romaine in *chilled* salad bowl. Drizzle with about ⅓ cup Garlic Olive Oil, then vinegar. Squeeze lemon over; break in eggs. Season with Worcestershire and salt. Grind pepper over; sprinkle with cheese. Toss lightly till dressing is well combined and romaine is coated. Add about 1 cup Caesar Croutons; toss once or twice. Serve immediately on *chilled* dinner plates. Garnish with anchovies, if desired. Serves 6 to 8.

*Garlic Olive Oil:* Slice 6 cloves garlic lengthwise in quarters; let stand in 1 cup olive or salad oil.

*Caesar Croutons:* Cut 3 slices of bread into ¾-inch cubes. Spread out on baking sheet; pour a little Garlic Olive Oil over bread. Heat at 225° about 2 hours. Sprinkle with grated Parmesan cheese. Store croutons, covered, in jar in refrigerator.

## Tomato-Egg Salad Star

4 medium tomatoes, cored
Seasoned salt
4 hard-cooked eggs, chopped
⅓ cup chopped, seeded cucumber

¼ cup chopped green pepper
2 tablespoons chopped green onion
¼ cup mayonnaise or salad dressing

Cut each tomato into six wedges, *cutting to, but not through* base. Pull apart slightly. Sprinkle cut surfaces with seasoned salt. Combine remaining ingredients. Spoon into centers of tomatoes. Serves 4.

## Buttermilk Coleslaw

¼ cup mayonnaise or salad dressing
¼ cup buttermilk
2 tablespoons vinegar
½ teaspoon salt

⅛ teaspoon Worcestershire sauce
Dash paprika
1 medium head cabbage, shredded (8 cups)

Combine mayonnaise or salad dressing, buttermilk, vinegar, salt, Worcestershire sauce, and paprika. Toss with cabbage. Serves 8 to 10.

## Spiced Peaches

1 29-ounce can peach halves
¼ cup sugar
1 tablespoon vinegar

6 inches stick cinnamon
½ teaspoon whole cloves
¼ cup brandy (optional)

Drain peaches; reserve syrup. Combine reserved syrup, sugar, vinegar, stick cinnamon, and cloves. Simmer, uncovered, 5 minutes. Add peaches; heat through. Cool. Stir in brandy, if desired. Store, covered, in refrigerator at least 48 hours before serving. Remove spices.

## Perfect Potato Salad

3 cooked potatoes, peeled,
    quartered, and sliced
    (3 cups)
1 teaspoon sugar
1 teaspoon vinegar
½ cup sliced celery
⅓ cup finely chopped onion

¼ cup chopped sweet pickle
1 teaspoon salt
1 teaspoon celery seed
¾ cup mayonnaise or salad
    dressing
• • •
2 hard-cooked eggs, sliced

In bowl sprinkle potatoes with sugar and vinegar. Add celery, onion, sweet pickle, salt, and celery seed. Add mayonnaise or salad dressing; toss to blend. Carefully fold in sliced eggs. Chill. Serves 4.

*Potatoes are traditional American favorites. One person who really liked them was Henry Ford — so much so that he had an 80-acre potato patch. He specialized in whoppers such as the two-pound Early Ohios he proudly displayed in the magazine. Over the years, potato lovers have devised many great recipes to use their potatoes. One is Perfect Potato Salad.*

## Orange and Green Salad

¼ pound spinach, torn in
    bite-size pieces
    (3 cups)
¼ bunch curly endive, torn
    in bite-size pieces
    (2 cups)
2 large oranges, peeled and
    sectioned (1½ cups)

1 small onion, thinly
    sliced
½ clove garlic, minced
6 tablespoons salad oil
2 tablespoons tarragon
    vinegar
1 teaspoon sugar
1 teaspoon paprika

Toss together torn spinach, torn curly endive, orange sections, and onion slices. Chill. In screw-top jar combine minced garlic, salad oil, tarragon vinegar, sugar, paprika, and 1 teaspoon salt. Cover and shake well. Pour dressing over the salad and toss lightly. Serves 6.

## Cherry-Grape Mold

⅔ cup sugar
2 envelopes unflavored
    gelatin
¼ teaspoon salt
1 6-ounce can frozen grape
    juice concentrate,
    thawed

2¼ cups water
⅓ cup lemon juice
1 17-ounce can pitted light
    sweet cherries, drained
    and halved
½ cup chopped celery
¼ cup chopped walnuts

Combine sugar, unflavored gelatin, and salt. Add grape juice concentrate; stir in water. Heat until gelatin is dissolved. Stir in lemon juice. Chill till partially set. Stir cherries, celery, and nuts into gelatin mixture. Pour mixture into 5½-cup mold. Chill till firm. Serves 8 to 10.

## Savory Herb Dressing

¾ cup salad oil
⅓ cup wine vinegar
2 teaspoons chopped pitted
    ripe olives
2 teaspoons chopped sweet
    pickle
1 teaspoon snipped chives

1 teaspoon snipped
    parsley
1 teaspoon salt
1 teaspoon dried tarragon,
    crushed
¼ teaspoon pepper

In screw-top jar combine salad oil, wine vinegar, olives, sweet pickle, chives, parsley, salt, tarragon, and pepper. Cover and shake vigorously. Serve dressing over mixed salad greens. Makes 1¼ cups dressing.

*Tarragon lends a distinctive flavor to many foods. This licorice-flavored herb is one of the fines herbes, and it blends well with tomatoes, egg dishes, fish, and salads. Tarragon is at its finest in Savory Herb Dressing.*

# Bread and Sandwich Favorites

## Crusty Cheese Squares

Cut crusts from top and sides of 1 loaf unsliced white bread. Trim top, if uneven. Make eight cuts crosswise and one cut lengthwise down the center of loaf *cutting to but not through* bottom crust. Blend ½ cup butter, softened, and two 5-ounce jars sharp process American cheese spread. Spread between every other slice and over top and sides of bread. Sprinkle top with poppy seed. Tie twine or heavy string around loaf to hold it together. Place on 15½x 10½x1-inch baking pan. Bake at 400° till cheese melts, 15 to 20 minutes. Makes 18 slices.

## Hot Cross Buns

*Hot Cross Buns are small yeast rolls with the shape of a cross snipped or frosted on the top. This Easter specialty has been a favorite of homemakers through the years, and* Better Homes and Gardens *has published it time and again with happy results. It's sure to be your favorite, too.*

3½ to 4 cups all-purpose
   flour
2 packages active dry yeast
½ to 1 teaspoon ground
   cinnamon
¾ cup milk

½ cup cooking oil
⅓ cup sugar
3 eggs
⅔ cup dried currants
1 slightly beaten egg white
   Frosting

In mixer bowl combine *2 cups* of the flour, yeast, and cinnamon. Heat milk, oil, sugar, and ¾ teaspoon salt till warm (115° to 120°). Add to dry mixture; add eggs. Beat at low speed of electric mixer for ½ minute, scraping bowl. Beat 3 minutes at high speed. By hand, stir in currants and enough remaining flour to make a soft dough. Shape into ball. Place in greased bowl; turn once. Cover; let rise in warm place till double (about 1½ hours). Punch down. Cover; let rest 10 minutes.

Divide in 18 pieces; form into balls. Place on greased baking sheet 1½ inches apart. Cover; let rise till double (30 to 45 minutes). Cut shallow cross in each; brush tops with egg white (reserve remaining). Bake at 375° for 12 to 15 minutes. Using pastry tube, pipe on crosses with Frosting. Makes 18 buns.

*Frosting:* Mix 1½ cups sifted powdered sugar, reserved egg white, ¼ teaspoon vanilla, and dash salt till smooth. Add milk, if necessary, to make of piping consistency.

## Batter Rolls

3 cups all-purpose flour
2 packages active dry yeast
½ teaspoon ground cinnamon
1¼ cups water
⅓ cup granulated sugar
⅓ cup shortening
1 teaspoon salt

1 egg
2 tablespoons grated orange
   peel
1 cup raisins
   • • •
1 cup sifted powdered sugar
1 to 2 tablespoons milk

In mixer bowl combine *1½ cups* of the flour, yeast, and cinnamon. Heat water, sugar, shortening, and salt just till warm (115° to 120°), stirring constantly to melt shortening. Add to dry mixture; add egg and peel. Beat at low speed of electric mixer for ½ minute, scraping bowl constantly. Beat 3 minutes at high speed. By hand, stir in remaining flour and raisins. Stir till flour is blended in. Cover; let rise in warm place till almost double (40 to 45 minutes). Stir down. Fill greased muffin pans ⅔ full. Let rise till almost double (about 25 minutes). Bake at 425° for 10 to 15 minutes. Cool slightly. Combine powdered sugar and milk; dip tops of rolls in icing. Makes 22 rolls.

Pull apart the sections of *Crusty Cheese Squares* and enjoy their tangy toasted cheese flavor. These golden squares are easy to prepare for a quick meal accompaniment or tasty midafternoon snack to serve with milk.

Plan to make cinnamon-spiced *Hot Cross Buns* a special part of your Easter morning breakfast or brunch menu. Piped-on frosting crosses add a decorative touch to these currant-filled buns.

## Brioche

1 package active dry yeast
½ cup butter or margarine
⅓ cup sugar
½ teaspoon salt

3½ cups all-purpose flour
½ cup milk
4 eggs
1 tablespoon sugar

Soften yeast in ¼ cup *warm* water (110°). Thoroughly cream butter, ⅓ cup sugar, and salt. Add *1 cup* of the flour and the milk to creamed mixture. Beat 3 eggs and 1 egg yolk together *(reserve egg white)*. Add softened yeast and beaten eggs to creamed mixture; beat well. Add remaining flour. By hand, beat for 5 to 8 minutes. Cover; let rise in warm place till double (about 2 hours). Stir down; beat well. Cover; chill overnight. Stir down; turn out on floured surface. Set aside ¼ of dough. Cut remaining dough into 6 pieces; form *each* into 4 balls. With floured hands, tuck under cut edges. Place in greased muffin pans. Cut reserved dough in 4 wedges; divide *each* into 6 pieces; shape into 24 balls. Make indentation in each large ball; brush with water. Press small balls into indentations. Cover; let rise till double (about 30 minutes). Slightly beat reserved egg white and mix with 1 tablespoon sugar; brush on tops. Bake at 375° about 15 minutes. Makes 24 rolls.

## Sugar-Cinnamon Loaf

3½ cups all-purpose flour
1 package active dry yeast
1¼ cups milk
¼ cup sugar
¼ cup shortening
1 teaspoon salt
1 egg

1 tablespoon milk
¼ cup sugar
1 teaspoon ground cinnamon
   Butter or margarine,
   melted
1½ tablespoons sugar
½ teaspoon ground cinnamon

In mixer bowl combine *1½ cups* of the flour and the yeast. Heat 1¼ cups milk, ¼ cup sugar, shortening, and salt just till warm (115° to 120°), stirring constantly. Add to dry mixture; add egg. Beat at low speed of electric mixer for ½ minute, scraping bowl constantly. Beat 3 minutes at high speed. By hand, stir in remaining flour. Knead lightly. Place in greased bowl; turn once. Let rise in warm place till almost double (about 1½ hours). Punch down. Turn out on floured surface. Cover; let rest 10 minutes. Roll to 18x7-inch rectangle. Brush with 1 tablespoon milk; sprinkle with ¼ cup sugar and 1 teaspoon cinnamon. Roll as for jelly roll, starting at small end. Seal edges. Place in a greased 9x5x3-inch loaf pan. Let rise till almost double (about 1 hour). Brush with butter; sprinkle with 1½ tablespoons sugar and ½ teaspoon cinnamon. Bake at 375° for 30 minutes. Makes 1.

## Onion-Cheese Supper Bread

½ cup chopped onion
3 tablespoons butter or
   margarine
½ cup milk
1 slightly beaten egg

1½ cups packaged biscuit mix
1 cup shredded sharp
   process American cheese
   (4 ounces)
1 tablespoon poppy seed

Cook onion in *1 tablespoon* of the butter till tender. Mix milk and egg. Add to biscuit mix; stir only till moistened. Add onion, and *half each* of the cheese and poppy seed. Spread in greased 8x1½-inch round baking dish. Sprinkle with remaining cheese and poppy seed. Melt remaining butter; drizzle atop. Bake at 400° about 20 minutes. Serves 8.

## Submarine Sandwich

Bake one giant brown-and-serve French roll (about 8 inches long) according to package directions. Split roll lengthwise, *cutting to but not through* bottom crust. Scoop out some of the center. Spread roll generously with prepared mustard, garlic butter, *or* mayonnaise mixed with curry powder. Line the bottom of roll with leaf lettuce. Pile on slices of corned beef, boiled ham, bologna, salami, pickled tongue, chicken, tuna, and herring as desired. Add slices of process American and Swiss cheese, onion, green and ripe olives, and dill pickle. Replace top of roll; anchor sandwich with wooden picks. Makes 1 serving.

## Bun-Steads

1 cup shredded process
   American cheese
1 6½- or 7-ounce can tuna,
   drained and flaked
½ cup mayonnaise
3 hard-cooked eggs, chopped
2 tablespoons chopped green
   pepper

2 tablespoons chopped onion
2 tablespoons chopped
   pimiento-stuffed green
   olives
2 tablespoons chopped sweet
   pickle
1 teaspoon prepared mustard
8 frankfurter buns, split

Combine cheese, tuna, mayonnaise, hard-cooked eggs, green pepper, onion, green olives, sweet pickle, and mustard. Divide mixture among frankfurter buns. Wrap each sandwich in foil. Heat at 300° till filling is hot, 25 to 30 minutes. Makes 8 sandwiches.

## Grilled Pizza Sandwiches

⅔ cup canned pizza sauce
8 slices white bread
8 small or 4 large slices
   salami

2 slices mozzarella cheese
   Dried oregano, crushed
   Butter or margarine,
   softened

Spread pizza sauce on one side of each bread slice. Top four slices of bread with 2 small or 1 large salami slice. Halve mozzarella cheese slices; place atop salami. Sprinkle lightly with oregano. Top with remaining bread slices, sauce side down. Spread butter generously on top and bottom of sandwiches. Grill both sides on griddle, sandwich grill, or in a skillet until sandwiches are toasted and cheese is melted, about 5 minutes on *each* side. Makes 4 sandwiches.

## Banana-Apricot Bread

⅓ cup shortening
⅔ cup sugar
2 eggs
1 cup mashed ripe banana
   (2 medium)
¼ cup buttermilk
1¼ cups all-purpose flour

1 teaspoon baking powder
½ teaspoon baking soda
½ teaspoon salt
1 cup whole bran cereal
¾ cup snipped dried
   apricots
½ cup chopped walnuts

Cream shortening and sugar. Add eggs and beat thoroughly. Combine mashed banana and buttermilk. Stir together thoroughly flour, baking powder, soda, and salt; add alternately with banana mixture to creamed mixture. Stir in bran, apricots, and nuts. Pour into greased 9x5x3-inch loaf pan. Bake at 350° for 50 to 60 minutes. Makes 1 loaf.

*On the West Coast it's called a Submarine Sandwich, a Hero on the East, and to many people all over, it's known as the Dagwood Bumstead, but it originated in a sandwich shop nestled among the wharfs of New Orleans where it's called a Poor Boy. Benny and Clovis Martin can take the credit for providing us with this substantial sandwich. Wishing to serve their regular customers — banana carriers and longshoremen — during the depression, they came up with a specially baked French bread (not really French, but long and thin and with little dough in the middle) on which they could ladle some roast beef or ham. It was a cheap, filling, and nutritious lunch for the hard-working wharf workers during years when money wasn't too available. In the '50s, that single layer of meat became alternate layers of meat, cheese, relish, and whatever is left over in the refrigerator, as popularized by the comic strip character, Dagwood Bumstead. But whatever you call it, this type of sandwich is guaranteed to fill the emptiest stomach.*

# A Decade of Desserts and Sweets

## Cheesecake Supreme

*The Cheesecake Supreme (pictured opposite), with five 8-ounce packages of cream cheese, similar to the famous Strawberry-Crowned Lindy's Cheesecake, which Broadwayites enjoyed after theater performances for many years, almost never made it into* Better Homes and Gardens. *It is so expensive that the food editor, Myrna Johnston, decided against it. However, she did decide to make one and take it to a friend who was sick. At the bedside, she met the Chairman of the Board, Fred Bohen, who sampled the cake. "Why not use this in the magazine?" he asked. "Because it's too expensive," Myrna said. "With a taste like this who cares about expense," Mr. Bohen replied. Once you've tasted this exquisite delight, you'll be glad the boss took that one bite.*

1 cup all-purpose flour
¼ cup sugar
1 teaspoon grated lemon peel
½ cup butter or margarine
1 slightly beaten egg yolk
¼ teaspoon vanilla
• • •
5 8-ounce packages cream cheese, softened
¾ teaspoon grated lemon peel
¼ teaspoon vanilla
1¾ cups sugar
3 tablespoons all-purpose flour
¼ teaspoon salt
4 large eggs
2 egg yolks
¼ cup whipping cream
Cherry Sauce *or* Strawberry Glaze (see photo, pages 6-7)

For crust combine 1 cup flour, ¼ cup sugar, and 1 teaspoon grated lemon peel. Cut in butter till crumbly. Add 1 slightly beaten egg yolk and ¼ teaspoon vanilla; mix well. Pat ⅓ of the dough on bottom of a 9-inch springform pan (sides removed). Bake at 400° about 8 minutes. Cool. Butter sides of springform pan; attach to the bottom. Pat remaining dough on sides of pan to a height of 1¾ inches.

For filling, beat cream cheese till creamy; add ¾ teaspoon grated lemon peel and ¼ teaspoon vanilla. Combine 1¾ cups sugar, 3 tablespoons flour, and ¼ teaspoon salt; gradually blend into cheese mixture. Add eggs and egg yolks one at a time, beating after each addition just to blend. Gently stir in whipping cream. Turn into crust-lined pan. Bake at 450° for 12 minutes. Reduce heat to 300°; bake till knife inserted off-center comes out clean, about 55 minutes longer. Remove from oven; cool 30 minutes. Loosen sides of cheesecake from pan with spatula. Cool 30 minutes more; remove sides of pan. Cool 2 hours. Meanwhile, prepare Cherry Sauce or Strawberry Glaze. Top cheesecake with sauce or glaze. Serves 12.

*Cherry Sauce:* In saucepan combine ½ cup sugar, 2 tablespoons cornstarch, and dash salt. Add one 20-ounce can frozen pitted tart red cherries, thawed. Cook and stir till thickened and bubbly. Reduce heat; simmer 10 minutes. Chill.

*Strawberry Glaze:* Crush 1 cup strawberries; add ¾ cup water. Cook 2 minutes; sieve. In saucepan combine ½ cup sugar and 2 tablespoons cornstarch; gradually stir in hot berry mixture. Bring to boiling, stirring constantly. Cook and stir till thick and clear. (Add red food coloring, if needed.) Cool to room temperature. Place 3 cups halved strawberries on cheesecake. Pour glaze over berries. Chill 2 hours.

## Crème Brûlée

3 slightly beaten eggs
¼ cup sugar
¼ teaspoon salt
2 cups light cream
½ teaspoon vanilla
½ cup packed brown sugar

In top of double boiler combine eggs, sugar, and salt. Stir in cream. Cook and stir over *hot, not boiling* water till custard coats a metal spoon. Cook 2 minutes longer. Cool quickly. Stir in vanilla. Pour into 1-quart shallow baking dish; chill. Sprinkle with brown sugar. Set in pan of ice cubes and a little cold water. Broil 8 inches from heat till bubbly crust forms, about 5 minutes. Serve warm or chilled. Serves 5 or 6.

186

## Feathery Fudge Cake

*Feathery Fudge Cake came from a Montana ranch wife who got the ice water that makes this cake feathery from her backyard running water stream. Originally three layers, this simplified version uses only two 9-inch round pans and is put together with some of the fudge frosting.*

2½ 1-ounce squares
    unsweetened chocolate
⅔ cup butter or margarine
1¾ cups sugar
1 teaspoon vanilla
2 eggs

2½ cups sifted cake flour
1¼ teaspoons baking soda
½ teaspoon salt
1¼ cups icy cold water
Fudge Frosting

Melt chocolate; cool. Cream butter. Gradually add sugar, creaming till light. Add vanilla. Add eggs, one at a time, beating after each. Blend in chocolate. Sift together cake flour, soda, and salt. Add to creamed mixture alternately with cold water, beating after each addition. Bake in 2 greased and lightly floured 9x1½-inch round baking pans at 350° till done, 35 to 40 minutes. Frost with Fudge Frosting.

*Fudge Frosting:* Butter the sides of a heavy 3-quart saucepan. In saucepan combine 3 cups sugar, 1 cup milk, two 1-ounce squares unsweetened chocolate, 3 tablespoons light corn syrup, and ¼ teaspoon salt. Cook mixture over low heat, stirring constantly, until sugar is dissolved and chocolate is melted. Cook to soft-ball stage (234°) without stirring. Remove frosting mixture from heat; add ¼ cup butter or margarine. Cool till warm (110°) without stirring. Add 1 teaspoon vanilla; beat with electric mixer until frosting is of spreading consistency.

## Banana Chiffon Cake

2¼ cups sifted cake flour
1½ cups sugar
3 teaspoons baking powder
1 teaspoon salt
½ cup cooking oil
5 unbeaten egg yolks
3 tablespoons cold water
1 cup mashed ripe banana

1 teaspoon grated lemon
    peel
8 egg whites (1 cup)
½ teaspoon cream of tartar
1 cup whipping cream
2 teaspoons sugar
1 banana
Lemon juice

Sift together flour, 1½ cups sugar, baking powder, and salt. Make well in center; add in order oil, egg yolks, water, mashed banana, and lemon peel. Beat till smooth. Beat egg whites with cream of tartar till *very stiff* peaks form. Pour batter evenly over egg whites; fold in gently. Bake in *ungreased* 10-inch tube pan at 325° about 55 minutes. Invert; cool. Whip cream with remaining sugar till soft peaks form. Frost cake with cream. Slice banana; dip in lemon juice and place on cake.

## Strawberry Angel Cake

1 package angel cake mix
1 3-ounce package
    strawberry-flavored
    gelatin
1 cup water

1 10-ounce package frozen
    sliced strawberries
    (1 cup)
1 cup whipping cream
1 tablespoon sugar

Prepare angel cake mix according to package directions. Cool; remove cake from pan. In saucepan combine gelatin and water. Heat mixture until gelatin is dissolved. Remove from heat; stir in frozen sliced strawberries. Chill till partially set. Whip ½ *cup* of the cream. Fold into gelatin mixture. Chill till mixture mounds. Cut cake crosswise into three equal layers. Fill cake layers with gelatin mixture; chill till firm. Just before serving, whip the remaining cream with sugar. Frost top of cake with whipped cream. Makes 16 servings.

## Date Cake

1½ cups chopped pitted dates
1 cup boiling water
½ cup shortening
1 cup sugar
1 egg

1 teaspoon vanilla
1½ cups all-purpose flour
1 teaspoon baking soda
¼ teaspoon salt
½ cup chopped walnuts

Combine dates and boiling water; cool to room temperature. Cream shortening and sugar till light. Add egg and vanilla; beat well. Stir together thoroughly flour, soda, and salt. Add to creamed mixture alternately with date mixture, beating after each addition. Stir in nuts. Bake in greased and lightly floured 13x9x2-inch baking pan at 350° for 25 to 30 minutes. If desired, serve with dollops of whipped cream.

## Raspberry Regal Dessert

12 ladyfingers, split
1 10-ounce package frozen
    raspberries, thawed
1 3-ounce package rasp-
    berry-flavored gelatin

1 cup tiny marshmallows
•  •  •
1 8¾-ounce can pineapple
    tidbits, drained
1 cup whipping cream

Line the sides of a 9-inch tube pan with split ladyfingers; place remaining ladyfingers on bottom of pan. Drain thawed raspberries, reserving syrup. Add water to syrup to make 1½ cups. Heat syrup mixture to boiling. Dissolve raspberry-flavored gelatin in hot liquid. Add marshmallows; stir till marshmallows are melted. Chill till partially set. Fold in raspberries and pineapple. Whip cream; fold into gelatin mixture. Pour into ladyfinger-lined pan. Chill till firm. Serves 8 to 10.

## Strawberry Pinwheel Bavarian

Dissolve one 3-ounce package strawberry-flavored gelatin and ¼ cup sugar in 1¼ cups boiling water. Stir in 1 cup tiny marshmallows; cool. Thaw one 10-ounce package frozen sliced strawberries; mash. Stir berries, 2 unbeaten egg whites, and 2 tablespoons lemon juice into gelatin mixture. Chill till partially set. Beat till fluffy. Whip ½ cup whipping cream; fold into gelatin mixture. Cut four or five 1-inch jelly roll slices in half; arrange, cut side down, around edge of 9-inch springform pan. Fill with gelatin mixture. Chill overnight. Serves 8 to 10.

*Strawberry Pinwheel Bavarian is a '50s adaptation of two classical favorites — the charlotte and the Bavarian cream. A charlotte is any dessert with a sweet filling surrounded by some type of cake or bread. And a Bavarian cream is a molded dessert made from custard, or gelatin and whipped cream. Strawberry Pinwheel Bavarian is elegant enough to serve after any meal.*

## Spicy Orange Diamonds

⅔ cup shortening
1 cup packed brown sugar
2 eggs
2 tablespoons grated orange
    peel
3 tablespoons orange juice
2 cups all-purpose flour

1 teaspoon baking soda
1 teaspoon ground cinnamon
½ teaspoon ground nutmeg
¼ teaspoon ground cloves
1 cup raisins
1 cup chopped walnuts
    Powdered sugar

Cream together shortening, brown sugar, and eggs. Blend in grated orange peel and orange juice. Stir together thoroughly the flour, baking soda, spices, and ½ teaspoon salt. Add to creamed mixture and mix well. Stir in raisins and nuts. Spread in greased 15½x10½x1-inch baking pan. Bake at 350° till done, 22 to 25 minutes. Cool; cut into diamonds or bars. Sprinkle with powdered sugar. Makes about 4 dozen.

## Snow Pudding

¾ cup sugar
5 tablespoons cornstarch
¼ teaspoon salt
2¼ cups water

⅓ cup lemon juice
2 stiffly beaten egg
  whites
Custard Sauce

Combine sugar, cornstarch, and salt. Blend in water. Heat to boiling; cook 5 minutes, stirring constantly. Cool. Stir in lemon juice; fold in egg whites. Pour into 4-cup mold; chill till firm. Serve pudding with Custard Sauce. Makes 6 servings.

*Custard Sauce:* In saucepan combine 2 slightly beaten egg yolks, ¼ cup sugar, and ⅛ teaspoon salt. Blend in 1½ cups milk. Cook and stir over low heat till mixture thickens. Stir in ½ teaspoon vanilla. Chill sauce till ready to serve.

## Choco-Mallow Ice Cream

½ of a 14-ounce can
  *sweetened condensed*
  milk (⅔ cup)
1 1-ounce square
  unsweetened chocolate

½ cup water
½ teaspoon vanilla
1 cup whipping cream
1 cup tiny marshmallows
½ cup chopped walnuts

In top of double boiler combine milk and chocolate; place over *hot, not boiling,* water. Cook, stirring often, till thick, about 10 minutes. Slowly add water and vanilla; mix well. Chill. Whip cream till thick and custardlike; fold into chocolate mixture. Pour into a 3-cup refrigerator tray; freeze till firm. Break mixture into chunks into a chilled bowl. Beat till smooth. Fold in marshmallows and nuts. Quickly return mixture to cold tray; freeze till firm. Makes about 1½ pints.

## Rocky Road Candy

2 8-ounce or 12 1⅜-ounce
  bars milk chocolate

3 cups tiny marshmallows
¾ cup broken walnuts

Slowly melt chocolate over low heat, stirring constantly. Remove from heat; beat till smooth. Stir in marshmallows and walnuts. Spread in buttered 8x8x2-inch baking pan. Chill. Makes 1½ pounds.

## Chocolate-Mint Cups

1 3½-ounce package after-
  dinner mints (¾ cup)
¾ cup milk
  Few drops green food
  coloring
1 cup whipping cream

1 1-ounce square
  unsweetened chocolate,
  grated
1 6-ounce package semisweet
  chocolate pieces
2 tablespoons shortening

In saucepan combine mints and milk. Stir over *low* heat till mints are melted. Stir in food coloring. Cool. Whip cream; fold into mint mixture. Pour into 3-cup refrigerator tray and freeze till mushy, stirring occasionally. Fold unsweetened chocolate into mint mixture; freeze till firm. Meanwhile, melt chocolate pieces and shortening over low heat; cool. Place 8 paper bake cups in muffin pans. With a teaspoon, swirl chocolate mixture around inside of cups. Cover entire surface with a layer of chocolate. Chill. When chocolate cups are hard, carefully tear off paper. Keep cold. Fill cups with scoops of mint filling. Serves 8.

## Crystal Cut Candies

2 cups sugar
½ cup light corn syrup
½ cup water
Dash salt

Few drops red *or* green
food coloring
Few drops oil of cinnamon
*or* oil of wintergreen

In heavy saucepan combine sugar, corn syrup, water, and salt. Bring mixture to boiling, stirring to dissolve sugar. Cook without stirring to soft-crack stage (290°). Add a few drops food coloring and flavoring. Gently swirl to blend. Pour into 8x8x2-inch baking pan. Let stand a few minutes till film forms over top. With a sharp knife, mark surface of candy in ¾-inch squares, starting from outside and working toward center. Using a flat metal spatula, press along the marked lines, being careful not to break through the film surface. (If lines do not hold shape, candy is not cool enough.) Continue pressing along marked lines toward center. While waiting for center candy to cool enough, retrace previous lines, pressing deeper but not breaking film. When spatula may be pressed to bottom of pan in all lines, candy will be shaped in puffs. Cool; turn out and break into pieces. Makes 60.

## Caramel-Nut Crunch

1⅓ cups sugar
1 cup butter or margarine
½ cup light corn syrup
1 teaspoon vanilla

8 cups popped corn
1 cup pecan halves, toasted
1 cup unblanched whole
almonds, toasted

Mix sugar, butter, and corn syrup. Bring to a boil, stirring constantly. Continue boiling, stirring occasionally, till mixture turns caramel color. Remove from heat; stir in vanilla. Place popped corn and nuts in buttered shallow baking pan; pour syrup over. Separate into clusters with 2 forks. Store in tightly closed container. Makes 2 pounds.

## Mrs. Claus' Fudge

In 3-quart saucepan cook 4 cups sugar, one 13-ounce can evaporated milk, and 1 cup butter to soft-ball stage (236°); stir frequently. Remove from heat. Stir in one 12-ounce package semisweet chocolate pieces, one 7- or 9-ounce jar marshmallow creme, 1 cup chopped walnuts, and 1 teaspoon vanilla till blended. Pour into buttered 13x9x2-inch baking pan. While warm, score into squares. Cool. Makes 54 pieces.

## Brown Sugar-Nut Roll

2 cups granulated sugar
1 cup packed brown sugar
1 cup evaporated milk

¼ cup light corn syrup
Dash salt
1 cup chopped pecans

Butter sides of heavy 2-quart saucepan. In pan combine granulated and brown sugars, milk, corn syrup, and salt. Cook and stir over medium heat till sugars dissolve and mixture boils. Cook to soft-ball stage (236°), stirring frequently. (Mixture may curdle but will become smooth when beaten.) Immediately remove from heat. *Do not* stir; cool to lukewarm (110°). Beat till candy begins to hold its shape. Turn out on buttered surface. Keeping hands well buttered, knead till candy can be shaped. Shape in two 7-inch long rolls. Roll immediately in nuts, pressing to coat well. Wrap; chill. Slice ½ inch thick. Makes 28 pieces.

*Candy conjures up thoughts of Christmas for many people, including Paul Engle who recalls one of his childhood Christmases in a 1958 issue of the magazine. "We made paper cones that were to hang on the tree and filled them with candy my sisters had boiled, and whipped and poured in the kitchen. My reward for cracking the nuts we had gathered in gunnysacks after the first frost on the farm (and for not eating all I had cracked) was scraping the pans. Somehow the bits and dribblings tasted better than the beautiful neat squares on their trays. This did not keep me from stealing a few solid pieces when my sisters were not looking. Since the candy had been made for a solemn holiday, my young conscience would give me a bad time —for about as long as it took to lift my hand and snatch the candy."*

The family IDEA magazine
November 1960 · 35c

# Better Homes and ~~Gardens~~

Do you need a
HOBBY
to give life
a fresh turn?
INSIDE
we have many
IDEAS for you
—plus a section on
PARTIES
that also will
lift you out
of the same
OLD RUT

Nothing about the '60s was passive. It was a time of searching, experimenting, and growing. Everywhere, people were reaching out for new sensations. The sight of men on the moon, the smell of incense, and the pulsating sound of electric rock all bombarded the senses. The search for new food sensations was no different. Americans of the '60s raced around the world discovering new cooking styles. From the French came the basics of haute cuisine. From the Orient came the wok and the hibachi. And from the Swiss came fondue. When Americans weren't busy enjoying the new foreign favorites, they were out in their backyards improving their barbecuing skills.

# THE 60s

If the forties were the tense, war-torn years and the fifties the more relaxed, easygoing decade, the sixties were a whole new 'bag', to use the vernacular of the time. The complacency of the previous decade had given way to a new American philosophy—one that advocated searching, experimenting, rejecting, and trying to establish new directions.

The year 1960 brought a new, young president with his dreams of a Camelot. The sixties also introduced the Peace Corps for those Americans who wanted to get out and do something constructive—and Haight-Ashbury for those who preferred to disassociate themselves from the 'establishment' and to counter the world's problems and hatreds with love-ins.

For most Americans there was enough time and money to allow for experimenting and searching for whatever was new and different. Everything reflected this, including fashions. Once again, the male was becoming the colorful component of the species, rejecting the conservative gray-flannel-suit image. On the female side, Twiggy modeled miniskirts that brought hemlines to an all-time high. Even 'see-throughs' became popular with some in an attempt to do what had not been dared before.

Music couldn't be relegated to background sounds anymore—the word was Rock! Amplified to earsplitting volumes and accompanied by psychedelic flashing lights, music was, like everything else, reaching for new sensations. And when, in 1963, four sheep dog-coiffured kids from England recorded "She Loves You," the world was bitten by Beatlemania, a musical malady with a variety of side effects.

Learning and exploration were very much a part of the sixties. Nearly everyone traveled. And while astronauts were traveling outer space preparing to stroll the lunar surfaces, other earthlings were traveling to the far reaches of our globe intent on learning from other cultures and bringing home what they'd learned.

In food, eating, and cooking styles, the thrust of the sixties was this same urgency to try the untried; maybe not to learn and progress toward smoother living, but simply to pack in more and different experiences. And the economy was good enough for this type of experimentation to thrive. An occasional disappointment when trying a new dish at a restaurant or when cooking an untried recipe at home was affordable. And, above all, it guaranteed the sensation of something new.

In that unrestrained rampage to experience everything, many less-than-superb dishes may have been given unwarranted acclaim. But if undeserved enthusiasm developed for such things as blazing skewer-swords, overcharred barbecued meats, and airy packaged puddings, this adventuring had its good side, too. It expanded our food vocabularies to include words such as Kiev, Veronique, smörrebrod, Bourguignon, cacciatore, gazpacho, and tempura, to mention just a few of the newcomers.

With travel increasing at a furious rate, interest in foreign cookery naturally burgeoned. Americans started boning up on French geography, culture, and cuisine—tried French dishes in restaurants, and worked hard to achieve the best of French foods in their own kitchens. Nor was France the only source for culinary explorations—Spain, Italy, Austria, Germany, China, Japan, India, and Hawaii all contributed their specialties to the American cook's repertoire of fine foods.

Ingredients became more exotic and cooking techniques more complicated. And along came the extensive use of the word "gourmet"—widely used—not so widely understood. In practice, it was applied to any dish that used a lot of herbs, wine, sour cream, or mushrooms. Gourmet, in its animate sense, came to mean someone who dined lavishly in the imagined rich

French manner: many courses and a conglomeration of dishes that were either highly sauced or terribly complicated. Only now is it becoming generally understood that a true gourmet also can be happy with simple meals and may consider a perfectly poached egg a genuine work of art.

**B**ut, despite the exotic food fancies of the sixties, simple foods were also coming front and center; and people were discovering that all ethnic food adventures didn't require passports. America's own black culture made its presence felt in many ways, and "black is beautiful" became the slogan symbolizing pride in being black. With the new awareness of America's black heritage, "soul food" became popular and introduced many non-blacks to still more new tastes.

The perspective on other countries and other cultures was changing. So was the perspective on the traditional husband-wife roles. In 1963 Betty Freiden authored *The Feminine Mystique,* a book that may or may not have triggered the Women's Liberation Movement. It undoubtedly did play a role in changing the thought processes in American marriages, and these changes exercised their influence in the kitchen, too.

Previously, the American husband would look askance at a new food offering or combination he couldn't identify as a variation on a familiar food theme. But the sixties required more than that of the man of the house. His experience with food was broader, and he began to enjoy ventures into the kitchen on his own. More men than ever began sharing in the marketing and the preparation of food. As a spin-off of this growing involvement by men, barbecuing continued to gain in popularity all over the country. It graduated from the bumbling enthusiasm stage to become a skill to be executed with excellence and élan. By 1965 barbecue cooks were fine-tuning the fire-cooking skills that they had begun 30 years before.

The art of entertaining was developing a new format, too. Informal, late-evening suppers replaced the formal sit-down dinners that had once been used to display the family's collection of china and crystal. Sunday brunches were replacing bridge luncheons, and the coffee klatch became an effective way to welcome new neighbors or to support a favorite political candidate. Tabletop appliances such as fondue pots and hibachi grills enabled guests to actively participate in the preparation of their food at a party. And the good old canapés of yesteryear took a backseat to easy 'nibblies' such as nuts and cereal mixes.

**W**ithout a doubt, fondue was the biggest entertaining hit of the sixties— and an entirely new concept in eating. It called for a new way of cooking, new utensils, even a new way of serving. And because guests had to gather around the fondue pot and dip their own French bread cubes into cheese, or beef cubes into hot oil, or fruit bites into melted chocolate, fonduing helped people get acquainted at many a party.

Throughout the period, interest in foods spanned two sometimes contradictory extremes. One of these was the endless search for any recipe or food that was new and exciting, the experimentation with a variety of tastes, complicated recipes, and new cooking techniques. The other was the trend toward preparation shortcuts, convenience cooking and products, and plan-ahead meals. *Better Homes and Gardens* responded to both of these interests while still helping home cooks to master basic cooking skills and classic cookery. It also responded to another paradox. Side by side with the attempt to try every new idea was the desire for in-depth expertise in the kitchen, and the pages of the magazine were filled with service articles and how-to help on everything from selecting cheese to maximum use of a wide variety of appliances.

And paradoxical is the only word that fits a time when nine million readers were in love with a floppy-eared dog named Snoopy, while the best-seller list was dominated by *Valley of the Dolls,* a novel that was panned by most critics but nonetheless read by millions of people. These were the years when Dr. Benjamin Spock, who in 1946 advised mothers on how to raise their babies, now advised these same babies-turned-adults on how best to avoid the draft. Together with war protests, peace marches, and moratoriums, there coexisted antiprotest protests and songs honoring the contemporary war heroes, the Green Berets. The world of art was set on its ear by Andy Warhol's $45,000 painting of a gigantic Campbell soup can. In the field of entertainment audiences felt the sharp, biting humor of "Laugh-In," and weren't really too sure whether Tiny Tim was to be taken seriously or considered an all-time great farce. And while many ghetto populations were rioting and burning in protest of social ills, America was planting its flag on the moon. A country was learning to be aware of the dangers of pesticides, the needs of minorities, and the power of "love conquers all"—that country also saw three great leaders assassinated. Nothing in the sixties was passive. Everything was charged with emotion, and everything was done with a sense of urgency and devotion to purpose.

Eating was no different. Americans, who had eaten their way through various countries, exotic cultures, a variety of new foods and taste sensations, suddenly realized they were bulging with more than new knowledge, so they plunged with enthusiasm into dieting away overweight. The great Metrecal age began in 1959. And in 1961 *Better Homes and Gardens* introduced its liquid formula diet plan, which allowed 1,000 calories a day and met daily nutritional needs.

Science was making many valuable contributions in the kitchen as well as in the laboratory. While perfecting laser beams, moon shots—even computerized marriage matches—scientists were also producing better tasting, more nutritious foods, leaner hogs, and broader-breasted turkeys. The faster-to-the-market broiler-fryers resulted in chicken breasts topping the sixties' popularity polls. Barbecuing equipment was engineered for greater efficiency and ease, and that cooking style reached an advanced state of refinement. The development of packaged foods was plotted according to surveys of food preferences, then perfected and popularized. One such item was the canned and frozen puddings that now appeared in the supermarkets from coast to coast.

Advances in transportation brought more new foods into American homes. Some of the most popular were artichokes, shallots, and a wide variety of lettuce to compete with the iceberg head lettuce that had previously held sway. Tangelos, mandarin oranges, kumquats, bing cherries, persimmons, and pomegranates became household words—and commodities.

The sixties may have been characterized by experimentation with the new and sensational in foods and cooking, but, rippling along behind this penchant for flashy food innovation, was a quiet, steady stream of fine home cooking. Though the headlines went to experiments, it was not uncommon for cooks to rally behind old-fashioned recipes more readily than the new ones. Articles on home-baked breads and other things homemade rated remarkable popularity, which may prove a point. In time of anxiety, busy hands are a comfort. When the concerns of a nation are fallout, repressed minorities, assassinated leaders, and relaxed morality—maybe kneading bread dough is a satisfying, momentary return to times that were less complex, when everything was less tempestuous, and when doing things well was more important than just getting the job done.

← *Unfold this section for three-page foldout illustration in full color*

AIR
TRIBAL LOVE-ROC
war
is not
healthy
children
introducing...
THE BEATLES
ENGLANDS No.1 VOCAL GROUP
VEE JAY
FOR MEN
SEPTEMBER 1966 • 75 CENTS
AYBOY
PORTRAIT OF OUR PLANET: III
THE ANTARCTIC
NEW ERA IN GOVERNMENT
THE VICTORIOUS
YOUNG KENNEDYS
NOVEMBER 21, 1960
DREAM

BLACK
IS
BEAUTIFUL
O'BRIEN
COMPETITION
This time Richard Nixon is mellower and wiser
I Had
By
Dr. Seuss
THE OFFICIAL
BOOK-AND-RECORD ALBUM
Everything you
always wanted to
know about sex
Also available
Play-Doh
Kitchen Play
I CAN'T
BELIEVE
I ATE THE
WHOLE
THING
TRY IT...
YOU'LL
LIKE IT!

# Recipe Features of the Sixties

### Fun with Fondue

Invite the gang to a fondue party and let them choose either beef or cheese fondue. Many parties of the sixties began like this. It's a great way for guests to get acquainted.

### International Main Dishes

Bring the flavor of Europe or the Orient into your dining room by preparing one of these International Main Dishes. The Americans of the sixties tried them all.

### Convenience Cooking

When you need a meal in a hurry, select one of these convenience dishes. Busy homemakers of the sixties needed quick and appetizing meals, so they invented these recipes.

### Myrna's Favorites

For that extra-special dinner party serve one of Myrna Johnston's favorites. During her many years as food editor, Mrs. Johnston found she enjoyed these recipes the most.

### Gourmet Cooking

Looking for something different? Any of these gourmet recipes of the sixties is sure to please. These foods are elegant, sophisticated, and sometimes complicated—but you'll find that they're worth the extra effort.

This kitchen of the sixties boasts a tile-topped cooking peninsula that extends over the cabinet on three sides to form a snack bar. The kitchen also has a built-in wall oven—one of the exciting innovations of this decade.

# Fun with Fondue

During the '60s, a new dish swept the country—fondue. Millions of Americans first saw this European classic in 'Cinerama Holiday,' one of the early wide-screen movies. From that time on, fondue was a hit. In addition to the traditional cheese fondue, beef fondue was also popular. Yet another new type was the dessert fondue in which pieces of fruit or cake were dipped into hot chocolate or butterscotch. Americans were quick to accept these new variations. Soon, fonduing became a new way of entertaining, and friends spent many happy hours together enjoying fondue.

*Credit the Swiss for the ingenious concoction of cheese fondue. Serve Classic Cheese Fondue (pictured opposite) as the main dish, accompanied with relishes or a salad, a beverage, and dessert, or plan to serve it as a snack.*

## Beef Fondue

**Cooking oil**
**1½ pounds trimmed beef**
    **tenderloin, cut in ¾-**
    **inch cubes**

**Caper Sauce**
**Mexican Hot Sauce**
**Garlic Butter**

Pour oil into metal fondue cooker to no more than ½ capacity or to a depth of 2 inches. Heat, uncovered, over range to 425°. Add 1 teaspoon salt. Transfer cooker to fondue burner. Have beef at room temperature. Spear meat with fondue fork; fry in hot oil to desired doneness. Transfer to dinner fork. Dip in Caper Sauce, Mexican Hot Sauce, or Garlic Butter. Serves 4.

*Caper Sauce:* In small mixing bowl combine 1 cup mayonnaise or salad dressing and 1 tablespoon undrained capers. Mix until thoroughly blended. Makes 1 cup.

*Mexican Hot Sauce:* In saucepan combine 1 cup chili sauce; ¼ cup chopped onion; 3 tablespoons vinegar; 1 tablespoon cooking oil; 1 teaspoon packed brown sugar; 1 clove garlic, crushed; ¼ teaspoon salt; ¼ teaspoon dry mustard; and ¼ teaspoon bottled hot pepper sauce. Bring to boiling; reduce heat and simmer 10 minutes, stirring often. Serve warm or cool. Makes 1¼ cups.

*Garlic Butter:* Cream ½ cup softened butter till fluffy. Add 1 small clove garlic, crushed. Let mellow at room temperature at least 1 hour before serving. Makes ½ cup butter.

*The honorable ancestor of Beef Fondue may have been Chinese rather than Swiss. In a brass kettle with a charcoal-filled chimney, the Chinese heated broth to cook vegetables and meats. They dipped with chopsticks; afterward, they drank the well-seasoned broth.*

## Classic Cheese Fondue

**3 cups shredded natural**
    **Swiss cheese (12 ounces)**
**1 cup shredded natural or**
    **process Gruyère cheese**
    **(4 ounces)**
**1½ teaspoons cornstarch**
**1 clove garlic, halved**

**1 cup sauterne**
**1 tablespoon lemon juice**
**Dash ground nutmeg**
**French or Italian bread,**
    **or hard rolls, cut in**
    **bite-size pieces, each**
    **with one crust**

Combine cheeses and cornstarch. Rub inside of heavy saucepan with garlic; discard garlic. Pour in sauterne and lemon juice. Warm till air bubbles rise and cover surface. (Don't cover or boil.)

Remember to stir vigorously and constantly from now on. Add a handful of cheeses, keeping heat medium (but do not boil). When melted, toss in another handful. After cheese is

blended and bubbling and while still stirring, add nutmeg and dash pepper. Quickly transfer to fondue pot; keep warm over fondue burner. (If fondue becomes too thick, add a little *warmed* sauterne.) Spear bread cube with fondue fork, piercing crust last. Dip bread into fondue and swirl to coat the bread. (The swirling is important to keep the fondue in motion.) Serves 4 to 6.

*Part of the fun of eating cheese fondue is the special dipping technique that keeps the cheese constantly moving. Each person pierces his cube of bread through the crust and swirls it in the cheese with a figure-eight motion. You don't have to use the hardened cheese and bread that the Swiss originally used in their Classic Cheese Fondue.*

## Fondued Flank Steak

1 pound beef flank steak
½ cup cooking oil
½ cup dry red wine
2 tablespoons catsup
2 tablespoons molasses

2 tablespoons finely
    snipped candied ginger
1 clove garlic, minced
½ teaspoon curry powder
    Cooking oil

Bias cut the flank steak in very thin 3x1-inch strips. Combine ½ cup cooking oil, wine, catsup, molasses, candied ginger, garlic, curry powder, and ½ teaspoon *each* salt and pepper. Pour marinade over flank steak. Cover; marinate 2 hours at room temperature. Drain well; pat dry with paper toweling. Thread on bamboo skewers accordion style.

Pour cooking oil into metal fondue cooker to no more than ½ capacity or to depth of 2 inches. Heat, uncovered, over range to 425°. Add 1 teaspoon salt. Transfer cooker to fondue burner. Have skewered meat strips at room temperature on serving plate. Fry meat in hot oil till desired doneness, 1 to 2 minutes. Makes 4 servings.

## Mexi-Meatball Fondue

¾ cup soft bread crumbs
    (about 1 slice bread)
¼ cup chili sauce
1 beaten egg
½ teaspoon instant minced
    onion

⅛ teaspoon garlic powder
¾ pound ground beef
    Cooking oil
    Mexican Hot Sauce (see
    recipe, page 202)
    Creamy Avocado Sauce

Combine the crumbs, chili sauce, egg, onion, garlic powder, and ½ teaspoon salt. Add ground beef and mix thoroughly. Shape meat mixture into about 30 meatballs. Pour cooking oil into metal fondue cooker to no more than ½ capacity or to depth of 2 inches. Heat, uncovered, over range to 375°. Add 1 teaspoon salt. Transfer cooker to fondue burner. Have meatballs at room temperature in serving bowl. Spear

meatball with fondue fork; fry in hot oil till done, 1 to 2 minutes. Transfer to dinner fork and dip into Mexican Hot Sauce or Creamy Avocado Sauce. Serves 3 or 4.

*Creamy Avocado Sauce:* Mix 1 cup mashed avocado, ½ cup dairy sour cream, 2 teaspoons lemon juice, ½ teaspoon grated onion, and ¼ teaspoon *each* salt and chili powder; chill. Stir in 3 slices bacon, crisp-cooked and crumbled.

## Fondue Italiano

*Serve Fondue Italiano, a variation of cheese fondue, at your next party. And be sure to follow these fondue traditions: any person who loses his bread cube in the fondue must kiss a friend of his choice; and the crusty cheese left in the bottom of the pot is for the person who gets through the whole meal without dropping a single cube of the bread.*

½ pound ground beef
1 15-ounce can tomato sauce
½ envelope spaghetti sauce
    mix
3 cups shredded natural
    Cheddar cheese
    (12 ounces)

1 cup shredded natural
    mozzarella cheese
    (4 ounces)
1 tablespoon cornstarch
½ cup chianti
    Italian bread, cut in
    bite-size pieces

In saucepan brown ground beef; drain off excess fat. Stir in the tomato sauce and the spaghetti sauce mix. Gradually add the shredded Cheddar cheese and shredded mozzarella cheese; stir over low heat till cheeses are melted. Blend together the cornstarch and chianti;

stir into the cheese mixture. Cook and stir till thickened and bubbly. Transfer cheese mixture to fondue pot; place over fondue burner. Spear bread cube with fondue fork; dip in fondue mixture, swirling to coat bread. (If fondue becomes thick, add a little *warmed* chianti.) Serves 6.

## Mexican Fondue

2 tablespoons finely
    chopped green pepper
2 tablespoons butter or
    margarine
2 tablespoons all-purpose
    flour
½ teaspoon chili powder
2 cups shredded sharp
    process American
    cheese (8 ounces)

1 10-ounce package frozen
    cream-style corn,
    thawed
1 8-ounce can tomatoes,
    cut up
1 well-beaten egg
    • • •
    French bread, cut in
      bite-size pieces, each
      with one crust

In saucepan cook green pepper in butter or margarine till tender. Stir in flour and chili powder. Add shredded cheese, thawed corn, and cut up tomatoes; stir till cheese melts. Blend small amount of hot mixture into beaten egg; return to saucepan. Cook and stir over low heat till thickened; *do not boil.* Transfer cheese mixture to fondue pot; place over fondue burner. Spear bread cube with a fondue fork; dip in cheese mixture, swirling to coat bread. Makes about 6 servings.

*Although fondue was invented by the Swiss, the origin of the word is French. It comes from 'fondre' which means to melt. Over the years, fondue has been enjoyed by many countries including Mexico. This recipe is for those who like their fondue south-of-the-border style.*

## Cheese-Sour Cream Fondue

6 slices bacon
¼ cup finely chopped onion
2 teaspoons all-purpose
    flour
4 cups shredded sharp
    process American
    cheese (16 ounces)

2 cups dairy sour cream
1 teaspoon Worcestershire
    sauce
    Rye bread, cut in bite-
      size pieces, each with
      one crust, *or* cooked
      mushrooms

In saucepan cook bacon till crisp; drain bacon, reserving 1 tablespoon drippings. Crumble bacon and set aside. Cook onion in reserved bacon drippings in saucepan till tender but not brown. Stir in the flour. Then, stir in the cheese, sour cream, and Worcestershire. Cook over low heat, stirring constantly, till cheese is melted. Transfer cheese-sour cream mixture to fondue pot. Top with reserved crumbled bacon. Place over fondue burner. Spear bread or mushroom dipper with fondue fork; dip in fondue, swirling to coat. Makes 6 to 8 servings.

## Monterey Jack Fondue

3 tablespoons butter or
    margarine
3 tablespoons all-purpose
    flour
⅛ teaspoon garlic powder
⅛ teaspoon cayenne
1 6-ounce can evaporated
    milk (⅔ cup)
½ cup chicken broth

1 teaspoon instant minced
    onion
1¼ cups shredded Monterey
    Jack cheese (6 ounces)
    • • •
    Cherry tomatoes
    Celery sticks
    Green pepper squares

In saucepan melt the butter; blend in the flour, garlic powder, and cayenne. Stir in the evaporated milk, chicken broth, and onion all at once. Cook, stirring constantly, until thickened and bubbly. Gradually add the shredded Monterey Jack cheese, stirring until cheese is melted. Transfer cheese mixture to a fondue pot; place over fondue burner. Spear cherry tomatoes, celery sticks, or green pepper squares with fondue fork; dip in fondue, swirling to coat. Serves 4.

*Monterey Jack cheese could be called the American mozzarella. Long known in California, it became nationally available in the late '60s. It is commonly used with many Mexican dishes, but it also makes a great cheese for fondue.*

206

## Cheese and Bean Dunk

*Not all fondues need to be made with natural cheese. Cheese and Bean Dunk, for example, contains a process cheese food. The garlic roll used in this recipe is a blend of fresh and natural cheeses pasteurized to prevent further ripening.*

1 6-ounce roll garlic
   cheese food
1 11½-ounce can condensed
   bean with bacon soup
1 cup dairy sour cream

2 tablespoons sliced green
   onion
Carrot sticks, celery
   sticks, *or* assorted
   crackers

Cut the roll of cheese into chunks. Place in saucepan with the soup. Stir over low heat till blended. Stir in the sour cream and green onion. Heat through. Transfer to fondue pot; place over fondue burner. Serve with vegetable dippers or crackers. Makes 2⅔ cups dip.

## Indian Curry Dip

1 tablespoon butter
1 teaspoon curry powder
¼ teaspoon salt
¼ teaspoon garlic powder
1 13¾-ounce can chicken
   broth (1¾ cups)

3 tablespoons cornstarch
¼ cup catsup
½ cup dairy sour cream
   Cooked turkey cubes,
   cooked shrimp, *or*
   assorted crackers

In saucepan melt the butter. Add the curry powder, salt, and garlic powder; mix well. Blend the chicken broth with the cornstarch; add to butter mixture. Cook, stirring constantly, till mixture thickens and bubbles. Pour curry mixture into fondue pot; set over fondue burner. Stir in the catsup; add the sour cream and heat through. Serve hot as a dip with turkey, shrimp, or crackers. Makes 2 cups dip.

## French-Fried Cheese

*Ordinarily, cheese fondue can be done in a ceramic pot. French-Fried Cheese, however, is an exception. Because the coated cheese cubes are cooked in hot oil, you'll need a sturdy metal pot. Be sure to add a teaspoon of salt to the oil to reduce spattering as the cheese browns.*

Cut assorted *natural* cheeses into ½-inch cubes. Use soft cheeses with a crust (Camembert or Brie), semihard (Bel Paese or brick), or hard (Cheddar, Edam, or Gouda) cheeses. For soft cheeses, shape crust around soft center as much as possible. Dip cheese in beaten egg; then roll in fine dry bread crumbs. Repeat for second layer. (A thick coating prevents cheese from leaking.)

Pour cooking oil into metal fondue cooker to no more than ½ capacity. Heat, uncovered, on range to 375°. Add 1 teaspoon salt. Transfer cooker to fondue burner. Spear cheese with fondue fork; fry in hot oil ½ minute. Cool slightly.

## Reuben Appetizers

1 3-ounce package cream
   cheese, softened
1 teaspoon instant minced
   onion
1 16-ounce can sauerkraut,
   well-drained

1 12-ounce can corned beef
1 cup fine dry bread crumbs
½ cup all-purpose flour
½ cup evaporated milk
   Cooking oil
1 teaspoon salt

Combine cheese and onion. Chop the sauerkraut. Add kraut, corned beef, and ¼ *cup* of the crumbs to cheese; mix well. Shape into 1-inch balls. Roll in flour; dip in milk, then in remaining bread crumbs.

Pour cooking oil into metal fondue cooker to no more than ½ capacity or to depth of 2 inches. Heat, uncovered, on range to 375°. Add salt. Transfer cooker to fondue burner. Have appetizers at room temperature in serving bowl. Spear with fondue fork; fry in hot oil for 1 to 2 minutes. Transfer to dinner fork. Makes about 100 appetizers.

## Fried Cream Squares

Line bottom and sides of 9x9x2-inch pan with foil. In saucepan combine ½ cup sugar, ½ cup cornstarch, and dash salt. Stir in 2 cups light cream and ½ cup milk. Cook and stir over medium heat till mixture thickens and bubbles. Stir small amount of hot mixture into 3 slightly beaten egg yolks. Return to hot mixture; cook and stir 2 minutes. Remove from heat; add few drops vanilla and few drops almond extract.

Spread *half* of the pudding mixture in the foil-lined pan. Arrange one 3-ounce package ladyfingers (8), split in half lengthwise, evenly over pudding; top with remaining pudding. Cool. Cover; chill well. Turn out onto waxed paper. Remove foil and cut into 1-inch squares. Dip squares into 2 beaten eggs; coat with a mixture of 1½ cups ground almonds and ¼ cup fine dry bread crumbs. Chill, uncovered, 1 hour.

Pour cooking oil into metal fondue cooker to no more than ½ capacity or to depth of 2 inches. Heat, uncovered, over range to 400°. Add 1 teaspoon salt. Transfer to fondue burner. Spear dessert square through cake layer with fondue fork; fry in hot oil till browned, a few seconds. Transfer to dinner fork before eating. Serves 14 to 16.

*Fondue makes any party more enjoyable. If you prefer informal dining, try a fondue buffet with different types of fondue for each course. If learning about wine is a new hobby, why not have a wine-tasting party followed by a fondue? For after-the-game parties, fondue is quick and easy to fix. And if you've drawn the dessert course in a progressive dinner, Fried Cream Squares may be just what you need.*

## French-Toasted Fondue

**French bread**
**2 well-beaten eggs**
**½ cup milk**

**¼ teaspoon salt**
**Cooking oil**
**Fluffy Maple Sauce**

Cut French bread into about 50 bite-size pieces, each with one crust. Combine eggs, milk, and ¼ teaspoon salt. Pour oil into metal fondue cooker to no more than ½ capacity or to depth of 2 inches. Heat, uncovered, over range to 375°. Add 1 teaspoon salt. Transfer cooker to fondue burner. Spear bread through crust with fondue fork; dip in egg mixture, letting excess drip off. Fry in hot oil till golden brown. Transfer to dinner fork; dip in Fluffy Maple Sauce. Serves 6 to 8.

*Fluffy Maple Sauce:* Thoroughly cream together 1½ cups sifted powdered sugar, ½ cup butter, ½ cup maple-flavored syrup, and 1 egg yolk. Fold in 1 stiffly beaten egg white. Chill. Makes 2 cups.

## Chocolate-Nut Fondue

In saucepan combine one 6-ounce package semisweet chocolate pieces, ½ cup sugar, and ½ cup milk. Cook, stirring constantly, till chocolate is melted. Add ½ cup chunk-style peanut butter; mix well. Pour into fondue pot; place over fondue burner. Spear fruit dipper (banana slices or apple slices), cake cube (pound cake or angel cake), or marshmallows with fondue fork; dip in sauce. Makes 6 to 8 servings.

*Originally invented to promote Swiss chocolate, chocolate fondue is the traditional dessert fondue. Serve it either as a dessert or as a party snack. Chocolate-Nut Fondue, a rich and filling variation, is a great ending to a light meal.*

## Butterscotch Fondue

**½ cup butter or margarine**
**2 cups packed brown sugar**
**1 cup light corn syrup**
**2 tablespoons water**

**1 14-ounce can *sweetened condensed* milk**
**1 teaspoon vanilla**
**Pound cake cubes**

In saucepan melt butter; stir in sugar, corn syrup, and water. Bring to boiling. Stir in milk; simmer, stirring constantly, till mixture reaches thread stage (230°). Add vanilla. Pour into fondue pot; place over fondue burner. Spear pound cake cube with fondue fork; dip in fondue. (If mixture becomes too thick, stir in a little water.) Serves 8.

# International Main Dishes

The prosperity of the '60s made Americans a traveling people. Servicemen and their families were stationed abroad, and the general public was taking vacations to all parts of the world. While on these trips, Americans began learning about new kinds of foods. They brought the memory of these dishes home and began serving them to family and friends. At first, the most well known of these foreign dishes were the Italian ones. But soon American tastes expanded to include French, Scandinavian, Spanish, Oriental, German, Greek, and Indian dishes.

*Are you looking for an Italian-inspired recipe for your next dinner party? Then plan the special-occasion menu around Olive-Spaghetti Sauce (pictured opposite) served with spaghetti cooked "al dente," meaning that it is cooked till tender, yet firm.*

## Beef in Burgundy

3 pounds lean beef chuck,
    cut in 1½-inch cubes
⅓ cup all-purpose flour
¼ cup butter
¼ cup olive oil
¼ cup cognac
8 medium carrots
6 small onions
3 slices bacon, cut up

1 cup chopped onion
1 clove garlic, minced
1 cup red Burgundy
1 cup beef broth
12 small mushroom caps
1 tablespoon butter
8 ounces small onions (8)
¼ cup red Burgundy
Snipped parsley

Coat beef with flour. Heat ¼ cup butter and olive oil in a large skillet. Brown beef on all sides in butter-oil mixture. Transfer the meat to a 5-quart Dutch oven. Add cognac and set aside. In the same skillet cook carrots, 6 small onions, bacon, chopped onion, and garlic till bacon is crisp and vegetables are browned, stirring frequently. Drain and place vegetable mixture in Dutch oven with meat. Add 1 cup Burgundy, beef broth, and ½ teaspoon salt.

Cover, bring to boil; reduce heat, and simmer till meat is tender, 1 to 1½ hours. In small skillet cook mushrooms in 1 tablespoon butter till tender, 2 to 3 minutes. Remove mushrooms; set aside. In the same skillet combine the 8 ounces onions and ¼ cup Burgundy. Simmer, covered, till tender, 15 to 20 minutes. Before serving, place cooked onions and mushrooms atop meat. Heat through. Top with parsley. If desired, serve with noodles. Serves 8.

## Olive-Spaghetti Sauce

1 pound ground beef
½ pound ground veal
¼ pound Italian sausage
1 28-ounce can tomatoes,
    cut up
2 6-ounce cans tomato paste
1½ cups red Burgundy
1 cup water
1 cup chopped onion
¾ cup chopped green pepper
2 cloves garlic, crushed

1½ teaspoons Worcestershire
    sauce
1 teaspoon sugar
½ teaspoon chili powder
3 bay leaves
1 6-ounce can sliced mush-
    rooms, drained (1 cup)
½ cup sliced pimiento-
    stuffed green olives
20 ounces spaghetti, cooked
    and drained

In large Dutch oven brown meats; drain off fat. Stir in remaining ingredients *except* mushrooms, olives, and spaghetti. Stir in 1 teaspoon salt and ⅛ teaspoon pepper. Simmer, uncovered, 2 hours; stir occasionally. Remove bay leaves. Add mushrooms and olives; simmer 30 minutes. Serve over spaghetti. Pass Parmesan cheese. Serves 8 to 10.

*The cooking styles of Italy are varied. In northern Italy dairy products, polenta, and rice are used and the seasonings are light. In the south around Naples, it's different. Most Americans know this type of Italian cooking. It features garlic, herbs, tomatoes, and pasta. Olive-Spaghetti Sauce is a good example.*

## Pastitsio

Sometimes called the Greek national dish, Pastitsio is a meat-tomato-cheese-macaroni dish that has a delicious custard topping. Cinnamon is the characteristic seasoning, both mixed with the meat and sprinkled on top. The flavor combination is so good you'll quickly discover why Pastitsio is a favorite recipe of Greek family and holiday meals and why it's often served on Greek ships as part of the elegant buffet suppers.

1½ pounds ground beef
1 cup chopped onion
1 16-ounce can tomatoes, cut up
1 6-ounce can tomato paste
¼ teaspoon dried thyme, crushed
1 7-ounce package elbow macaroni

4 slightly beaten egg whites
½ cup cubed feta cheese or process American cheese
½ cup butter or margarine
½ cup all-purpose flour
¼ teaspoon ground cinnamon
4 cups milk
4 slightly beaten egg yolks

In skillet cook beef and onion till meat is browned; drain off excess fat. Add tomatoes, tomato paste, thyme, and 1 teaspoon salt. Simmer, covered, 30 minutes; stir often.

Meanwhile, cook macaroni according to package directions; drain well. Stir slightly beaten egg whites and cheese into the drained macaroni; stir in the meat mixture. Turn into a 13x9x2-inch baking dish. In large saucepan melt butter. Blend in flour, cinnamon, and 1 teaspoon salt. Add milk all at once. Cook, stirring constantly, till thickened and bubbly. Remove from heat. Gradually stir some of the hot sauce into the slightly beaten egg yolks; blend well. Return yolk mixture to sauce, stirring rapidly. Pour over meat mixture in baking dish. Sprinkle lightly with additional cinnamon, if desired. Bake at 375° till heated through, 35 to 40 minutes. Let stand 10 minutes before serving. Makes 12 servings.

## Sauerbraten

2½ cups water
1½ cups red wine vinegar
2 medium onions, sliced
½ lemon, sliced
12 whole cloves
6 bay leaves

6 whole peppercorns
1 tablespoon sugar
¼ teaspoon ground ginger
1 4-pound beef rump roast
2 tablespoons shortening
Gingersnap Gravy

In large bowl or crock combine water, vinegar, onions, lemon, cloves, bay leaves, peppercorns, sugar, ginger, and 1 tablespoon salt. Add rump roast, turning to coat. Cover and refrigerate meat about 36 hours; turn meat at least twice daily. Remove meat; wipe dry. Strain and reserve marinade. In Dutch oven brown meat in hot shortening; add strained marinade. Cover and cook slowly till tender, about 2 hours. Remove meat. Prepare Gingersnap Gravy. Serves 10.

Gingersnap Gravy: Combine 1½ cups meat juices and ½ cup water; add ⅔ cup broken gingersnaps. Cook and stir till thickened.

## Kima (Curried Beef Skillet)

Kima is Pakistani Pilaf, a rice dish steamed with meat, shellfish or fish, and/or vegetables. Native to Near East and Middle Eastern countries, it has been adopted by America's rice-growing South.

1 pound ground beef
1 cup chopped onion
1 clove garlic, minced
2 raw potatoes, peeled and cubed
2 tomatoes, peeled and cubed

1 10-ounce package frozen peas, broken apart
2 teaspoons curry powder
1½ teaspoons salt
Dash pepper
Flaked coconut
Hot cooked rice

In skillet cook beef, onion, and garlic till meat is browned. Drain off excess fat. Stir in remaining ingredients except coconut and rice. Cover; reduce heat and simmer till vegetables are tender, 20 to 25 minutes. Sprinkle with coconut. Serve with rice. Makes 6 servings.

## Chicken Kiev

4 large whole chicken
    breasts, boned and
    skinned
1 tablespoon chopped green
    onion
1 tablespoon snipped
    parsley

Salt
1 ¼-pound stick butter,
    chilled
All-purpose flour
1 beaten egg
½ cup fine dry bread crumbs
Fat for frying

Halve chicken breasts lengthwise. Place chicken, boned side up, between two pieces of clear plastic wrap. Working out from center, pound to ¼-inch thickness. Peel off wrap; sprinkle with onion, parsley, and salt. Cut butter into 8 sticks; place a stick at end of each chicken piece. Roll as for jelly roll, tucking in sides. Press ends to seal. Coat rolls with flour and dip in mixture of egg and 1 tablespoon water; then roll in bread crumbs. Chill well, at least 1 hour. Fry in deep hot fat (375°) till golden brown, about 5 minutes. Serves 4 to 8.

*Chicken Kiev, named after a Russian city, is a sure way to please guests at any party. The important thing to remember is to tuck the meat securely around the butter stuffing so it doesn't ooze out during browning.*

## Mexican Casserole

Cook 1½ pounds ground beef and 1 cup chopped onion till meat is browned. Drain off fat. Stir in one 16-ounce can tomatoes, cut up; one 8-ounce can tomato sauce; ½ cup raisins; 3 hard-cooked eggs, chopped; ¾ teaspoon salt; ¼ teaspoon Worcestershire sauce; and dash bottled hot pepper sauce. Boil, uncovered, 5 minutes. Meanwhile, using 2 cups packaged biscuit mix, prepare dumplings following directions on package. Turn boiling meat mixture into a 12x7½x2-inch baking dish; top with dumplings. Sprinkle dumplings with cornmeal. Bake, uncovered, at 400° till dumplings are done, 20 minutes. Serves 8.

## Puffy Tortilla Bake

¾ cup chopped onion
2 tablespoons cooking oil
1 16-ounce can tomatoes,
    cut up
1 8-ounce can tomato sauce
1 clove garlic, minced
1 to 1½ teaspoons finely
    chopped canned green
    chili peppers
1½ teaspoons chili powder
1 teaspoon sugar

¾ pound ground beef
1 clove garlic, minced
½ cup sliced green onion
3 tablespoons chopped
    pitted ripe olives
2 teaspoons chili powder
Puffy Tortillas
1½ cups shredded sharp process American cheese
¼ cup pitted ripe olives,
    sliced lengthwise

Cook chopped onion in *1 tablespoon* oil till tender. Add tomatoes, tomato sauce, next 4 ingredients, and ½ teaspoon salt. Simmer, uncovered, 30 minutes; set aside. Cook beef and 1 clove garlic in remaining 1 tablespoon oil till beef is browned. Add green onion, chopped olives, 2 teaspoons chili powder, and ½ teaspoon salt; stir to blend. With browned side down, fill each Puffy Tortilla with *2 to 3 tablespoons* meat mixture and *1 tablespoon* cheese; roll up. Arrange in 12x7½x2-inch baking dish. Pour sauce over; sprinkle with remaining cheese and sliced olives. Bake at 350° for 25 to 30 minutes. Makes 4 to 6 servings.

*Puffy Tortillas:* Stir together ¾ cup all-purpose flour, ¾ cup yellow cornmeal, and ¼ teaspoon salt. Add 1¾ cups water and 1 beaten egg. Beat smooth. For each tortilla, pour 3 tablespoons batter into hot greased 6-inch skillet; cook till browned on bottom and just set on top, 2 to 3 minutes. Remove to paper toweling. Makes 12.

*Since ancient times, the tortilla has been the national bread of Mexico. Originally, making tortillas was a long process involving cooking corn kernels with lime and then grinding this mixture to make flour. Today, you can make tortillas from either corn or wheat flour. Simply shape the dough into large and small pancakes, then fry them. Use the large tortillas for bread, and the small ones as the basis for Mexican favorites such as Puffy Tortilla Bake.*

212

212

*Flamboyant as flamenco, Spanish Paella is a colorful extravaganza of rice, vegetables, chicken, and seafood. It receives its rich yellow color from saffron, one of the world's most expensive spices.*

*This spice comes from the stamens of purple crocuses, which cover Spanish hillsides. Because of the delicate nature of the stamens, each must be plucked by hand—two or three per flower.*

*So expensive is this hand-operation, and consequently the price to the stores, that early food departments kept only empty packets of saffron on the shelves. You selected the packet and exchanged it for a full one at the check-out counter—after you had paid for the privilege of using these purple crocus wonders.*

*The dish is named for the pan in which it's cooked—a shallow Spanish skillet about 15 inches wide, with two handles.*

## Spanish Paella

¼ cup all-purpose flour
1 teaspoon salt
  Dash pepper
1 2½- to 3-pound ready-to-cook broiler-fryer chicken, cut up
¼ cup olive *or* cooking oil
2 cups chicken broth
2 medium onions, quartered
2 carrots, peeled and sliced lengthwise
1 stalk celery with leaves

⅔ cup long-grain rice
¼ cup diced canned pimiento
¼ teaspoon ground oregano
¼ teaspoon ground saffron
1 clove garlic, minced
12 ounces fresh or frozen shelled shrimp
12 *small* clams in shells, well-scrubbed
1 9-ounce package frozen artichoke hearts, thawed

Mix flour, salt, and pepper in plastic or paper bag. Add a few chicken pieces at a time; shake to coat. In heavy skillet brown chicken in hot oil about 20 minutes. Transfer to large kettle. Add next 9 ingredients and ½ teaspoon salt; simmer, covered, 30 minutes. Add remaining ingredients; simmer, covered, 20 minutes more. Serves 6 to 8.

## Swedish Cabbage Rolls

1 beaten egg
⅔ cup milk
¼ cup finely chopped onion
1 teaspoon salt
1 teaspoon Worcestershire sauce
½ pound ground beef

½ pound ground pork
¾ cup cooked rice
6 large cabbage leaves
1 10¾-ounce can condensed tomato soup
1 tablespoon brown sugar
1 tablespoon lemon juice

In a bowl combine egg, milk, onion, salt, Worcestershire, and dash pepper; mix well. Add beef, pork, and cooked rice; beat together with fork. Immerse cabbage leaves in boiling water just till limp, about 3 minutes; drain. (Slit heavy center vein of leaf about 2½ inches, if necessary.) Place ½ cup meat mixture on each leaf; fold in sides and roll ends over meat. Place rolls in 12x7½x2-inch baking dish. Blend together tomato soup, brown sugar, and lemon juice; pour mixture over rolls. Bake at 350° for 1¼ hours. Baste once or twice with sauce. Serves 6.

*Hungarian Goulash probably began as a hot spicy stew eaten by shepherds and herdsmen. The word goulash comes from 'gulyas' meaning 'herdsman's meat.' This dish is a classic of Hungarian cuisine. It features the paprika, sour cream, and hot noodles that are characteristic of Hungarian cooking.*

## Hungarian Veal Goulash

2½ pounds veal, cut in ¾-inch cubes
2 tablespoons cooking oil
1 cup chopped onion (about 2 medium onions)
1 clove garlic, minced
¼ cup all-purpose flour
1 tablespoon paprika
1½ teaspoons salt

1 teaspoon sugar
¼ teaspoon pepper
¼ teaspoon dried thyme, crushed
2 bay leaves
1 16-ounce can tomatoes, cut up
1 cup dairy sour cream
  Hot buttered noodles

Brown meat, half at a time, in hot oil. Reduce heat. Add onion and garlic; cook till onion is tender but not brown. Stir in *2 tablespoons* of the flour, paprika, salt, sugar, pepper, thyme, and bay leaves. Add tomatoes and ½ cup water. Cover; simmer, stirring occasionally, till meat is tender, about 1 hour. Stir often toward the end of cooking. Remove bay leaves. Combine sour cream and remaining flour. Stir into meat mixture; heat through. Serve over noodles. Serves 6 to 8.

## Sukiyaki

2 tablespoons cooking oil
1 pound beef tenderloin,
    sliced paper-thin
    across the grain
2 tablespoons sugar
½ cup beef stock *or* canned
    condensed beef broth
⅓ cup soy sauce
2 cups bias-cut green
    onions (2-inch lengths)
1 cup bias-cut celery
    slices (1-inch lengths)
5 cups small spinach leaves

1 16-ounce can bean
    sprouts, drained
12 to 16 ounces bean curd,
    cubed* (optional)
1 cup thinly sliced
    mushrooms
1 5-ounce can water chest-
    nuts, drained and
    thinly sliced
1 5-ounce can bamboo
    shoots, drained
Hot cooked rice
Soy sauce

Preheat large skillet, electric skillet, or wok; add oil. Add beef; cook quickly, turning meat over and over, just till browned, 1 to 2 minutes. Sprinkle with sugar. Combine stock or broth and ⅓ cup soy sauce; pour over meat. Push meat to one side. Let soy mixture bubble.

Keeping in separate groups, add onions and celery. Continue cooking and toss-stirring *each group* over high heat about 1 minute; push to one side. Again keeping in separate groups, add spinach, bean sprouts, bean curd, mushrooms, water chestnuts, and bamboo shoots. Cook and stir *each food* just till heated through. Let guests help themselves to some of everything. Serve with rice. Pass soy sauce. Serves 4.

*Bean curd (tofu) may be found at Oriental food shops.

*Take a make-believe trip to the Sukiyaki houses that flourished in San Francisco after World War II. These were take-off-your-shoes places where guests sat around a long table on pillows. Kimono-clad Japanese waitresses prepared Sukiyaki at the table. Guests chose from thinly sliced beef, bias-cut celery, fresh spinach, mushrooms, bamboo shoots, bean sprouts, and water chestnuts — all cooked in hot oil and served over rice. The crowning touch was the soy sauce passed 'round and 'round the table.*

## Chinese Chicken Almond

In large heavy skillet quickly cook 2 cups finely sliced raw chicken breasts in ¼ cup hot cooking oil.* Stir in 3 cups chicken broth; 2 cups diced celery; two 5-ounce cans bamboo shoots, drained and diced; two 5-ounce cans water chestnuts, drained and sliced; 1 cup diced bok choy (Chinese cabbage) *or* romaine: and 2 tablespoons soy sauce. Bring to boil; cook, covered, over low heat till crisp-tender, about 5 minutes. Blend ½ cup cold water and ⅓ cup cornstarch; add to chicken mixture. Cook and stir till thickened and bubbly. Salt to taste. Top with ½ cup toasted almond halves. Serve over hot cooked rice. Serves 6 to 8.

*High heat and quick stirring are essential to avoid over-cooking.

## Chinese Peas and Shrimp

12 ounces fresh or frozen
    shelled shrimp
2 tablespoons cooking oil
1 7-ounce package frozen
    Chinese pea pods,
    thawed, *or* 2 cups fresh
    Chinese pea pods
2 tablespoons thinly sliced
    green onion with tops

2 teaspoons shredded
    peeled gingerroot *or*
    ½ teaspoon ground
    ginger
1 clove garlic, minced
1 teaspoon cornstarch
½ teaspoon sugar
½ teaspoon salt
1 teaspoon soy sauce

Thaw frozen shrimp. In heavy skillet cook shrimp quickly in hot oil till pink, 3 to 5 minutes. Add pea pods, onion, gingerroot or ginger, and garlic; toss and cook over high heat 1 minute. Combine cornstarch, sugar, and salt. Add soy sauce and 2 teaspoons cold water, mixing till smooth. Pour over shrimp mixture; toss and cook till thickened and clear, about 1 minute. Pass soy sauce, if desired. Serves 3 or 4.

*Oriental cooking is an art that began in China some 20,000 years ago. The quick-cooking technique of the Chinese saves fuel, preserves nutrients, and helps flavor. Foods are added to a mixed dish in a given order. Those ingredients that take longer to cook go in first. As a result, Chinese food stays crisp and attractive. Try Chinese Peas and Shrimp and see.*

# Convenience Cooking

Convenience cooking is creating meals with products that have part of the food preparation already done—anything from condensed soup to complete dinners. Although convenience cooking has long been a part of the cooking scene, it finally reached full blossom in the '60s. One reason it was so popular was that women were starting to leave the kitchen. Cooking for the family was no longer the homemaker's chief function. She wanted and needed time to work outside the home or to become involved in community projects. Convenience cooking was a quick and easy answer to her problem. Recognizing that the cooking style of their readers was changing, *Better Homes and Gardens* in 1964 sponsored a contest looking for new ways of using convenience foods. Using the results of this contest as well as other research, they published a wide variety of time-saving ideas. The dishes in this section are some of the very best of these recipes.

## Vegetable-Meat Cups

*Fast new twists that cut preparation time to a minimum in this Vegetable-Meat Cups recipe are the instant potatoes, frozen peas, and Cheddar cheese soup used for sauce. This one-dish meal containing meat and vegetables typifies a food style that became popular in the '60s.*

1 beaten egg
¼ cup milk
¼ cup coarsely crushed saltine crackers
½ teaspoon Worcestershire sauce
1 pound ground beef
Packaged instant mashed potatoes (enough for 4 servings)

2 tablespoons sliced green onion
• • •
½ of a 10¾-ounce can condensed Cheddar cheese soup (⅔ cup)
3 tablespoons milk
½ of a 10-ounce package frozen peas, cooked and drained

Combine egg, ¼ cup milk, crackers, Worcestershire, ¾ teaspoon salt, and dash pepper. Add beef; mix well. On waxed paper shape into 4 patties with 5-inch diameter. Shape each over an inverted 5-ounce custard cup; discard paper. Chill 1 hour. Place inverted cups in shallow baking pan; bake at 375° for 20 minutes. Prepare potatoes following package directions; stir in onion. Lift baked meat cups from custard cups and turn upright; fill with potatoes. In saucepan mix Cheddar cheese soup with 3 tablespoons milk; stir in cooked peas. Heat through. Spoon sauce over meat cups. Makes 4 servings.

## Sweet-Sour Meatballs

*This Sweet-Sour Meatballs recipe came from a reader in California. It took the Grand Prize in the magazine's convenience food contest. Try it; you'll discover why.*

1 8¾-ounce can pineapple tidbits
¼ cup packed brown sugar
2 tablespoons cornstarch
¼ cup vinegar
1 teaspoon soy sauce
1 15-ounce can meatballs in gravy (2 cups)

1 8-ounce can water chestnuts, drained and thinly sliced (1 cup)
1 medium green pepper, cut in strips (1 cup)
• • •
Hot cooked rice
1 tomato, cut in wedges

Drain pineapple, reserving ⅓ cup syrup. In saucepan combine brown sugar and cornstarch. Blend in pineapple syrup, vinegar, soy sauce, and ¾ cup water. Cook and stir over low heat till mixture thickens and bubbles. Carefully stir in the meatballs in gravy, sliced water chestnuts, green pepper strips, and pineapple tidbits. Heat to boiling. Serve over rice. Garnish with tomato wedges. Makes 4 servings.

Turn ground meat into something special and prepare *Vegetable-Meat Cups.* The cup which holds the instant potatoes is a ground meat mixture shaped over custard cups. Canned soup, milk, and frozen peas make up the sauce to complete this dish.

Next time it's your turn to furnish the refreshments, prepare *Lemon Pudding Pound Cake* (see recipe, page 219). It's a simple-to-make dessert that starts with a cake mix and a pudding mix. Garnish the cake with fresh lemon slices, if desired.

## Shrimp and Rice Supreme

1 cup milk
1 10½-ounce can condensed
  cream of celery soup
1 4½-ounce can shrimp
1 12-ounce package frozen
  rice and peas with
  mushrooms

2 tablespoons snipped
  parsley
1 teaspoon curry powder
• • •
4 frozen patty shells,
  baked
Toasted slivered almonds

In 2-quart saucepan gradually stir the milk into the soup. Drain the shrimp. Add the drained shrimp, frozen rice and peas with mushrooms, parsley, and curry powder to the soup mixture. Cover and simmer gently for 30 minutes; stir occasionally. Serve shrimp mixture in baked patty shells. Garnish with toasted almonds. Makes 4 servings.

## Saucy Pork Chops

6 pork chops, cut ½ to ¾
  inch thick
Salt
Pepper
1 medium onion, thinly
  sliced

1 10½-ounce can condensed
  cream of chicken soup
¼ cup catsup
2 to 3 teaspoons Worcestershire sauce

Trim fat from chops and cook in skillet till 1 tablespoon fat accumulates. Discard trimmings; brown chops on both sides in drippings. Season with salt and pepper. Top with onion. Combine soup, catsup, and Worcestershire; pour over chops. Simmer, covered, 45 to 60 minutes. Remove chops to warm platter. Spoon sauce over. Serves 6.

## Ginger Beans with Luncheon Meat

Combine two 16-ounce cans pork and beans in tomato sauce, ¾ cup finely crushed gingersnaps (10 to 12), ¼ cup catsup, 2 tablespoons light molasses, and ½ teaspoon salt. Turn into a 1½-quart casserole. Cut one 12-ounce can luncheon meat in 6 slices; place on top of beans. Bake, covered, at 350° about 30 to 35 minutes. Makes 4 to 6 servings.

## Ham and Chicken Stack-Ups

1 cup pancake mix
1 cup milk
1 slightly beaten egg
2 tablespoons cooking oil
1 5-ounce can boned
  chicken, drained

1 10½-ounce can condensed
  cream of mushroom soup
1 4-ounce can chopped mushrooms, drained
1 4½-ounce can deviled ham
½ cup dairy sour cream

In mixing bowl combine pancake mix, milk, egg, and oil; beat with rotary beater till smooth. Bake 12 pancakes on lightly greased griddle, using about 2 tablespoons batter for each. Remove to towel-covered baking sheet and keep warm.

Cut up canned chicken. Combine chicken, *half* of the soup, and drained mushrooms. Place 4 pancakes in a 12x7½x2-inch baking dish. Spread chicken-mushroom mixture evenly over each pancake in baking dish. Top each with second pancake; spread each evenly with deviled ham. Top with remaining 4 pancakes. Combine remaining soup with sour cream; spoon over stacks. Bake at 350° till heated through, 10 to 15 minutes. Serves 4.

## Taco Salad

1 pound ground beef
½ envelope dry onion soup
   mix (¼ cup)
1 small head lettuce, torn
   in bite-size pieces
   (about 4 cups)
1 4-ounce package shredded
   sharp natural Cheddar
   cheese

1 large tomato, cut in
   wedges
1 small onion, sliced and
   separated in rings
½ cup sliced pitted ripe
   olives
¼ cup chopped green pepper
1 6-ounce package corn
   chips

In skillet brown beef. Sprinkle onion soup mix over meat; stir in ¾ cup water. Simmer mixture, uncovered, 10 minutes. In salad bowl combine lettuce, cheese, tomato, onion, olives, and green pepper; toss well. Spoon meat over; top with corn chips. Makes 4 to 6 servings.

## Hot Frank 'n Potato Salad

½ envelope dry onion soup
   mix (¼ cup)
1 tablespoon all-purpose
   flour
1 tablespoon sugar

4 or 5 frankfurters
2 tablespoons vinegar
2 16-ounce cans sliced
   potatoes, drained
½ cup dairy sour cream

In skillet mix soup mix, flour, sugar, and dash pepper. Cut franks in ½-inch pieces. Add with vinegar and ½ cup water to skillet. Cook and stir till boiling. Add potatoes. Reduce heat; simmer, covered, 10 minutes. Add sour cream; heat, but *do not boil*. Makes 6 servings.

## Swedish Vegetable Salad

1 10-ounce package frozen
   cauliflower, cooked,
   drained, and
   cooled
1 16-ounce can sliced
   carrots, drained
1 16-ounce can cut green
   beans, drained

1 14-ounce can artichoke
   hearts, drained and
   halved
1 cup chopped celery
1 tablespoon instant minced
   onion
½ cup French salad dressing
   Chili-Dill Dressing

Cut cooked cauliflower into flowerets. Arrange well-drained canned vegetables with cauliflower and celery in large salad bowl. Add onion to French dressing. Drizzle over vegetables; chill 2 hours. Drain. Serve drained vegetables in lettuce cups, if desired. Pass Chili-Dill Dressing. Serves 10 to 12.

*Chili-Dill Dressing:* Combine ½ cup mayonnaise, ¼ cup chili sauce, 1 tablespoon lemon juice, 2 teaspoons dried dillweed, ½ teaspoon salt, and dash pepper. Chill well.

## Harvest Fruit Mold

Cover one 11-ounce package mixed dried fruits with 2 cups water. Bring to boiling. Reduce heat; simmer, covered, 30 minutes. Add ¼ cup sugar; cook 5 minutes. Drain fruit, reserving syrup. Add water to reserved syrup to equal 2 cups. Dissolve two 3-ounce packages orange-flavored gelatin in 2 cups boiling water; stir in reserved syrup. Chill till partially set. Pit prunes; cut up all fruit. Fold into gelatin. Pour into 6½-cup ring mold. Chill till firm. Serves 8.

*What's in a name? Frankfurters, dachshunds, hot dogs, or wieners have come a long way since they were first served with catsup and mustard in a long bun at Coney Island. Originally called frankfurters or dachshunds because they were introduced by a butcher from Frankfurt, Germany, they picked up their nickname, hot dog, from a New York sportscaster who had difficulty getting his vowels around dachshund. He was helped by an enterprising vendor who heated the normally cold frankfurters or dachshunds for baseball fans who were watching an early-season baseball game. But if you subscribe to the theory that these long, skinny sausages originated in Vienna, you call the sausage a Wiener.*

## Quick Swedish Rye Bread

1 13¾-ounce package
   hot roll mix
2 eggs
2 tablespoons molasses

1 tablespoon packed brown
   sugar
¾ cup rye flour
1 teaspoon caraway seed

In large mixing bowl dissolve the yeast from the roll mix in ¾ cup warm water (110°). Stir in eggs, molasses, and brown sugar. Combine flour from roll mix, rye flour, and caraway seed. Add to yeast mixture; blend well. Cover and let rise in a warm place till nearly doubled (about 1 hour). Turn out on lightly floured surface, tossing lightly to coat dough with flour. Divide dough in two parts. Shape in two round loaves and place on greased baking sheet. Let rise in a warm place until double (30 to 45 minutes). Bake at 350° for 30 minutes. Makes 2 loaves.

## Orange-Nut Ring

Separate rolls from 2 packages refrigerated orange Danish rolls with icing (16 rolls). Arrange 1 package (8 rolls), flat side down, around bottom of an ungreased 6½-cup ring mold. Stagger remaining package of rolls on top of first layer, covering seams of rolls on bottom layer. Bake at 375° for 20 to 25 minutes. Invert immediately on serving plate. Spread top and sides with frosting included in packages. Sprinkle with ¼ cup chopped pecans. Serve warm with butter. Makes 8 servings.

## Honey Crunch Loaf

*Honey has served man well as a food, medicine, love potion, sacred offering, and money. The Greeks believed it gave wisdom, health, and long life. In Rome, many a wife won her husband's heart with honey. Today, it adds a naturally sweet flavor to any food—especially Honey Crunch Loaf.*

1 round or oval loaf un-
   sliced white bread
½ cup butter, melted
½ cup honey

½ cup presweetened crisp
   rice cereal
½ cup flaked coconut
½ cup packed brown sugar

Slice bread 4 or 5 times in each direction, *cutting to, but not through, bottom crust.* Place loaf on foil on a baking sheet; turn up edges of foil. Combine butter with ¼ *cup* of the honey; spoon over top of loaf and let excess drizzle between sections. Combine cereal, coconut, and sugar; sprinkle on top of loaf and between sections. Drizzle with remaining honey. Heat at 350° till lightly browned, about 20 minutes.

## Cherry Cream Puffs

1 stick piecrust mix
⅔ cup boiling water
2 eggs
1 21-ounce can cherry pie
   filling

2 cups frozen whipped
   dessert topping,
   thawed
½ cup flaked coconut

In saucepan crumble piecrust mix into boiling water; cook and stir vigorously till pastry forms a ball and leaves sides of pan. Cook and stir 1 minute over low heat. Add eggs, one at a time, beating with electric mixer at low speed for 1 minute after each addition. Drop about 3 tablespoons mixture onto greased baking sheet for each cream puff. Bake at 400° till golden brown and puffy, 30 to 35 minutes. Remove from baking sheet. Cool on rack. Cut off tops; remove excess webbing. Set aside ½ *cup* pie filling. Fold dessert topping and coconut into remaining pie filling; fill cream puffs with mixture. Cover with tops of cream puffs; spoon reserved pie filling over. Makes 8 puffs.

## Lazy Day Grasshopper Pie

Chocolate wafers
1 7- or 9-ounce jar
    marshmallow creme
¼ cup milk

6 or 7 drops green food
    coloring
4 drops peppermint extract
1 cup whipping cream

Line bottom of 9-inch pie plate with chocolate wafers, filling in spaces between whole cookies with pieces of cookie. Line sides of the pie plate with half cookies.

In mixing bowl combine marshmallow creme, milk, food coloring, and peppermint extract; whip till fluffy. Whip cream. Fold into marshmallow mixture. Spoon filling into cookie crust. Freeze till firm, 8 hours or overnight. Garnish with dollops of additional whipped cream, if desired. Serves 6 to 8.

*The grasshopper, a popular after-dinner drink of the '50s, includes green creme de menthe and white creme de cacao. Consequently, any combination of these liqueur flavors — mint and chocolate — earns a dessert the name grasshopper. This Grasshopper Pie is 'Lazy Day' because marshmallow creme saves the work of making a chiffon-type filling; chocolate cookies provide an easy crumb crust.*

## Crunchy Apricot Cake

1 21-ounce can apricot pie
    filling
1 package 1-layer-size
    yellow cake mix

1 egg
½ cup flaked coconut
½ cup chopped pecans
½ cup butter, melted

Spread pie filling in bottom of 9x9 x2-inch baking pan. Combine cake mix, egg, and ⅓ cup water. Using electric mixer, beat 4 minutes on medium speed. Pour over pie filling; sprinkle with coconut and pecans. Drizzle melted butter over top. Bake at 350° for 40 minutes. Cut into squares and serve apricot side up. Serve warm. Makes 9 servings.

## Lemon Pudding Pound Cake *(see photo, page 215)*

4 eggs
1 package 2-layer-size
    yellow cake mix
1 3¾- or 3⅝-ounce package
    *instant* lemon
    pudding mix

¾ cup water
⅓ cup cooking oil
• • •
2 cups sifted powdered
    sugar
⅓ cup lemon juice

Beat eggs till thick and lemon-colored. Add cake mix, pudding mix, water, and oil; beat 10 minutes at medium speed on electric mixer. Pour into *ungreased* 10-inch tube pan with removable bottom. Bake at 350° about 50 minutes. Meanwhile, combine sugar and lemon juice; heat to boiling. *Leaving cake on pan bottom,* remove sides of pan from hot cake. Using 2-tined fork, prick holes in top of cake. Brush hot lemon mixture over top and sides of cake. Cool. Remove pan bottom.

*This Lemon Pudding Pound Cake was the recipe used by the magazine to launch its convenience food contest in 1964 — held to celebrate the publishing of 10,000,000 copies of the* Better Homes and Gardens Cook Book, *now called the* New Cook Book, *and to urge readers to be creative with convenience foods of all types.*

## Easy Chocolate Fudge

½ cup butter or margarine
1 5½- or 6-ounce package
    *regular* chocolate
    pudding mix
½ cup milk

4¾ cups sifted powdered
    sugar
½ cup chopped walnuts
½ teaspoon vanilla
Walnut halves (optional)

In medium saucepan melt butter or margarine; stir in dry pudding mix and milk. Bring to boiling; boil for 1 minute, stirring constantly. Remove from heat; beat in powdered sugar. Stir in nuts and vanilla. Turn into buttered 10x6x2-inch baking dish. Garnish with walnut halves, if desired. Chill; cut in 1½-inch squares. Makes 1¾ pounds.

# Myrna's Favorites

Young homemakers may not know the name of Myrna, but to millions of cooks-in-the-home Myrna Johnston was the Food Editor of *Better Homes and Gardens* magazine and the person who brought to them all the latest and best in food news. For more than thirty years, Myrna sat at her desk in Des Moines, Iowa, endured train rides across the continent in the days before the airplane, and jetted about the nation in search of the finest recipes or food help for her millions of fans. Myrna always aimed to serve and inspire her readers. She stresses that every recipe is an opportunity to win a friend — so it had better be good! Mrs. Johnston also believes that pictures are an important part of the success of a recipe in that they help the homemaker visualize the dish. As a grandmother of three, Myrna enjoys cooking for her family. An example is this Christmas smorgasbord. But Myrna's favorites go beyond these foods. They cover foods ranging from guacamole to light as a cloud biscuits to almond torte.

Myrna's holiday smorgasbord features a glazed ham decorated with cream cheese, *Swedish Brown Beans, Swedish Meatballs* (pictured opposite), boiled potatoes trimmed with dill, a molded fruit salad, lingonberry sauce, stuffed eggs and celery, *Fruit Soup* (see recipe, page 223), an apple salad, and pickled herring with red onion rings. Coffee, cider, cheese, and cookies are served on the dessert table.

## Swedish Meatballs

¾ pound lean ground beef
½ pound ground veal
¼ pound ground pork
1½ cups soft bread crumbs
1 cup light cream
½ cup chopped onion
1 tablespoon butter
1 egg

¼ cup finely snipped
    parsley
1¼ teaspoons salt
    Dash pepper
    Dash ground ginger
    Dash ground nutmeg
2 tablespoons butter
    Gravy

Have meats ground together twice. Soak bread crumbs in cream about 5 minutes. In saucepan cook onion in 1 tablespoon butter till tender but not brown.

Mix meats, crumb mixture, cooked onion, egg, parsley, salt, pepper, ginger, and nutmeg. Beat 5 minutes at medium speed on electric mixer, or mix by hand until well combined. Shape into 1-inch balls. (Mixture will be soft. For easier shaping, wet hands or chill the mixture first.) In skillet brown meatballs in 2 tablespoons butter. Remove from skillet and prepare Gravy. Add meatballs to Gravy. Cover; cook *slowly*, about 30 minutes. Baste the meatballs occasionally. Makes about 4 dozen.

*Gravy:* Melt 2 tablespoons butter in skillet with drippings. Stir in 2 tablespoons all-purpose flour. Dissolve 1 beef bouillon cube in 1¼ cups boiling water. Add bouillon and ½ teaspoon instant coffee powder to flour mixture. Cook and stir till thickened and bubbly.

*The smorgasbord, which means bread and butter table, is an elaborate luncheon or buffet dinner composed of several different kinds of dishes, each eaten from a separate plate. Traditional Swedish smorgasbord selections include herring dishes; other fish and cold egg recipes; cold meats and salads; and hot dishes such as omelets, rice puddings, and Swedish Meatballs.*

## Swedish Brown Beans

1 pound dry Swedish brown
    beans
3 inches stick cinnamon
1½ teaspoons salt

⅓ cup packed brown sugar
¼ cup vinegar
2 tablespoons dark corn
    syrup

Rinse beans; drain. Add 6 cups cold water. Cover; let stand overnight. (Or, bring water and beans slowly to boiling; simmer 2 minutes. Cover; let stand 1 hour.) Add cinnamon and salt. Cover; simmer till beans are about tender, 1½ to 2 hours. Add sugar and vinegar. Cook, uncovered, till tender and desired consistency, about 30 minutes; stir occasionally. Remove cinnamon. Stir in syrup. Serves 6.

## Guacamole

2 ripe medium avocados,
   peeled and pitted
2 tablespoons lemon juice
2 to 4 tablespoons chopped
   canned green chili
   peppers

1 thin slice of a small
   onion
1 clove garlic, crushed
⅛ teaspoon ground white
   pepper
Crisp vegetable dippers

In blender container combine all ingredients except dippers. Add ½ teaspoon salt. Blend till smooth, scraping down sides of container as necessary. Serve as a dip with vegetables. Makes 1 cup.

## Barbecued Ribs with Warren's Sauce

*The zippy barbecue sauce that goes with these ribs was the specialty of Warren Johnston, the husband of Myrna. An avid barbecue fan, he had settled on this sauce as the best for all types of meat after years of grilling and tasting under the watchful eye of his wife, the famous food editor.*

4 pounds pork loin back
   ribs
1 cup catsup
1 cup water
¼ cup vinegar
1 tablespoon sugar

1 tablespoon Worcestershire
   sauce
1 teaspoon salt
1 teaspoon celery seed
2 or 3 dashes bottled hot
   pepper sauce

Lace ribs on barbecue spit accordion style, and secure with holding forks. Adjust on rotisserie above drip pan. Let ribs rotate over *medium-slow* coals. Meanwhile, in saucepan combine remaining ingredients. Bring the mixture to boiling; reduce heat and simmer, uncovered, 30 minutes. After ribs cook 40 minutes, baste well with sauce; add damp hickory to coals, if desired. Cook till ribs are well done, about 20 minutes longer. Pass remaining sauce with ribs. Makes 4 or 5 servings.

## Moo Burgers

*Moo Burgers get their name from the dairy sour cream that's used to make them. Myrna says they're light and fluffy and lots of fun to eat.*

1½ pounds ground beef
1 cup dairy sour cream
¼ cup Worcestershire sauce
1 tablespoon instant minced
   onion

1½ teaspoons salt
1½ cups corn flakes
• • •
8 hamburger buns, split
   and toasted

Combine beef, sour cream, Worcestershire, onion, and salt. Crush corn flakes slightly by hand; stir into meat. Shape mixture into 8 patties about ¾ inch thick. Grill over *slow* coals 5 minutes. Turn and grill till done, 3 to 4 minutes longer. Serve in buns. Makes 8 sandwiches.

## Beef Filets with Royal Mushroom Sauce

6 beef filets, cut 1 inch
   thick
2 tablespoons butter
½ cup chopped mushrooms
¼ cup chopped green onion

4 teaspoons cornstarch
1 cup red Burgundy
½ cup water
2 tablespoons snipped
   parsley

In skillet brown beef steaks quickly in butter. Cook, uncovered, over medium-high heat, turning occasionally. Cook about 9 to 10 minutes for rare and 11 to 12 minutes for medium. Remove steaks from skillet. Season with salt and pepper; keep hot. Add mushrooms and onion to skillet. Cook till tender. Blend in cornstarch. Add wine, water, parsley, 1 teaspoon salt, and dash pepper; cook and stir till thick and bubbly. Cook 1 minute longer. Serve over steaks. Serves 6.

## Swedish Fruit Soup *(see photo, page 220)*

In a large saucepan combine 4 cups water, one 11-ounce package mixed dried fruits, ½ cup light raisins, and 3 to 4 inches stick cinnamon. Simmer, uncovered, till fruits are tender, about 30 minutes. Add one 18-ounce can unsweetened pineapple juice; 1 medium unpeeled orange, thinly sliced and halved; ½ cup currant jelly; ¼ cup sugar; 2 tablespoons quick-cooking tapioca; and ¼ teaspoon salt. Simmer, covered, over low heat, 15 minutes longer, stirring occasionally. Remove the stick cinnamon. Serve warm or chilled. Makes 8 to 10 servings.

## Cloud Biscuits

2 cups all-purpose flour
4 teaspoons baking powder
1 tablespoon sugar
½ cup shortening
1 beaten egg
⅔ cup milk*

Stir together dry ingredients and ½ teaspoon salt; cut in shortening till mixture resembles coarse crumbs. Combine egg and milk; add to flour mixture all at once. Stir till dough follows fork around bowl. Turn out on lightly floured surface; knead gently with heel of hand about 20 strokes. Roll dough ¾ inch thick. Cut with floured 2¼-inch biscuit cutter. Place on ungreased baking sheet. If desired, chill 1 to 3 hours. Bake at 450° till golden brown, 10 to 14 minutes. Makes 12.

*For Drop Biscuits:* Increase milk to ¾ cup; omit kneading. Drop dough from tablespoon onto ungreased baking sheet. Bake.

## Almond Brittle Torte

1½ cups all-purpose flour
¾ cup sugar
8 egg yolks (½ cup)
¼ cup cold water
1 tablespoon lemon juice
1 teaspoon vanilla
8 egg whites (1 cup)
1 teaspoon cream of tartar
¾ cup sugar
2 cups whipping cream
1 tablespoon sugar
2 teaspoons vanilla
Almond Brittle Topping
½ cup toasted almond halves

In a mixing bowl thoroughly combine flour and ¾ cup sugar. Make a well in center and add egg yolks, water, lemon juice, and 1 teaspoon vanilla. Beat till batter is smooth. Beat egg whites with cream of tartar and 1 teaspoon salt till very soft peaks form. Add ¾ cup sugar gradually, 2 tablespoons at a time. Continue beating till stiff peaks form.

Fold egg yolk batter gently into egg white mixture. Pour batter into *ungreased* 10-inch tube pan. Carefully cut through batter, going around tube 5 or 6 times with knife to break large air bubbles. Bake at 350° till top springs back when touched lightly about 45 to 50 minutes. Invert pan; cool. Remove cake. Cool well. Split crosswise in 4 equal layers. *Just before serving,* whip cream with 1 tablespoon sugar and 2 teaspoons vanilla. Spread *half* the whipped cream between cake layers and the remainder over top and sides. Cover with Almond Brittle Topping; insert almonds into frosting porcupine style.

*Almond Brittle Topping:* In saucepan mix together ¾ cup sugar, 2 tablespoons light corn syrup, 2 tablespoons water, and ½ teaspoon instant coffee crystals. Cook the mixture to soft-crack stage (285° to 290°). Remove the mixture from heat; immediately add 1½ teaspoons baking soda. Stir vigorously, but only till mixture blends and pulls away from sides of saucepan.

Quickly pour the mixture into a buttered 8x8x2-inch baking pan. *Do not spread or stir.* Cool. Tap bottom of pan to remove the candy. Crush the candy into coarse crumbs.

*Almond Brittle Torte is the candy cake of a famous San Francisco sweet shop, a birthday favorite that the chef stumbled onto accidentally. It's also a good example of how some recipes just happen instead of being created in a home economist's brain. While making nougat by caramelizing sugar, the chef accidentally knocked some baking soda into the syrupy sugar. It fizzed and foamed. Grabbing it off the stove, he turned it out on his marble slab. When cool, it became porous and hard. He decided to crush the brittle and decorate a whipped cream frosted cake with the brittle and almonds.*

# Gourmet Cooking

Gourmet cooking flourished in the '60s. Americans, not always satisfied with eating on the run, learned to appreciate the art of elegant dining. They began using their spare time to prepare fancier and more complicated foods. Weekend chefs began adapting many of the international dishes to American tastes. A growing interest in wines, both foreign and domestic, brought about a whole group of new dishes using wine. People discovered the world of herbs and began creating new flavor combinations. Soon a new way of entertaining developed and couples with an interest in fine foods formed gourmet clubs that met once a month. By the end of the '60s the adventure of gourmet dining had firmly captured the imagination of many Americans all across the country.

*The appetizer, although relatively new on the American scene, is well-known around the world. The French have hors d'oeuvres, which are usually small pieces of cheese, meat, fish, or olives. The Zakouska, usually served with large amounts of wine and liquor, is typical of many Slavic countries, especially Russia. In Scandinavian countries, the smorgasbord is used as the appetizer course, and in Italy, foods served before the meal are called antipasto.*

## Shrimp Appetizers

2 pounds fresh or frozen
    shrimp in shells
2 tablespoons olive oil
2 tablespoons butter or
    margarine
½ teaspoon salt

¼ teaspoon freshly ground
    pepper
¼ cup dry vermouth
2 tablespoons lemon juice
• • •
Lemon wedges

Thaw shrimp if frozen; shell and clean. In skillet blend olive oil and butter over medium heat. Add shrimp, salt, and pepper; cook till shrimp turn pink and become opaque, 5 to 6 minutes. Add vermouth and lemon juice; cook over high heat for 1 minute, stirring constantly. Serve hot as an appetizer with lemon wedges. Serves 8.

## Chicken Jubilee

6 small whole chicken
    breasts, skinned and
    boned
1 20-ounce can pineapple
    slices
2 tablespoons butter
1 cup finely chopped fully
    cooked ham
2 tablespoons chopped onion
¼ cup coarsely crushed
    saltine crackers

¼ teaspoon ground ginger
¼ cup butter or margarine
¾ cup chicken broth
2 tablespoons vinegar
½ teaspoon salt
1 tablespoon cornstarch
    Butter or margarine
1 8¾-ounce can pitted dark
    sweet cherries,
    drained
¼ cup brandy, heated

Place chicken pieces, boned side up, on cutting board. Working from center out, pound chicken lightly till about ¼ inch thick. Drain pineapple, reserving ½ cup syrup. Dice *4 slices* and cook in the 2 tablespoons butter with ham and onion. Add crackers and ginger; mix well.

Divide stuffing evenly among chicken pieces. Tuck in sides of each and roll up as for jelly roll. Skewer or tie. In skillet brown slowly in ¼ cup butter. Add chicken broth, vinegar, and salt. Cover; cook 20 minutes. Mix cornstarch with reserved pineapple syrup. Stir into sauce in skillet. Cook, uncovered, till tender, about 15 minutes. Remove chicken to serving dish.

Brown remaining pineapple lightly in a little butter. Add to chicken with cherries. Pour sauce into heatproof dish. At table, pour heated brandy over sauce and ignite. Spoon flaming sauce over chicken. Serves 6.

*If you were playing the French game of naming dishes for the province of which the garnish is typical, Roast Pork Tangerine would be à la Florida or Californie because that's where the fruit grows. So would Roast Duckling with Grenadine Sauce because pomegranates from which grenadine syrup sometimes comes also grow there (and 'round the Mediterranean and in China, too). Actually, generous use of fruits with meats is more American than European, though the French do duckling with oranges and Montmorency cherries and the Scandinavians use prunes and apples with goose. It makes sense to use fruits to cut the richness of meat or poultry.*

## Roast Pork Tangerine

1 5- to 6-pound pork loin roast
1 teaspoon dry mustard
1 teaspoon dried marjoram, crushed
2 teaspoons grated tangerine peel
½ cup tangerine juice

1 tablespoon brown sugar
3 tablespoons all-purpose flour
⅛ teaspoon dry mustard
Dash dried marjoram, crushed
2 tangerines, peeled and sectioned

Place pork, fat side up, on rack in shallow roasting pan. Mix 1 teaspoon mustard, 1 teaspoon marjoram, and 1 teaspoon salt; rub over meat. Roast at 325° for 2½ hours. Skim fat from pan. Combine peel, juice, and brown sugar; spoon over roast. Continue roasting till meat thermometer registers 170°, about 1 hour more; baste often. Remove meat to platter. Pour off all but 3 tablespoons fat. Blend flour, ⅛ teaspoon dry mustard, and dash marjoram into reserved fat. Add 1½ cups water, stirring constantly. Cook and stir till thickened and bubbly. Season to taste. Add tangerines to gravy; pass with pork. Serves 10.

## Tuna-Cream Puff Bowl

4 hard-cooked eggs
1 9¼-ounce can tuna
1 tablespoon lemon juice
1 cup sliced celery
¼ cup sliced pimiento-stuffed green olives

¼ cup finely chopped onion
¼ teaspoon salt
½ cup mayonnaise or salad dressing
Cream Puff Bowl
2 cups shredded lettuce

Sieve 1 egg yolk and slice 1 whole egg; reserve. Chop remaining eggs and white. Drain and flake tuna; sprinkle with juice. Add celery, olives, onion, salt, and dash pepper. Fold in mayonnaise and chopped eggs; chill. Before serving, cover bottom of Cream Puff Bowl with lettuce; fill with tuna salad. Trim with reserved egg. Serves 6.

*Cream Puff Bowl:* Melt ¼ cup butter in ½ cup boiling water. Add ½ cup all-purpose flour, ¼ teaspoon celery seed, and dash salt all at once; stir vigorously. Cook, stirring constantly, over low heat till mixture forms a ball that doesn't separate. Cool slightly. Add 2 eggs, one at a time, beating till smooth after each. Spread batter evenly over bottom and sides of greased 9-inch pie plate. Bake at 450° for 15 minutes; reduce heat to 325° and bake 30 minutes. Turn oven off; leave cream puff in oven to dry, about 20 minutes. Remove from oven; cool.

*In France, Leek Lorraine would be known as Quiche Normande because leeks, which replace onions in this version of the Alsace-Lorraine's cheese-custard pie, thrive in Normandy. Leeks were known to Frenchmen as the 'asparagus of the poor' because they were prepared in the same way, but leeks cost much less.*

## Leek Lorraine

1 unbaked 9-inch pastry shell
1 envelope leek soup mix
1½ cups milk
½ cup light cream
3 slightly beaten eggs

1½ cups shredded natural Swiss cheese (6 ounces)
1 teaspoon dry mustard
1 4½-ounce can deviled ham
2 tablespoons fine dry bread crumbs

Bake pastry shell at 450° for 7 minutes. In saucepan combine soup mix and milk. Cook and stir till boiling; cool slightly. Stir in cream. Combine eggs, cheese, dry mustard, and dash pepper. Slowly stir in soup mixture. Mix ham and crumbs. Spread on bottom and sides of pastry shell. Pour in soup mixture. Bake at 325° till knife inserted in center comes out clean, 45 minutes. Let stand 10 minutes. Serves 6.

## Roast Duckling with Grenadine Sauce

2 4-pound ready-to-cook
domestic ducklings
1¼ cups chicken broth
¾ cup chopped onion
½ cup chopped carrot
½ cup chopped celery
¾ cup grenadine syrup

1 tablespoon butter or
margarine
1 tablespoon sugar
2 tablespoons lemon juice
2 teaspoons cornstarch
¼ cup orange-flavored
liqueur

Reserve giblets from ducklings. Prick ducklings to allow fat to escape; tie legs to tail. Roast on rack in roasting pan at 375° for 1½ hours; then, roast at 425° till legs move easily in sockets, about 15 minutes. Spoon off fat once or twice during roasting. Meanwhile, combine giblets, broth, and vegetables. Cover; simmer 1 hour. Strain, reserving liquid. Add ½ *cup* of the grenadine syrup; boil to reduce to ¾ cup liquid. Melt butter; blend in sugar and cook till brown. Add lemon juice and remaining grenadine. Stir till smooth. Stir in reduced grenadine mixture. Blend cornstarch with liqueur; add to sauce. Cook and stir 3 minutes. Serve with ducklings. Serves 4 to 6.

*Grenadine is what makes this roast duckling different from all others. Formerly, grenadine was made of pomegranate juice; today, however, it's usually a mixture of fruit juices or artificial flavoring and coloring.*

## Ham with Green Grapes

1 tablespoon butter
2 tablespoons sugar
Dash ground ginger
1 fully cooked ham slice,
cut ¾ to 1 inch thick
(about 2 pounds)

¾ cup rosé
1 tablespoon cornstarch
¼ cup cold water
• • •
1 cup seedless green
grapes, halved

Melt butter in skillet. Sprinkle in sugar and ground ginger. Brown ham quickly in mixture. Remove ham. Blend wine into sugar mixture; cook and stir till boiling. Combine cornstarch and the cold water. Add to wine mixture. Cook and stir till thickened and bubbly. Return ham to skillet; cover and simmer 15 minutes. Add grapes; cook 1 to 2 minutes longer. Spoon sauce over ham on platter. Makes 6 servings.

## Lamb with Vegetables

4 lamb steaks, cut ½ inch
thick
½ teaspoon dried rosemary,
crushed
¼ teaspoon salt
Dash pepper
1 tablespoon shortening
¼ cup chopped onion
2 tablespoons chopped green
pepper

1 clove garlic, crushed
1 3-ounce can sliced
mushrooms, drained
(½ cup)
2 medium tomatoes, sliced
¼ cup dry white wine
• • •
2 tablespoons cold water
1 tablespoon all-purpose
flour

Season lamb with a mixture of the rosemary, salt, and pepper. In skillet brown lamb on both sides in hot shortening. Add onion, green pepper, and garlic; cook till vegetables are tender. Add mushrooms, tomatoes, and wine. Cook, covered, over low heat for 30 minutes; uncover and simmer till meat is tender, about 15 minutes more. Remove meat and vegetables to serving dish. Pour pan juices into a measuring cup. Add enough water to make 1 cup liquid; return to skillet. Blend together water and flour; stir into pan juices. Cook and stir till thickened and bubbly. Serve sauce with lamb. Makes 4 servings.

*Today's cooks turn to wine, mushrooms, and herbs such as rosemary for lamb. Rosemary thrives best where fog rolls in from the ocean, as along the California coast, which probably accounts for its original meaning, 'dew of the sea.' Its leaves look like inch-long pine needles and are available only in this whole form. The fresh sprigs of this evergreen shrub of the mint family also make an aromatic addition to charcoal when barbecuing lamb or a brush for marinade.*

## Papaya Ring Mold

2 3-ounce packages lemon-flavored gelatin
2 cups boiling water
1 cup cold water
1 8¼-ounce can crushed pineapple
3 tablespoons lemon juice

2 3-ounce packages cream cheese, chilled
1 large papaya, peeled, seeded, and diced *or* 1 15-ounce can papaya, drained and diced
2 medium oranges, peeled, sectioned, and cut up

Dissolve lemon-flavored gelatin in boiling water. Stir in cold water, undrained pineapple, and lemon juice. Chill till partially set. Dice cream cheese. Fold cheese, papaya, and oranges into gelatin mixture. Pour into 6½-cup ring mold; chill till firm. Unmold. Serves 8 to 10.

## Curry Salad

½ teaspoon beef-flavored gravy base
1 cup mayonnaise or salad dressing
1 tablespoon curry powder
1 clove garlic, minced
¼ teaspoon Worcestershire sauce

6 to 8 drops bottled hot pepper sauce
6 cups torn mixed salad greens
4 cups torn spinach
2 7-ounce cans artichoke hearts, chilled, drained, and halved
¼ cup sliced radishes

Dissolve gravy base in ¼ cup hot water; blend in mayonnaise. Stir in curry powder, garlic, Worcestershire sauce, and hot pepper sauce. Chill. Combine remaining ingredients in a large salad bowl. Toss lettuce mixture lightly with chilled dressing. Makes 10 servings.

## Coffee Éclairs

½ cup butter or margarine
1 cup water
1 cup all-purpose flour
4 eggs
1 quart vanilla *or* coffee ice cream
1 cup light corn syrup

1 tablespoon instant coffee powder
3 tablespoons cornstarch
2 tablespoons butter or margarine
1 teaspoon vanilla
½ cup chopped pecans

In saucepan combine ½ cup butter and 1 cup water; bring to boiling. Add flour all at once, stirring rapidly. Reduce heat. Cook and stir till mixture leaves sides of pan and gathers around spoon in a smooth, compact mass. Remove from heat. Add eggs, one at a time, beating vigorously after each. Continue beating till mixture looks satiny and breaks off when spoon is raised. For each éclair, drop ¼ *cup* dough onto *ungreased* baking sheet about 2 inches apart, leaving about 6 inches space between rows. Shape each into a 4x1-inch rectangle, rounding sides and piling dough on top. Bake at 400° till golden brown, about 40 minutes. Cool on rack. Cut in half lengthwise and remove webbing. Fill bottom halves with ice cream; replace tops. Cover and freeze. At serving time, pour corn syrup into saucepan. Combine 1½ cups cold water and coffee powder; blend in cornstarch. Stir into corn syrup. Cook and stir till thick and bubbly; cook 2 minutes more. Remove from heat; add 2 tablespoons butter and vanilla. Stir till butter melts; stir in pecans. Serve warm sauce over éclairs. Serves 10 to 12.

## Crepes Frangipane

⅓ cup all-purpose flour
1 tablespoon sugar
  Dash salt
¾ cup milk
1 egg
1 egg yolk
1 tablespoon butter, melted

**Almond Cream Filling**
2 tablespoons butter,
  melted
½ of a 1-ounce square
  unsweetened chocolate
Powdered sugar
Whipped cream

Combine flour, sugar, salt, milk, egg, egg yolk, and 1 tablespoon butter in mixing bowl. Beat with rotary beater till smooth. Lightly grease a 6-inch skillet; heat till drop of water sizzles. Lift skillet off heat and pour in 2 tablespoons batter. Quickly tilt from side to side till batter covers bottom evenly. Return skillet to heat and cook till underside is lightly browned, about 1½ minutes. To remove, invert skillet over paper toweling. Repeat.

Spread about 3 tablespoons Almond Cream Filling on unbrowned side of each crepe; roll up and place folded side down in 13x9x2-inch baking dish. Brush crepes with the 2 tablespoons melted butter and bake at 350° till hot, 20 to 25 minutes. Grate chocolate; sprinkle atop crepes. Sift powdered sugar over all. To serve, spoon whipped cream over warm crepes. Makes 10.

*Almond Cream Filling:* In saucepan mix 1 cup sugar and ¼ cup all-purpose flour. Add 1 cup milk; cook and stir till thickened, then cook and stir 1 to 2 minutes longer. Beat 2 eggs and 2 egg yolks slightly. Stir some of the hot mixture into eggs; return to hot mixture. Cook and stir just till boiling; remove from heat. Beat till smooth. Stir in ½ cup ground toasted almonds, 3 tablespoons butter, 2 teaspoons vanilla, and ½ teaspoon almond extract. Cool to room temperature.

*Frangipane is the almond cream filling used in these crepes. It was named for an Italian gourmand living in Paris at the time of Louis XIII. Traditionally, the almond flavoring in this filling comes from crushed macaroons, but here ground toasted almonds add an extra-special touch.*

## Zabaglione au Madeira

6 egg yolks
½ cup sugar

¼ cup Chablis
¼ cup Madeira

In top of a double boiler beat together egg yolks and sugar with an electric mixer till very thick and lemon colored, 3 to 4 minutes. Gradually beat in Chablis and Madeira. Set pan over *hot, not boiling* water in bottom of double boiler. The water should not touch the top pan. Cook, beating constantly, till mixture becomes smooth and thick, about 10 minutes. Spoon into individual dessert dishes. Serves 8 to 10.

*Zabaglione is the Italian egg-froth dessert the French call Sabayon. Eat it warm or cold from sherbet glasses. It's also a sauce for peaches, or a yeast cake called Savarin.*

## Flaming Pears Melba

2 29-ounce cans pear halves
1 3-ounce package cream
  cheese, softened
2 tablespoons chopped
  walnuts

1 tablespoon sugar
1 tablespoon cornstarch
1 10-ounce package frozen
  raspberries, thawed
¼ cup brandy

Drain 12 pear halves. (Use any remaining pears and syrup another time.) Combine softened cream cheese, chopped walnuts, and sugar. Spoon 1 rounded tablespoon of the cream cheese mixture into cavity of 6 pear halves. Top with 6 more pear halves. Press the pear halves together, making 6 whole pears.

In saucepan blend cornstarch and ¼ cup cold water; stir in the raspberries. Cook and stir till mixture is thickened and bubbly; sieve. To serve, warm brandy in a small saucepan; pour atop warm raspberry sauce. Ignite. Immediately spoon flaming sauce over pears in individual dessert dishes. Serves 6.

*Pears Melba is a delightful variation of the classic Peaches Melba. This peach dessert with raspberry purée was created by the famed French chef Escoffier in honor of Dame Nellie Melba, an Australian opera star he met in London. Today, almost any ice cream dessert that includes a raspberry purée can be called Melba.*

# Good Eating during the Sixties

## Best-Ever Appetizers and Beverages

Food was a vital part of entertaining in the sixties, and these dips, spreads, appetizers, and beverages were favorites.

## Menu Headliners

Add to your collection of main dishes by trying some of these shrimp, scallop, lamb, veal, beef, pork, and chicken recipes.

## Vegetable Harvest

Capture the goodness of fresh-from-the-garden vegetables all year long with any of these delightful vegetable dishes.

## Salads the Year Round

Surprise your luncheon guests with a salad bar, and serve several of these refreshingly different salads.

## Tempting Bread Ideas

Breads are good any time of day, whether in a sandwich, spread with butter or jam, or shaped into a coffee cake.

## Sweets from the Sixties

Make your family smile. Carry them back to a world of sugarplums and lollipops by preparing these shortcake, dumpling, parfait, pie, mousse, cookie, and candy recipes.

Accompany savory *Steak au Poivre* (see recipe, page 237) with flavorful *Tomato-Bean Combo* (see recipe, page 248) and elegant *Cherries Portofino* (see recipe, page 258) to create a colorful, tempting dinner menu that will please everyone.

# Best-Ever Appetizers and Beverages

### Hilo Hot Dog Appetizers

1 12-ounce jar apricot
    preserves (1 cup)
½ of an 8-ounce can tomato
    sauce (½ cup)
⅓ cup vinegar
¼ cup dry sherry

2 tablespoons soy sauce
2 tablespoons honey
1 tablespoon cooking oil
¼ teaspoon salt
¼ teaspoon ground ginger
2 pounds frankfurters

In saucepan combine apricot preserves, tomato sauce, vinegar, dry sherry, soy sauce, honey, oil, salt, and ginger. Slice frankfurters on the bias into thirds and thread on skewers. Broil slowly 4 to 5 inches from heat about 6 minutes; turn and baste often with sauce. Heat remaining sauce to serve with franks. Makes 48 to 60 appetizer franks.

### Tuna Pâté

In a mixer bowl thoroughly beat together one 8-ounce package cream cheese, softened; 2 tablespoons chili sauce; 2 tablespoons snipped parsley; 1 teaspoon instant minced onion; ¼ teaspoon bottled hot pepper sauce; and few drops Worcestershire sauce. Add two 6½- or 7-ounce cans tuna, well drained; beat with electric mixer until thoroughly blended. Pack tuna mixture into a small (1 quart) bowl. Chill thoroughly. Remove from refrigerator and unmold onto serving plate. Top with drained capers. Serve with assorted crackers. Makes 3 cups.

### Clam-Cheese Dip

1 7½-ounce can minced
    clams
1 8-ounce package cream
    cheese, softened
½ cup crumbled blue cheese
    (2 ounces)

1 tablespoon snipped chives
    *or* green onion tops
¼ teaspoon salt
    Bottled hot pepper sauce
    Crackers *or* chips

Drain clams, reserving liquid. Combine cheeses, chives or onion tops, salt, and hot pepper sauce to taste. Beat mixture till smooth. Stir clams into cheese mixture. Add enough reserved clam liquid to make of spreading consistency. (Add milk, if necessary.) Chill; remove from refrigerator 15 minutes before serving. Pass crackers. Makes 1⅔ cups.

### Hot Beef Spread

In a medium bowl blend one 8-ounce package softened cream cheese and 2 tablespoons milk. Stir in one 2½-ounce jar sliced dried beef, finely snipped; 2 tablespoons instant minced onion; 2 tablespoons finely chopped green pepper; and ⅛ teaspoon pepper. Mix ingredients thoroughly. Stir in ½ cup dairy sour cream. Spoon the beef mixture into an 8-inch pie plate or small shallow baking dish. Sprinkle ¼ cup coarsely chopped walnuts over the top of the beef mixture. Bake at 350° about 15 minutes. Serve the hot beef spread with assorted crackers.

## Ham-Cheese Logs

1 cup shredded sharp
    natural Cheddar cheese
1 8-ounce package cream
    cheese, softened
1 4½-ounce can deviled ham

½ cup chopped pitted ripe
    olives
½ cup finely chopped pecans
    Crackers

Have the Cheddar cheese at room temperature. In a small mixer bowl beat together the shredded Cheddar cheese and cream cheese until blended. Beat in the deviled ham; stir in olives. Chill thoroughly. Shape into two 8-inch logs. Roll in pecans. Serve with crackers.

## Stuffed Mushroom Appetizers

12 large mushrooms (about 6
    ounces)
1 tablespoon finely chopped
    onion
1 tablespoon butter or
    margarine

1 2¼-ounce can deviled ham
1 teaspoon prepared mustard
¼ teaspoon Worcestershire
    sauce
½ cup soft bread crumbs

Thoroughly wash the mushrooms; trim off tips of mushroom stems. Carefully remove the stems. Finely chop stems. In saucepan cook the stems and the chopped onion in butter or margarine until tender. Remove the saucepan from the heat. Stir in the deviled ham, prepared mustard, and Worcestershire sauce. Stir in soft bread crumbs. Mound the stuffing mixture into mushroom crowns. Place the mushrooms on sheet of heavy foil; bring the foil sides up and pinch together loosely, leaving room for expansion of steam. Heat the stuffed mushrooms on grill over *hot* coals till mushrooms are tender, 12 to 15 minutes. Makes 12.

*These stuffed mushrooms are so good that after eating them even a juicy steak is a letdown.*

## Broiled Grapefruit

2 large grapefruit, halved
    Butter or margarine
⅓ cup sugar

1 teaspoon ground cinnamon
4 chicken livers
1 tablespoon butter

Have grapefruit at room temperature. Cut around every section of grapefruit halves, close to membrane (fruit should be completely loosened from shell). Cut a hole in center of each grapefruit and dot with butter or margarine. Combine sugar and cinnamon; sprinkle over grapefruit halves. Place grapefruit in shallow baking pan, and broil 4 inches from heat just till tops are browned, 8 to 10 minutes. Meanwhile, cook chicken livers in the 1 tablespoon butter or margarine. Place a liver in center of each grapefruit. Serve hot. Serves 4.

*From the heart of Florida's citrus country comes Broiled Grapefruit. This specialty of Chalet Suzanne in Lake Wales has a cinnamon-sugar glaze and is topped with a plump chicken liver.*

## Cappuccino

½ cup whipping cream
3 tablespoons instant
    espresso
2 cups boiling water

Ground cinnamon
Ground nutmeg
Grated orange peel

Whip cream. Dissolve espresso in boiling water. Pour coffee into small cups, filling cup only half full. Add a large spoonful of whipped cream to each cup. Top each with cinnamon, nutmeg, and orange peel. Gently stir cream into coffee till melted. Makes 6 or 7 servings.

*Cappuccino is a bit of sheer romance in a fancy cup. This elegant beverage is one of the favorites of the coffeehouse era that has stood the test of time.*

# Menu Headliners

### Veal Roll-Ups

1½ to 1¾ pounds veal round steak, cut ¼ inch thick, *or* 6 veal cutlets
6 thin slices boiled ham
3 slices process Swiss cheese
1 slightly beaten egg

2 tablespoons milk
¾ cup fine dry bread crumbs
1 10½-ounce can condensed cream of mushroom soup
½ cup milk
2 tablespoons dry white wine
Paprika

If using round steak, cut into 6 pieces. Pound each steak piece or cutlet to ⅛-inch thickness. Top each piece with a ham slice. Cut each cheese slice into 4 strips; place 2 strips on each ham slice. Roll meat around cheese; secure with wooden picks. Mix beaten egg and 2 tablespoons milk. Dip meat rolls in egg mixture; roll in fine dry bread crumbs. Place rolls, seam side down, in 13x9x2-inch baking dish. In small saucepan combine cream of mushroom soup, ½ cup milk, and dry white wine. Heat the mixture till bubbly; pour around meat. Cover baking dish with foil; Bake at 350° till tender, about 1 hour. Uncover; sprinkle meat rolls with paprika. Bake 10 minutes more to brown crumbs. Transfer to a warm serving platter. Spoon the sauce over meat rolls. Trim with parsley, if desired. Serves 6.

Add a continental flair to your meal by serving impressive *Veal Roll-Ups* to your guests. A combination of veal, ham, and Swiss cheese makes for an elegant entrée.

## Crab Bisque

Blend one 10½-ounce can condensed cream of asparagus soup, one 10½-ounce can condensed cream of mushroom soup, 2 soup cans of milk, and 1 cup light cream. Heat to boiling.

Stir in one 7½-ounce can crab meat, drained, flaked, and cartilage removed, and ⅓ cup dry sherry; heat through. Garnish with butter pats and snipped parsley. Serves 6 to 8.

*Crab Bisque has the sound of an elegant, hours-in-the-kitchen type soup. Elegant describes it, but preparation is shamefully easy. Get out the family soup tureen and ladle the bisque in bowls with a flourish.*

## Shrimp Quiche

10 ounces fresh or frozen
   shelled shrimp
1 cup shredded process
   Swiss cheese (4 ounces)
1 cup shredded Gruyere
   cheese (4 ounces)
1 tablespoon all-purpose
   flour

3 eggs
1 cup light cream
½ teaspoon prepared mustard
¼ teaspoon Worcestershire
   sauce
   Dash bottled hot pepper
   sauce
   Pastry for 6 tart shells

Thaw frozen shrimp. Dice shrimp; set aside. Toss together cheeses and flour. Beat together eggs, cream, mustard, Worcestershire, hot pepper sauce, ¼ teaspoon salt, and dash pepper. Line 6 individual bakers with pastry. Divide about ¾ of cheese-flour mixture among bakers; add shrimp and remaining cheese. Pour in egg mixture. Bake at 400° till knife inserted off-center comes out clean, about 30 minutes. If desired, garnish with whole cooked shrimp and parsley. Serves 6.

Heighten the taste appeal of a meal by featuring individual *Shrimp Quiche.* For an attractive garnish use whole shrimp and a sprig of parsley.

## Zippy Lamb Shanks

| | |
|---|---|
| 4 lamb shanks (about 2½ pounds) | ½ cup catsup |
| Salt | ½ cup water |
| Pepper | 1 small clove garlic, minced |
| 2 tablespoons shortening | 1½ teaspoons Worcestershire sauce |
| 1 medium onion, sliced | Hot cooked rice |
| ½ cup sliced celery | |

Season the lamb shanks with salt and pepper. In a skillet brown the shanks in hot shortening. In a small bowl combine the onion, celery, catsup, water, garlic, and Worcestershire sauce; add mixture to the meat. Simmer, covered, till meat is tender, about 1½ hours. Skim off excess fat. Serve the lamb shanks with hot cooked rice. Serves 4.

## Scallops Mornay for Two

*Mornay Sauce is a Bechamel (or white sauce) made with stock from fish or shellfish, cream, and finely grated cheese, often thickened with egg yolks. These Scallops Mornay would make a good Coquilles St. Jacques if baked in scallop shells and sprinkled with buttered bread crumbs and grated Parmesan instead of putting cheese in the sauce.*

| | |
|---|---|
| ¾ cup water | 1 tablespoon butter or margarine |
| ½ cup sauterne | 1½ tablespoons all-purpose flour |
| ¼ teaspoon instant minced onion | ½ cup milk |
| ¼ teaspoon salt | ¼ cup shredded process Swiss cheese |
| Dash pepper | 1 to 2 tablespoons snipped parsley |
| 8 ounces fresh or frozen scallops | |
| ½ cup sliced mushrooms | |

Combine water, sauterne, onion, salt, and pepper in saucepan; simmer 5 minutes. (Halve or quarter large scallops.) Add scallops and mushrooms to sauterne mixture. Cover; simmer 5 minutes. Remove scallops and mushrooms; set aside while preparing sauce. For sauce, cook liquid in pan till reduced to ½ cup, about 15 minutes. Melt butter in another saucepan; stir in flour. Stir in reduced liquid and milk; cook and stir till thickened and bubbly. Add cheese, stirring till melted. Season with salt and pepper, if needed. Remove from heat; add scallops and mushrooms. Spoon into 2 individual baking dishes. Bake at 375° for 15 to 20 minutes. Trim with parsley. Serves 2.

## Best Beef Brisket

| | |
|---|---|
| 1 3-pound boneless fresh beef brisket | 3 medium onions |
| 1½ teaspoons salt | 6 medium potatoes, peeled and halved lengthwise |
| Dash pepper | ½ teaspoon salt |
| Dash paprika | Dash pepper |
| 1 bay leaf | Prepared horseradish |

Trim excess fat from brisket. Place meat in Dutch oven with tight fitting cover. Sprinkle 1½ teaspoons salt, dash pepper, and paprika over meat. Add bay leaf. Cut onions in thick slices; arrange over meat. (Do not add water.) Cover; bake at 325° for 3 hours. Arrange potatoes around meat; sprinkle potatoes with ½ teaspoon salt and dash pepper. Cover; bake till done, about 1 hour longer, turning and basting potatoes every 15 minutes. (If meat and potatoes need more browning, uncover and continue baking till browned. Turn and baste potatoes.)

Skim off excess fat; remove bay leaf. Serve brisket with meat juices or thickened gravy. To carve, cut across grain, slanting knife slightly and making thin slices. Pass prepared horseradish. Serves 9.

## Beef Teriyaki

⅔ cup soy sauce
¼ cup dry sherry
2 tablespoons sugar
1 teaspoon ground ginger

1 clove garlic, minced
2 pounds beef sirloin
    steak, cut ½-inch
    thick

In a large bowl combine soy sauce, dry sherry, sugar, ginger, and garlic. Cut the beef sirloin steak into 6 to 8 serving-size pieces. Add the steak to the soy sauce mixture. Marinate the steak at room temperature about 30 minutes. Remove the steak from marinade mixture. Drain, reserving the marinade.

Broil the sirloin steak 3 inches from the heat for 5 to 7 minutes on *each* side, basting the steak with the marinade 2 or 3 times while cooking. Makes 6 to 8 servings.

*Teriyaki marinades are culinary wonders from Japan that adapt well to broiling meat over charcoal or in a broiler oven. Traditionally, the meat is cut in thin strips before marinating, but those who prefer steak in one piece will like the good flavor from the soy-ginger-sake (or sherry) mixture.*

## Steak au Poivre *(see photo, page 230)*

2 tablespoons cracked black
    pepper
2 pounds beef sirloin
    steak, cut 1½-inches
    thick

2 tablespoons cooking oil
½ cup beef broth
1 tablespoon brandy
    (optional)
¼ cup snipped parsley

Press the cracked black pepper into both sides of the beef sirloin steak. In a large skillet brown the sirloin steak in hot cooking oil. Lower the heat and cook steak to the desired doneness. (Allow about 20 minutes for medium.) Remove the steak to a warm platter; keep warm. Pour off the excess cooking oil. Stir in the beef broth and brandy. Bring the mixture to a boil, scraping the skillet. Pour the broth mixture over the steak. Sprinkle the steak with snipped parsley. Makes 6 servings.

*Steak au Poivre and Pepper Steak are not the same thing, although they translate that way. The first is a French recipe, the second an oriental version. In Steak au Poivre the steak is thick, and the pepper is the freshly cracked black spice that is rubbed into the surface of the meat. In Pepper Steak thin strips of beef are cooked with thin strips of green pepper in a teriyaki sauce.*

## Cheesy Beef Pie *(see photo, page 238)*

1 pound ground beef
½ cup chopped onion
1 8-ounce can tomato sauce
¼ cup snipped parsley
1 3-ounce can chopped mush-
    rooms, drained (½ cup)
¼ teaspoon dried oregano,
    crushed
⅛ teaspoon pepper

2 packages refrigerated
    crescent rolls (8
    rolls in each)
2 eggs
1 egg white
6 slices sharp process
    American cheese
1 egg yolk
1 tablespoon water

In skillet cook beef and the chopped onion till beef is browned and onion is tender; drain. Stir in tomato sauce, parsley, mushrooms, oregano, and pepper; set the beef mixture aside. Unroll *one* package of crescent rolls. Place the four sections of the dough together, forming a 12x6-inch rectangle. Seal the edges and perforations together. Roll into a 12-inch square. Fit the dough into a 9-inch pie plate; trim. Beat the two eggs with the one egg white. Spread *half* of the beaten eggs over the dough in the pie plate. Spoon the beef mixture into the pastry shell. Arrange cheese slices atop the ground meat mixture; spread remaining egg mixture over the cheese slices. Mix the egg yolk and water together; brush mixture lightly on edge of the pastry. Reserve remaining egg yolk mixture.

Roll the second package of rolls to 12-inch square as before. Place atop the filling. Trim edge, seal, and flute edge; cut a few slits in pastry. Brush top with remaining egg yolk mixture. Bake at 350° for 50 to 55 minutes. If pastry browns too fast, cover with foil. Let stand 10 minutes before serving. Serves 6.

*Cherry-Almond Glazed Pork* (see recipe, page 240) features a boneless rolled roast with a tangy glaze of cherry preserves, red wine vinegar, and slivered almonds. Accompany the roast pork with extra cherry-almond glaze.

What could be more special than *Cheesy Beef Pie* (see recipe, page 237) for a family supper menu? This main dish pie makes excellent use of refrigerated crescent rolls for a quick-to-fix crust.

Out of the Southwest has come *Brunch Eggs Ranchero* (see recipe, page 241). You'll love the zesty flavor of eggs baked in a mixture of crisp bacon, garlic, chilies, and tomatoes. Serve with rolled, buttered tortillas.

The next time you are giving a dinner party, prepare colorful *Ham with Nectarines* (see recipe, page 240). Nectarine slices and a tangy sweet-sour sauce accent the ham flavor.

## Cherry-Almond Glazed Pork *(see photo, page 238)*

1 3-pound boneless pork
  loin roast
Salt
Pepper
1 12-ounce jar cherry
  preserves
¼ cup red wine vinegar

2 tablespoons light corn
  syrup
¼ teaspoon ground cinnamon
¼ teaspoon ground nutmeg
¼ teaspoon ground cloves
¼ cup slivered almonds,
  toasted

Rub loin roast with a little salt and pepper. Place the meat on rack in a shallow roasting pan. Roast, uncovered, at 325° for 2 to 2½ hours. Meanwhile, in saucepan combine the cherry preserves, red wine vinegar, corn syrup, cinnamon, nutmeg, cloves, and ¼ teaspoon salt. Heat and stir the mixture till boil-ing; reduce the heat and simmer 2 minutes. Add the almonds. Keep the sauce warm. Spoon some sauce over the roast to glaze. Return the roast to the oven till meat ther-mometer registers 170°, about 30 minutes, basting roast with sauce several times. Pass remaining sauce with the roast. Makes 8 servings.

## Ham with Nectarines *(see photo, page 239)*

*When yesterday's exotic fruits such as nectarines began appearing with regularity in local markets, readers wanted to know more about this smooth-skinned relative of the peach. Since this luscious fruit complements meat, it was presented in a sauce for ham.*

1 fully cooked center-cut
  ham slice, cut 2 inches
  thick (about 3 pounds)
1 cup sugar
2 tablespoons cornstarch
2 teaspoons seasoned salt
2 teaspoons dry mustard
½ teaspoon paprika

⅓ cup orange juice
¼ cup vinegar
2 slightly beaten egg yolks
2 or 3 nectarines, sliced
  (about 1½ cups) *or*
1 12-ounce package
  frozen sliced peaches,
  thawed and drained

Slash edges of ham slice. Place ham on rack in shallow baking pan; bake at 350° for 40 minutes.

Meanwhile, in a saucepan mix sugar, cornstarch, seasoned salt, dry mustard, and paprika. Blend in orange juice, vinegar, and 1 cup cold water. Cook over low heat, stirring constantly, till thickened and bubbly. Stir a small amount of hot mixture into egg yolks; return quickly to hot mixture. Cook and stir 1 minute more. Add nectarines.

Place the ham slice on a warm serving platter; spoon on some of the hot nectarine sauce. Pass the remaining sauce with the ham slice. Makes 8 to 10 servings.

## Pork Chops in Sour Cream

6 pork chops, cut ½
  inch thick
¾ teaspoon dried sage,
  crushed
½ teaspoon salt
2 tablespoons shortening
2 medium onions, sliced

1 beef bouillon cube
¼ cup boiling water
½ cup dairy sour cream
1 tablespoon all-purpose
  flour
2 tablespoons snipped
  parsley

Rub chops with a mixture of sage, salt, and dash pepper. Brown chops lightly on both sides in hot short-ening. Drain off excess fat; add onions. Dissolve bouillon cube in boiling water. Pour over chops. Cover and simmer 30 minutes. Re-move meat to warm serving platter. Prepare gravy by combining sour cream and flour in small bowl. Slowly stir in meat drippings. Re-turn mixture to skillet; cook and stir till heated through. (Do not boil.) Add water till desired con-sistency. Serve over pork chops; garnish with parsley. Serves 6.

## Chicken Veronique

1 2½- to 3-pound ready-to-cook broiler-fryer chicken, cut up
1 lemon, halved

⅓ cup butter or margarine
⅓ cup sauterne
1 cup seedless green grapes
Paprika

Rub chicken well with the lemon; sprinkle with salt. Let dry on rack 15 minutes. In skillet brown chicken in hot butter, about 10 minutes. Add sauterne; spoon over chicken. Cover; simmer till chicken is tender, 30 to 40 minutes. About 3 minutes before end of cooking, add grapes. Dash chicken generously with paprika; pass sauce. Serves 4.

## Rolled Chicken Breasts

3 large whole chicken breasts, skinned and boned
6 thin slices boiled ham
6 ounces natural Swiss cheese, cut in 6 sticks
¼ cup all-purpose flour
2 tablespoons butter or margarine

1 3-ounce can sliced mushrooms, drained (½ cup)
⅓ cup sauterne
1 teaspoon chicken-flavored gravy base
2 tablespoons all-purpose flour
Toasted sliced almonds

Halve chicken breasts lengthwise. Place chicken, boned side up, between two pieces of clear plastic wrap. Working from center out, pound chicken lightly with mallet to ¼ inch thickness. Sprinkle with salt. Place a ham slice and a cheese stick on each chicken piece. Tuck in sides of each, and roll up as for jelly roll, pressing to seal well. Skewer or tie securely. Coat rolls with the ¼ cup flour; brown in butter. Remove chicken to 11x7½x1½-inch baking pan. In same skillet combine mushrooms, sauterne, gravy base, and ½ cup water. Heat, stirring in any crusty bits from skillet. Pour mixture over chicken. Cover and bake at 350° till tender, 1¼ hours. Remove chicken to warm platter. Blend 2 tablespoons flour with ½ cup cold water. Add to gravy in baking pan. Cook and stir till thick. Pour some gravy over chicken; garnish with almonds. Pass the remaining gravy. Serves 6.

*Chicken, as purchased at the meat counter, is definitely not just the sum of its parts. The availability of all drumsticks, all thighs, or all breasts packed together brought forth recipes like Rolled Chicken Breasts.*

## Brunch Eggs Ranchero *(see photo, page 239)*

5 slices bacon, cut up
1 16-ounce can tomatoes, cut up
2 tablespoons chopped canned green chili peppers (about 2)

1 clove garlic, minced
4 eggs
Salt
Pepper
4 slices bacon
Tortilla Rolls

In skillet cook 5 cut-up bacon slices till crisp; drain off fat. Add undrained tomatoes, chili peppers, and garlic; heat through. Divide among 4 individual bakers. Carefully slip one egg atop mixture in each baker. Season lightly with salt and pepper. Bake at 325° till eggs are set, 20 to 25 minutes. Cook 4 slices of bacon till done, *but not crisp.* Insert tines of fork into one end of bacon slice. Turn fork to wind bacon around it; remove fork. Top each egg with a bacon curl. Serve with Tortilla Rolls. Serves 4.

*Tortilla Rolls:* Heat canned or frozen tortillas according to package directions. Spread one side of each tortilla with butter or margarine. Roll up with butter inside. Place on oven-proof pan. Cover; heat at 325° for 5 to 10 minutes.

# Vegetable Harvest

## Sour Cream Baked Potatoes

*By the '60s, sour cream had become a staple kept on hand for chip dips and to replace the butter pat on a baked potato, to blend with blue cheese for salad dressing, and to swirl over cheesecake. Then came sour cream sauce mix, with an even longer shelf life and no refrigeration needed, and we had a new baked potato treat.*

5 medium baking potatoes
1 envelope sour cream
   sauce mix (enough for
   1 cup sauce)
⅔ cup milk

¼ teaspoon ground cumin
   seed
¾ teaspoon salt
2 tablespoons butter
5 slices bacon

Scrub potatoes; prick with fork. Bake at 425° for 50 to 60 minutes. Blend together sauce mix, milk, cumin, salt, and dash pepper; set aside for 10 minutes. Cut thin slice from top of potatoes and discard. Scoop out center of potatoes; add to sauce mixture. Add butter. Beat till fluffy, adding more milk, if necessary. Spoon mixture back into potato shells. Sprinkle with paprika, if desired. Bake at 375° for 20 to 25 minutes. Cook bacon till done, *but not crisp.* Wind bacon slice around fork; remove fork. Top potatoes with bacon curls. Serves 5.

## Glazed Sweet Potatoes

In 12-inch skillet dissolve one 3-ounce package orange-flavored gelatin, ¼ cup packed brown sugar, and dash salt in ¾ cup water. Add ¼ cup butter. Bring to a boil, stir-ring constantly. Add two 17-ounce cans sweet potatoes. Simmer, uncovered, basting frequently, till syrup thickens and potatoes are glazed, about 15 minutes. Serves 8.

Bursting with a rich, tangy flavor, *Sour Cream Baked Potatoes* are a delicious addition to any meal. Sprinkle the potatoes with paprika and garnish with bacon curls.

## Asparagus Spears with Hollandaise Sauce

1½ pounds asparagus spears*
   Boiling water

• • •

4 egg yolks
½ cup butter, cut in thirds

2 to 3 teaspoons lemon
   juice
Dash salt
Dash white pepper
Hard-cooked egg slices

To clean fresh asparagus, wash the stalks thoroughly and scrape off the scales. To remove the woody base, break the stalks; they will snap where the tender part starts.

To cook asparagus standing up, fasten asparagus in a bundle, using a band of foil, and stand the stalks upright with the tips extending 1 inch or more above boiling salted water in a tall glass percolator or a deep kettle. If stalks tend to fall over, prop up bundle with crumpled foil. Cover and cook the asparagus spears till tender, 10 to 15 minutes. The asparagus tips cook in the steam while the asparagus stalks cook in boiling water.

To prepare hollandaise sauce: place egg yolks and one-third of the butter in top of double boiler.

Cook over *hot, not boiling* water till butter melts; stir rapidly. (Upper pan should not touch water.) Add another one-third of the butter and continue stirring. As mixture thickens and butter melts, add remaining butter, stirring constantly.

When butter is melted, remove pan from hot water; stir rapidly 2 minutes. Stir in lemon juice, a teaspoon at a time; season with salt and pepper. Heat over hot water, stirring till thick. Remove from heat at once. If sauce curdles, immediately beat in 1 to 2 tablespoons boiling water. Serve over asparagus. Top with egg slices. Serves 4.

*If desired, substitute two 10-ounce packages frozen asparagus spears. Cook according to package directions. Drain well.

*Harbinger of spring, fresh asparagus was nicknamed Marcus Aurelius by Thomas Jefferson's grandchildren because the Roman emperor liked the vegetable, too. They'd run in shouting, "The Marcus Aurelius is up!"*

*The Dutch always served the tender shoots with melted butter and lemon juice. The French borrowed the recipe, thickened it with egg yolks, and dubbed the golden, velvety-smooth sauce Hollandaise.*

Delight your guests by serving a year-round favorite, *Asparagus Spears with Hollandaise Sauce.* Top the asparagus spears with a rich hollandaise sauce, and trim with hard-cooked egg slices.

## Asparagus Casserole

2 tablespoons butter or
  margarine
2 tablespoons all-purpose
  flour
½ teaspoon salt
½ teaspoon prepared mustard
  Dash pepper
2 cups milk

2 pounds asparagus, cut in
  1½-inch pieces, cooked,
  and drained
3 hard-cooked eggs, sliced
¼ cup finely crushed
  saltine crackers
2 tablespoons butter or
  margarine, melted

Melt 2 tablespoons butter; blend in flour, salt, mustard, and pepper. Add milk; cook and stir quickly till thickened and bubbly. Arrange *half* of the asparagus in an 8x8x2-inch baking dish. Top with egg slices; season egg with salt and pepper. Spoon *half* of the sauce mixture evenly over all. Top with remaining asparagus and sauce. Toss crumbs with 2 tablespoons melted butter; sprinkle evenly atop sauce. Bake, uncovered, at 350° till heated, 25 to 30 minutes. Serves 6.

## Lemon Turnips

3 medium turnips, peeled
  and cut into sticks
2 tablespoons butter or
  margarine

1 tablespoon snipped
  parsley
1 teaspoon chopped onion
1 teaspoon lemon juice

In saucepan cook turnips in boiling salted water till almost tender, 10 to 15 minutes. Drain. Add butter, parsley, onion, and lemon juice. Toss to coat. Season with salt and pepper. Makes 4 servings.

## Cauliflower Scallop

2 10-ounce packages frozen
  cauliflower
1 10½-ounce can condensed
  cream of celery soup
2 beaten eggs
½ cup shredded sharp
  process American cheese

½ cup soft bread crumbs
¼ cup snipped parsley
¼ cup chopped canned
  pimiento
1 tablespoon instant minced
  onion
½ teaspoon salt

Cook cauliflower according to the package directions, *except* omit salt. Drain and cut in pieces. Mix together the remaining ingredients and dash pepper. Stir in cauliflower. Pour vegetable mixture into 10x6x-2-inch baking dish. Bake at 350° till set, 30 minutes. Serves 6 to 8.

## Scalloped Corn Supreme

1 17-ounce can cream-
  style corn
1 cup milk
1 well-beaten egg
1 cup coarsely crumbled
  saltine crackers

¼ cup finely chopped onion
3 tablespoons chopped
  canned pimiento
½ cup coarsely crumbled
  saltine crackers
1 tablespoon butter, melted

Heat corn and milk. Gradually stir in egg. Add 1 cup crumbs, onion, pimiento, ¾ teaspoon salt, and dash pepper. Mix well. Pour into greased 8x1½-inch round baking dish. Combine ½ cup crumbs and butter. Sprinkle over corn. Bake at 350° for 20 minutes. Serves 6.

*Al Capp's comic-strip character, Li'l Abner, credits much of his strength to having eaten 'turnip preserves' since he was a baby. This is not so remarkable, as turnips are rich in vitamin C. But this was not the reason why people clamored for Lemon Turnips in the '60s. The full-flavored taste was more important than the vitamin content.*

## Brussels Sprouts Soufflé

¼ cup butter or margarine
¼ cup all-purpose flour
1 cup milk
4 egg yolks
1 cup shredded natural
    Cheddar cheese

1 10-ounce package frozen
    Brussels sprouts,
    cooked, drained, and
    finely chopped
    (1½ cups chopped)
4 egg whites

Melt butter in saucepan; blend in flour. Add milk. Cook and stir till thickened and bubbly. Beat egg yolks till thick and lemon-colored. Blend a moderate amount of the hot mixture into egg yolks; return to hot mixture and stir rapidly. Stir in shredded cheese and chopped Brussels sprouts. Remove from heat. Beat egg whites till stiff peaks form; fold into vegetable mixture. Turn into an *ungreased* 2-quart soufflé dish. Bake at 350° for 40 minutes. Serve immediately. Serves 4 to 6.

## Broccoli Parmesan

2 pounds broccoli or
    2 10-ounce packages
    frozen broccoli spears
2 tablespoons butter
¼ cup chopped onion

1 10½-ounce can condensed
    cream of chicken soup
½ cup milk
⅓ cup grated Parmesan
    cheese

Cook broccoli in boiling *unsalted* water till tender; drain well. Melt butter in saucepan; add the chopped onion and cook over medium heat till tender but not brown. Blend in soup, milk, and Parmesan cheese. Heat through. Serve sauce over hot broccoli. Makes 6 to 8 servings.

## Vegetable-Rice Pilaf

⅓ cup long grain rice
1 tablespoon finely chopped
    onion
2 tablespoons butter or
    margarine

1 teaspoon instant chicken
    bouillon granules
¼ teaspoon salt
1 8½-ounce can mixed
    vegetables, drained

Cook rice and onion in butter till lightly browned, about 5 to 10 minutes, stirring frequently. Add 1 cup water, bouillon granules, and salt. Bring to a boil, stirring to dissolve granules. Reduce heat; cover and cook slowly till liquid is absorbed and rice is fluffy, about 20 minutes. Stir in mixed vegetables; heat through. Makes 2 servings.

*Pilaf, pilaff or pilau, it's rice. Native to the Orient, pilaf is also indigenous to America's southeast coast between Wilmington, North Carolina, and Savannah, Georgia, all of which was once the colony of Carolina. An ancestor of jambalaya, pilaf is traditionally a savory dish of long grain white rice, onions, tomatoes, bacon, spices, and shellfish. But just as spelling and pronunciation can vary, so can the ingredients.*

## Spinach Elegante

2 10-ounce packages frozen
    chopped spinach
1 6-ounce can sliced
    mushrooms, drained
3 slices bacon, crisp-
    cooked and crumbled

1 tablespoon butter
¼ teaspoon dried marjoram,
    crushed
1 cup dairy sour cream
½ cup shredded sharp
    process American cheese

Cook spinach according to package directions; drain well. Stir in mushrooms, bacon, butter, marjoram, and dash pepper. Spread in a 10x6x 2-inch baking dish. Bake at 325° for 25 minutes. Spread sour cream over top of spinach; sprinkle with the shredded cheese. Return to oven till cheese melts, about 3 to 5 minutes. Makes 6 servings.

# Salads the Year Round

## Frosted Cheese Mold

2 envelopes unflavored
  gelatin
1 cup milk
2 12-ounce cartons cream-
  style cottage cheese
½ cup crumbled blue cheese
  (2 ounces)
1 6-ounce can frozen
  limeade concentrate,
  thawed

½ cup broken pecans
6 drops green food coloring
1 cup whipping cream
  Melon balls
  Orange sections
  Frosted Grapes (see recipe
  page 113)
  Mint sprigs
  Lime wedges

In saucepan soften gelatin in milk. Place over low heat and stir till gelatin is dissolved. Remove from heat. With electric mixer beat cottage cheese and blue cheese together till well blended. Stir in gelatin mixture. Stir in limeade concentrate, nuts, and food coloring. Chill till mixture mounds. Whip cream; fold into cheese mixture. Turn into a 6½-cup ring mold; chill till firm. Unmold on serving plate. Fill center with melon balls and orange sections. Garnish with frosted grapes and mint sprigs. Pass lime wedges. Serves 12 to 16.

Delightful is the word for *Frosted Cheese Mold* (pictured opposite). This elegant salad combines cottage cheese with limeade concentrate, a flavor accent. Fill the center of the molded salad with fruit and mint sprigs. Wreathe the salad with additional mint.

## Fruit and Orange Fluff

1 3⅝- or 3¾-ounce package
  *instant* vanilla
  pudding mix
2 cups cold milk
1 cup dairy sour cream
½ teaspoon grated orange
  peel
¼ cup orange juice

Sliced unpeeled pears*
Quartered nectarines *or*
  peaches*
Whole strawberries
Seedless green grape
  clusters
Dark sweet cherries
Blueberries

To prepare dressing, slowly beat pudding mix and milk in mixing bowl with rotary beater till well blended, about 1 to 2 minutes. Gently beat in sour cream. Fold in orange peel and juice. Chill the mixture. To serve, center small bowl of dressing in large shallow bowl. Arrange fruits around. To keep cool place fruit bowl atop bowl of crushed ice. Makes 3 cups dressing.

*To keep fruit bright, use ascorbic acid color keeper or dip in lemon juice mixed with a little water.

*Greek mythology becomes reality when you squeeze orange juice for Fruit and Orange Fluff. Oranges were the golden apples in the mythological Garden of Hesperides on an island near Mount Atlas in northern Africa. Planted in the sunken area of a stone quarry, this garden possessed an unusual climate due to its protected location. Curiously enough, this same spot is still used for growing oranges.*

## Orange-Apricot Ring

1 17-ounce can unpeeled
  apricot halves
2 3-ounce packages orange-
  flavored gelatin

Dash salt
1 6-ounce can frozen orange
  juice concentrate
1 cup cold water

Drain apricots, reserving syrup. Put apricots in blender container; blend till apricots are pureed. Add enough water to reserved syrup to make 1½ cups. Combine reserved syrup, gelatin, and salt. Heat to boiling, stirring to dissolve gelatin.

Remove from heat. Add concentrate and stir till melted. Stir in apricot purée and cold water. Pour into 5-cup ring mold and chill till firm. Unmold on a platter. If desired, fill center with lettuce and orange sections. Makes 8 to 10 servings.

## Berry-Peach Marble

1 3-ounce package straw-
   berry flavored gelatin
1 cup boiling water
1 cup cold water
2 cups sliced strawberries
• • •
1 16-ounce can peach slices

1 envelope unflavored
   gelatin
2 tablespoons lemon juice
1 2-ounce package dessert
   topping mix
2 3-ounce packages cream
   cheese, softened

Dissolve strawberry-flavored gelatin in boiling water; stir in cold water. Chill till partially set. Fold in sliced strawberries.

Meanwhile, drain peaches, reserving syrup. Dice peaches. Add enough water to peach syrup to make 1 cup. In saucepan soften unflavored gelatin in syrup mixture; heat and stir till gelatin is dissolved. Stir in lemon juice. Cool. Prepare dessert topping mix following package directions; beat in cream cheese. Fold in unflavored gelatin mixture and peaches. Chill till partially set.

Layer the strawberry and cream cheese mixtures in 7½-cup mold. Swirl a knife gently through to marble. Chill till firm. Serves 10.

## Creamy Broccoli Mold

1 envelope unflavored
   gelatin
1 10-ounce package frozen
   chopped broccoli
2 chicken bouillon cubes
1 tablespoon instant minced
   onion

½ cup dairy sour cream
½ cup chopped celery
¼ cup chopped canned
   pimiento
2 tablespoons snipped
   parsley
2 tablespoons lemon juice

Soften unflavored gelatin in ¾ cup cold water. Cook package of frozen chopped broccoli following package directions, *adding* bouillon cubes and onion to cooking water. *Do not add salt. Do not drain.* Add softened gelatin to broccoli mixture and stir till gelatin is dissolved. Cool. Stir in sour cream.

Fold in the celery, chopped pimiento, snipped parsley, and lemon juice. Pour the gelatin mixture into 5½-cup ring mold; chill till firm. Makes 6 to 8 servings.

## Spinach-Avocado Bowl

*In the Midwest, where the only lettuce was garden variety in spring and iceberg in winter, the crisp deep green leaves of raw spinach were a welcome addition to the salad bowl. Plenty of greens are available now, but Spinach-Avocado Bowl remains a favorite.*

Place 10 ounces fresh spinach, torn in bite-size pieces, in salad bowl. Arrange over spinach 2 medium avocados, peeled and sliced; ½ pound bacon, crisp-cooked and crumbled; and ½ cup chopped peanuts. Serve the salad with Russian salad dressing. Serves 8 to 10.

## Tomato-Bean Combo *(see photo, page 230)*

1 16-ounce can cut green
   beans, drained
2 medium tomatoes, peeled,
   chopped, and drained
¼ cup finely chopped onion

½ cup dairy sour cream
¼ cup Italian salad
   dressing
   Romaine leaves
   Tomato wedges

Combine beans, chopped tomato, and onion. Blend together sour cream and Italian salad dressing; add to bean mixture and toss lightly. Chill at least 2 to 3 hours. At serving time, spoon salad into romaine-lined salad bowl. Garnish with tomato wedges. Makes 6 servings.

## Nearly-A-Meal Salad

½ cup salad oil
2 tablespoons vinegar
2 tablespoons lemon juice
2 teaspoons sugar
1 teaspoon paprika
1 teaspoon prepared mustard
½ teaspoon salt
1 medium head lettuce, torn
    in bite-size pieces
1 16-ounce can whole or cut
    green beans, drained

2 cups diced, peeled,
    cooked potatoes
1 6½- or 7-ounce can tuna,
    drained and broken up
2 medium tomatoes, peeled
    and sliced
2 hard-cooked eggs, cut in
    wedges (optional)
Salt
Pepper

In a screw-top jar combine the salad oil, vinegar, lemon juice, sugar, paprika, prepared mustard, and salt; cover and shake vigorously till thoroughly blended. Chill the salad dressing. Just before serving, arrange lettuce in salad bowl. Shake dressing again and drizzle a few tablespoons over lettuce. Arrange beans, potatoes, tuna, and tomatoes atop lettuce. Garnish with egg wedges, if desired. Season with salt and pepper. Pour remaining dressing over salad. Makes 6 servings.

*Taking a cue from the dramatic salads of southern France, potatoes, fish, and vegetables at hand are combined into a salad that is nearly a meal. For an equally delicious main course, substitute rice for the potatoes. A special hint from this playground of the rich and famous — the longer you marinate with the dressing the better the salad will be.*

## Shrimp in Avocado Ring

1 3-ounce package lemon-
    flavored gelatin
1 cup boiling water
1 cup mayonnaise or salad
    dressing
1 to 2 tablespoons lemon
    juice

½ teaspoon salt
1 cup whipping cream
2 medium avocados, peeled
    and sieved (1 cup)
Lettuce
Cleaned and cooked shrimp

Dissolve the lemon-flavored gelatin in boiling water. Chill till partially set; whip the gelatin till fluffy. Stir in mayonnaise, lemon juice, and salt. Whip cream. Fold cream and sieved avocado into gelatin mixture. Pour mixture into 5½-cup ring mold *or* six to eight ½-cup ring molds. Chill till firm.

Unmold on lettuce-lined platter or plates. Fill center with cooked shrimp. Makes 6 to 8 servings.

## Green Goddess Salad

1½ cups mayonnaise
¼ cup finely snipped chives
2 tablespoons tarragon
    vinegar
2 tablespoons snipped
    parsley
1 tablespoon dried
    tarragon, crushed
4 anchovy fillets, chopped
1 green onion, finely
    snipped
6 cups torn romaine,
    chilled

3 cups torn curly endive,
    chilled
1 9-ounce package frozen
    artichoke hearts,
    cooked, drained, and
    chilled
2 medium tomatoes, cut in
    wedges
½ cup pitted ripe olives,
    sliced
1 2-ounce can rolled anchovy
    fillets

Combine mayonnaise, chives, vinegar, parsley, tarragon, anchovy fillets, and onion; mix well. Chill. At serving time combine remaining ingredients in large salad bowl. Top with desired amount of dressing. Roll-toss the salad until the greens are well coated. Serves 6.

Brighten up your family's breakfast by serving *Double-Deck Orange Coffee Cake.* Top this fragrant, warm-from-the-oven coffee cake with a delicious orange glaze.

Spicy-hot *Yankee Tostadas* (see recipe, page 253) are a fast sandwich to fix and great for informal entertaining. Top the muffins with beans, lettuce, seasoned meat mixture, and shredded sharp Cheddar cheese.

# Tempting Bread Ideas

## Double-Deck Orange Coffee Cake

2½ cups packaged biscuit mix
3 tablespoons sugar
⅓ cup milk
1 egg

3 tablespoons cooking oil
Orange Filling
Orange Glaze
Shredded orange peel

Mix biscuit mix, sugar, milk, egg, and oil with fork; beat 15 strokes. Turn out onto lightly floured surface and knead 8 to 10 times. Divide dough in 2 *almost-equal* parts. Roll larger part to 8-inch circle; place in greased 9-inch pie plate, patting dough up about ½ inch on sides. Sprinkle with Orange Filling.

Roll remaining dough to 7-inch circle; place atop filling. With scissors, snip 1-inch slashes around edge of top layer. Bake at 375° till light brown, 25 to 30 minutes. Drizzle with Orange Glaze. Sprinkle with orange peel. Serve hot.

*Orange Filling:* Mix ⅓ cup packed brown sugar, ⅓ cup chopped walnuts, 2 tablespoons flour, 1 tablespoon grated orange peel, and 2 tablespoons melted butter.

*Orange Glaze:* Add 1 to 1½ tablespoons orange juice to 1 cup sifted powdered sugar. Mix till smooth.

## Orange-Mince Muffins

In a mixing bowl thoroughly combine ½ cup prepared mincemeat, ½ cup apple juice, and 1 beaten egg. Add one 14-ounce package orange muffin mix; stir the mixture just till moistened. Fill 12 paper bake cups or greased muffin pans ⅔ full. Bake the muffins at 400° till golden brown, about 15 minutes. Remove from the pans immediately. Prepare the frosting by blending 1 cup sifted powdered sugar with 4 teaspoons milk and ¼ teaspoon rum extract *or* ¼ teaspoon vanilla. Drizzle the frosting over the warm muffins. Serve warm. Makes 12 muffins.

## French Onion Bread

4½ to 5 cups all-purpose
   flour
1 package active dry yeast
1 envelope onion soup mix
2 tablespoons sugar

2 tablespoons grated
   Parmesan cheese
2 tablespoons shortening
   Cornmeal
1 egg white

In large mixer bowl combine *2 cups* of the flour and the yeast. In a saucepan combine onion soup mix and 2¼ cups water; cover and simmer 10 minutes. Add sugar, cheese, shortening, and 1 teaspoon salt, stirring constantly. Cool till warm (115° to 120°). Add to dry mixture. Beat at low speed with electric mixer for ½ minute, scraping sides of bowl. Beat 3 minutes at high speed. By hand, stir in enough of the remaining flour to make a moderately stiff dough. Turn out on lightly floured surface. Knead till smooth and elastic (8 to 10 minutes). Place in a lightly greased bowl, turning once to grease surface. Cover; let rise in a warm place till almost double (1¼ to 1½ hours). Punch down, divide in half. Cover; let rest 10 minutes. Shape in two long loaves, tapering ends. Place each loaf diagonally on a greased baking sheet. Sprinkle with cornmeal. Gash tops diagonally, ⅛- to ¼-inch deep. Cover; let rise till almost double (about 1 hour). Bake at 375° for 20 minutes. Brush with mixture of egg white and 1 tablespoon water. Bake 5 to 10 minutes longer. Makes 2 loaves.

*French Onion Bread is an extension of the baguette, the ordinary family-size loaf of crusty French bread used in the French marketman's 4 a.m. breakfast. Then, the bread was torn apart and dropped into a steaming bowl of onion soup and flavored with grated Parmesan cheese. Here, the bread is seasoned with dried onion soup mix and Parmesan cheese before baking.*

## Dilly Bread

2 tablespoons chopped
onion
1 tablespoon butter or
margarine
2 cups all-purpose flour
1 package active dry yeast
2 teaspoons dillseed
¼ teaspoon baking soda

1 cup cream-style cottage
cheese
¼ cup water
2 tablespoons sugar
1 teaspoon salt
1 egg
Butter or margarine,
softened

Cook onion in 1 tablespoon butter till tender. In a large mixer bowl combine ¾ *cup* of the flour, yeast, dillseed, and soda. To onion mixture add cottage cheese, water, sugar, and salt; heat just till warm (115° to 120°), stirring constantly. Add to dry mixture in mixer bowl; add egg. Beat at low speed with electric mixer for ½ minute, scraping sides of bowl constantly. Beat 3 minutes at high speed. By hand, stir in enough of the remaining flour to make a stiff dough. Cover; let rise in warm place till almost double (1 to 1¼ hours). Stir dough down. Turn into a well-greased 8½x4½x2½-inch loaf pan. Let rise till almost double (25 to 30 minutes). Bake at 350° for 35 to 40 minutes. Cover with foil last 20 minutes. Brush with butter. Makes 1 loaf.

## Sally Lunn

*Sally Lunn is a simplified brioche, baked in a Turk's head mold, that came to Virginia with early English colonists. Originally, it was a bun made and sold in a bake shop in Bath, England, or on the streets to the cry of "Solet Lune". This was a corruption of the French "soleillune" or sun and moon which described the golden tops and white bottoms of the buns. These became Sally Lunns in America.*

1 package active dry yeast
¼ cup warm water (110°)
¾ cup warm milk (110°)
6 tablespoons butter or
margarine

3 tablespoons sugar
2 eggs
3 cups all-purpose flour
1¼ teaspoons salt

Soften yeast in warm water. Add warm milk and set aside. Cream butter and sugar. Add eggs, one at a time, beating after each addition. Combine flour and salt; add to creamed mixture alternately with yeast mixture. Beat well after each addition. Beat dough till smooth. Cover dough; let rise in a warm place till almost double (about 1 hour). Beat down and pour dough into a well greased Turk's head mold or 9-inch tube pan. Let rise till almost double (about 30 minutes). Bake at 350° for 40 to 45 minutes. Remove coffee cake from the tube pan. Serve coffee cake either warm or cool. Makes 1 coffee cake.

## Olive Pizza Bread

1 slightly beaten egg
2 cups shredded process
American cheese
(8 ounces)
1 cup pitted ripe olives,
cut in large pieces
⅓ cup butter or margarine,
melted
1 tablespoon instant minced
onion

1 teaspoon Worcestershire
sauce
Dash bottled hot pepper
sauce
• • •
3 cups packaged biscuit mix
1 cup milk
1 teaspoon caraway seed
(optional)

Mix egg, cheese, olives, butter, onion, Worcestershire sauce, and bottled hot pepper sauce. Set aside while preparing dough. Combine biscuit mix and milk; stir to a soft dough. Spread in a greased 12-inch pizza pan. Spoon olive topping over dough; sprinkle with caraway seed. Bake at 425° for 20 to 25 minutes. Cut in 8 to 10 wedges; serve hot.

## Spicy Fruit Puffs

| | |
|---|---|
| 2 cups all-purpose flour | 2 beaten eggs |
| 3 teaspoons baking powder | ⅔ cup milk |
| ½ teaspoon ground cinnamon | ¼ cup shortening, melted |
| ¼ teaspoon ground nutmeg | and cooled |
| 1 cup shredded peeled apple | 1 cup whole wheat *or* bran |
| ⅔ cup packed brown sugar | flakes, coarsely |
| ¼ cup chopped walnuts | crushed |

Stir together flour, baking powder, cinnamon, nutmeg, and 1 teaspoon salt. Stir in shredded apple, brown sugar, and walnuts. Combine beaten eggs, milk, and shortening; add to apple mixture all at once, stirring just to blend. Fold in wheat or bran flakes. Fill greased muffin pans ⅔ full. Bake at 400° for 15 to 20 minutes. Makes 12 muffins.

## Swiss Yodelers

| | |
|---|---|
| 2 cups shredded process | 1 3-ounce can chopped mush- |
| Swiss cheese | rooms, drained |
| ½ cup whipping cream | 3 slightly beaten eggs |
| 12 slices white bread | ½ cup milk |
| 9 slices bacon, cooked and | Butter or margarine |
| drained | |

Mix together cheese and cream. Spread mixture on 6 bread slices (about 2 tablespoons on each). Halve bacon slices. Place bacon pieces and mushrooms on top of cheese. Top with remaining bread. Combine eggs and milk. Dip sandwiches in egg-milk mixture, coating both sides. Brown sandwiches in butter, turning once. Makes 6 sandwiches.

*Swiss Yodelers are French-toasted Swiss cheese sandwiches dressed up with bacon and mushrooms.*

## Yankee Tostadas *(see photo, page 250)*

| | |
|---|---|
| ¾ pound ground beef | 1 11-ounce can baked beans |
| ¼ cup chopped onion | in molasses sauce |
| 1 cup bottled barbecue | 4 English muffins, split |
| sauce | and toasted |
| ½ teaspoon dried oregano, | 1½ cups shredded lettuce |
| crushed | 1 cup shredded sharp |
| ½ teaspoon garlic salt | natural Cheddar cheese |

Brown ground beef with onion; drain off excess fat. Add barbecue sauce, oregano, and garlic salt. Simmer 5 minutes. In saucepan heat beans. Top *each* muffin half with 3 tablespoons beans, 3 tablespoons lettuce, ¼ cup meat mixture, and 2 tablespoons cheese. Serves 8.

*Like a hot breeze from the southwest, Mexican foods fanned out over the United States in the '60s. In a sharp Yankee trade, Boston-style beans were substituted for frijoles, the mashed beans that usually accompany this Mexican sandwich.*

## Stroganoff Sandwich

Cut 1 unsliced loaf of French bread in half lengthwise; wrap in foil. Heat at 375° for 10 to 15 minutes. In skillet cook 1 pound ground beef with ¼ cup chopped green onion till meat is browned; drain off fat. Stir in 1 cup dairy sour cream, 1 tablespoon milk, 1 teaspoon Worcestershire sauce, ¾ teaspoon salt, and ⅛ teaspoon garlic powder. Heat, but *do not boil.* Cut 2 tomatoes into slices and 1 green pepper into rings. Spread softened butter or margarine on cut surfaces of bread.

Spread *hot* meat mixture on bread. Alternate tomatoes and green pepper atop meat. Sprinkle with 1 cup shredded process American cheese. Place on baking sheet; heat at 375° for 5 minutes. Serves 8.

# Sweets from the Sixties

One glance at this delicious *Strawberry Shortcake* (pictured opposite), and you'll want to try it immediately. Sugared strawberries, rich shortcake layers, and fluffy whipped cream make this a special dessert.

## Blueberry Dumplings

2½ cups fresh or frozen
    blueberries
⅓ cup sugar
1 tablespoon lemon juice
1 cup all-purpose flour

¼ cup sugar
2 teaspoons baking powder
2 tablespoons butter or
    margarine
½ cup milk

In Dutch oven with tight fitting lid bring blueberries, ⅓ cup sugar, 1 cup water, and dash salt to boiling. Cover and simmer 5 minutes. Add lemon juice. Stir together flour, ¼ cup sugar, baking powder, and ¼ teaspoon salt. Cut in butter till like coarse meal. Add milk; stir only till moistened. Drop from tablespoon into bubbling sauce, making 6 dumplings. Cover tightly; simmer 15 minutes without uncovering. Serve hot. Sprinkle with sugar, if desired. Serves 6.

Calorie rich and color blessed, Strawberry Shortcake has been a perennial favorite for years. Just check the magazine cover statistics. One with a shortcake on it is tops with the consumer everytime—and for good reason. The rich biscuit dough, split in two layers, buttered, and stacked with sugared and moisture-ripe berries lusciously decorated with dollops of cream, is good tasting and good to look at. With such a combination, it's no secret why this American tradition fits into the '60s—or any decade.

## Strawberry Shortcake

2 cups all-purpose flour
2 tablespoons sugar
3 teaspoons baking powder
½ teaspoon salt
½ cup butter or margarine
1 beaten egg

⅔ cup light cream
    Butter or margarine
3 to 4 cups sliced
    strawberries
    Sugar
1 cup whipping cream

Stir together thoroughly flour, sugar, baking powder, and salt; cut in ½ cup butter till mixture resembles coarse crumbs. Combine egg and light cream; add to dry mixture, stirring just to moisten.

    Spread dough in greased 8x1½-inch round baking pan, building up edges slightly. Bake at 450° for 15 to 18 minutes. Remove shortcake from pan; cool on rack 5 minutes. Split in 2 layers; lift top off carefully. Spread bottom layer with butter. Sweeten berries with sugar. Whip cream. Spoon berries and cream between layers and over top. Serves 6.

## Nectarine Grape Compote

4 cups sliced, peeled
    nectarines
2 cups seedless green
    grapes

1½ cups white grape juice
3 tablespoons orange-flavored
    liqueur
1 pint pineapple sherbet

In serving bowl combine the nectarines and grapes. Add grape juice and liqueur; stir gently. Chill. To serve, spoon into dessert dishes; top each serving with a scoop of pineapple sherbet. Makes 8 servings.

## Ribbon Fudge Parfait

In saucepan combine ½ package low-calorie chocolate pudding mix (1 envelope) and 2 teaspoons instant coffee powder; slowly stir in 1¾ cups skim milk. Cook and stir till mixture boils. Remove from heat. Cool; beat smooth. Fold in 2 stiffly beaten egg whites. Prepare ½ of 2½-ounce package low-calorie dessert topping mix (1 envelope) following package directions. Fold ½ *cup* topping into pudding. Alternately spoon pudding and topping into parfaits. Chill. Serves 6.

*Two things—improved instant coffee powder and a new interest in coffeehouses—came along at the same time to popularize coffee-flavored desserts in America. Sprinkled into whipped cream in place of rum, coffee powder made Italian Tortoni a new treat. Strewn with almonds and put into paper cups to freeze, it's just easy ice cream.*

## Coffee-Nut Tortoni

1 cup whipping cream
6 tablespoons sugar
2 teaspoons instant coffee
    powder
1 teaspoon vanilla
2 to 3 drops almond extract

1 egg white
¼ cup finely chopped
    toasted almonds
¼ cup flaked coconut,
    toasted
8 maraschino cherries

Combine cream, *4 tablespoons* of the sugar, coffee, vanilla, and almond extract; stir till coffee is dissolved. Whip till custardlike. Beat egg white to soft peaks. Gradually add remaining sugar; beat to stiff peaks. Mix nuts and coconut. Fold egg white and *half* the nut mixture into whipped cream. Spoon into custard cups. Sprinkle with remaining nut mixture. Freeze. To serve, top with cherries. Serves 6.

## Frosty Fudge Mousse

1 cup whole wheat flakes
½ cup chopped walnuts
¼ cup packed brown sugar
1 stiffly beaten egg white
4 cups tiny marshmallows
1 cup milk

2 1-ounce squares unsweet-
    ened chocolate
Dash salt
1 slightly beaten egg yolk
1 teaspoon vanilla
1 cup whipping cream

Finely crush flakes. Fold flakes, nuts, and brown sugar into egg white. Spread in 10x6x2-inch baking dish. Bake at 300° for 10 minutes. Cool. Heat marshmallows, milk, chocolate, and salt over low heat; stir till melted. Stir moderate amount of hot mixture into yolk; return to hot mixture. Cook and stir over low heat 1 minute. Stir in vanilla. Chill till almost set; stir occasionally. Whip cream; fold into chilled mixture. Pour into crust. Freeze firm. Serves 10 to 12.

## Red Cherry Pie

¾ cup juice from cherries
3 cups canned pitted tart
    red cherries
    (water pack)
1 cup sugar
2 tablespoons quick-
    cooking tapioca

10 drops red food coloring
3 to 4 drops almond extract
Dash salt
Pastry for 9-inch
    lattice-top pie
1 tablespoon butter
    or margarine

Combine cherry juice, cherries, sugar, tapioca, red food coloring, almond extract, and salt. Let stand 20 minutes. Line 9-inch pie plate with pastry; fill with cherry mixture. Dot with butter. Adjust the lattice crust; crimp edge high. Bake at 400° for 50 to 55 minutes.

## Buttery Caramels

In heavy 3-quart saucepan, melt 1 cup butter or margarine. Add 2¼ cups packed brown sugar and dash salt; stir till thoroughly combined. Stir in 1 cup light corn syrup; mix well. Gradually add one 14-ounce can *sweetened condensed* milk, stirring constantly. Cook and stir over medium heat till candy reaches firm-ball stage (245°), 15 to 20 minutes. Remove candy from heat; stir in 1 teaspoon vanilla. Pour candy into buttered 9x9x2-inch baking pan. Cool. Cut into squares. Wrap individual candy pieces before storing. Makes about 2¾ pounds.

## Pfeffernuesse

Combine ¾ cup light molasses and ½ cup butter. Cook and stir till butter melts. Cool to room temperature. Stir in 2 beaten eggs. Stir together 4 cups all-purpose flour, ½ cup sugar, 1½ teaspoons ground cinnamon, 1¼ teaspoons baking soda, ½ teaspoon ground cloves, ½ teaspoon ground nutmeg, ¼ teaspoon ground ginger, and dash pepper. Stir into molasses mixture. Chill. Shape into 1-inch balls. Bake on ungreased cookie sheet at 375° for 10 to 12 minutes. Roll in powdered sugar while warm. Cool; reroll in powdered sugar. Makes 54.

*Pfeffernuesse (pepper nuts) are holiday cookies of the gingerbread family brought by German settlers to this country. In communities with brick hearth ovens, as in the Amanas in Iowa, the German communities in Pennsylvania, and the Moravian kitchens of Winston-Salem, North Carolina, Pfeffernuesse dough was mixed at home, then taken to the bakery to be baked after the bread came out.*

## Stuffed Date Drops

8 ounces pitted dates (40)
⅔ cup walnut *or* pecan
　　halves (40)
¼ cup shortening
¾ cup packed brown sugar
1 egg

½ cup dairy sour cream
1¼ cups all-purpose flour
½ teaspoon baking powder
½ teaspoon baking soda
¼ teaspoon salt
　　Golden Frosting

Stuff each date with a nut half; set aside. Cream shortening and brown sugar till light; beat in egg. Stir in sour cream. Stir together dry ingredients; add to creamed mixture. Mix well. Stir in dates. Drop dough onto greased cookie sheet (having one stuffed date in each cookie). Bake at 400° for 6 to 8 minutes; remove immediately from cookie sheet. Spread with Golden Frosting. Makes about 40 cookies.

*Golden Frosting:* Heat 6 tablespoons butter till lightly brown; remove from heat. Gradually beat in 2 cups sifted powdered sugar and ½ teaspoon vanilla. Slowly add hot water, beating till spreadable.

## Layer Bar Cookies

½ cup butter or margarine
1 cup finely crushed
　　graham crackers
1 6-ounce package semi-
　　sweet chocolate pieces
1 6-ounce package butter-
　　scotch pieces

1 3½-ounce can flaked
　　coconut (1⅓ cups)
½ cup chopped walnuts
　　• • •
1 14-ounce can *sweetened
　　condensed* milk

Melt butter in a 13x9x2-inch baking pan. Sprinkle graham crackers evenly over butter. Layer the top with chocolate pieces, butterscotch pieces, coconut, and nuts. Pour the condensed milk over all. Bake the cookies at 350° for 30 minutes. Cool; cut in bars. Makes about 45.

## Southern Pralines

2 cups sugar
¾ teaspoon baking soda
1 cup light cream

1½ tablespoons butter or
　　margarine
2 cups pecan halves

In 3-quart saucepan combine sugar and soda; mix well. Stir in cream. Bring to boiling over medium heat, stirring constantly. Cook and stir to soft-ball stage (234°). (Mixture caramelizes slightly as it cooks.) Remove from heat; add butter. Stir in pecans; beat the candy till thick enough to drop from spoon (takes only 2 to 3 minutes). Drop from tablespoon on waxed paper. If the candy becomes too stiff to drop, add a little hot water to make the right consistency. Makes 2 dozen pieces.

258

## Cherries Portofino *(see photo, page 230)*

*(see photo, page 230)*

*Cherries Portofino refers to the fine port wine used with the Bing cherries rather than to an Italian seaport. By the '60s, production of these dark, sweet cherries had increased enough to make them a national fruit staple rather than a West Coast only treat.*

1 16-ounce can pitted
    dark sweet cherries
    (2 cups)
½ cup port

2 3-ounce packages rasp-
    berry-flavored gelatin
2 cups boiling water
    Whipped cream

Drain the cherries, reserving the syrup. In a bowl combine the drained cherries and port; set aside about 3 hours. Dissolve the raspberry-flavored gelatin in the boiling water. Drain cherries, reserving the port. Combine port with the reserved cherry syrup and enough cold water to make 1½ cups. Stir in the dissolved gelatin. Chill the gelatin mixture till partially set. Fold in the cherries. Pour into 12x7½x2-inch baking dish. Chill till firm. To serve gelatin mixture, cut into cubes; spoon into sherbet glasses. Top gelatin with dollops of whipped cream. Serve with sugar cookies, if desired. Makes 6 to 8 servings.

## Pizza Peach Pie

*America's love affair with the Italian snack of meats, cheese, and tomato sauce on a crisp dough in the '50s was broadened to take in pizza dessert by the '60s. Pizza Peach Pie is a shimmering delight of currant jelly glaze over a bed of peaches. The French would call it a flan.*

½ cup butter or margarine
¼ cup sifted powdered
    sugar
1 cup all-purpose flour
• • •
2 tablespoons cornstarch
2 tablespoons granulated
    sugar

¼ teaspoon ground mace
⅔ cup orange juice
½ cup red currant jelly
• • •
1 29-ounce can peach
    slices, well drained
    Whipped cream

In small mixer bowl cream together butter or margarine and powdered sugar using an electric mixer. Blend in flour to make a soft dough. Pat dough evenly onto bottom and sides of 12-inch pizza pan; prick the dough well with a fork. Bake the crust at 350° for 15 to 20 minutes. For filling, in a small saucepan combine cornstarch, granulated sugar, and ground mace. Stir in orange juice; add the jelly. Cook and stir till mixture thickens and bubbles; cook and stir 2 minutes longer. Cool slightly. Arrange peaches in a single layer in the baked shell, forming circles, one inside the other. Spoon jelly mixture over peaches. Chill. Trim pie with dollops of whipped cream. Makes 10 to 12 servings.

## Butterscotch Pie

¾ cup packed brown sugar
⅓ cup all-purpose flour
    *or* 3 tablespoons
    cornstarch
¼ teaspoon salt
2 cups milk

3 slightly beaten egg yolks
3 tablespoons butter
1 teaspoon vanilla
1 *baked* 9-inch pastry
    shell, cooled
    Meringue

In saucepan combine sugar, flour, and salt; stir in milk. Cook and stir over medium heat till thickened and bubbly. Cook and stir 2 minutes more. Remove from heat.

Stir a moderate amount of the hot mixture into beaten yolks; immediately return to hot mixture. Cook 2 minutes, stirring constantly. Remove from heat. Add butter and vanilla. Pour into cooled baked pastry shell. Spread Meringue atop hot pie filling and bake at 350° for 12 to 15 minutes. Cool.

*Meringue:* Beat 3 egg whites with ½ teaspoon vanilla and ¼ teaspoon cream of tartar till soft peaks form. Gradually add 6 tablespoons sugar, beating till stiff and glossy peaks form and all sugar is dissolved. Spread meringue over hot filling, sealing to edge of pastry.

*Lemon Meringue Pie* is a recipe classic. A puff of meringue baked to golden perfection covers a pleasantly tart, creamy lemon filling. It's an elegant dessert that's suitable for any occasion.

## Lemon Meringue Pie

1½ cups sugar
3 tablespoons cornstarch
3 tablespoons all-purpose
   flour
Dash salt
1½ cups hot water
3 slightly beaten
   egg yolks

2 tablespoons butter
   or margarine
½ teaspoon grated
   lemon peel
⅓ cup lemon juice
1 *baked* 9-inch pastry
   shell, cooled
Meringue

In a medium saucepan thoroughly combine the sugar, cornstarch, all-purpose flour, and salt. Gradually add the hot water to the mixture, stirring constantly. Cook and stir over high heat till the mixture comes to boiling. Reduce the heat; cook and stir 2 minutes more.

Stir a moderate amount of the hot mixture into slightly beaten egg yolks, then immediately return to remaining hot mixture in saucepan. Bring filling to boiling and cook 2 minutes, stirring constantly. Remove from heat. Add butter or margarine and grated lemon peel. Slowly add lemon juice while stirring constantly. Pour hot filling into cooled pastry shell. Spread Meringue atop hot filling. Bake the pie at 350° till peaks are golden brown, about 12 to 15 minutes. Cool.

*Note:* For a creamier lemon filling thoroughly combine the sugar, cornstarch, flour, salt, and hot water. Cook and stir for 8 minutes over low heat after mixture comes to a boil. Stir a moderate amount of the hot mixture into slightly beaten egg yolks, then immediately return to hot mixture. Cook 4 minutes after the mixture boils.

*Meringue:* In a mixer bowl combine 3 egg whites, ½ teaspoon vanilla, and ¼ teaspoon cream of tartar. Beat with electric mixer till soft peaks form. Gradually add 6 tablespoons sugar, beating the meringue till stiff and glossy peaks form and all the sugar is dissolved. Spread the meringue over the hot lemon pie filling; carefully seal all around the edge of the pastry so there will be no shrinking.

*Years ago, James Beard attempted to obtain from Myrna Johnston,* Better Homes and Gardens *food editor, the recipe for the Lemon Meringue Pie that appeared on the magazine's cover. Now, you can have the secret for this handsome recipe: remove the filling from the heat as soon as it has thickened and before stirring in the lemon juice and butter. Not only does this keep the fresh lemon flavor, but it prevents the filling from becoming runny. Good ten and twenty years ago — it's good today.*

CIRCULATION 7,777,777

April 1971 50¢

# Better Homes

## and Gardens.

Auto Pollution: What Can We Really Do About It?

Great Family Vacation Ideas Off The Beaten Path

Favorite Desserts: Vanilla, Chocolate, Strawberry

Dahlias: The Big Color Flower Anyone Can Grow

## COLOR
### AND HOW YOU CAN LIVE WITH IT

With one foot planted in the past and one in the future, Americans are propelling themselves forward into the '70s. In all areas of life there is a paradoxical blending of past and future—especially in food. Homemakers are performing a modern juggling act. On one hand, they are using foods that are quick, easy, and convenient. While, on the other hand, they are going back to many of the old, time-tested cooking techniques that their grandmothers used. Out of all this comes such diverse ideas as microwave cooking, making your own breads, computerized meal planning, and organic gardening. What lies in the future? Whatever it is, it's sure to be the best of both worlds— the nostalgic old one of the past and the bright new one of the future.

# THE 70s

When the seventies take their place in American history, they may well be recorded as the decade of concerned awareness at a time when the nation was fighting to control pollution and to conserve its diminishing natural resources. The seventies also may be recorded as a time of technological advances unequaled in any other 10-year period. The potential of the laser, fusion power, geothermal energy, a new generation of appliances stemming from microelectronics, and a whole galaxy of advances to make living easier are all part of the seventies.

Foods, marketing, and cooking are influenced by technology, too, as it produces brand-new products as well as improvements to old products. Formulated foods will show up in beverages, table spreads, snacks, and desserts. These specially designed foods may be similar to familiar products in texture, flavor, and nutritional characteristics or they may be an entirely new food idea. The design of the food may also include boosting its nutritional value. In some cases, processors will fortify or reinforce nutrients already present as they do with bread or cereal products. Or manufacturers may add a nutrient—vitamin C or iron, for example—to jelly, catsup, or other popular foods to give them the nutritional value they lack.

Canned and packaged groceries also will take on different characteristics. Convenience is a watchword of the seventies, so supermarket shelves will display more and more packaged casseroles and combination dishes that allow a homemaker to add one or two ingredients for the taste of a 'scratch' meal while she enjoys the convenience of a packaged dinner. Shoppers also will see a group of shelf-stable products containing "intermediate moisture," a development that will move from Sky Lab to supermarket with "all systems go." These foods look fresh and are slightly soft to the touch, indicating that not all of the moisture has been removed during processing.

Special interest sections abound in the seventies supermarket. Whole-grain cereals and flours are grouped along with honey, nuts, carob powder, and related products under the banner of natural foods. Artificially sweetened or water-packed fruits and vegetables await the dieter in a display of low-calorie foods. In many parts of the country Mexican, Oriental, and other ethnic foods rate spotlight treatment.

The seventies may be headlined by technology and scientific advances —it's also a decade that appreciates the old. While science is developing optoelectronics to send printed messages over telephone wires or producing three-dimensional photography called holography— a brand-new interest is rising in a very old technique, acupuncture, the ancient Chinese method of therapy through puncturing the body with tiny needles. At a time when textured soy protein forms roasts, burgerlike products, and other meat substitutes, cooks are turning back the calendar and making homemade yogurt, bagels, and sourdough bread.

The stress is on convenience and labor-saving products and equipment. It is also on "doing your own thing." The local beverage mart may be only minutes from home, yet 'doing' Americans are making their own wine as crafts and hobbies become a regular part of family life in the seventies. The time to pursue these activities may be the result of work-saving conveniences—but more probably it's the result of a different concept of evaluating and budgeting time. This is the decade of "unisex" work responsibilities. *His* and *hers* jobs lose their labels when both husband and wife go off to work, so the first one home shops, starts dinner, does the laundry, or mows the lawn. Shortcuts and timesaving appliances get the routine jobs out of the way quickly, leaving more time for leisure.

ON                    MICROWAVE

OFF                   INFRARED

*Thermatronic*
• THERMADOR

Ms.

Jonathan
Livingston
Seagull

RICHARD
BACH

PHOTOGRAPHS
BY RUSSELL
MUNSON

BACH JONATHAN LIVINGSTON SEAGULL          Macmillan

FutureShock  by Alvin Toffler

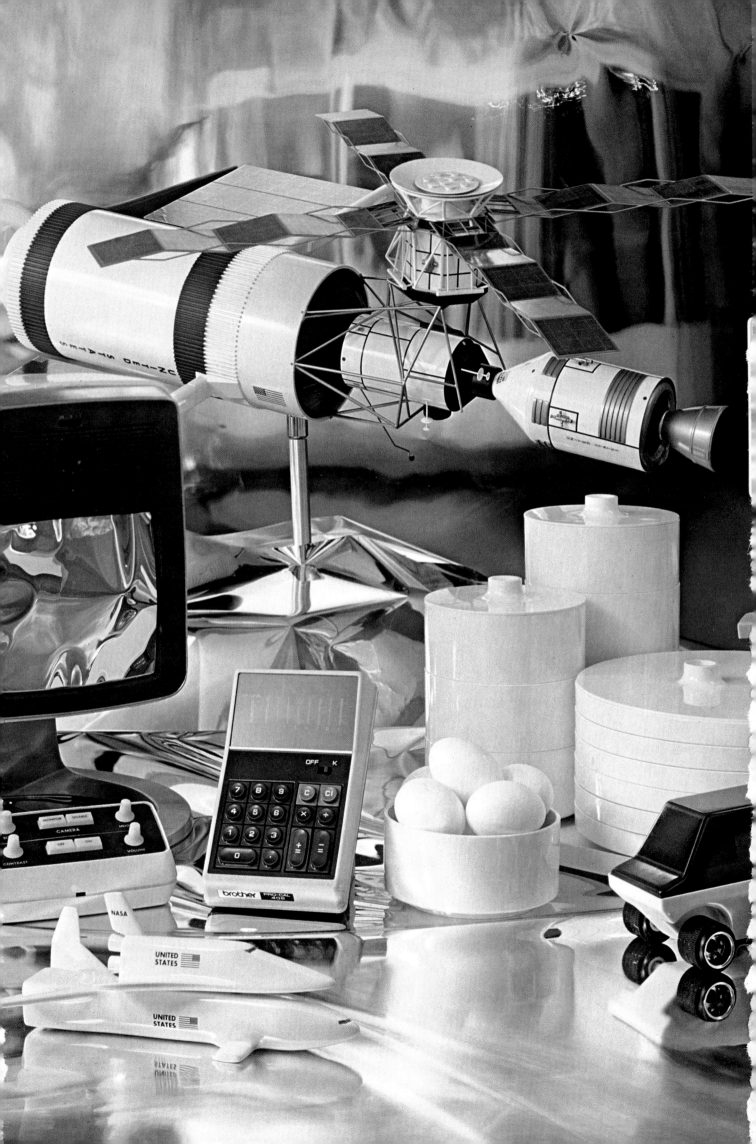

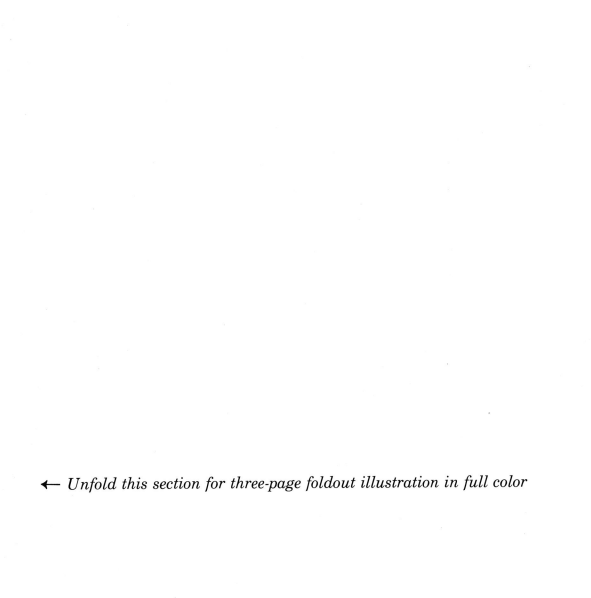

← *Unfold this section for three-page foldout illustration in full color*

Not all shopping will be done by home-based computers. But even at the supermarkets, technology will eliminate the wait at the check-out counter. Purchases will be placed on a conveyor belt and a laser beam will scan the coded price symbol, then feed the data into a minicomputer, which figures the bill in a flash and then produces a receipt listing prices, taxes, bottle return refunds, etc.

Supermarket shoppers will see changes in product packaging and labeling, too. Many wrappings will be designed to self-destruct or be eaten. Odorless, tasteless wrapping films and materials may melt or evaporate during cooking to 'dissolve' the problem of disposing of packaging materials. Along the same line, coffee stirrers made of a sweetener and/or creamer disappear as they stir hot coffee.

The seventies should see a standardization of food labeling as well as a change in the way weights are printed on packages. In the meat department, whether meat is fresh or frozen, standard names will appear on all cuts, thus a shopper from Maine will see the same names on beef and pork in Georgia or California. A listing of nutrients will appear on the label, too. Calorie counts are there, of course, but so are the vitamin, mineral, and protein content of an average serving of the product. Having the information handy takes on added importance as partially or fully prepared foods are incorporated more frequently into meals, and snacking becomes a national pastime.

Another change is seen in the weight printed on the package. It will appear in metric units—grams or liters. Metrics will be the new math of the seventies with the changeover, starting late in the decade, scheduled in stages over a 10-year period. At home, metric spoons and utensils will replace old standbys, and cook books will print recipes using the new measurements. But the ramifications of the metric system are not limited to food products. Almost everything we purchase or use is weighed or measured, and though the peck and the rod won't be missed much, the inch and the ounce die hard. What was previously purchased in gallons will be bought in liters and the need to learn a new metric system, combined with shortages of gasoline and concern over pollution, may just be enough to drive auto owners into the electric car waiting in the wings.

There is no need to despair of learning the metric system; new educational methods will make it as easy as possible. In most cities, community antenna television will offer fifteen to twenty different channels for information or entertainment and even larger potential is in store. People will be able to use their TV sets for hobby instruction, professional training, education, and an almost endless variety of other purposes. Video tapes, received through the mail, will be used in place of ads and catalogs to display available merchandise right in a consumer's home.

Shopping from the home, being entertained at home, even being educated at home may have a great sociological effect on Americans—bringing families closer together as more creative and social activities are centered around the home. And nothing fits into this home-based life-style better than the art of cooking. Though foods and eating styles have changed through the years, cooking has always been an enjoyable, rewarding pursuit. It is now. It will continue to be. And the recipes of the seventies provide a wondrous blending of the classic and the convenient—of the nostalgic and the 'now.' To the young, the old is new. To the cooks of previous decades, and the cooks of tomorrow, the best of everything is available, with more to come.

Travel ranks high on the list of leisure time activities in the seventies. Besides the enjoyment of seeing different places and sampling other foods and cultures, travel fills another need. It expands the living space of dwellers in apartments and small houses. The race for space isn't only to the planets—in this decade it's a pursuit of more living room, more fresh air, and more natural living in cities that are becoming overcrowded and suburbs that are no longer wide-open spaces.

A new feeling for the outdoors seems to be part of the search of the seventies. Some people find it by puttering in a garden or bicycling in a nearby park. An alternative for many is renting or buying a second home in the mountains or near a man-made lake created by flood control projects or land developers.

Wherever people turn for recreation, the landscape is dominated by hamburger and pizza places, gourmet restaurants, and every type of eating place in between. Although eating out is part of the family food pattern, dinner at home is more the norm. And never in American history has the family dinner been more informal. In fact, dinner may even be in a series of sittings, depending on scheduled school, sport, or social events for each family member. Dining becomes more leisurely and a touch more formal, perhaps, when guests are included.

Paradoxical though it seems, creative cookery and hurry-up meals mesh very well in American kitchens, thanks to a staff of appliance helpers that chop, mix, heat, or cool foods as needed. Microwave cooking, an offshoot of wartime radar technology, no longer limited to restaurant and hospital kitchen use, moved into home kitchens to cut cooking times from hours to minutes. Self-cleaning ovens save time and work, as does the cool-top range that cooks by means of an oscillating magnetic field created by the power source—or 'air speed' infrared cooking in which infrared energy is used to cook food while air heated to 350° is blown across it. And the trash compactor, considered by many merely a mechanized foot in the wastebasket, nonetheless, does save many hours of 'footwork' per year.

Food preparation is no longer an entirely kitchen job. Portable and compact equipment makes cooking possible in almost any room of the house. Even greater mobility is in store as buildings become equipped with power-pack systems that snap in and out of place and move easily within a room, from room-to-room, or house-to-house. The appliances attached have built-in sensing or monitoring devices to diagnose service problems or indicate when maintenance care is needed.

The small battery-operated calculators of the early seventies were forerunners of the household computer destined to change some time-honored patterns of 'keeping house.' In the future, the permanent investment in home furnishings may be in the computer center, while previously important investments such as fine furniture and accessories may be replaced by bookracks, headboards, and tables made of tubes of recycled paper—or sofas and chairs of corrugated cardboard. The emphasis may shift from having material possessions to getting things done efficiently in order to allow time for enjoying family, activities, and surroundings.

Among its other duties, the home-computer system will keep an inventory of food in the freezer, refrigerator, or kitchen shelf. If asked, it will plan meals that are balanced nutritionally. It will print out a shopping list—even order items from the store. And, by prior arrangement with a bank, the computer allows the store to deduct the total expenditure from the family's bank balance.

# Recipe Features of the Seventies

## Doing Your Own Thing

Whenever you get the urge to be creative, do your own thing. This series of recipes is one where you start at the very beginning and build up. Have you ever wanted to ferment your own liqueurs, grind your own sausage, bake your own sourdough bread, or make your own yogurt and cottage cheese? If you have, then these recipes are just right for you.

## Natural Foods

If you're eager to try something new, go natural. Each of the recipes in this section begins with a natural food. They reflect the interest in the seventies of avoiding processed foods and going back to natural ones. You can choose such foods as yogurt, wheat germ, soy grits, bulgur wheat, sunflower seeds, honey, nuts, or dried fruits.

## Microwave Cooking

Move into the world of microwave cooking. The new electronic ovens will open up a whole new cooking experience for you—one in which dishes that used to take a half hour or more to prepare now take only minutes. If you've ever wanted to fix chicken in a hurry or make a baked custard in minutes, microwave cooking is the answer.

The colorful kitchens of the seventies make eating a more pleasant experience. This kitchen features a double-door refrigerator and a serving peninsula. The acrylic plastic furniture and vinyl border give a look of the future.

# Doing Your Own Thing

Doing your own thing is perhaps one of the distinguishing characteristics of the '70s. The modern homemaker is eager to create new things especially when it comes to food. The challenge of making foods from scratch gives a satisfying sense of creativity. As a result old crocks come out of hiding, bakery bread gives way to homemade, and cheese comes from the kitchen not the dairy case. This collection of recipes represents just a few of the foods homemakers can make for themselves.

## Homemade Yogurt

Heat 2 cups skim milk to just below boiling point (200°). Cool to 115°. Place 2 tablespoons plain yogurt in mixing bowl; blend in warm milk. Put 2 *tablespoons* mixture in a custard cup to use in place of plain yogurt as a starter next time. (To make *Fruited Yogurt:* Add ¼ cup crushed fresh or frozen fruit and 2 tablespoons sugar to mixture after removing starter.) Cover the yogurt and starter with clear plastic wrap and a towel. Place in bowl of warm water (115°). Let the yogurt stand till firm when shaken gently, 6 to 8 hours for plain, 3 to 5 hours for fruited. Change the water occasionally, keeping the temperature constant at about 115°. Chill yogurt and starter. Makes 2 cups.

## Winter Rumtopf

3 medium pears, cored
    and chopped
3 oranges, peeled,
    sectioned, and chopped

1 cup maraschino cherries
1 cup sugar
1 cup rum
    Fruit, sugar, rum

In crock combine pears, oranges, and cherries. Stir in the 1 cup sugar; pour in 1 cup rum. Loosely cover with cheesecloth. Refrigerate 2 weeks. For every cup of fruit removed, add 1 cup of fruit, ⅓ cup sugar, and ⅓ cup rum. Serve over ice cream or pound cake, if desired.

## Orange-Flavored Liqueur

4 medium oranges
    Water

2 cups sugar
2 cups vodka *or* rum

Squeeze juice from oranges; reserve peel from 1 orange. Scrape white membrane from reserved peel; cut peel into strips. Add water to juice to make 2 cups. In saucepan combine orange juice, peel, and sugar. Bring to boiling; reduce heat and simmer over low heat 5 minutes. Cool. Pour into jar. Stir in vodka or rum. Cover with lid. Let stand at room temperature for 3 to 4 weeks. Strain. Makes 5 cups.

## Coffee-Flavored Liqueur

In saucepan combine 2 cups water, 1½ cups granulated sugar, and 1½ cups packed brown sugar. Simmer gently, uncovered, 10 minutes. Remove from heat. Stir in ⅓ cup instant coffee powder. Cool. Pour into 2-quart jar. Stir in one ⅘-quart bottle vodka and 2 teaspoons vanilla. Cover. Let stand at room temperature 2 weeks. Makes 5½ cups.

*The first cordials were discovered purely by accident. They were created by black-robed alchemists who were supposedly working with the devil to produce gold. These magicians became the first medieval distillers, producing the fragrant concoctions for which the rest of the world is grateful. One descendant of these early cordials that you can make is Orange-Flavored Liqueur.*

## Cranberry Cordial

1 16-ounce package
    cranberries (4 cups)

3 cups sugar
1 pint gin (2 cups)

Coarsely chop cranberries. Place in a ½-gallon jar or crock. Add sugar and gin. Seal with screw-top lid or cover tightly with foil. Store in cool place. Turn the jar over each day for 3 weeks. (If in crock, stir gently.) Store in tightly-covered quart jars. Strain before serving. Serve cordial well chilled. Makes about 3¼ cups cordial plus 3 cups drained cranberries. Use cranberries in Christmas Glogg, recipe below, or freeze in ice ring for holiday punch bowl.

*Homemade cranberry liqueur is just right for entertaining guests. Serve it in cordial glasses, over ice, or create your own special Christmas Glogg. Whatever way you serve this Sandinavian cordial, it will surely bring you many compliments.*

## Christmas Glogg

6 whole cloves
6 inches stick cinnamon
4 whole cardamon, shelled
1 32-ounce bottle cranberry
    juice cocktail (4 cups)

1 cup drained cranberries
    from Cranberry Cordial
¼ to ½ cup sugar
1 cup Cranberry Cordial
1 cup dry red wine

Tie cloves, cinnamon, and cardamon in cheesecloth bag and place in saucepan. Add *2 cups* of the cranberry juice cocktail, the drained cranberries, and sugar. Bring to boiling. Simmer, uncovered, for 10 minutes. Remove spices. Before serving, add remaining cranberry juice cocktail, Cranberry Cordial, and wine. Heat almost to boiling. Serve in mugs topped with a few cranberries. Makes about 6 cups.

End a special dinner right by serving your own after-dinner drinks. *Orange-Flavored Liqueur, Coffee-Flavored Liqueur,* and *Cranberry Cordial* are quick to fix up and become more flavorful as they mellow. Liqueurs and cordials are meant to be sipped and lingered over.

274

## Homemade Mincemeat

*Mincemeat, an old New England favorite, originally came from Europe. Large crocks of it were made in the fall to help preserve meat for the winter. New Englanders and Europeans alike found it a great alternative to drying or smoking meats.*

1 pound beef stew meat
4 pounds apples, peeled, cored, and cut up
4 ounces suet
1 15-ounce package raisins
2½ cups sugar
2 cups dried currants
½ cup diced candied fruits and peels

1 teaspoon grated orange peel
1 cup orange juice
1 teaspoon grated lemon peel
¼ cup lemon juice
1 teaspoon salt
½ teaspoon ground nutmeg
¼ teaspoon ground mace

Simmer beef, covered, in water till tender, about 2 hours. Cool; put through coarse blade of food chopper with apples and suet. Combine with remaining ingredients and 2½ cups water in large kettle. Cover; simmer 1 hour. Stir to prevent sticking. Pack hot mincemeat into hot pint or quart jars, leaving 1-inch headspace. Wipe rims. Adjust lids. Process in pressure canner at 10 pounds pressure for 20 minutes. Makes 6 pints.

## Potato Sausage

*Potato Sausage or Doppa is the star attraction at many Scandinavian Christmas Eve suppers. It gets its name from the word meaning 'to dip in the kettle' because the original custom was to sop up the broth left from cooking the sausage with rye bread.*

Sausage casings
1½ pounds boneless beef with fat trimmed
1 pound boneless pork with fat trimmed

6 potatoes, peeled and cut up
1 medium onion, cut up
1 tablespoon salt
1 teaspoon ground allspice

Rinse casings; soak 2 hours or overnight in water. Grind meats with coarse blade of meat grinder; combine with remaining ingredients and ¼ teaspoon pepper. Attach sausage stuffer to grinder; push casing onto stuffer letting some extend beyond end of attachment. Using coarse blade, grind meat mixture into casings till firm but not overly full. When links are 18 inches long, tie ends with string. To cook links, prick filled casing with wooden pick in several places so fat can escape. Cook in water to cover in a covered kettle for 30 to 40 minutes. Serve warm. Store leftovers covered with water in refrigerator. To serve leftovers, drain; reheat in skillet. Makes 5 pounds.

## Bagels

4¼ to 4½ cups all-purpose flour
2 packages active dry yeast

1½ cups warm water (110°)
4 tablespoons sugar
1 tablespoon salt

In large mixer bowl combine *1½ cups* of the flour and yeast. Combine water, *3 tablespoons* of the sugar, and salt; add to flour mixture. Beat at low speed with electric mixer for ½ minute, scraping sides of bowl constantly. Beat 3 minutes at high speed. By hand, stir in enough of the remaining flour to make a moderately stiff dough. Knead on lightly floured surface till smooth (8 to 10 minutes). Cover; let rest 15 minutes. Cut in 12 portions; shape into smooth balls. Punch a hole in center of each. Pull gently to enlarge hole, working each into uniform shape. Cover; let rise 20 minutes. (Optional step for glossy surface: place raised bagels on *ungreased* baking sheet and broil 5 inches from heat for 1½ to 2 minutes on each side.) In kettle bring 1 gallon water and remaining sugar to boiling. Reduce to simmering; cook 4 bagels at a time for 7 minutes, turning once. Drain. Place on greased baking sheet. Bake at 375° for 30 to 35 minutes. (If broiled, bake broiled bagels 25 minutes.) Makes 12.

## Sourdough Bread

1 package active dry yeast
1½ cups warm water (110°)
5½ to 6 cups all-purpose
   flour

1 cup Sourdough Starter
   (room temperature)
2 teaspoons sugar
½ teaspoon baking soda

In mixer bowl soften yeast in warm water. Blend in *2½ cups* of the flour, Sourdough Starter, sugar, and 2 teaspoons salt. Combine *2½ cups* of the flour and the soda; stir into flour-yeast mixture. Add enough remaining flour to make a stiff dough. Knead on floured surface till smooth (5 to 7 minutes). Place in greased bowl; turn once. Cover; let rise till double (about 1½ hours). Punch down; divide in half. Cover; let rest 10 minutes. Shape into 2 round loaves. Place on greased baking sheets. With sharp knife, make diagonal slashes on tops. Let rise till double (1 to 1½ hours). Bake at 400° for 35 to 40 minutes. Remove from baking sheets; cool. If desired, brush with butter. Makes 2.

*Sourdough Starter:* Soften 1 package active dry yeast in ½ cup *warm* water (110°). Stir in 2 cups *warm* water, 2 cups all-purpose flour, and 1 tablespoon sugar. Beat smooth. Cover with cheesecloth; let stand at room temperature 5 to 10 days, stirring 2 or 3 times a day. (If room is warm, fermentation time will be shorter than if room is cool.) Cover; refrigerate till used.

*To keep Starter going:* After using some Starter, add ¾ cup water, ¾ cup all-purpose flour, and 1 teaspoon sugar to remainder. Let stand at room temperature till bubbly, at least 1 day. Cover and refrigerate. If not used within 10 days, add 1 teaspoon sugar. Repeat adding sugar every 10 days.

*What makes Sourdough Bread different from any other is that a fermented starter is used. This method of leavening was popular among early prospectors and cowboy cooks who saved a piece of dough to use as starter for next time. The word even became a nickname for Alaskan gold miners who always had sourdough as part of their gear.*

## Norwegian Lefse

2 cups hot mashed potatoes
2 tablespoons butter or
   margarine, softened

1 tablespoon milk
1 teaspoon salt
1 cup all-purpose flour

Beat together potatoes, butter, milk, and salt. Cover and chill thoroughly. Turn out on floured surface. Sprinkle with *half* of the flour. Knead for 8 to 10 minutes, gradually kneading in remaining flour. Divide dough into 8 or 16 portions; shape into balls. On floured surface, roll each small ball to 6-inch paper-thin circle, large balls to a 9-inch circle. Roll dough around rolling pin to transfer to hot, greased skillet. Cook till lightly browned, 2 to 3 minutes. Turn and brown second side, 2 to 3 minutes more. (Should be limp, not crisp.) Repeat with remaining dough. Spread with butter and sprinkle with sugar, if desired; fold in quarters. Makes 8 large or 16 small.

*Potato Lefse is a traditional Norwegian favorite. This mashed potato pancake is rolled very thin and baked on a griddle. To eat it, spread it with butter, sprinkle with sugar, and then roll or fold the soft pancake into a shape that's easy to pick up and eat with your fingers.*

## Cottage Cheese

¼ tablet rennet *or* 1 tablespoon dairy sour cream
2 quarts milk

¼ cup buttermilk
½ cup light cream
½ teaspoon salt

Dissolve rennet in 2 tablespoons water. Heat milk till just cool to touch (no more than 80°). Add rennet and buttermilk. Cover; let stand at room temperature till milk solidifies to a smooth curd, 12 to 24 hours (longer in winter). Break curd into chunks. Heat all to 100°; hold at this temperature in pan of hot water 20 to 30 minutes, stirring occasionally. Line colander with several layers of cheesecloth; place in large bowl. Pour curds into cheesecloth; drain off whey, 4 to 6 hours. Turn out cheese; break into curds. Add cream and salt. Makes 1 pound.

# Natural Foods

"Getting back to nature" is a strong trend in the early '70s. This is especially true with food. Foods that once were consigned to the 'health nuts' are now in vogue for everyone. Yogurt, wheat germ, sunflower seeds, bean sprouts, bulgur wheat, brown rice, honey, and dried fruits all fit into this general category of health foods.

Much of this trend comes from a fear that processed foods—those you pick up from the supermarket in a packet—lose much of the nutrients in a food. While this is not necessarily true, many people go the long route and are attempting to use only health foods instead of trying to decide for themselves what is good and what is deficient.

This interest has led to many good things—the development of soy products, for example. This versatile vegetable can be used as beans, grits, and with meats.

Health foods may not be your bag, but their impact on the '70s cannot be ignored. Try some of the recipes in the next section. You'll find that you'll enjoy them whether you go the health food route or not.

The assortment of natural foods include *Fruited Granola* (pictured opposite), *Sunflower Seed Bread* (see recipe, page 279), and *Spinach Salad* (see recipe, page 278), sprinkled with toasted sesame seeds.

## Chilled Yogurt Soup

1 cup plain yogurt
1 large unpeeled cucumber, cut in pieces
1½ tablespoons cooking oil
1½ teaspoons lemon juice

1 small clove garlic
¼ teaspoon dried dillweed
¼ teaspoon salt
Fresh mint *or* parsley

In blender container combine yogurt, cucumber, oil, lemon juice, garlic, dillweed, and salt; blend till smooth. Chill. Serve in chilled mugs. Garnish with chopped fresh mint or parsley, if desired. Serves 4.

*Yogurt, one of the oldest natural foods, dates back thousands of years to the early nomads of the Middle East. It was valuable for them because it could be carried in goatskins through the desert all day and would still be safe to eat. Today, yogurt is no longer carried around in goatskins, but it is used in many recipes including Chilled Yogurt Soup.*

## Bulgur Pilaf

1 cup bulgur wheat
2 tablespoons cooking oil
1 14-ounce can beef broth
½ cup chopped onion

1 4-ounce can mushroom stems and pieces
½ teaspoon salt
¼ teaspoon dried oregano, crushed

In skillet cook wheat in oil till slightly toasted, stirring frequently. Add broth, onion, mushroom pieces with liquid, salt, and oregano. Cover and simmer till tender, about 20 minutes. Makes 4 servings.

## Fruited Granola

1½ cups quick cooking rolled oats
½ cup chopped unroasted peanuts
½ cup chopped blanched almonds

½ cup wheat germ
½ cup raisins
⅓ cup snipped dried apricots
⅓ cup packed brown sugar
Light cream *or* milk

Combine oats, peanuts, almonds, and wheat germ. Spread in a 15½x10½x1-inch baking pan. Toast at 400° for 10 minutes; stir once. Stir in raisins, apricots, and brown sugar. Serve with cream. Serves 4.

*Granola, the darling of health food lovers, is a crunchy mixture of oats, peanuts, wheat germ, raisins, apricots, and brown sugar. This flavorful combination can be eaten plain as a snack or with milk as a breakfast cereal.*

## Macroburger

*Macroburgers, the food of the young health food enthusiasts at a Berkeley, California commune, are soybean burgers on homemade bread. With fresh garden vegetable salad and avocado dressing, herbal tea, or ice-cold fresh orange juice, the meal is very nutrition-wise too.*

1 cup dry soybeans
3½ cups cold water
½ cup millet
2 cups water
• • •
¼ cup soy sauce
3 tablespoons cooking oil
¾ teaspoon dried dillweed, crushed
¾ teaspoon dried thyme, crushed
½ teaspoon chili powder
¼ teaspoon ground cumin seed

⅛ teaspoon cayenne
2 cloves garlic, minced
1 cup finely chopped onion
¾ cup fine dry bread crumbs
½ cup finely chopped celery
½ cup grated carrot
2 tablespoons finely chopped green pepper
Monterey Jack cheese
Shortening
Whole wheat bread, toasted
Lettuce leaves
Tomato slices

Wash soybeans; combine soybeans and the 3½ cups cold water. Soak overnight. Or bring to a boil and simmer 2 minutes; let stand at least 1 hour. Cover and cook till tender, about 3 hours. Drain. Meanwhile, combine millet and the 2 cups water in saucepan. Bring to a boil; reduce heat. Cover and cook, stirring occasionally, till tender, 40 to 45 minutes. Add more water if necessary to prevent sticking. In blender container combine drained soybeans, soy sauce, cooking oil, dillweed, thyme, chili powder, cumin, cayenne, and garlic; blend thoroughly. Mix in millet, onion, crumbs, celery, carrot, and green pepper. Using ⅓ cup mixture for each, form into patties. Brown on both sides in hot shortening, about 3 minutes on each side. Top with a slice of cheese when browning second side. Serve patties between slices of toasted bread with lettuce and tomato. Serves 8 to 10.

## Vegetable and Soy Macaroni Soup

*The interest in natural foods has led to the rediscovery of the economy and protein possibilities of lentils and soy products. Vegetable and Soy Macaroni Soup is a meal in a bowl that goes well with a piece of cheese for dessert.*

1 cup dry lentils
5 cups water
1 28-ounce can tomatoes, cut up
2 cups shredded cabbage
¾ cup chopped onion

½ cup chopped carrot
4 vegetable bouillon cubes
1 clove garlic, minced
• • •
1 cup uncooked soy macaroni
Salt

Rinse lentils; drain and place in soup kettle. Add water, undrained tomatoes, cabbage, chopped onion, carrot, vegetable bouillon cubes, and minced garlic. Cover and simmer about 1 hour. Add uncooked soy macaroni and cook, covered, till vegetables and soy macaroni are done, about 20 minutes. Season to taste with salt. Makes 6 servings.

## Spinach Salad *(see photo, page 276)*

1 pound spinach
½ small head lettuce
1 green onion and top, sliced
⅓ cup olive oil

3 tablespoons lemon juice
1 tablespoon honey
• • •
1 tablespoon toasted sesame seeds

Wash spinach and pat dry with paper toweling. Tear spinach into a salad bowl. Tear lettuce into bite-size pieces. Toss spinach and lettuce with onion. In screwtop jar combine olive oil, lemon juice, and honey; shake well. Just before serving, add dressing to salad and toss to coat. Sprinkle sesame seeds atop salad. Makes 6 servings.

## Enriched Meat Loaf

1 beef bouillon cube
1 slightly beaten egg
1 8-ounce can stewed
   tomatoes
½ cup wheat germ

½ cup nonfat dry milk
   powder
⅓ cup finely chopped onion
¼ cup soy grits
1 pound ground beef

Dissolve bouillon cube in ½ cup boiling water. In bowl combine egg, bouillon, tomatoes, wheat germ, milk powder, onion, soy grits, and ¾ teaspoon salt. Thoroughly mix in ground beef. Turn into 8½x4½x2½-inch loaf pan. Bake at 350° for 1 hour. Drain off fat. Serves 6.

## Sunflower Seed Bread *(see photo, page 276)*

3½ to 4 cups unbleached
   white flour
1 package active dry yeast
½ cup milk
3 tablespoons sugar
2 tablespoons butter

1 egg
1 tablespoon grated orange
   peel
½ cup orange juice
⅔ cup shelled sunflower
   seeds

In large mixer bowl combine *1½ cups* of the flour and the yeast. Heat milk, sugar, butter, and 1½ teaspoons salt till warm (115° to 120°), stirring constantly to melt butter. Add to dry mixture in mixer bowl; add egg, orange peel, and juice. Beat at low speed with electric mixer for ½ minute, scraping bowl. Beat 3 minutes at high speed. By hand, stir in sunflower seeds and enough remaining flour to make a stiff dough. Knead on floured surface till smooth (5 to 8 minutes). Place in greased bowl; turn once. Cover; let rise till double (about 1½ hours). Punch down. Cover; let rest 10 minutes. Shape into loaf; place in greased 8½x4½x2½-inch loaf pan. Cover; let rise till double (45 to 60 minutes). Brush top with butter, if desired. Bake at 375° about 40 minutes. Remove from pan; cool. Makes 1 loaf.

*Homemade bread is part of the scene in the '70s, and suddenly, plain bread is out of style. After years of bleaching flour, milling companies are marketing an unbleached product, too. Sunflower seeds, wheat germ, and other seeds or nuts are often stirred into the dough for special flavor and nutritional interest.*

## Protein Plus Muffins

1¼ cups soy flour
⅔ cup nonfat dry milk
   powder
2 teaspoons baking powder
½ cup chopped pitted dates
¼ cup chopped nuts

2 slightly beaten eggs
1 teaspoon grated orange
   peel
¾ cup orange juice
2 tablespoons cooking oil
2 tablespoons honey

Stir together dry ingredients and ½ teaspoon salt. Add dates and nuts. Mix remaining ingredients; stir into dry ingredients till moistened. Fill 12 greased muffin pans ⅔ full. Bake at 350° for 30 minutes.

## Nut Butter

½ cup unroasted cashews
¼ cup shelled sunflower
   seeds

¼ cup sesame seeds
3 tablespoons cooking oil
2 tablespoons honey

In blender container combine cashews, seeds, oil, and ¼ teaspoon salt. Blend at highest speed till nearly smooth, stopping blender often to scrape down sides. Remove mixture from container. Stir in honey. If desired, stir in ⅓ cup chopped raisin. Makes about ⅔ cup.

# Microwave Cooking

Just as the gas range revolutionized cooking in the 1800s, so too the microwave oven in the '70s. Up-to-the-minute in style, these ovens cook clean, fast, and all the way through. No messy ovens, or roasts cooked on the outside but underdone on the inside are possible with this ultra-modern cooking aid. At present, the microwave oven is intended not to replace conventional cooking but to be used along with it. Many steps now done on top of the range in pans can be done in the microwave oven in glass or paper utensils. Since several steps can be done in the same container, the amount of dishwashing is cut down. As an owner of a microwave oven you will have the fun of doing your own experimenting. Remember that seconds count. Use the timing listed in the recipe as your starting point.

## Easy Chicken Bake

*Easy Chicken Bake is a good way to use your microwave oven. If you've ever wondered how a chicken gets cooked so fast, here's how. Your electronic oven has a vacuum tube called a magnetron that generates electromagnetic waves. These waves penetrate the chicken, causing the moisture molecules in the chicken to vibrate, resulting in friction. This friction produces heat which causes the chicken to cook in practically no time.*

1 2⅜-ounce package
    seasoned coating mix
    for chicken
2 tablespoons grated
    Parmesan cheese
2 tablespoons snipped
    parsley
4 small whole chicken
    breasts
¼ cup milk

Place coating mix, cheese, and parsley in plastic bag. Dip chicken in milk; shake in bag to coat. Place in 12x7½x2-inch *glass* baking dish. Cover with clear plastic wrap. Cook in microwave oven 23 minutes. Uncover. Cook till done, about 5 minutes more. Serves 4.

## Cheeseburger-Vegetable Casserole

1 pound ground beef
½ cup chopped onion
    • • •
¼ cup butter or margarine
¼ cup all-purpose flour
1 teaspoon salt
1½ cups milk
1½ cups shredded sharp
    process American cheese
1 teaspoon Worcestershire
    sauce
1 10-ounce package frozen
    mixed vegetables
¼ cup chopped canned
    pimiento
    Packaged instant mashed
    potatoes (enough for 4
    servings)

In *glass* mixing bowl crumble beef. Add onion. Cook in microwave oven till meat is browned, about 5 minutes, stirring twice during cooking. Drain off fat. Place butter in 4-cup *glass* measuring cup; cook in microwave oven till melted, about 25 seconds. Stir in flour, salt, and dash pepper. Gradually stir in milk. Cook in microwave oven for 2 minutes. Stir. Cook till thickened and bubbly, about 2 minutes more. Stir in *1 cup* of the cheese and the Worcestershire sauce. Add to meat mixture. Break up frozen vegetables. Stir vegetables and pimiento into meat mixture. Spoon into 8x8x2-inch *glass* baking dish. Cover with clear plastic wrap.* Cook in microwave oven for 10 minutes. Prepare potatoes according to package directions *except* use ¼ cup less water. Spoon around edge of casserole. Sprinkle remaining cheese over potatoes. Cook in microwave oven till cheese is melted, about 1 minute more. Serves 4 to 6.

*Or, cover and freeze. Cook frozen casserole in microwave oven for 7 minutes. Stir, breaking up chunks. Cook till hot, about 7 minutes. Top with potatoes and cheese as above.

Mixed vegetables, hamburger, and instant mashed potatoes all go into *Cheeseburger-Vegetable Casserole*. With the help of a microwave oven this tempting casserole can go from freezer to table in just minutes.

## Baked Chocolate Custard

1⅓ cups milk
⅓ cup semisweet chocolate
    pieces
2 beaten eggs

3 tablespoons sugar
½ teaspoon vanilla
    Dash salt

Measure milk in 4-cup *glass* measuring cup; add chocolate pieces. Cook in microwave oven till milk is very hot and chocolate is softened, about 2 minutes. Stir till chocolate is melted. If necessary, beat smooth with a rotary beater. Combine remaining ingredients; blend in hot milk mixture. Pour into four *glass* 6-ounce custard cups. Place in 8x8x2-inch *glass* baking dish. Add very hot water to depth of 1 inch. Cook in microwave oven for 2½ minutes. Turn baking dish halfway around. Cook 2½ minutes more. Remove cups from baking dish. (Custard will set up upon standing.) Serve warm or chilled. Serves 4.

## Raisin-Filled Apples

⅓ cup raisins
¼ cup packed brown sugar
2 tablespoons chopped
    walnuts

¼ teaspoon ground cinnamon
4 large baking apples,
    cored

Combine raisins, sugar, nuts, and cinnamon. Peel off a strip around top of apples. Place apples in a 2-quart *glass* casserole. Fill centers with the raisin mixture. Cover dish with clear plastic wrap. Cook in microwave oven till just tender, 4 to 5 minutes. Serve warm. Serves 4.

*Microwave ovens can be a help in many types of cooking situations. If you cook for one or two, it's ideal because it cooks small amounts quickly. It's also a help for families whose members eat at different times. Each person can eat his own portion when he's ready to eat. The microwave is great for entertaining, too. It lets you be with your guests rather than in the kitchen.*

# Good Eating during the Seventies

## Main Dishes for Moderns

Keep in step with the seventies by serving one of these inviting main dishes. These recipes reflect the diversity of the time. Some are modern and quick. Others are classic and elegant. All are easy to prepare and fun to eat. Choose from beef, crab, turkey, tuna, shrimp, chicken, and pork dishes. They're all-star attractions for the seventies.

## Rounding Out the Meal

Plan a seventies party. Once you've invited your guests and chosen a main dish, it's time to think about the rest of your menu. This section offers you a wide variety of colorful and appetizing recipes to choose from. Start by selecting a mushroom, oyster, or cheese appetizer. Then move on to salads. Decide on one of the fruit or vegetable salads. Add warm homemade bread, and top off the meal with something sweet. These desserts vary from fruit desserts to candies. They'll keep your guests coming back for more.

Try these seventies favorites: *Steak Dip Sandwiches* (see recipe, page 288) is perfect for buffets; *Tossed Zucchini Salad* (see recipe, page 293) goes well with Italian food; and *Butterscotch Crunch* (see recipe, page 294) ends any meal.

# Main Dishes for Moderns

## Steaks Bertrand

6 beef cube steaks
⅔ cup dry red wine
1 6-ounce can whole
   mushrooms, drained
¼ cup snipped parsley

Dash garlic powder
6 tablespoons butter or
   margarine
3 slices process Swiss
   cheese, halved

Place steaks in clear plastic bag; set in deep bowl. Combine wine, mushrooms, parsley, and garlic powder; pour over meat. Close bag, eliminating air. Marinate 30 minutes at room temperature or 2 hours in the refrigerator. Drain meat, reserving marinade.

In large skillet melt butter. Quickly cook *half* of the meat in butter, about 2 minutes on each side. Remove meat to blazer pan of chafing dish; keep warm. Repeat with remaining meat. Add marinade to skillet and bring to boiling; pour over meat. Top meat with cheese slices. Cover and place on chafing dish stand; cook over low heat till cheese melts. Serve sauce with meat. Serves 6.

## Tomato Beef

*The already high interest in Chinese food received a boost when President and Mrs. Nixon visited Peking in 1972. Chinese dishes from all over China are now being enjoyed in American homes. Especially popular is food from the southern province of Canton where recipes like Tomato Beef began.*

1½ pounds boneless beef sirloin, cut in ½-inch-
   thick slices
   • • •
1 tablespoon cornstarch
3 tablespoons soy sauce
2 tablespoons cooking oil
Dash freshly ground
   pepper

½ teaspoon grated, fresh
   gingerroot or ground
   ginger
1 green pepper, sliced
¼ pound mushrooms, sliced
6 green onions, cut in
   ½-inch pieces
2 small tomatoes, cut in
   wedges

Partially freeze beef slices; cut meat diagonally in ¼-inch strips. In a bowl combine the cornstarch, soy sauce, *1 tablespoon* of the oil, and freshly ground pepper. Add beef; toss to coat well. Let stand several hours in the refrigerator. Drain and reserve marinade. Heat ginger in remaining oil in electric wok or skil-let at 350°. Add beef to oil and stir-fry till meat is brown, 5 to 6 minutes; push meat to one side. Add green pepper, mushrooms, and onion pieces. Cook till crisp-tender, 2 to 3 minutes; push to one side. Add tomatoes; cover and cook 2 minutes. Pour marinade over meat; cook and stir till thick. Serves 4.

## Skillet Enchiladas

*The enchilada, a traditional Mexican dish, is composed of a fried tortilla rolled with a filling and covered with a sauce. Many variations of this old favorite have crossed the border and are now part of the cuisine referred to as Tex-Mex food. One is Skillet Enchiladas.*

In skillet brown 1 pound ground beef and ½ cup chopped onion; drain off excess fat. Stir in one 10½-ounce can condensed cream of mushroom soup, one 10-ounce can enchilada sauce, ⅓ cup milk, and 2 tablespoons chopped canned green chili peppers. In a small skillet dip 8 frozen or canned tortillas, one at a time, in a little hot cooking oil just till tortillas are limp. Drain. Using 2 cups shredded sharp process American cheese, place ¼ *cup* cheese on each tortilla. Using ½ cup chopped pitted ripe olives, sprinkle each tortilla with some of the olives and roll up. Place rolled tortillas in sauce in the skillet. Cover and cook till heated through, about 5 minutes. Sprinkle with an additional ½ cup shredded sharp process American cheese; cover and cook till cheese melts, about 1 minute. Makes 4 servings.

*Skillet Enchiladas* are cheese- and olive-filled tortillas cooked in a ground beef sauce seasoned with green chili peppers. These hot little peppers should have the seeds rinsed out before using. Serve the enchiladas with a cool tossed salad and smooth guacamole dressing of avocado.

Electric woks are tabletop cooking favorites that give impetus to informal entertaining in the '70s. Guests can watch as the hostess cooks *Tomato Beef* to be served over fluffy white rice. Eating with chopsticks is optional.

## Hollandaise Turkey Roast

6 slices cooked turkey
1 chicken bouillon cube
3 tablespoons butter
¼ cup all-purpose flour
½ cup milk

1 3-ounce can sliced mushrooms, drained
2 egg yolks
1 tablespoon lemon juice
¼ cup butter, melted

Put turkey in 10x6x2-inch baking dish. Dissolve bouillon cube in ½ cup water. In saucepan melt 3 tablespoons butter; blend in flour and ¼ teaspoon salt. Add bouillon and milk. Cook and stir till thick and bubbly. Stir in mushrooms. Pour over turkey. Bake at 350° about 15 minutes. Put egg yolks, lemon juice, ¼ teaspoon salt, and dash pepper in blender container; blend till thick. At low speed, slowly add ¼ cup *hot* butter. Pour over turkey; broil till golden. Makes 6 servings.

## Teriyaki Tenderloin

*Teriyaki Tenderloin is right in swing with the '70s. It's a variation of an old Japanese method of cooking in which meat is marinated in a soy sauce-sake mixture, giving the meat a sweet flavor. In this '70s version, sake has been replaced by sherry, and onion soup mix adds zest to the soy marinade.*

½ cup dry sherry
¼ cup soy sauce
2 tablespoons brown sugar

2 tablespoons dry onion
soup mix
1 2-pound beef tenderloin

Combine sherry, soy sauce, brown sugar, and soup mix. Place beef in plastic bag; set in deep bowl. Add marinade and close bag. Chill 8 to 24 hours. Occasionally, press bag against meat to distribute marinade. Remove meat from marinade; reserve marinade. Place meat on rack in roasting pan. Roast at 425° for 50 minutes; baste often with *half* the marinade. Combine remaining marinade and 2 tablespoons water. Bring to boiling. Slice meat; spoon sauce over. Serves 6 to 8.

## London Broil

1½ pounds top-quality beef
flank steak
¾ cup Italian salad
dressing

2 tablespoons soy sauce
⅛ teaspoon onion juice
⅛ teaspoon lemon pepper
Salt

Score steak on both sides. Place in shallow pan. Blend dressing, soy sauce, onion juice, and lemon pepper; pour over steak. Cover. Let stand at room temperature for 2 to 3 hours; turn several times. Place steak on rack of broiler pan. Broil 3 inches from heat for 5 minutes; season with salt. Turn; broil 5 minutes more for medium rare. Season with salt. Slice *very thin* diagonally across grain. Serves 6.

## Polka-Dot Tuna

1 8-ounce package frozen
mixed vegetables with
onion sauce
1⅔ cups milk
1 tablespoon cornstarch
1 6½- or 7-ounce can tuna,
drained and flaked

1 3-ounce can sliced
mushrooms, drained
2 tablespoons chopped
canned pimiento
4 English muffins, split,
toasted, and buttered

In saucepan combine vegetables and milk. Blend cornstarch and 1 tablespoon water; add to vegetables. Cook and stir till thickened and bubbly. Stir in tuna, mushrooms, and pimiento; heat through. Spoon over muffins. Top with toasted almonds, if desired. Serves 4.

## Shrimp and Eggplant

8 ounces fresh or frozen
    shelled shrimp, cooked
½ cup chopped onion
2 tablespoons chopped green
    pepper
1 clove garlic, minced
¼ cup butter or margarine
1 medium eggplant

1 8-ounce can tomatoes
1 teaspoon salt
½ teaspoon ground thyme
    Dash pepper
1½ cups cooked rice
2 tablespoons butter or
    margarine
1½ cups soft bread crumbs

Split cooked shrimp lengthwise; set aside. In skillet cook onion, green pepper, and garlic in ¼ cup butter till tender but not brown. Peel eggplant and cut into ½-inch cubes. Dice tomatoes; add to mixture in skillet with eggplant, salt, thyme, and pepper. Cover and simmer till eggplant is tender, about 10 minutes. Stir in shrimp and cooked rice. Spoon mixture into 4 individual casseroles. Melt the 2 tablespoons butter; stir in bread crumbs. Sprinkle crumbs over shrimp-eggplant mixture. Bake at 400° till golden, 10 to 15 minutes. Serves 4.

*Eggplant, one of the most interesting of all vegetables, is actually a fruit. Obscure in origin, it was believed to cause insanity and was therefore nicknamed the 'mad apple.' Called eggplant because the first varieties were the size of an egg, it was used only as a table decoration until it was proven safe to eat. Today, eggplant can be enjoyed in many dishes including Shrimp and Eggplant.*

## Shellfish Newburg

1½ pounds fresh or frozen
    shrimp in shells
3 10½-ounce cans condensed
    cream of mushroom soup
1 cup light cream
3 beaten egg yolks
½ cup dry white wine

1 tablespoon lemon juice
1 6-ounce package frozen
    crab meat, thawed,
    flaked, and cartilage
    removed
Patty shells *or* toast
    points

In large saucepan bring 1 quart water and 1½ tablespoons salt to boiling. Add shrimp. Heat to boiling; reduce heat and simmer till shrimp turn pink, 1 to 3 minutes. Drain. Peel shrimp and remove black vein under cold running water. Split peeled shrimp lengthwise. In large saucepan blend soup and cream. Heat just to boiling, stirring occasionally. Stir a moderate amount of hot sauce into egg yolks. Return to sauce. Stir over low heat till thickened. Stir in wine and lemon juice. Add shrimp and crab. Heat through. Serve sauce in patty shells. Garnish with parsley, if desired. Serves 10 to 12.

## Chicken Skillet

⅓ cup all-purpose flour
1 teaspoon salt
1 teaspoon paprika
¼ teaspoon ground sage
1 2½- to 3-pound ready-to-
    cook broiler-fryer
    chicken, cut up
¼ cup shortening

1 teaspoon sugar
1 13¾-ounce can chicken
    broth
1 cup sliced carrots
1 medium onion, sliced
2 tablespoons snipped
    parsley
1 tablespoon lemon juice

Combine flour, salt, paprika, sage, and ¼ teaspoon pepper in paper or plastic bag; add chicken, a few pieces at a time, and shake. Reserve excess flour mixture. In skillet brown chicken on all sides in hot shortening. Remove chicken from skillet. Stir reserved flour mixture and sugar into pan drippings; add chicken broth. Cook and stir till thick and bubbly. Add carrots, onion, parsley, and lemon juice. Arrange chicken atop vegetable mixture. Cover and cook till vegetables and chicken are tender, 40 to 45 minutes; stir occasionally. Serves 4.

Choose *Beef Wellington* for a special occasion, and you will impress any guest. Cover the tender beef tenderloin with liver pâté, a flaky pastry casing, and pastry cutouts for this elegant main dish.

*Beef Wellington was a chef's delight of the '60s. Chefs in restaurants everywhere were using this costly and difficult recipe as a show-off piece. By the '70s, homemakers were beginning to experiment with it at home, and the* Better Homes and Gardens *Test Kitchens developed this recipe.*

## Beef Wellington

1 4-pound beef tenderloin
2 cups all-purpose flour
½ teaspoon salt
⅔ cup shortening
⅓ to ½ cup cold water

2 2¾-ounce cans liver
   pâté
1 beaten egg
   Parsley
   Gravy

Place beef on rack in shallow roasting pan. Roast at 425° till meat thermometer registers 130°, about 45 minutes. Reserve drippings. Cool meat. Stir flour and salt together; cut in shortening till mixture resembles coarse crumbs. Slowly add cold water, tossing with fork till moistened. Form ball. Roll to 14x12-inch rectangle; spread pâté to within ½ inch of edges. Center meat, top down, on pastry. Draw up long sides; overlap. Brush with egg; seal. Trim ends; fold up. Brush with egg; seal.

Place on greased baking sheet, seam down. Add pastry cutouts. Brush with egg. Bake at 425° for 35 minutes. Trim with parsley. Serve with Gravy. Serves 12.

*Gravy:* Combine reserved drippings, 1½ cups water, and 2 beef bouillon cubes in saucepan. Heat and stir till bouillon dissolves. Blend ¼ cup all-purpose flour and ½ cup cold water; add to pan with ⅓ cup Burgundy and ½ teaspoon dried basil, crushed. Cook and stir till bubbly. Season to taste.

## Steak Dip Sandwiches *(see photo, page 282)*

Grill 6 pieces beef sirloin steak, cut ¼ inch thick (about 1½ pounds) in lightly greased skillet for 2 to 3 minutes on each side. In small saucepan combine ½ cup butter, ¼ cup water, 3 tablespoons bottled steak sauce, 2 tablespoons sliced green onion with tops, 1 tablespoon Worcestershire sauce, and ¼ teaspoon salt. Heat through. Toast 6 slices of French bread, cut 1½ inches thick, in broiler. Dip toast in sauce; place on serving plate or tray. Top each toast slice with a grilled steak. Spoon remaining sauce over tops of sandwiches. Makes 6 servings.

## Cheese Manicotti

¼ cup chopped onion
1 clove garlic, crushed
2 tablespoons cooking oil
1 16-ounce can tomatoes,
    cut up
1 8-ounce can tomato sauce
1 teaspoon sugar
1 teaspoon dried oregano,
    crushed
¼ teaspoon dried thyme,
    crushed

1 small bay leaf
12 manicotti shells
2 beaten eggs
1½ cups fresh ricotta *or*
    cream-style cottage
    cheese (12 ounces)
1 8-ounce package shredded
    mozzarella cheese
½ cup grated Parmesan
    cheese
¼ cup snipped parsley

In saucepan cook onion and garlic in oil till tender but not browned. Add tomatoes, tomato sauce, sugar, oregano, thyme, bay leaf, ⅓ cup water, and ¼ teaspoon salt. Bring to boiling; simmer, uncovered, for 45 minutes. Remove bay leaf.

Cook manicotti shells in boiling, salted water just till tender; drain. Rinse in cold water. Combine eggs, ricotta, *half* the mozzarella, Par-

mesan, parsley, ¼ teaspoon salt, and dash pepper. Spoon cheese mixture into shells. Pour *half* the tomato mixture into a 13x9x2-inch baking dish; top with stuffed shells. Pour remaining sauce over shells. Sprinkle with remaining mozzarella. Bake, covered, at 350° for 30 minutes. (If desired, refrigerate casserole up to 24 hours. Bake, covered, 45 minutes.) Serves 6.

*Italian foods are as popular in the '70s as they have been in the past. However, Americans are becoming interested in dishes other than just spaghetti and pizza. Some of the lesser-known and more difficult dishes are now popular. One of these is Manicotti. This dish, literally meaning 'little puffs', is made with long macaroni rolls filled with a ricotta mixture.*

## Spoon Bread with Creamed Chicken

1 cup yellow cornmeal
3 cups milk
2 tablespoons cooking oil
1 teaspoon baking powder
1 teaspoon salt
3 well-beaten egg yolks
3 stiffly beaten egg whites
½ cup chopped celery

¼ cup butter or margarine
⅓ cup all-purpose flour
1 13¾-ounce can chicken
    broth
2 cups cubed, cooked
    chicken
2 tablespoons chopped
    canned pimiento

Prepare spoon bread by cooking cornmeal and *2 cups* of the milk till the consistency of mush. Remove from heat; stir in remaining 1 cup milk, oil, baking powder, and salt. Add the egg yolks; fold in beaten egg whites. Pour into a greased 1½-quart casserole. Bake at 325° for

1 hour. Meanwhile, cook celery in butter till tender. Blend in flour. Stir in chicken broth. Cook and stir till thickened and bubbly. Add chicken, pimiento, and salt to taste; heat through. To serve, ladle creamed chicken over hot spoon bread. Makes 6 servings.

## Pork Chop and Wild Rice Skillet

4 loin pork chops, cut ¾
    inch thick
½ cup chopped onion
1 cup uncooked wild rice,
    well washed

1 10½-ounce can condensed
    beef broth
1⅓ cups water
    Salt and pepper
1 medium tomato, sliced

Trim fat from chops and cook trimmings in skillet till 2 tablespoons drippings accumulate; discard trimmings. Brown chops on both sides; remove. Cook onion in pan drip-

pings till tender but not brown. Add rice, broth, and water. Return chops to skillet; season. Cover; simmer till tender, 1 hour. Top with tomato; heat through. Serves 4.

*Wild rice comes from the northern parts of Minnesota and Wisconsin. Here, Indians shake the grains of this wild grass into the bottoms of their canoes. Because wild rice is harvested by hand, it is very expensive. If it's a little too much for your budget, substitute long grain and wild rice mix, and this pork chop skillet will still be a bountiful meal.*

# Rounding Out the Meal

## Mushroom Cocktail

Mushrooms are a natural for low-calorie dishes such as *Mushroom Cocktail* (pictured opposite). This appetizer, with its zesty sauce, adds only 38 calories to the day's tally.

⅓ cup catsup
1 tablespoon vinegar
¼ teaspoon prepared
    horseradish

Lettuce leaves
1½ cups shredded lettuce
12 medium mushrooms,
    washed and sliced

Blend catsup, vinegar, and horseradish. Chill. Line 6 sherbets with lettuce leaves; layer with shredded lettuce. Arrange mushrooms atop each. Chill. To serve. Drizzle each with 1 tablespoon sauce. Serves 6.

## Oysters Bienville

*For an elegant way to start off any party, serve Oysters Bienville. This tasty appetizer from the South was named for the French governor of the Louisiana Territory who founded the city of New Orleans.*

18 oysters in shells
½ cup chopped green
    onion
1 clove garlic, minced
2 tablespoons butter
2 tablespoons all-purpose
    flour
⅔ cup chicken broth
1 egg yolk
⅓ cup dry white wine

1 3-ounce can sliced mush-
    rooms, drained
2 tablespoons snipped
    parsley
Dash bottled hot pepper
    sauce
½ cup soft bread crumbs
½ tablespoon butter, melted
2 tablespoons grated
    Parmesan cheese

Open oyster shells. With knife, remove oysters. Wash shells. Place each oyster in deep half of the shell. Arrange on bed of rock salt in a shallow pan; set aside. Cook onion and garlic in 2 tablespoons butter till tender. Blend in flour and ¼ teaspoon salt. Add chicken broth all at once. Cook and stir till mixture thickens and bubbles. Beat egg yolk and wine together. Add a little of the hot mixture to egg mixture; return to hot mixture. Stir in mushrooms, parsley, and hot pepper sauce. Cook over low heat, stirring, till mixture almost boils. Toss crumbs with melted butter. Stir in Parmesan cheese. Heat oysters at 400° for 5 minutes. Top each oyster with 1 tablespoon of the sauce mixture and 1 teaspoon crumb mixture. Bake till heated through and crumbs are lightly browned, 10 to 12 minutes longer. Serves 6.

## Flaming Greek Cheese

*If you like adventure, Flaming Greek Cheese is an appetizer for you. Kasseri cheese is the headliner in this spectacular dish. Although originally from Greece, this cheese now is also made in America. Made from sheep's milk, it has a flavor similar at once to both Cheddar and Parmesan. To add to the excitement, it also tastes faintly like a light, sparkling wine.*

4 ounces kasseri cheese
2 tablespoons metaxa, or
    another brandy

½ lemon
Thin slices Italian or
    French bread, toasted

Slice kasseri ¼ inch thick; place on sizzle platter, oven-going skillet, or pie pan. Broil till cheese is just soft and surface bubbles slightly, about 7 minutes. Heat metaxa; flame and pour over cheese. Squeeze lemon over cheese. Spread on toasted bread. Makes 4 servings.

## Smoky Cheese Ball

Combine two 8-ounce packages cream cheese, softened; 2 cups shredded smoky Cheddar cheese; ½ cup butter or margarine, softened; 2 tablespoons milk, and 2 teaspoons steak sauce. Beat till fluffy. Chill slightly. Shape into ball; coat with 1 cup finely chopped toasted almonds.

## Honey-Oatmeal Bread

4½ to 4¾ cups whole wheat
  flour
3 packages active dry yeast
2 cups milk
⅓ cup honey

¼ cup cooking oil
½ cup quick-cooking
  rolled oats
Quick-cooking rolled oats
1 beaten egg white

In large mixer bowl combine *2 cups* of the flour and the yeast. In saucepan heat milk, honey, oil, and 1 tablespoon salt just till warm (115° to 120°). Add to dry mixture. Beat at low speed with electric mixer for ½ minute, scraping bowl. Beat 3 minutes at high speed. By hand, stir in ½ cup oats and enough remaining flour to make a stiff dough. Turn out onto lightly floured surface and knead till smooth and elastic (5 to 6 minutes). Place in lightly greased bowl; turn once. Cover; let rise in warm place till double (45 to 60 minutes). Punch down; turn out on lightly floured surface. Divide in half. Cover; let rest 10 minutes. Coat *each* of two well-greased 8½x4½x2½-inch loaf pans with 2 tablespoons oats. Shape dough into loaves. Place in pans. Cover; let rise in warm place till double (35 to 45 minutes). Brush with a mixture of egg white and 1 tablespoon water; sprinkle tops lightly with rolled oats. Bake at 375° for 35 to 40 minutes. Cover with foil the last 15 minutes if tops brown too fast. Remove from pans; cool. Makes 2.

## Perfect White Bread

*The story of bread is as old as civilization itself. Beginning as a flat product, bread wasn't leavened until Egyptian times. One day, a baker set some dough aside and later found that it had risen from yeast in the air. He baked it anyway and created the first leavened bread. Since then, breadmaking has improved a great deal; today's homemaker can serve her family fine-textured breads such as Perfect White Bread.*

5¾ to 6¼ cups all-purpose
  flour
1 package active dry yeast

2¼ cups milk
2 tablespoons sugar
1 tablespoon shortening

In large mixer bowl combine *2½ cups* of the flour and the yeast. In saucepan heat together milk, sugar, shortening, and 2 teaspoons salt just till warm (115° to 120°), stirring constantly. Add to dry mixture in mixer bowl. Beat at low speed with electric mixer for ½ minute, scraping sides of bowl constantly. Beat 3 minutes at high speed. By hand, stir in enough of the remaining flour to make a moderately stiff dough. Turn out onto a lightly floured surface and knead till smooth and elastic (8 to 10 minutes). Shape in a ball. Place in lightly greased bowl; turn once to grease surface. Cover; let rise in warm place until double (about 1¼ hours). Punch dough down; turn out on lightly floured surface. Divide dough in two portions. Cover; let rest 10 minutes. Shape into two loaves; place in two greased 8½x 4½x2½-inch loaf pans. Cover and let rise in warm place till double (45 to 60 minutes). Bake at 375° about 45 minutes. If tops brown too fast, cover with foil last 15 minutes. Remove from pans; cool. Makes 2.

## Corn-Mushroom Bake

¼ cup all-purpose flour
1 16-ounce can cream-style
  corn
1 3-ounce package cream
  cheese, cut in cubes
½ teaspoon onion salt

1 16-ounce can whole kernel
  corn, drained
1 6-ounce can sliced
  mushrooms, drained
½ cup shredded process
  Swiss cheese (2 ounces)

Stir flour into cream-style corn. Add cream cheese and onion salt; heat and stir till cheese melts. Stir in remaining ingredients. Pour into 1½-quart casserole; top with buttered crumbs, if desired. Bake, uncovered, at 400° for 30 to 35 minutes. Serves 6 to 8.

## Crunch-Top Potatoes

Preheat oven to 375°. Pour ¼ cup melted butter into 13x9x2-inch baking pan. Add two 16-ounce cans sliced potatoes, drained, in a single layer; turn once in butter. Mix 1 cup shredded natural Cheddar cheese (4 ounces), ¾ cup crushed cornflakes, and 1 teaspoon paprika; sprinkle over potatoes. Bake at 375° about 20 minutes. Makes 6 servings.

*Timesaving recipes are a big part of the cooking of the '70s. With more and more women working outside the home, recipes that can be done in a hurry fill an important need. The next time you need hurry-up potatoes, try Crunch-Top Potatoes.*

## Cherry-Cranberry Salad

1 20-ounce can frozen pitted
   tart red cherries
1 3-ounce package cherry-
   flavored gelatin
1 8-ounce can jellied
   cranberry sauce
1 3-ounce package lemon-
   flavored gelatin

1 3-ounce package cream
   cheese, softened
⅓ cup mayonnaise
1 8¼-ounce can crushed
   pineapple, undrained
½ cup whipping cream
1 cup tiny marshmallows
2 tablespoons chopped nuts

Thaw and drain cherries; reserve syrup. Add water to syrup to make 1 cup; bring to boil. Remove from heat. Stir in cherry gelatin till dissolved. Break up cranberry sauce; add to gelatin and stir till smooth. Add cherries. Turn into 9x9x2-inch baking dish; chill till *almost* firm.

Dissolve lemon gelatin in 1 cup boiling water. Beat cream cheese with mayonnaise; stir in lemon gelatin and pineapple. Chill till partially set. Whip cream; fold into lemon mixture with marshmallows. Spread atop *almost set* cherry layer; top with nuts. Chill till firm. Serves 12.

## Tossed Zucchini Salad *(see photo, page 282)*

In a screw-top jar combine ⅓ cup salad oil, 3 tablespoons vinegar, 2 teaspoons sugar, ¼ teaspoon salt, dash garlic powder, and dash pepper; shake. In bowl combine 1 cup thinly sliced zucchini and 2 tablespoons sliced green onion. Pour dressing over zucchini mixture; chill 1 to 2 hours. Drain; reserve marinade. Combine 3 cups torn lettuce; 1½ cups torn romaine; 2 tomatoes, cut in wedges; and drained zucchini. Toss with desired amount of marinade. Serves 6.

## Apple-Orange Toss

1 11-ounce can mandarin
   orange sections,
   chilled
2 large apples, cored and
   cut in bite-size pieces

¼ cup walnut pieces
½ cup orange-flavored
   yogurt
2 tablespoons orange
   marmalade

Drain mandarin oranges; combine with apples and walnuts. Stir together yogurt and marmalade; toss with apple mixture. Serves 6.

## Dairy Garden Salad

1 cup large curd, cream-
   style cottage cheese
½ cup dairy sour cream

¼ cup sliced radishes
¼ cup sliced green onion
6 tomato slices

Blend cottage cheese with sour cream. Stir in radishes and green onion. Season with salt and pepper. Spoon over tomatoes. Serves 6.

The '70s brought with it renewed concern over watching calories and losing weight. Out of this concern have come a whole group of low-calorie recipes. One of these is Honeydew-Lime Mold (pictured opposite).

## Honeydew-Lime Mold

¼ cup sugar
1 envelope unflavored gelatin
1 cup low-calorie lemon-lime carbonated beverage

¼ cup lime juice
3 or 4 drops green food coloring
1 drop peppermint extract
¼ cup evaporated skim milk
1 cup honeydew melon balls

In saucepan mix sugar and gelatin. Add ½ cup cold water. Heat till gelatin dissolves. Stir in ¼ *cup* of the carbonated beverage, lime juice, food coloring, and extract. Add skim milk to ⅓ *cup* gelatin mixture. Chill till partially set; whip till fluffy.

Pour into a 4½-cup mold. Chill till *almost* firm. Combine remaining carbonated beverage with remaining gelatin; chill till partially set. Fold in melon balls. Pour over whipped layer. Chill till set. Unmold. Makes 6 servings.

## Plum-Cherry Compote

Drain one 17-ounce can whole un-pitted purple plums and one 16-ounce can pitted dark sweet cherries, reserving syrups. Place the purple plums and cherries in a bowl.

In saucepan blend 2 tablespoons sugar and 1 tablespoon cornstarch. Gradually stir in ½ cup orange juice and reserved fruit syrups. Add 5 inches stick cinnamon and 1 thin lemon slice. Cook over medium heat, stirring constantly, till mix-

ture thickens and bubbles. Cook and stir 2 to 3 minutes longer. Remove from heat; discard the cinnamon stick and lemon slice. Cool slightly. Stir in ⅓ cup dry sherry. Pour over fruit. Cover and refrigerate till thoroughly chilled, stirring occasionally. Spoon the fruit mixture into individual dessert dishes. Using ½ cup dairy sour cream, top individual servings with a dollop of sour cream. Makes 8 servings.

Candy fans of the '70s sometimes take time out for an old-fashioned treat such as penuche. The name for this brown sugar candy comes from the Spanish word panocha or 'raw sugar.' If you like penuche but don't have a lot of time to spend in the kitchen, prepare Quick Walnut Penuche.

## Quick Walnut Penuche

½ cup butter or margarine
1 cup packed brown sugar
¼ cup milk

1¾ to 2 cups sifted powdered sugar
1 cup chopped walnuts

In saucepan melt butter. Stir in brown sugar. Cook and stir over low heat for 2 minutes. Add milk; bring to boiling. Cool to room tempera-

ture. Beat in powdered sugar till like fudge. Stir in nuts; pour in buttered 8x8x2-inch pan. Chill till firm enough to cut. Makes 32 pieces.

## Butterscotch Crunch *(see photo, page 282)*

¾ cup packed brown sugar
2 tablespoons cornstarch
¼ teaspoon salt
2 cups milk
2 slightly beaten egg yolks
2 tablespoons butter

1 teaspoon vanilla
2 chocolate-coated English toffee bars (1⅛ ounce each), chilled
¼ cup toasted flaked coconut

In saucepan combine sugar, cornstarch, and salt; add milk. Cook and stir till thickened and bubbly. Cook 2 minutes more; remove from heat. Stir a moderate amount of hot mixture into egg yolks; return to hot

mixture. Cook and stir till just boiling. Remove from heat; stir in butter and vanilla. Cover; cool. Crush candy in plastic bag; add coconut. In four sherbets alternate pudding and coconut mixture. Serves 4.

# INDEX

## A-B

## D-F

# R-S